Cambridge English

Complete First for Schools

Student's Book **with** answers

Guy Brook-Hart with Helen Tiliouine

Cambridge University Press
www.cambridge.org/elt

Cambridge Assessment English
www.cambridgeenglish.org

Information on this title: www.cambridge.org/9781107661592

© Cambridge University Press and UCLES 2014

This publication is in copyright. Subject to statutory exception
and to the provisions of relevant collective licensing agreements,
no reproduction of any part may take place without the written
permission of Cambridge University Press.

First published 2014

20 19 18 17 16 15 14 13 12

Printed in Dubai by Oriental Press

A catalogue record for this publication is available from the British Library

ISBN 978-1-107-67516-2 Student's Book without answers with CD-ROM
ISBN 978-1-107-66159-2 Student's Book with answers with CD-ROM
ISBN 978-1-107-68336-5 Teacher's Book
ISBN 978-1-107-67179-9 Workbook without answers with Audio CD
ISBN 978-1-107-65634-5 Workbook with answers with Audio CD
ISBN 978-1-107-69533-7 Class Audio CDs (2)
ISBN 978-1-107-68529-1 Presentation Plus DVD-ROM
ISBN 978-1-107-64039-9 Student's Pack (Student's Book without answers with CD-ROM,
Workbook without answers with Audio CD)

The publishers have no responsibility for the persistence or accuracy of URLs
for external or third-party internet websites referred to in this publication, and
do not guarantee that any content on such websites is, or will remain, accurate
or appropriate. Information regarding prices, travel timetables, and other
factual information given in this work is correct at the time of first printing but
the publishers do not guarantee the accuracy of such information thereafter.

Contents

Map of the units	4
Introduction	6
Cambridge English: First for Schools overview	7
1 A family affair	8
2 Leisure and pleasure	18
Vocabulary and grammar reviews Units 1 and 2	28
3 Happy holidays?	30
4 Food, glorious food	40
Vocabulary and grammar reviews Units 3 and 4	50
5 Study time	52
6 My first job	62
Vocabulary and grammar reviews Units 5 and 6	72
7 High adventure	74
8 Dream of the stars	84
Vocabulary and grammar reviews Units 7 and 8	94
9 Secrets of the mind	96
10 On the money	106
Vocabulary and grammar reviews Units 9 and 10	116
11 Medical matters	118
12 Animal kingdom	128
Vocabulary and grammar reviews Units 11 and 12	138
13 House space	140
14 Fiesta!	150
Vocabulary and grammar reviews Units 13 and 14	160
Language reference	162
Writing reference	186
Speaking reference	194
Answer key	199
Acknowledgements	248

Map of the units

Unit title	Reading and Use of English	Writing	Listening
1 A family affair	Part 6: 'Parents are human too' Part 2: 'Do you help with household chores?'	Part 1 An essay: Teenagers and young people should share housework equally with their parents. Do you agree? Expressing opinions Using *although, however, on the other hand* and *whereas*	Part 1: Young people talking about their families and activities
2 Leisure and pleasure	Part 1: 'My first bike' Part 4: Key word transformation	Part 2 An article: A leisure-time activity you really enjoy Writing compound and complex sentences	Part 2: A talk from a games developer
Vocabulary and grammar reviews Units 1 and 2			
3 Happy holidays?	Part 3: 'A bus journey' Part 7: 'My nightmare holiday!'	Part 2 A story: A trip I'll never forget	Part 3: Five young people talking about their holidays
4 Food, glorious food	Part 6: 'Can chocolate make you smarter?' Part 1: 'Moso Moso' – a restaurant review	Part 2 A review: A local restaurant, café or snack bar	Part 4: A radio interview about eating insects
Vocabulary and grammar reviews Units 3 and 4			
5 Study time	Part 7: 'At school abroad' Part 3: 'Culture shock for language exchange students'	Part 2 The set text: The most interesting character in the book you have read Writing opening paragraphs Using linking words and phrases	Part 1: People talking about studying and school
6 My first job	Part 5: 'Lucy's first job' Part 2: 'A new summer programme'	Part 2 A letter or email: Describe the weekend jobs teenagers do in your country Commonly misspelled words	Part 3: Five people talking about their holiday job
Vocabulary and grammar reviews Units 5 and 6			
7 High adventure	Part 6: 'Are you ready for an adventure race?' Part 4: Key word transformation	Part 2 An article: A great way to keep fit	Part 2: A talk about adventure racing Part 4: A radio interview with a paraglider
8 Dream of the stars	Part 7: 'Four young actors' Part 1: 'YouTube millionaire celebrities'	Part 1 An essay: There are both advantages and disadvantages to a career as a musician or an actor. Writing a balanced essay	Part 2: A talk about a television quiz show
Vocabulary and grammar reviews Units 7 and 8			
9 Secrets of the mind	Part 5: 'Happiness or Harvard?' Part 4: Key word transformation	Part 2 A story: Barbara just couldn't stop smiling	Part 1: People talking about different aspects of psychology
10 On the money	Part 2: 'Online shopping? No thanks!' Part 5: 'My greatest influence'	Part 2 A review: Something you have been given or bought recently Words/Phrases to build up more complex sentences	Part 4: A student interview about a new shopping centre
Vocabulary and grammar reviews Units 9 and 10			
11 Medical matters	Part 4: 'What would you like to do?' Part 3: 'Is there a doctor on board?'	Part 1 An essay: Modern lifestyles can seriously endanger our health. Do you agree? Writing concluding paragraphs An essay: Young people generally don't pay enough attention to their health and fitness. Do you agree?	Part 3: Five people talking about visits to the doctor
12 Animal kingdom	Part 1: 'My sister's circus' Part 7: 'Surviving an animal attack'	Part 2 A letter or email: Advice to a visitor to your country Giving advice	Part 1: People talking about animals in different situations
Vocabulary and grammar reviews Units 11 and 12			
13 House space	Part 5: 'My new home in Venice, 1733' Part 2: 'Living on a houseboat'	Part 2 An article: My ideal home	Part 2: A talk about a haunted house
14 Fiesta!	Part 6: 'The world's highest festival?' Part 3: 'My local festival'	Part 1 An essay: Is it better to watch films at the cinema or at home? *it, this, that* and *they* for reference	Part 4: A radio interview with a street performer
Vocabulary and grammar reviews Units 13 and 14			

Speaking	Pronunciation	Vocabulary	Grammar
Part 1: Talking about yourself, your home and your family Giving extended answers	Word stress (1): Stress in words with two or more syllables	Phrasal verbs: *get on with, do up*, etc. Collocations with *make* and *do*	Present perfect simple and continuous
Part 2: Comparing photos of free-time activities Using discourse markers to structure the answer	Sentence stress (1): Stress on words carrying the most meaning	Phrasal verbs and expressions: *take up, sum up*, etc.	Making comparisons Adjectives with *-ed* and *-ing*
Part 3: Discussing the benefits of different kinds of trip Phrases to involve partners in discussion Strategies for dealing with the second section of Part 3	Intonation (1): Indicating when you have/haven't finished speaking	*travel, journey, trip* and *way* Adjective suffixes	Past simple, past continuous and *used to* *at, in* or *on* in time phrases Past perfect simple and continuous
Part 4: Discussing diet, food and health Supporting opinions with reasons and examples	Grouping words and pausing (1)	*food, dish* and *meal* Adjectives to describe restaurants	*so* and *such* *too* and *enough*
Part 1: Talking about your studies Giving reasons, offering several possible ideas	Word stress (2): Shifting word stress	Phrasal verbs: *get over, live up to*, etc. *find out, get to know, know, learn, teach* and *study*; *attend, join, take part* and *assist* Forming nouns from verbs	Zero, first and second conditionals
Part 2: Comparing photos of different kinds of work Describing similarities and differences when comparing	Sentence stress (2): Contrastive sentence stress	*work/job; possibility/occasion/opportunity; fun/funny* Collocations with *work* and *job*	Countable and uncountable nouns Articles
Part 3: Discussing ways of encouraging people to do more sport Suggesting ideas, asking opinion, agreeing and disagreeing	Intonation (2): Showing attitude	Verb collocations with sporting activities *look, see, watch, listen* and *hear*	Infinitive and verb + *-ing*
Part 4: Discussing different aspects of media and celebrity Giving balanced, general answers Expressing agreement/disagreement	Grouping words and pausing (2)	Verb collocations with *ambition, career, experience* and *job* *play, performance* and *acting; audience, (the) public* and *spectators; scene* and *stage*	*at, in* and *on* in phrases expressing location Reported speech
Part 2: Comparing photos of different kinds of feeling and emotion Speculating about photos using *look, seem* and *appear*	Sentence stress (3): Using sentence stress for emphasis	*achieve, carry out* and *devote* *stay, spend* and *pass; make, cause* and *have*	Modal verbs to express certainty and possibility
Part 1: Talking about what kind of shops you go to Strategies for answering Part 1 questions	Linking (1): Linking to increase fluency	*arrive, get* and *reach* Phrasal verbs: *come up with, pull in*, etc.	*as* and *like* Modals expressing ability
Part 2: Comparing photos of situations related to health Strategies for dealing with difficulties: finding the right word	Intonation (3): Showing certainty/uncertainty	Idiomatic expressions: *taken aback*, etc. Health vocabulary: *illness, infection*, etc.	Relative pronouns and relative clauses
Parts 3 and 4: Discussing topics related to animals Commenting on the question Expressing other people's opinions Expressing agreement/disagreement	Word stress (3): Strong and weak forms	*avoid, prevent* and *protect; check, control, keep an eye on* and *supervise* Negative prefixes	Third conditional and mixed conditionals *wish, if only* and *hope*
Part 2: Comparing photos of people in different locations	Linking (2): Linking with consonant sounds	*space, place, room, area, location* and *square*	Causative *have* and *get* Expressing obligation and permission
Parts 3 and 4: Discussing different topics related to festivals and celebrations	Improving fluency	Vocabulary for festivals: *celebrate, commemorate*, etc. Suffixes to form personal nouns	The passive

Introduction

Who this book is for

Complete First for Schools is a stimulating and thorough preparation course for students wishing to take the revised **Cambridge English: First for Schools** exam from 2015. It teaches you the reading, writing, listening and speaking skills which are necessary for the exam, how to approach each exam task, as well as essential grammar and vocabulary. The book also teaches you the language knowledge and develops the skills you need to reach an upper-intermediate B2 level in the Common European Framework of Reference. *Complete First for Schools* is official Cambridge English preparation material for the exam.

What the book contains

In the **Student's Book** there are:

- 14 units for classroom study. Each unit contains:
  - at least one part of each of the Writing, Speaking and Listening papers and two parts of the Reading and Use of English paper. The units provide language input, skills practice and exam technique to help you to deal successfully with each of the tasks in the exam.
  - essential information and advice on what each part of the exam involves and the best way to approach each task.
  - a wide range of enjoyable and stimulating speaking activities designed to increase your fluency and your ability to express yourself.
  - detailed advice and practice of strategies to perfect your performance in the Speaking paper.
  - a pronunciation section working on stress, intonation, pausing, linking and fluency.
  - a step-by-step approach to doing Cambridge English: First for Schools writing tasks.
  - grammar activities and exercises with the grammar you need to know for the exam. When you are doing grammar exercises you will sometimes see this symbol: . These are exercises which are based on research from the Cambridge English Corpus and they deal with areas which cause problems for many candidates in the exam.
  - vocabulary input needed for success at Cambridge English: First for Schools based on the English Vocabulary Profile (EVP) at B2 level. When you see this symbol: **EP**, the exercise is based on EVP research. When you see this symbol next to a vocabulary exercise, the exercise is based on research from the Cambridge English Corpus and focuses on words which candidates often confuse or use wrongly in the exam.

- 14 Vocabulary and grammar reviews. These contain exercises which revise the grammar and vocabulary that you have studied during the unit.

- A **Language reference section** which clearly explains all the main areas of language, including grammar, word formation, spelling and punctuation, which you need to know for the Cambridge English: First for Schools exam.

- **Writing and Speaking reference sections**. These explain the possible tasks you may have to do in the Speaking and Writing papers, and they give you examples, language and advice on how best to approach them.

- A **CD-ROM** provides extra practice, with all the activities linked to the topics in the Student's Book.

Also available are:

- **two audio CDs** containing listening material for the 14 units. The listening material is indicated by these icons in the Student's Book:
  ▶ 00

- a **Workbook** to accompany the Student's Book, with four pages of exercises for each unit. The Workbook is also accompanied by an **audio CD**.

Cambridge English: First for Schools overview

Part / timing	Content	Test focus
Reading and Use of English 1 hour 15 minutes	**Part 1** A modified cloze text containing eight gaps and followed by eight multiple-choice items **Part 2** A modified open cloze text containing eight gaps **Part 3** A text containing eight gaps. Each gap corresponds to a word. The stems of the missing words are given beside the text and must be changed to form the missing word. **Part 4** Six separate questions, each with a lead-in sentence and a gapped second sentence to be completed in two to five words, one of which is given as a 'key word' **Part 5** A text followed by six multiple-choice questions **Part 6** A text from which six sentences have been removed and placed in a jumbled order after the text. A seventh sentence, which does not need to be used, is also included. **Part 7** A text, or several short texts, preceded by ten multiple-matching questions	In tasks 1–4 candidates are expected to demonstrate the ability to apply their knowledge of the language system by completing the first four tasks. In tasks 5–7 candidates are also expected to show understanding of specific information, text organisation features, tone, and text structure.
Writing 1 hour 20 minutes	**Part 1** One compulsory essay question presented through a rubric and short notes **Part 2** Candidates choose one task from a choice of four questions. The task types are: • an essay • an article • a letter or email • a review • a story • a task based on a set text	Candidates are expected to be able to write using different degrees of formality and different functions: advising, comparing, describing, explaining, expressing opinions, justifying, persuading, recommending and suggesting.
Listening Approximately 40 minutes	**Part 1** A series of eight short unrelated extracts from monologues or exchanges between interacting speakers. There is one three-option multiple-choice question per extract. **Part 2** A short talk or lecture on a topic, with a sentence-completion task which has ten items **Part 3** Five short related monologues, with five multiple-matching questions **Part 4** An interview or conversation, with seven multiple-choice questions	Candidates are expected to be able to show understanding of attitude, detail, function, genre, gist, main idea, opinion, place, purpose, situation, specific information, relationship, topic, agreement, etc.
Speaking 14 minutes	**Part 1** A conversation between the examiner (the 'interlocutor') and each candidate (spoken questions) **Part 2** An individual 'long turn' for each candidate, with a brief response from the second candidate (visual and written stimuli, with spoken instructions) **Part 3** A discussion question with five written prompts **Part 4** A discussion on topics related to Part 3 (spoken questions)	

A family affair

Starting off

Work in pairs

- Which of the activities in the photos look the most fun? Why?
- Do you do any activities like these with your family?
- Write a list of five activities you enjoy doing with your family and a list of five activities you enjoy doing with your friends. Then discuss: How different are the two lists? Why do you think this is?

Listening Part 1

EXAM INFORMATION

In Listening Part 1, you:
▶ listen to people talking in eight different situations which may be either a conversation between two or more people, or just one person speaking.
▶ answer one question for each situation by choosing A, B or C;
▶ hear each piece twice.

1 Work in pairs. You will hear people talking in eight different situations. Before you listen, read questions 1–8 and <u>underline</u> the main idea in each. An example has been done for you.

1 You hear part of a conversation with a boy called Patrick. He thinks his <u>mother helps</u> him <u>because</u>
  A she enjoys it.
  B she worries about him.
  C she has plenty of time.

2 You hear a girl called Tracey talking to a friend. What is her family doing to the house at the moment?
  A extending it
  B painting it
  C cleaning it

3 You hear a girl called Vicky taking part in a class discussion. How often does she do sporting activities with her father?
   A more often than before
   B the same as before
   C less often than before

4 You hear a boy called Kostas talking about family celebrations. How does he feel about them?
   A bored
   B embarrassed
   C amused

5 You hear a boy called Rajiv talking to his sister on the phone. He is annoyed with her because
   A she has taken something without permission.
   B she has gone out without telling him.
   C she has lost something he needs.

6 You hear a boy called Marco talking to a friend. He is tired because he has done too much
   A studying.
   B exercise.
   C travelling.

7 You hear a girl called Samin leaving a telephone message for her mother. She is phoning to
   A explain something.
   B complain about something.
   C ask permission for something.

8 You hear an interview with a young musician called Pau. Why does he say he chose to play the trumpet?
   A It was the only instrument available.
   B It was his favourite instrument.
   C It was a family tradition.

2 🎧 02 Listen and choose the best answer (A, B or C).

3 Work in pairs. Correct the mistakes in questions 1–6 on the tablet.

1 How much you help around the house?
   How much do you help around the house?
2 How often you all doing things together as a family?
3 You ever do sports with other people in your family?
4 Are you enjoy family celebrations?
5 How other members of the family annoy you?
6 You have any family traditions?

4 Now take turns to ask and answer questions 1–6 in Exercise 3.

Vocabulary
Phrasal verbs

1 EP Match these phrasal verbs (1–6) from Listening Part 1 with their definitions (a–f).

1 get on with — a collect (or go and get) someone or something
2 do up   b continue
3 clear up   c continue doing something, especially work
4 go on
5 wear out   d make a place tidy by removing things from it or putting them where they should be
6 pick up
                 e make someone extremely tired
                 f repair or decorate a building so that it looks attractive

2 Complete these sentences by writing a phrasal verb from Exercise 1 in the correct form in each of the gaps.

1 I need to *get on with* my homework project, otherwise I won't finish it for tomorrow.
2 Mati had a little sleep because she felt .... after spending all morning .... the mess in her room.

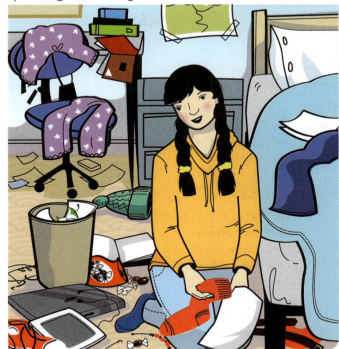

3 I got bored with the film because it .... for too long.
4 We'll need to .... some more pots of paint if we're going to .... your room this weekend.

Unit 1

Reading and Use of English Part 6

1 **EP** Work in pairs. You are going to read an article giving advice to teenagers about talking to adults. Before you read, write these adjectives in the most appropriate column below.

> ~~aggressive~~ anxious bad-tempered concerned
> critical enthusiastic hard-working impatient
> impolite mature organised reasonable
> responsible self-confident sensitive strict
> understanding unreliable

usually positive	usually negative	could be either
	aggressive	

2 Add one of these prefixes *dis-*, *un-*, *im-*, *ir-*, *in-* to each of these words to make opposites.

> critical *uncritical* concerned enthusiastic mature
> organised reasonable responsible sensitive

➡ page 181 Language reference: Word formation – adding prefixes

3 Work in pairs. Which of the adjectives in Exercise 2 describe typical attitudes of parents to teenagers? Why? Which describe typical attitudes of teenagers to parents? Why?

4 Work in groups.
- Make a list of things teenage children sometimes say about their parents.
  They never listen to me!
  They never let me do what I want!
  They're very unreasonable.
  They work really hard.
  They help me when I have problems at school.
- What can you do to live happily with your parents?
  Be honest with them and respect their point of view.

5 Read the article carefully, ignoring the gaps, and make a note of the main idea of each paragraph.
An example has been done for you.

Parents are humans too!

It's hard for teenagers to talk to their parents.

Talking to parents, can be difficult, but a little understanding on both sides can make it easier.

Do you ever get the feeling that your parents just don't listen to you? They'd rather discuss how much you're studying and how long you've been playing computer games this evening than helping you book tickets to see your favourite band. It's not that your parents ignore you completely; it's more that they don't see things in quite the same way as you. When you talk to them, they may give the impression that they're taking in what you say. **1** It's as if the words are going in, but the meaning just isn't getting through to them. And this isn't the only problem you may face.

As you grow up, your personality is developing and you're trying to become more independent, so naturally you have more questions and opinions about all aspects of your life. You start wondering whether your parents actually know what they're talking about. **2** That's often because it's the first time they've been responsible for a teenager and they're learning to cope!

Obviously, it's important to respect your parents and you should try to understand why they might have a different point of view from yours. Their priority is to provide you with a structured environment, where they can guide and support you. It's crucial for them to know what you're doing and that you're safe. However, it's vital that they

10

A family affair

try and see your point of view. **3** ☐ After all, in only a few years you'll probably leave home and have to look after yourself!

Although this situation is absolutely normal, it doesn't make it any easier. Ideally, your home should be a place where things can be discussed reasonably and constructively. However, parents are human too and can be hurt by what you say to them. Try to remember that in every family there are good times and bad times, but your parents are there for you throughout. **4** ☐ You'll be taking steps to earn their trust, and they might be prepared to be more tolerant.

Be sensitive! If there is something you really have to talk about, don't bring it up just before your Mum or Dad goes to work or just before bedtime. Think about what you are going to say and during the discussion, keep calm and be open and honest. Avoid talking about how your friends' parents behave in similar situations. **5** ☐ Reminding yourself that many other teenagers are having the same problems can, however, offer the best way of coping with such feelings.

The important thing is to keep talking. **6** ☐ Remember that there's no reason why people should automatically understand all your views. The more you can discuss things with your parents in a mature way, the happier you will feel. On the other hand, if you really find it impossible to talk to your parents, it might be a good idea to find a family member, teacher or professional counsellor who can help you. Above all, stay positive and remember that it won't be long before you'll be able to make your own decisions.

6 Six sentences have been removed from the article. Choose the correct sentence (A–G) which fits each gap (1–6). There is one extra sentence which you do not need. Use the underlined words and phrases in the sentences and in the text to help you.

A These doubts can lead to arguments and it's hard for parents to know how to deal with this.
B But that doesn't mean they're right on this occasion.
C They also need to give you the freedom to make your own decisions.
D In fact they're often not actually doing so at all.
E And don't take yourself too seriously!
F It won't help your attempts to communicate and may only increase the frustrations you're experiencing.
G As long as you show them that you appreciate this, they will begin to realise that you're not trying to cause trouble.

EXAM INFORMATION

In Reading and Use of English Part 6, you read a text of 500–600 words with six gaps where sentences have been removed. You choose one sentence from a list of seven sentences A–G for each gap; there is one sentence you will not need.

Unit 1

7 Work in groups of four. Two students should take the role of parents and two students should take the role of teenagers.

- Work with the student who has the same role as you. Read your role and prepare what you are going to say.
- When you are ready, change partners and have your conversations.

Parents

Your son's/daughter's teacher has called you because your son/daughter is not handing in their homework on time. You are annoyed because:
- they spend ages in their room and you thought they were doing their homework.
- you think they should have told you if they were having problems with their school work.

Have a conversation with your teenage son/daughter. Find out what happened and decide how to avoid this situation in the future.

Teenage son/daughter
- You have not been handing in your homework on time recently.

Have a conversation with your parents. Explain what has been happening and discuss how to avoid this situation in the future.

Grammar
Present perfect simple and continuous

1 Look at each of the pairs of sentences in *italics* and answer the questions that follow.

1 a *I've broken my personal record playing virtual tennis.*
  b *I've been playing virtual tennis all evening.*

Which sentence (a or b) talks about …
1 the result of an activity?
2 the length of an activity?

2 a *I've been learning how to do carpentry.*
  b *I've phoned her more than six times, but she never answers the phone.*

Which sentence (a or b) talks about …
1 how many times something has been repeated?
2 changes or developments which are not finished?

3 a *I've been helping my mum while her assistant is on holiday.*
  b *We've lived in this house since I was a small child.*

Which sentence (a or b) talks about something which is …
1 temporary?
2 permanent?

→ page 178 Language reference: Verb tenses – present perfect simple and continuous

2 Complete these sentences by writing the verbs in brackets in the correct form (present perfect simple or continuous) in the gaps.

1 I *'ve been visiting* (visit) friends, so I haven't spoken to my parents yet today.
2 My mum .... (ask) me to tidy my room several times.
3 I .... (clean) the kitchen, so what would you like me to do next?
4 Our neighbour .... (play) the violin for the last three hours and it's driving me mad!
5 Congratulations! You .... (pass) the exam with really high marks!
6 Adriana doesn't know many people in our town yet. She .... (only live) here for a few weeks.
7 We .... (spend) every summer in Crete since I was a child, so it'll be sad if we don't go there this year.
8 I'm really tired because I .... (cook) all day!

A family affair

3 👁 Candidates often make mistakes with the present perfect simple and continuous. Correct one of the wrong underlined verbs in each of these sentences.

1 I <u>was</u> interested in it since I <u>was</u> a child.   *have been*
2 In the last three weeks, I <u>learned</u> so many interesting things which I <u>didn't know</u> how to do before.
3 This <u>isn't</u> the first time I <u>fix</u> the brakes on my bike.
4 My name <u>is</u> Hannah and I <u>play</u> tennis for three years.
5 Since I <u>started</u> the project, I <u>had been doing</u> research on someone famous from my country.
6 Vicky and Kostas <u>are</u> friends for many years. They actually <u>met</u> at primary school.
7 They <u>had been</u> talking about it for weeks, but nothing <u>has been done</u> up to now.
8 I <u>dance</u> since I <u>was</u> very young and now I <u>am working</u> very hard to fulfil my dream of becoming a famous dancer.

Reading and Use of English Part 2

1 Work in pairs. You will read an article about housework. Before you read, match the verbs (1–8) with the nouns (a–h) to make phrases for common household chores.

1 do   a the beds
2 do   b the dinner ready
3 dust   c the floor
4 get   d the furniture
5 hang   e the ironing
6 lay   f the table
7 make   g the washing out to dry
8 sweep   h the washing-up

2 Work in groups.
- Who does each of the chores in Exercise 1 in your family, and why?
  We all do our own ironing because we're all very busy. My dad gets the dinner ready because he says it helps him relax.
- Which of the chores do you not mind doing? Which would you prefer to avoid?

3 Read the text quickly. Why do teenagers do housework?

4 Complete the text by writing one word in each gap. Make sure that you spell the word correctly.

Do you help with household chores?

If you help your parents with the housework, do you just do it **(0)** ...*for*... pocket money, or do you see it **(1)** .... a way of helping your busy parents? According to a recent study of teenagers, many feel they have a duty to help their parents because it is fair, especially if their parents work.

More than two-thirds of the young people who were surveyed, clean floors **(2)** .... least once a week and more than 80% regularly set the table for meals or **(3)** .... the washing-up. Girls are more likely than boys to wash **(4)** .... own clothes.

(5) .... are, however, a few teens who only do the housework because they are made **(6)** .... by their parents. They argue that they should **(7)** .... be expected to help out at home because in their view, their teenage years are a period which should be enjoyed **(8)** .... than interrupted with household responsibilities. What do you think?

13

Unit 1

5 Now check or complete your answers by using these clues.

1 This preposition is used with *see* to mean *believe it is (that thing)*. Other verbs which are followed by this preposition are *consider* and *regard*.
2 In other words, they clean floors a minimum of once a week.
3 Which verb do we use with *washing-up*?
4 Whose clothes do they wash?
5 This word is often used to introduce a sentence before the verb *be*.
6 *Their parents make them do the housework* = They are made .... do the housework by their parents.
7 Do you understand that a *minority of teens* mentioned in this paragraph believe they should help?
8 This word is part of a two-word phrase which means *instead of*.

EXAM INFORMATION

In Reading and Use of English Part 2, you read a text of 150–160 words with eight gaps where words have been removed. You write one word in each gap. You are given an example (0).

6 Work in pairs. Do you think what the text says about teenagers and household chores is true in your country as well?

Vocabulary
Collocations with *make* and *do*

1 **EP** Complete the third column of the table below by writing these words and phrases in the correct row.

> an activity   an appointment   an arrangement
> the bed   business   a change   a choice
> the cleaning   a course   a decision   an effort
> an excuse   (an) exercise   a favour   friends
> homework   housework   an impression   a job
> a mistake   money   a noise   a phone call   a plan
> progress   a promise   the shopping   (a) sport   work

verb	definition	common collocation
make	to create or produce something	*make an appointment*
do	to perform an activity or job	

2 Candidates often confuse *make* and *do*. Complete these sentences by writing *make* or *do* in the correct form in the gaps.

1 According to a recent study of teenagers, most of them .... not do housework just for pocket money.
2 I always .... my own bed in the morning, but I don't .... any cleaning.
3 Our teacher said she had to .... a lot of phone calls to .... all the arrangements for the school trip.
4 A few changes have been .... to the computer game and the company say they'll try to avoid .... similar mistakes in the future.
5 People who .... language courses tend to .... a lot of friends at the same time.
6 When my mum came back from .... the shopping, she helped me to .... my homework.

3 Work in pairs. Each choose five words/phrases from the box in Exercise 1 and think about when you did or made each of these things. Then take turns to tell your partner about each of them.

I had to make a choice between going away with my family, or doing a language course during the summer. Although it was a difficult choice to make, I decided to do the language course and miss my holiday.

A family affair

Speaking Part 1

EXAM INFORMATION

In Speaking Part 1, the examiner asks you questions about yourself. These may include questions about your life or studies, your plans for the future, your family and your interests, etc.

1 Look at these two questions, which the examiner may ask you in Speaking Part 1.

- Where are you from?
- What do you like about the place where you live?

1 Which question asks you to give your personal opinion? Which asks you for personal information?
2 Which question can be answered with quite a short phrase? Which question needs a longer answer?

2 ▶ 03 Listen to two candidates, Irene and Peter, answering the questions above. Who do you think gives the best answers? Why?

3 In the exam, you will get higher marks if you use a range of appropriate vocabulary. Work in pairs. Which of these phrases can you use to describe the place where you live?

a a large industrial city
b a relaxed atmosphere
c lively cafés
d in the middle of some great countryside
e a pleasant residential district
f good live music venues
g plenty of sports facilities
h a lot of historic buildings
i a lot of attractive buildings
j some pretty good shopping
k a busy city centre
l wonderful beaches nearby

4 Which of the phrases (a–l) can you use with … ?

It is … *a large industrial city*
It has …

(In some cases, both are correct.)

5 **Pronunciation:** word stress (1)

In the Speaking paper, you will get higher marks if your pronunciation is clear. In words of more than one syllable, one syllable is stressed more than the others. If you stress the wrong syllable, the word becomes difficult to understand. In dictionaries the stressed syllable is marked like this: in'dustrial.

1 Underline the stressed syllable in each of these words and phrases.

industrial   relaxed atmosphere   wonderful
facilities   historic

2 ▶ 04 Listen and check your answers. Then work in pairs and take turns to read the words aloud.

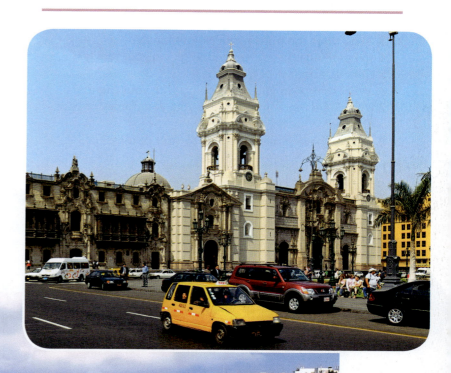

15

Unit 1

6 How can you extend your answers to these two questions below? Think about Irene's extended answers you heard in (Speaking) Exercise 2, and use the frameworks given to help you.

> Examiner: Where are you from?
> Student: I'm from … It's a … which …

> Examiner: What do you like about the place where you live?
> Student: Well, it's … , so … , but … and … Also …

7 Work in pairs. Take turns to ask and answer the questions in Exercise 6. Use some of the vocabulary from (Speaking) Exercise 3.

8 Read questions 1–8.
- Spend a little time thinking about how you can give extended answers.
- Work in pairs and take turns to ask and answer the questions.

1. Do you come from a large family?
2. What do you like about being part of a large/small family?
3. Who does the housework in your family?
4. What things do you enjoy doing with your family?
5. Tell me about your friends.
6. What things do you enjoy doing with your friends?
7. Which are more important to you: your family or your friends?
8. Do you have similar interests to your parents?

➡ page 194 Speaking reference: Speaking Part 1

Writing Part 1 — An essay

EXAM INFORMATION

In Writing Part 1, you:
▶ write an essay in which you discuss a question or topic. After the essay title, there are some notes which you must use.
▶ must also include your own ideas.
▶ must write between 140 and 190 words.

1 Read this writing task and <u>underline</u> the points you must deal with.

In your English class, you have been talking about how much teenagers and young people should help with the housework.
Now your English teacher has asked you to write an essay. Write an essay using **all** the notes and give reasons for your point of view.

Essay question
Teenagers and young people should share housework equally with their parents. Do you agree?

Notes
Write about:
1. who has more time for housework
2. who does housework better
3. … (your own idea)

Write your **essay**.

2 Work in groups. Discuss the task and try to find two or three things you can say about each of the notes 1–3.

3 Read Violetta's answer to the task, ignoring the gaps. Which of her ideas do you agree with and which do you disagree with?

> **(1)** .... it is fashionable to say that everyone should share the housework equally, in many homes parents do most of it. **(2)** .... , I believe people of all ages should do their fair share.
>
> It is true that young people spend most of the day at school or college and they also have large amounts of homework to do when they come home. **(3)** .... , parents go out to work and come home tired. In my view, family life is more pleasant when everyone shares the responsibility for cleaning and tidying because it takes less time.
>
> People often argue that parents do the cooking and ironing better. **(4)** .... in my opinion, young people should learn to do them as preparation for the future.
>
> Finally, housework is boring if you do it alone **(5)** .... when families do it together, it gives parents and children a chance to talk to each other about the things that matter to them. This greatly improves family life and makes young people more cooperative and responsible.
>
> For all these reasons, I think that family life is more pleasant when everyone shares the chores.

4 Complete this plan for Violetta's essay by matching the notes (a–e) with the paragraphs (1–5).

> Para. 1: intro: ....
> Para. 2: ....
> Para. 3: ....
> Para. 4: ....
> Para. 5: conclusion: ....

a life more enjoyable doing things together
b time: young people studying, parents working, chores finished more quickly
c get practice – you improve
d sharing work together – better family life
e parents do most of it + my opinion

5 It is important to express your opinions in an essay. Find four phrases which Violetta uses to introduce her personal opinions.

6 When you write an essay, you should try to present contrasting points of view. Complete Violetta's essay by writing *although*, *however*, *on the other hand* or *whereas* in each of the gaps 1–5. Then check your answers by reading the Language reference.

→ page 168 Language reference: Linking words for contrast

7 Complete these sentences by writing *although*, *however*, *on the other hand* or *whereas* in the gaps. In some cases, more than one answer may be possible.

1 Adults tend to worry more about their health, ... young people are more concerned about money.
2 .... I am happy to do some of the cooking, I don't want to do it all.
3 My mum and dad have similar tastes. .... , mine are completely different.
4 .... my parents give me a lot of freedom, I would prefer to have even more independence.
5 Young people often spend many hours a week on their social life. .... , older people are often too busy.
6 I enjoy making beds. .... , I'm not at all keen on doing the ironing.

8 Write your own answer to the writing task in Exercise 1. Before you write, use the notes you made in Exercise 2 to write a plan. Write between 140 and 190 words.

- Use Violetta's answer in Exercise 3 as a model, but express your own ideas and the ideas which came up during your discussion.

→ page 186 Writing reference: Part 1 Essays

2 Leisure and pleasure

Starting off

Work in pairs.
1 Which of the activities in the photos have you done?
2 Which do you think is …
   A the most enjoyable?
   B the cheapest?
   C the healthiest?
   D the most relaxing?
   E the least active?
   F the best one to do with friends?
   G the most popular among young people?
3 Which would you like to try? Why?

Listening Part 2

1 Work in groups. You are going to hear a games developer talking about his life and work. Before you listen, complete the advantages and disadvantages of video or computer games by writing a word from the box in the gaps.

> concentrate   contribute   develop   distract
> encourage   make   require   solve   waste

Advantages
1 They .... people to be more creative.
2 They can .... you from your problems.
3 People learn to .... on complicated tasks.
4 They .... many skills, such as hand and eye coordination.
5 They teach people how to .... problems.

Disadvantages
6 People .... little imagination to play them.
7 They .... people less sociable.
8 They .... to violence in society.
9 People .... time doing something which is not very useful.

2 Which sentences do you agree with? Why?

EXAM INFORMATION

In Listening Part 2, you hear a talk or lecture by one speaker. You:
▶ listen and complete ten sentences with a short word or phrase.
▶ write words you actually hear and try to spell them correctly.
▶ hear the recording twice.

3 Work in pairs. Read the listening task text below. What type of information do you need to complete each sentence?

Games Developer

As a child, Mike's main interests were playing video games and reading (1) ....

Mike's original ambition was to become a (2) .... , not a games developer.

The name of the club he formed with other students at school was '(3) ....'.

He worked in his summer holidays in order to get (4) ....

One thing he enjoys is doing (5) .... to find solutions for games.

He likes working with people who have both (6) .... that are unlike his.

He has worked on many successful games and one is now a (7) ....

Mike says the information in Dark Snake is very (8) ....

Large games need (9) .... to develop, so he prefers working on smaller ones.

Mike travelled to (10) .... recently.

4 🔊 **05** You will hear a man called Mike Selby, who works as a games developer, talking about his job. Now listen to the talk and complete the sentences in Exercise 3 with a word or short phrase.

5 Work in groups.
1 Which video games do you find …
  • most entertaining?
  • best for passing the time or taking a break?
  • most educational or informative?
2 Are there any video games you would recommend?
3 Mike talked about how he made his hobby into his career. Is this something you would like to do? If so, what hobby would you like to make into a career?

Leisure and pleasure

Grammar
Making comparisons

1 Circle the correct phrase in *italics* in these extracts from Listening Part 2. Then listen again to check your answers.

1 My mum and dad hoped I'd become *a bit more / some more* interested in my school work.
2 It was a *more safer / much safer* career choice.
3 At the time, it was the *most / more* exciting thing in my life.
4 And then I had this opportunity which was even *best / better*.
5 I worked *much harder / more hardly* than I ever worked at school.
6 Games development is the *more / most* creative thing you can imagine.
7 One of the *very big / biggest* thrills for me was when one of my games, Dark Snake, was made into a film.
8 I don't want to spend *as many / so much* time on things.

➔ page 169 Language reference: Making comparisons

2 👁 Candidates often make mistakes with comparisons. Complete the sentences with the correct form of the adjective in brackets.

1 There are lots of ways to keep fit, but I think .... (*healthy*) of all is zumba.
2 Playing chess is .... (*cheap*) than playing video games.
3 Team games are .... (*sociable*) than biking because you meet and speak to a lot of people.
4 When you play chess, you have to think .... (*hard*) than when you're playing video games.
5 For me, parachute jumping is the .... (*thrilling*) of all sports.
6 Speaking for myself, I find team sports the .... (*not interesting*).
7 Mountain biking is .... (*good*) for getting exercise than most sports.

3 Complete these sentences with your own ideas.
1 Learning to ride a bicycle is not as …
2 In team games, the most …
3 I'm much better at …
4 My friends are far …
5 Computer games are not nearly …

19

Unit 2

Reading and Use of English Part 1

EXAM INFORMATION

In Reading and Use of English Part 1, you:
- read a text of 150–160 words.
- fill in the gaps with the best option A, B, C, D.

1 You are going to read an extract from a blog by a teenager about how he started riding motorbikes. Before you read, work in pairs. What do you think people most enjoy about riding motorbikes?

2 Read the extract quickly, to find out who encouraged the writer's interest in motorbikes.

My first bike

When I first **(0)** ...*took up*... riding motorbikes, I was only ten. My biking beginnings could be summed up in three words: sheer good **(1)** .... Most of my friends' parents won't let them take any risks at all, but knowing how **(2)** .... I was to have a go, my dad got hold of a little red Honda 50cc. I **(3)** .... my mum a series of promises about how careful I was going to be. I actually had no intention of keeping them – they were all made up. My dad and I took the bike to a field **(4)** .... to a friend, and **(5)** .... I didn't have a clue how to ride a bike, I got on and managed to start it. There were two piles of straw **(6)** .... of me, with a tiny gap between them. As I raced through the **(7)** .... gap, I was thrilled to **(8)** .... my dad yell 'Stop!' It was incredibly exciting and I knew I was hooked.

3 For questions 1–8, read the extract again and decide which answer (A, B, C or D) best fits each gap. There is an example at the beginning (0).

0	A (took up)	B start	C thought	D came
1	A chance	B luck	C accident	D occasion
2	A worried	B upset	C troubled	D desperate
3	A made	B did	C said	D told
4	A borrowing	B owning	C belonging	D lending
5	A even	B however	C despite	D although
6	A forward	B ahead	C towards	D front
7	A narrow	B thin	C slender	D fine
8	A hear	B listen	C sound	D catch

4 Work in pairs.

Student A
You are a teenager. You want to buy a motorbike, but you need your parents to lend you the money.
Think of reasons why you want a motorbike and then try to persuade your father/mother to lend you the money you need.

Student B
You are one of Student A's parents. You don't want him/her to buy a motorbike. Think of reasons why he/she shouldn't buy a motorbike and try to persuade him/her not to do so.

Leisure and pleasure

Vocabulary
Phrasal verbs and expressions

1 **EP** Match these phrasal verbs and expressions from the extract (1–8) with their definitions (a–h).

1 take up (line 1)
2 sum up (line 2)
3 take risks (line 4)
4 have a go (line 5)
5 get hold of (line 5)
6 keep a promise (line 8)
7 make up (lines 8 and 9)
8 not have a clue (line 10)

a describe the important facts or characteristics about something or someone
b do what you said you would do
c say or write something which is not true
d start doing a particular job or activity
e be completely unable to guess, understand, or deal with something
f try to do something
g do something even though something bad might happen because of it
h obtain something

2 Complete these sentences by writing a phrasal verb or expression from Exercise 1 in the correct form in the gaps.

1 I'd never do something like sky-diving because I don't enjoy ....
2 How would you .... her personality in just a few words?
3 Hans let me .... on his new bike, and now I want to get one myself!
4 Sometimes when I arrive home late, I .... an excuse to tell my parents why I am late.
5 Diego .... how to answer the questions in yesterday's exam because he simply hadn't studied.
6 People won't trust you unless you can .... and do what you say you're going to do.
7 I need to get more exercise, so I'm thinking of .... jogging.
8 We could play football this afternoon if I can .... a ball.
9 When.. her holiday, she told me that it had been extremely stressful and expensive.
10 I couldn't .... him on his mobile and he didn't reply to any of my emails.

3 Work in pairs. Take turns to answer the following questions. Make a note of your partner's answers.

- How would you sum up your personality in three words?
- What new activity would you most like to have a go at?
- Do you enjoy taking risks? Why? / Why not?
- Are you good at keeping promises?
- Do you ever make things up? Why? / Why not?

Now work with another pair and tell them about your partner.

Unit 2

Grammar
Adjectives with -ed and -ing

1 Look at these sentences from the extract and answer the questions below.

> As I raced through the narrow gap, I was <u>thrilled</u> to hear my dad yell 'Stop!' It was incredibly <u>exciting</u> and I knew I was hooked.

1 Which of the <u>underlined</u> words refers to how the boy felt?
2 Which of the <u>underlined</u> words refers to what made him feel like that?

➔ page 163 Language reference: Adjectives with -ed and -ing

2 Candidates often confuse adjectives with *-ed* and adjectives with *-ing*. Circle the correct adjective in *italics* in these sentences.

1 When we went to Disneyland, I think we found it more *amused / amusing* than our parents.
2 It can be very *irritated / irritating* when friends arrive late for a film.
3 You will never get *bored / boring* at night in Berlin because the nightlife is wonderful.
4 My teachers find it very *irritated / irritating* when people arrive late for class.
5 The situation was very *embarrassed / embarrassing* for me and I felt uncomfortable.
6 I was really *excited / exciting* and wanted to see as much of the city as possible.

3 **EP** Use the word given in capitals at the end of these sentences to form a word with *-ed* or *-ing* that fits the gap.

1 Everyone watches Pietro at parties because he's just an .... dancer. **ASTONISH**
2 We were quite .... by the attitude of the other students. **PUZZLE**
3 It's very .... to be able to apply things we learn in the classroom to our free-time activities. **MOTIVATE**
4 Anita looked quite .... when she left the police station. **WORRY**
5 The film was not particularly .... **AMUSE**
6 We were pretty .... by the time we got to the top of the mountain. **EXHAUST**

Leisure and pleasure

For questions 1–6, complete the second sentence so that it has a similar meaning to the first sentence, using the word given. Do not change the word given. You must use between two and five words, including the word given.

4 ▶ 06 You will hear a girl talking about one of these experiences a–g. Listen and decide which experience she is talking about.

a She rode a motorbike for the first time.
b She was punished for something she didn't do.
c She had to study all weekend for an exam.
d She broke a bone.
e She was trapped in a lift.
f She won a competition.
g She did a parachute jump.

5 Listen again. Which adjectives did she use to describe how she felt …

1 about the whole experience: *amazing*
2 after studying: …………… and ……………
3 about her best friend's suggestion: ……………
4 about the thought of breaking a bone: ……………
5 in the plane: …………… and ……………
6 about the jump itself: ……………

6 Work in pairs. Look at the experiences a–g in Exercise 4. Have you done any of these or have any of them happened to you? How did you feel about them? Take turns to describe your experience.

Reading and Use of English Part 4

EXAM INFORMATION

In Reading and Use of English Part 4, you:
▶ complete six sentences with between two and five words so that they mean the same as the sentences printed before them
▶ use a word given in CAPITALS without changing it in any way.

0 He doesn't enjoy running as much as cycling.
 MORE
 He likes *cycling more than* running.
1 It is easier to learn the guitar than most other musical instruments.
 ONE
 The guitar is …………………………… musical instruments to learn.
2 Olivia finds watching TV more boring than reading.
 NOT
 For Olivia, watching TV is …………………………… reading.
3 Maria's brothers are better tennis players than her.
 AS
 Maria doesn't …………………………… her brothers.
4 No one in the class makes as much noise as Peter.
 PERSON
 Peter …………………………… the class.
5 In general, cars are more expensive than motorbikes.
 NOT
 In general, cars are …………………………… motorbikes.
6 It took Janusz longer to finish the game than Sarah.
 MORE
 Sarah finished the game …………………………… Janusz.

Unit 2

Speaking Part 2

EXAM INFORMATION

In Speaking Part 2, you and the other candidate take turns to speak on your own for a minute during which you:
► compare two photos which the examiner gives you.
► answer a question connected with both photos.
► answer a question quite briefly about your partner's photos.

1 Work in pairs. Look at the examiner's instructions and the question and photos below. Then discuss what you can say to compare them.

> Here are your photographs. They show people doing different activities in their free time. I'd like you to compare the photographs, and say how you think the people can benefit from spending their free time doing these different activities.

How can the people benefit from spending their free time doing these different activities?

2 ▶ 07 Listen to an examiner giving this task to a candidate called Martyna. According to Martyna, how can people benefit from each activity?

3 Listen again and tick ✓ this checklist.

Martyna	Yes	No
1 introduces her talk.		✓
2 describes each photo in detail.		
3 deals with each photo in turn.		
4 spends most of the time answering the printed question.		
5 refers to the first photo when talking about the second photo.		
6 talks about things not connected with the question.		
7 speaks until the examiner says 'Thank you'.		

4 Work in pairs. Complete the sentences from Martyna's answer which begin with these words and phrases.
1 I think they benefit from …
2 Firstly …
3 At the same time …
4 Also …
5 I think they also benefit because …

5 Which word(s)/phrase(s) (1–5) in Exercise 4 does Martyna use to:
a introduce her answer to the examiner's question?
b introduce the first point she wants to make?
c add additional points?

6 Which of these words/phrases could also be used for b and c in Exercise 5?

> Besides   First of all   In addition
> To start with   What is more

24

Leisure and pleasure

7 Pronunciation: sentence stress (1)

We stress the words in sentences that we particularly want our listeners to hear, the words which carry the most meaning. These are usually nouns, verbs or adjectives, not small grammar words like articles or prepositions.

1 Underline the words you think are stressed in these sentences. Then listen to check your answer.

1 <u>Firstly</u>, they're getting some <u>exercise</u>, which is always <u>good</u> for you.
2 It's great for your health and helps you to relax.
3 At the same time, they're having fun together …
4 … which is important because it builds up their social relationships and their friendships.
5 Also, it's good to see boys and girls doing a bit of sport together instead of separately.
6 I think it helps break down social boundaries between boys and girls.

2 Work in pairs. Take turns to read the sentences aloud using the same sentence stress.

3 Work in pairs. Take turns to read these extracts.

- Firstly, they're getting some exercise, which is always good for you because it's great for your health and helps you to relax.
- At the same time, they're having fun together, which is important because it builds up their social relationships and their friendships. Also, it's good to see boys and girls doing a bit of sport together instead of separately because I think it helps to break down social boundaries between boys and girls.

8 Change partners and take turns to do the Speaking Part 2 task in (Speaking) Exercise 1.

- Try to speak for a minute.
- Try to use some of the words and phrases from (Speaking) Exercise 4.
- Use your own ideas and Martyna's ideas.
- While you are listening to your partner, use the checklist in (Speaking) Exercise 3 and give feedback when your partner has finished.

9 Work in pairs and take turns to do this Speaking Part 2 task.

The photographs show people doing different free-time activities.
Compare the photographs, and say what you think the people enjoy about doing these different activities.

What do the people enjoy about doing these different activities?

➡ page 195 Speaking reference: Speaking Part 2

Unit 2

Writing Part 2 — An article

1 Look at this writing task and underline the points you must write about.

> You have seen this announcement in an English-language magazine for teenagers.
>
> **A great way to spend your free time!**
> Tell us about a leisure-time activity you really enjoy.
> • How did you get started?
> • Why do you enjoy it so much?
> We will publish the most interesting articles in next month's issue.
>
> Write your article.

2 Work in pairs. Tell your partner about one of your free-time activities. While speaking, answer the questions in the writing task above.

3 Work in pairs. The article in the next column would lose marks in the exam because it is not divided into paragraphs.
  1 Divide it into four paragraphs.
  2 Say what the main idea is in each paragraph.

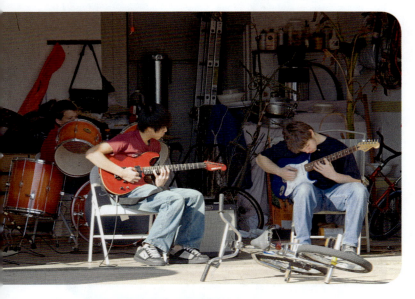

EXAM INFORMATION

In Writing Part 2:
▶ you do one writing task from a choice of four.
▶ the possible tasks are an article, a letter or email, a review, a story or an essay. The fourth task is always the set-book option.
▶ you must write between 140 and 190 words.

Playing the electric guitar – it's creative and fun!

I've always loved music, but I first got interested in playing the electric guitar last summer. I was staying with my cousin, who is a keen guitarist, and I wanted to have a go as well. She started by teaching me a few chords and some very simple tunes. I found I really enjoyed playing the guitar and I was soon trying things that were a little more complicated. It wasn't always easy, but my cousin was great and helped me so much. She even gave me one of her old guitars, which she didn't need any more. When I got back home, my parents let me do guitar lessons and now I'm becoming quite a competent player. Some of my friends also play musical instruments, like the drums and the bass guitar. When they come round to my house, we play music together because we find it satisfying and relaxing. I find learning to play new tunes fascinating and it's wonderful when we can all play something really well. I'd recommend it as a hobby because for me it's one of the most sociable, creative and entertaining hobbies that anyone can have.

➡ page 193 Writing reference: Writing Part 2 Articles

4 You can write compound sentences by joining two sentences with *and*, *but* and *because*. Which two sentences are joined in these compound sentences?
  1 I've always loved music, but I first got interested in playing the electric guitar last summer.
  2 I found I really enjoyed playing the guitar and I was soon trying things that were a little more complicated.
  3 It wasn't always easy, but my cousin was great and helped me so much.
  4 When they come round to my house, we play music together because we find it satisfying and relaxing.
  5 I'd recommend it as a hobby because for me it's one of the most sociable, creative and entertaining hobbies that anyone can have.

5 Write compound sentences by joining these sentences with *and*, *but* and *because*. Use pronouns (*he, she, it*, etc.) to avoid repetition.

1 I'd like to learn to fly. I think learning to fly is too expensive. *I'd like to learn to fly, but I think it's too expensive.*
2 I got interested in flying when I was about 14. My father took me to an airshow.
3 My parents don't want me to fly. They think flying is dangerous.
4 One of my friends is learning to fly. My friend has asked me to come with him. My friend thinks I'd like flying.

6 You can write complex sentences by joining two sentences with words such as *when*, *who*, *which* and *that*. Write these complex sentences as two separate sentences.

1 I was staying with my cousin, who is a keen guitarist. *I was staying with my cousin. My cousin is a keen guitarist.*
2 I was soon trying things that were a little more complicated.
3 She even gave me one of her old guitars, which she didn't need any more.
4 When I got back home, my parents let me do guitar lessons.
5 When they come round to my house, we play music together.

7 Join these sentences using *when*, *who*, *which* and *that*.

1 I was 13. I started running seriously.
2 My aunt encouraged me. My aunt's a keen athlete.
3 I go running most days. I've finished school and done my homework.
4 Running is a sport. Running gets you really fit.

8 Join these sentences using *and*, *because*, *but*, *when*, *which* and *who*. Use pronouns (*he, she, it*, etc.) to avoid repetition.

1 I started windsurfing. I was 13. I was staying with friends by the sea.
2 One of my friends is a keen windsurfer. She encouraged me to start. She thought I would enjoy it.
3 I kept falling into the sea to start with. It was a fairly windy day. There were a lot of waves.
4 I didn't enjoy it at first. I had to concentrate quite hard. I carried on trying.
5 I started to windsurf quite fast. It was exciting. I started to find it quite enjoyable.

9 Find adjectives in the article which describe the following:

1 the writer's feelings about playing the electric guitar with friends:
.... , ...
2 playing the electric guitar as a hobby:
.... , ... , ...
3 the writer's ability to play the electric guitar:
....

10 **EP** Complete the table below by writing these words and phrases in the correct column.

astonishing   competitive   delightful   demanding
depressing   dreadful   economical   entertaining
exhausting   incredible   irritating   popular   superb
time-consuming   tremendous   unbelievable

feelings about an activity	the type of activity

11 You are going to write your own article to answer the writing task in Exercise 1. Before you write:
- decide on a title for your article which will encourage people to read it.
- decide how many paragraphs you need, the subject of each paragraph and write a short plan.
- think about some of the vocabulary you can use.

12 When you are ready, write your article using between 140 and 190 words.

Vocabulary and grammar review Unit 1

Vocabulary

1 Complete the sentences below by writing an adjective in the gaps. Choose from the adjectives or their opposites in the exercises in Reading and Use of English Part 6 on page 10. In some cases, more than one answer may be possible.

1 Juan's parents are very ....*strict*.... and don't allow him to do everything he wants.
2 You need to be careful what you say to my brother, as he can be rather .... in the morning.
3 Pascale is very .... , so she's bound to finish her part of the project on time.
4 David is so .... that you can never trust him to do what he says he's going to do.
5 Melanie tries to act confidently even when she's feeling very .... about things.
6 I wouldn't have criticised you if I had known how .... you were!
7 Helen is very young, but she behaves in a .... and responsible way.
8 We're all feeling rather .... about Luis, because he's been looking rather depressed recently.

2 Complete these sentences with a phrasal verb in the correct form.

1 Your room is such a mess! Could you .... it .... before you go out?
2 Dad will .... you .... from the station when you arrive.
3 I must .... the housework, otherwise I'll never finish it.
4 I need a rest – all this shopping has .... me ....
5 We'll need to .... the flat before we move in – the paintwork is very old.
6 The game .... for about two hours, but I won in the end.

3 Complete these sentences with the correct form of *make* or *do*.

1 Could you .... me a favour and let me copy your notes from the last class?
2 Do you mind if I use your phone? I've got to .... an urgent phone call.
3 I'll .... the shopping on my way home this evening.
4 My mum's .... an English course in the evenings, and I sometimes help her with her homework.
5 I've got so much homework to .... that I can't come out with you tonight.
6 Marco has .... a big effort with his students, so I'm afraid he's a bit disappointed with their results.
7 Sarah wasn't enjoying the party, so she .... an excuse and left.
8 We phoned the police because our neighbours were .... too much noise.

Grammar

4 Complete these sentences by writing the verbs in brackets in the correct form (present perfect simple or continuous). In some cases, both forms are possible.

1 I'm celebrating because my team has .... (*win*) the league!
2 At last you .... (*arrive*) – we .... (*expect*) you for ages.
3 Of course I'm annoyed. I .... (*spend*) ages preparing for this party and no one .... (*turn up*) yet.
4 We .... (*have*) a really interesting time. Gavin .... (*tell*) us about his trip round the world. There are a few countries he still .... (*not tell*) us about, but I get the impression he .... (*see*) almost everything!
5 Kate .... (*lose*) weight recently because she .... (*get*) more exercise.
6 I wonder if Irina .... (*finish*) reading that book yet. I .... (*wait*) to read it for ages.
7 Tatiana is so greedy! She .... (*eat*) all the cakes and she .... (*not leave*) any for us.
8 Paolo .... (*look*) very tired recently. I think it's because he .... (*study*) too hard.

Vocabulary and grammar review Unit 2

Vocabulary

1 Complete these sentences by writing a phrasal verb or expression from the Vocabulary section on page 21 in the correct form in the gaps.

1 If you can't ...., no one will ever trust you.
2 I just don't like ...., so I'd never get a motorbike.
3 Mario is thinking of .... jogging, as he doesn't feel he's getting enough exercise.
4 Instead of reading to the children, I think I'll just .... a story for their bedtime.
5 I'll .... all our ideas in just a few words to save time.
6 I .... how to solve this maths problem; would you like to .... and see if you can do it?

Grammar

2 Join these sentences to form compound and complex sentences. More than one answer may be possible.

1 Katya took up karate. She was seven years old. She was interested in karate.
2 Her father is a professional karate instructor. He taught her karate. She progressed quickly. She soon became junior regional champion.
3 She did karate with other children. The other children were the same age as her. None of them was as good as her. She felt dissatisfied.
4 Last year, she participated in the national championship. She did not win. She was injured during one of the matches.
5 She hopes to become a professional karate instructor. She hopes to work in the same sports centre as her father. Her father has too many students.
6 Some of her father's students have been studying karate for several years. Her father thinks they would benefit from a different teacher. They are too familiar with his style of karate.

3 For questions 1–6, complete the second sentence so that it has a similar meaning to the first sentence, using the word given in capitals. Do not change the word given. You must use between two and five words, including the word given.

1 This motorbike is not as noisy as my previous one.
MADE
My previous .... this one.
2 Small towns are safer than large cities.
NOT
Small towns .... as large cities.
3 No one in the team plays better than Gemma.
PLAYER
Gemma .... in the team.
4 She looks more relaxed than she did before the exam.
STRESSED
She does not look .... she did before the exam.
5 Tatiana does not speak nearly as clearly as Irina.
MUCH
Irina speaks .... Tatiana.
6 None of the other sofas in the shop are as comfortable as this one.
ANY
This sofa is .... the others in the shop.

Word formation

4 **EP** Use the word given in capitals at the end of each sentence to form a word that fits in the gap.

1 What an .... band! I never expected they'd be that good. **AMAZE**
2 They found the journey so .... that they fell asleep as soon as they arrived. **EXHAUST**
3 It's a .... problem – I don't really know what to do about it. **PUZZLE**
4 Jake felt .... with his exam results. He had hoped to do better. **DISAPPOINT**
5 You can't expect children to work hard if they don't feel .... **MOTIVATE**
6 We were .... by the way they shouted at us. **ASTONISH**

3 Happy holidays?

Starting off

1 Work in pairs. Complete the table below by writing the words and phrases from the box in the most appropriate column.

> camping holiday   at a campsite   walking and climbing
> at a luxury hotel   a beach holiday   on a cruise ship
> meeting new people   sunbathing   a sightseeing tour
> relaxing   a cruise   at a youth hostel   by the sea
> in the mountains   backpacking   visiting monuments
> in the city centre   at the seaside   seeing new places

types of holiday	holiday locations and places to stay	holiday activities

2 Choose one of the photos but don't tell your partner which one. Imagine you are on this kind of holiday. Ask each other questions to guess which pictures you have chosen. You can only answer 'yes' or 'no'.

Happy holidays?

Listening Part 3

EXAM INFORMATION

In Listening Part 3, you:
▶ listen to five different speakers talking about the same topic. You must match each speaker with one of eight sentences A–H. There are three extra sentences you don't need.
▶ hear each speaker twice.

1 You are going to hear five people talking about the holiday they took last year. Before you listen, <u>underline</u> the main idea in each statement A–H.

A I didn't <u>enjoy</u> it much <u>at first</u>.
B I didn't mind the discomfort.
C I got to know lots of people.
D I'd done something similar before.
E I wanted a low-cost holiday.
F I improved my language skills.
G I wasn't in as much danger as some people imagined.
H I went on the trip as a break from my parents.

2 🔊 09 Now listen and, for questions 1–5, choose from the list (A–H) in Exercise 1 what each speaker says about their holiday. Use the letters only once. There are three extra letters which you do not need to use.

1 Francesca	1
2 Mike	2
3 Sally	3
4 Paul	4
5 Katie	5

3 Work in groups.
What do you like about holidays with your:
• family?
• friends?

Grammar
Past simple, past continuous and *used to*

1 🔊 09 Complete these extracts from Listening Part 3 by writing the verbs in brackets in the correct form in the gaps. Then listen again to check your answers.

• ... on family holidays we always (1) .... (*go*) to the same campsite and lie on the same beach ...
• My dad (2) .... (*be*) a climber when he (3) .... (*be*) younger ...
• Still, there was an upside because while we (4) .... (*go*) round yet another museum, I (5) .... (*get*) to meet this Polish girl called Jolanta.
• ... so we just (6) .... (*dump*) our parents and (7) .... (*go*) off for the day together. We (8) .... (*have*) a really great time ...
• ... we (9) .... (*stay*) with her aunt in a small town near Rome. We were allowed to go out to cafés together in the evenings, as long as the grown-ups knew what we (10) .... (*do*).

➡ page 179 Language reference: Verb tenses – past simple, past continuous and *used to*

2 Circle the correct form of the verb in *italics* in each of these sentences.

1 When he *walked / was walking* home, he found a wallet with a huge amount of money in it!
2 When I was at primary school, I *was doing / used to do* about one hour's homework a day.
3 As soon as Mandy *was getting / got* Simon's text, she *was jumping / jumped* on her bike and *was riding / rode* round to his house to speak to him.
4 When I was younger, we *used to spend / were spending* our holidays in my grandparents' village.
5 Luckily, we *walked / were walking* past a shopping centre when the storm *began / was beginning*.
6 My mum *used to visit / was visiting* lots of exotic places when she *was / was being* a tour guide.

3 👁 Candidates often make spelling mistakes when adding *-ed* to past tense verbs. Add *-ed* to each of these words.

> develop   enjoy   happen   mention   occur   open
> plan   prefer   stop   study   travel   try

➡ page 176 Language reference: Spelling

Unit 3

Vocabulary
travel, journey, trip and way

1. 👁 Candidates often confuse the following nouns: *travel, journey, trip* and *way*. Look at these sentences from the recording script in Listening Part 3 and complete the extract below by writing *travel, journey, trip* or *way* in the gaps.

   - I went on one of those **journeys** overland to Kenya …
   - … one day we went on a **trip** to the nearest town – it was only half an hour's drive away.
   - We were on our **way** back down the mountain when we got caught in this really big storm.
   - My parents aren't really into foreign **travel**, so it was the first time I'd ever been abroad.

   travel, journey, trip or *way*?
   - A (1) .... is a journey in which you visit a place for a short time and come back again.
   - '(2) ....' refers only to the route that you take to get from one place to another.
   - The noun '(3) ....' is a general word which means the activity of travelling.
   - Use '(4) ....' to talk about when you travel from one place to another.

2. 👁 Circle the correct word in *italics* in each of these sentences.
   1. She met plenty of interesting people during her weekend *travel / trip* to Montreal.
   2. We stopped at the supermarket on the *way / trip* to the beach to pick up some cold drinks.
   3. My mum and dad have booked a *journey / trip* to Greece for our holidays this August.
   4. My mum is away on a business *journey / trip*, so the house is really quiet at the moment.
   5. People spend far more on foreign *travel / journeys* than they did 50 years ago.
   6. The *travel / journey* to my village will take about three hours.
   7. 'Have a good *travel / trip* to Budapest!' 'Thanks! See you next week when I get back!'
   8. You can't get to school by bicycle if the *journey / way* is too long – over 30 kilometres, for example.
   9. Excuse me, I'm a bit lost. Can you tell me the best *journey / way* to the bus station?

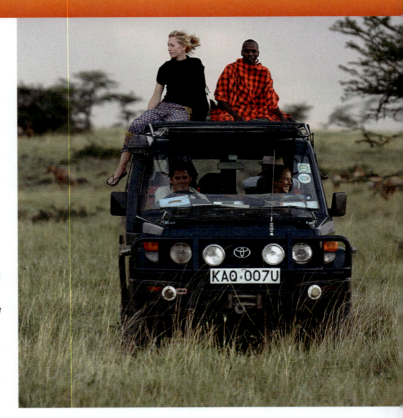

3. Complete each of the sentences by writing an adjective from the box. In some cases, more than one answer may be possible.

   > a(n) homeward/outward/hard/dangerous **journey**
   > a business/sightseeing/shopping/day/forthcoming/round **trip**
   > a(n) outward/pleasant/successful/safe/extended/overnight **journey/trip**

   1. I hope you have a(n) .... journey.
   2. I'm going on a(n) .... trip to Zurich, so I won't be back till tomorrow.
   3. The .... journey wasn't nearly as hard as the homeward one.
   4. They've gone on a(n) .... trip, so I guess they'll come home with lots of new clothes.
   5. What are you going to do on your .... trip to New York? Is it for business or pleasure?
   6. Have a(n) .... journey and don't drive too fast!

4. Work in groups. Imagine you are planning a trip together this weekend. Decide:
   - where to go
   - how to get there
   - what to do when you arrive.

Reading and Use of English Part 3

1 **EP** Form adjectives from these nouns and verbs by adding a suffix.

	noun (n) or verb (v)	adjective
1	nature (n)	*natural*
2	adventure (n)	
3	friend (n)	
4	memory (n)	
5	mystery (n)	
6	risk (n + v)	
7	crowd (n + v)	
8	thrill (n + v)	
9	doubt (n + v)	
10	success (n)	
11	remark (n + v)	
12	access (n + v)	

→ page 181 Language reference: Word formation – adding suffixes

2 **EP** Form adjectives from the nouns and verbs in the box. In some cases, more than one answer may be possible. When you have finished, use your dictionary to check your answers.

> artist   caution   colour   educate   emotion   energy
> mass   predict   reason   respond   storm   thought
> wealth

EXAM INFORMATION

In Reading and Use of English Part 3, you read a text of 150–160 words with eight gaps and one example (0). You write the correct form of the word given in **CAPITALS** at the end of the line in each gap.

In the test, the words will be a mix of nouns, adjectives, adverbs and verbs.

3 **EP** Read the text on the right. Use the word given in capitals at the end of some of the lines to form a word that fits in the gap in the same line. When you have finished, use your dictionary to check your answers.

Happy holidays?

A bus journey

Tasha climbed onto a (0) ......*crowded*...... bus which was going to take her to a nearby village. The wooden seats looked quite (1) .... , so she decided to stand, even though a (2) .... passenger offered her a seat. As the bus moved through the countryside, it filled with women dressed in bright, (3) .... clothes on their way to market to do their weekly shopping. 'This is an (4) .... experience,' thought Tasha, who was beginning to feel (5) .... about her journey.
More passengers climbed aboard laughing and chatting, and the noise became (6) .... Gradually, the bus grew hotter and Tasha began to feel a little (7) .... that she might not get to the door when the bus reached her stop. Fortunately, though, a (8) .... passenger saw her problem and shouted to the other passengers to let her pass and suddenly everyone made room for her to get off.

CROWD

COMFORT

THOUGHT

COLOUR

FORGET

OPTIMIST

CONSIDER

ANXIETY

SYMPATHY

4 Work in groups. Have you ever felt nervous or anxious on a journey? Why?

Unit 3

Grammar
at, in or on in time phrases

1 **Complete these sentences from Listening Part 3 by writing *at*, *in* or *on* in the gaps.**

   1 We got up .... about nine every morning and went swimming in the lake, even .... days when it was cloudy.
   2 We also went for walks in the forest .... night.
   3 We were allowed to go out to cafés together .... the evenings ...
   4 I went off with a couple of my friends .... March.

→ page 172 Language reference: Prepositions – *at in* and *on* in time expressions

2 👁 **Candidates often make mistakes with *at*, *in* and *on* in time phrases. Make sentences.**

Lots of people go to the beach		July.
		December.
The best time to visit my country is		summer.
		spring.
My mother's birthday's	at	autumn.
The roads here are usually busy	on	winter.
	in	the morning.
I always do my homework		Sunday evenings.
It's a good idea to start hiking early		night.
		the weekend.
		the afternoons.
		14 September.

Reading and Use of English Part 7

EXAM INFORMATION

In Reading and Use of English Part 7, you will read either one long text divided into four to six sections, or four to six separate short texts. The total length will be 500–600 words. There are ten questions which you must match with the different texts or sections.

1 **Work in groups.** You are going to read about four people's nightmare trips. Before you read, discuss what things sometimes spoil people's holidays.

2 **Read questions 1–10 carefully and underline the key words in each question.**

Which person

had to hide from danger?	1
found an employee intimidating?	2
didn't have time to appreciate the places they were in?	3
missed their home comforts?	4
worried about how strong something was?	5
found someone unsympathetic?	6
had a painful experience?	7
was unhappy about the weather?	8
was unaware of the danger in what they were doing?	9
realised on arrival that the trip was a mistake?	10

3 **For questions 1–10, choose from the people (A–D). Each person may be chosen more than once.**

4 **Work in groups.** Which of the holidays sounds the worst to you? Take turns to tell each other about a memorable holiday you have had. Then decide which of you had the most interesting holiday.

MY NIGHTMARE TRIP!

Happy holidays?

A Pauline Vernon — Malaysia

My dad was teaching in Kota Bharu, Malaysia. When my mum and I flew out to visit him for three weeks, he had already organised our stay in great detail. On our first evening we had a party on the beach. It was an idyllic scene: a beautiful empty beach, palm trees, white sand, the warm gentle waters of the South China Sea. I swam in the shallow water thinking 'this is the life', when a jellyfish swam between my legs. The sting, on both legs, was agony, and it was only then I discovered that two people had died from jellyfish stings that year and until that point no one had bothered to mention the sea-snakes, for whose bite there is no cure. I now understood why the beach was deserted.

C Nola Tracey — Yorkshire, UK

It had seemed like such a good idea three months beforehand, which was when I'd persuaded my parents to let me go on the geography trip, but when we actually got off the coach in the drizzle and made our way into the youth hostel where we were staying, I just wanted to be curled up in my own warm bed at home. The hostel was run by a rather scary woman, who checked that we'd tidied our rooms every morning before we went out for the day. The teachers were really nice, but even they couldn't do anything about the endless rain. Of course they'd imagined us all walking in the hills in glorious sunshine – well that never happened! Instead we stood in our waterproofs and wellies in freezing streams taking measurements for hours on end. I got used to not being able to feel my toes!

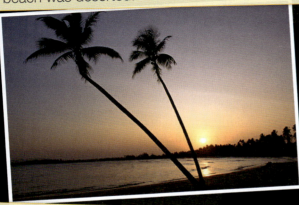

B Sandy Henderson — the USA

I was camping in Yosemite National Park in California with a friend, when I awoke to the sound of screaming. I looked out of my tent and saw my friend trying to get out of his sleeping bag, with a giant black bear rearing up behind him. Quite possibly the quickest I've ever got out of bed, I scrambled up and we both sprinted in no particular direction. By pure chance, we'd passed a small cabin a little way back on the trail and we made a dash for that, jumped inside and locked the door. Seconds later, the bear was scraping at the door as we cowered inside, afraid that the whole thing might fall off. After quite a long time, the bear lost interest and we were able to leave the shelter.

D Harry Green — Denmark

I went to Denmark with my friend Dan's family on a cycling holiday. I'd wondered what the weather would be like, but I needn't have worried. It was lovely and sunny! What was a problem, though, was how far we had to cycle every day. My friend's family are all incredibly fit, and although I'm fairly sporty too, I struggled to keep up, even though I'd had a great night's sleep. My friend's dad just kept saying, 'Serves you right for spending so much time playing computer games!' He didn't seem to understand how hard I was finding it. We were in a beautiful part of Denmark, but we never had the chance to stop and look at anywhere properly. And in the evenings, all I wanted to do was sleep!

Unit 3

Grammar
Past perfect simple and continuous

1 Look at this sentence from Reading and Use of English Part 7 (A Pauline Vernon) and answer the questions below.

> When my mum and I flew out to visit him for three weeks, he had already organised our stay in great detail.

1 Which of these actions happened first?
   A He had organised their stay.
   B They flew out to visit him.
2 Which verb form is used to indicate that something happened before something else in the past?
3 Compare the sentence above with the one below. What does the sentence below suggest about when the stay was organised?
   When my mother and I flew out to visit him for three weeks, he organised our stay in great detail.

➡ page 179 Language reference: Verb tenses – past perfect simple

2 Work in pairs. Find at least six other examples of the past perfect (*had been / had done*) in Reading and Use of English Part 7. Why is the past perfect used in each case, i.e. what is the event or situation in the past simple? e.g. *A Pauline Vernon – I discovered that two people had died from jellyfish stings that year – I discovered this.*

3 Complete these sentences by writing the verb in brackets in the correct form (past simple or past perfect) in the gaps.

1 We were feeling hungry although we .... (*eat*) lunch only an hour before.
2 I didn't know my way around the city because I .... (*never be*) there before.
3 The party, which our hosts .... (*organise*) before we arrived, was one of the most enjoyable parts of our trip.
4 When I .... (*arrive*) in Nairobi, I wasn't allowed into the country because I .... (*lose*) my passport.
5 I .... (*recognise*) her from the photograph, although I .... (*never speak*) to her before.
6 He helped to raise money to repair homes which the hurricane .... (*damage*).

4 Look at sentences A and B below.

1 Which sentence focuses on the length of time spent travelling?
2 Is the underlined verb in the past perfect simple or past perfect continuous?

A Paul was tired because he'<u>d been travelling</u> all day.
B Paul went to the information office because he'<u>d never travelled</u> in the region before.

➡ page 179 Language reference: Verb tenses – past perfect continuous

5 Complete these sentences by writing the verb in brackets in the correct form (past perfect simple or continuous) in the gaps.

1 The storm damaged the house where she .... (*live*) since she left school.
2 We .... (*walk*) up the mountain for about three hours when suddenly it .... (*begin*) to rain.
3 I .... (*already finish*) the work when she .... (*offer*) to help me.
4 I .... (*only speak*) for 30 seconds when he interrupted me with a question.
5 I was tired and dirty when I .... (*get*) home because I .... (*walk*) in the country all afternoon.

Happy holidays?

Speaking Part 3

EXAM INFORMATION

In Speaking Part 3:
- you and the other candidate must discuss a situation or problem together and reach a decision.
- the examiner gives you a page with a task consisting of a question and five different word prompts.
- you have 15 seconds to think about the task and then you have two minutes to discuss your ideas.
- the examiner then asks you another question (which is not written down) so that you can summarise your thoughts. You will have one minute to do this.

1 Work in pairs. Read the examiner's instructions and look at the task. Which phrases in the box below could you use to talk about each option?

> I'd like you to imagine that your school has won first prize in a competition – a trip for all the students. Here are some ideas for trips that students could do and a question for you to discuss. Talk to each other about how these different trips could benefit the students.

become more self-confident
become more independent
learn to work in a team
cope in another language   be educational
make a change from their everyday lives
get a real thrill   have new experiences
appreciate other cultures   learn teamwork
tough conditions   get away from their daily routine

2 ▶ 10 Listen to two candidates, Miguel and Antonia, beginning this task. What benefits do they mention for three of the options?

3 In Speaking Part 3, it's important for candidates to react to each other's ideas and suggestions. You can do this by asking each other questions. Complete the students' questions below by writing a word or phrase from the box in the gaps. Then listen again to check your answers.

> about that   don't you   shall   think   this one
> what about

1 .... we start with .... ?
2 How do you .... a sightseeing tour of a city might be good for students?
3 .... this sort of activity holiday in the mountains?
4 Yes, and they learn to be more independent because they're away from home and their families, ... think?
5 And the 'Beach activity day', what .... ?

37

Unit 3

4 Pronunciation: intonation (1)

You can indicate that you have finished speaking, or that you have more to say by making your voice rise or fall. This is called **intonation**. A **falling intonation** shows that you have finished speaking, while a **rising intonation** often indicates that you have more to say.

The speaker's voice falls or rises most on words which are stressed.

1 Listen to these extracts from the conversation. Decide if the speaker's voice rises or falls on the underlined words.

 1 How do you think a sightseeing tour might be <u>good for students</u>?
 2 I think you can learn a lot about <u>architecture</u> and <u>history</u> and <u>things like that</u>.
 3 Yes, and also you can visit somewhere very <u>different</u> and learn about other <u>cultures</u>.
 4 What about this sort of <u>activity</u> holiday in the <u>mountains</u>?
 5 I think it can give young people exciting <u>experiences</u> and <u>adventures</u>, things they don't get in their everyday <u>lives</u>.

2 Work in pairs. Take turns to read sentences 1–5 aloud.

3 Write two sentences of your own, explaining the benefits of two of the options in the speaking task. Decide which words you should stress and whether your voice should rise or fall on the stressed words. When you are ready, work in pairs and
 - take turns to read your sentences aloud
 - react to what your partner says with your own ideas.

5 Work in pairs. Do the first part of the task yourselves.
 - Ask each other the questions from (Speaking) Exercise 3.
 - Talk about each of the options from the speaking task in turn. Take two minutes to do this.
 - Try to use the words and phrases from the box in (Speaking) Exercise 1.

6 Work in pairs. Look at the examiner's instruction for the second part of the task and the list of strategies (1–6) which follow. Then:
 - decide together which strategies would be good for this part of the task. Write Y (yes) or N (no) next to each strategy
 - give reasons for your answers.

> Now you have a minute to decide which trip the school should choose.

 1 Talk about each of the options in turn again.
 2 Suggest which option you would choose, say why, and ask your partner if he/she agrees.
 3 Agree with the first option your partner suggests.
 4 Disagree with the first option your partner suggests, say why you disagree, then suggest another option and say why.
 5 Agree with the first option your partner suggests, but then suggest an alternative and say why.
 6 Disagree with everything your partner says in order to make the discussion longer.

7 ▶ 12 Listen to two pairs of candidates, Miguel and Antonia, and Irene and Nikolai, doing this part of the task. Which of the strategies from Exercise 6 (1–6) does each speaker use?

 - Miguel: ……… Antonia: ………
 - Irene: ……… Nikolai: ………

8 Match each of these phrases (1–7) with their function (a–e). Some functions can be matched with more than one phrase.

 1 In my opinion, the best choice is … because …
 2 I think we should choose … because …
 3 What do you think?
 4 Yes, I think you're right, but … because …
 5 You might be right, but I think we should also consider … because …
 6 I think … is a better option because …
 7 I think your suggestion would be fine if … , but …

 a suggest an option and say why
 b ask your partner if they agree
 c disagree with a suggestion and say why
 d suggest a different option
 e agree with a suggestion, but suggest a different option and say why

9 Now work in pairs and do the second part of the task using phrases from Exercise 8.

➡ page 197 Speaking reference: Speaking Part 3

Writing Part 2 — A story

EXAM INFORMATION

In Writing Part 2, you may be asked to write a short story. This task usually gives you the words you must use to start or end your story. The task tests your ability to:
- structure your writing.
- use a variety of tenses, grammatical structures and vocabulary.

1 Look at the following writing task and underline:
- the words you must use to start your story
- the two elements you must include in your story
- where the story will appear, so that you know who is going to read it.

Your teacher has asked you to write a story for the English-language magazine at your school. The story must begin with this sentence:
It was a trip I'll never forget.

Your story must include:
- a group of people
- a surprise

Write your **story**.

2 🔊 **13** Now listen to five people talking about trips and journeys they will never forget. For questions 1–5 below, choose the trip or journey from the list (A–F). Use the letters only once. There is one extra letter which you do not need to use.

A A family excursion	Jean	1
B A first flight	Mark	2
C A school trip	Maya	3
D A frightening voyage	Patrick	4
E A visit to a relative	Sarah	5
F A long car journey		

3 Listen again. Which stories include a group of people and a surprise?

4 Work in pairs. Which of the stories you heard do you think would make the most interesting contribution to the school magazine?

➡ page 189 Writing reference: Writing Part 2

5 Read the story on the right and circle the best alternative 1–10 in *italics*.

Happy holidays?

It was a trip I'll never forget. We **(1)** *(were feeling)* / *had felt* very excited as we climbed into the rather ancient bus. With 40 noisy kids and three nervous teachers, it was very crowded. I was still at primary school and our teachers **(2)** *had decided* / *were deciding* to organise an excursion to a nearby wildlife park.

We found the tour round the park fascinating because we were seeing animals we **(3)** *had only read* / *only read* about in books before, such as zebras and elephants. It was brilliant to see them in real life.

Anyway, just after we **(4)** *had entered* / *were entering* the part where the monkeys lived, the bus **(5)** *had* / *was having* a puncture. While we **(6)** *were waiting* / *had waited* for the driver to change the wheel, a whole group of monkeys **(7)** *approached* / *had approached* the bus and started climbing all over it. We **(8)** *had never seen* / *were never seeing* such a cool thing before and we **(9)** *started* / *were starting* laughing and shouting even more. I think the teachers felt relieved when the driver **(10)** *managed* / *had managed* to change the wheel and continue the tour. All in all, it was a very memorable trip.

6 Work in pairs.
1 How many paragraphs are there and what is the subject of each paragraph?
2 What adjectives does the writer use?
3 What things do you think made the journey memorable for the writer?

7 Write your own story for the school magazine in 120–180 words.
- Before you write, think about what you want to say and make a plan of what to include in each paragraph. Your story can be true or invented.
- When you write, think what tenses you can use, and try to use a variety.
- Include adjectives to describe your feelings.
- When you have finished, check your writing for mistakes.

4 Food, glorious food

Starting off

1 Work in groups. Complete the predictions below (1–4) about food in the future by writing a word or phrase from the box in the gaps. Then check your answers on page 42.

> a chocolate   b insects
> c meat grown in a laboratory

1 .... from stem cells will one day replace meat from farm animals in our diet.
2 In many parts of the world, people eat .... , which are a great source of protein. They will soon become part of everyone's diet.
3 There may be a connection between eating .... and increased intelligence: people will eat more of it.
4 Eating .... will help prevent disease.

2 Match each sentence with a photo.

Which of the foods in Exercise 1 would you …
a be happy to eat or use?
b be ready to try?
c absolutely refuse to eat or use?

3 Work in pairs.

- What's the most delicious food you've ever eaten?
- What's the most unpleasant food you can imagine?
- If you could fill a large bowl with food that you really enjoy, what would you fill it with?

Reading and Use of English Part 6

1 Work in groups. You are going to read an article about the effects of eating chocolate. Do you think chocolate is good for you or bad for you? Why?

2 Read the article *Can chocolate make you smarter?* carefully and note down the topic of each paragraph. An example has been done for you.

3 Six of the seven sentences below have been removed from the article. There is one extra sentence you do not need to use. <u>Underline</u> the words and phrases in the sentences which refer to something in another part of the article. (Sentences A and B have been done for you as examples.)

A <u>In other words</u>, higher cognitive performance could stimulate chocolate consumption.
B <u>So</u> the next time you feel like eating chocolate, remind yourself that it's really for the benefit of your country.
C It only shows that the two are connected.
D Otherwise, the benefits of chocolate wouldn't be so obvious.
E The good news for chocolate lovers is that the two are linked.
F In short, the more chocolate we eat, the cleverer we get.
G Instead, I found my information in a respected medical journal.

40

Food, glorious food

CAN CHOCOLATE MAKE YOU SMARTER?

Research suggests that eating chocolate may actually boost intelligence.

Did you know that if you want to become more intelligent, then according to some scientists, you're going to have to make real sacrifices and start eating more chocolate? It isn't actually such a crazy idea. Some types of food are connected to increased intelligence and I've discovered that chocolate is one of them. You may not believe me, but I've researched this carefully. And I don't mean I clicked on the 'learn about chocolate' section on a chocolate manufacturer's website.

What research is about

1 ☐ Apparently, it all has to do with a substance called 'flavanols'. Flavanols have been shown to slow or reverse the drop in cognitive performance that often accompanies aging (and yes, even teenagers are aging!) It so happens that cocoa, the basic ingredient in chocolate, is a rich source of flavanols.

The researcher, Dr Franz H. Messerli, figured that if a country has a high chocolate consumption, then its population should, in theory, have overall better brain function. But how do you measure the brain function of a population? Messerli's ingenious answer is that the per capita number of Nobel Prize winners that a country has produced provides a rough indicator of the cognitive performance of its population. **2** ☐ Switzerland has the highest number of Nobel Prize winners and also has the highest chocolate consumption of the 22 other countries that have produced Nobel Prize winners.

The all-important question though, is how much extra chocolate do we have to eat to increase our brain power? Messerli estimates that the minimally effective chocolate dose is around 2 kg per year, and the benefits don't seem to stop even at the highest chocolate-dose level of 11 kg per year. **3** ☐

However, given that so many people don't eat chocolate for various reasons, some of us will have to compensate and do more than our fair share of the work. **4** ☐ And although it's such important work, for the sake of your teeth, you should do it at the end of a meal and then brush them!

Of course, Messerli's research doesn't show that eating chocolate *causes* an increase in national intelligence. **5** ☐ There are other possible explanations for the relationship between a country's level of chocolate consumption and the number of Nobel Prize winners that it has produced. One explanation is the existence of a third factor, such as a country's socio-economic status, or geographic and climatic conditions. Messerli says that even if these factors play a role in intelligence, they do not fully explain why the link is so close between chocolate consumption and the number of Nobel Prize winners.

Another explanation is that smart populations eat more chocolate. **6** ☐ As Dr Messerli explains: 'It is conceivable that people with superior cognitive function are more aware of the health benefits of the flavanols in dark chocolate and are therefore prone to increasing their consumption.' This is still good news for chocolate lovers, since it means that eating chocolate should now be recognised as 'increasing one's daily intake of cognitive enhancers'. Clearly this is an area for more research. MUCH more research. My favourite dishes have always been desserts and I'm always happy to push forward the boundaries of science.

4 Choose from the sentences A–G the one which fits each gap (1–6). When you place a sentence, check what the words and phrases which you <u>underlined</u> refer to.

5 Work in groups.
- Why do you think countries where people produce a lot of chocolate also produce more Nobel Prize winners?
- Do you believe these claims about the benefits of chocolate?
- Are there other types of food which people say can increase your intelligence? If so, which?
- The writer is being humorous when she says 'you're going to have to make real sacrifices and start eating more chocolate'. Why is this funny?
- Can you find other phrases in the article that are intended as jokes?

EXAM ADVICE

▶ Read the text carefully before you look at the gaps, so you know what each paragraph is about. It helps to make a brief note in the margin.
▶ Read the sentences carefully one by one; can you recognise from the idea expressed in the sentence where it should go?
▶ Use words and phrases in the sentences which refer to something in the article to help you.

Unit 4

Vocabulary
food, dish and *meal*

1 👁 Candidates often confuse *food, dish* and *meal*. Read the definitions on page 183. Then complete these sentences by writing one of the words, in the correct form, in the gaps.
   1 Some types of .... are connected to increased intelligence.
   2 For the sake of your teeth you should do it at the end of a ....
   3 My favourite .... have always been desserts.

2 👁 Each of these sentences contains a word which is often used wrongly by candidates. Cross out the wrong word and write the correct word.
   1 I'm quite surprised, but I'm really enjoying English ~~meal~~. *food*
   2 Moussaka is one of the most delicious meals you can eat in my country.
   3 This beef food is really tasty, isn't it?
   4 The meal in my country is delicious.
   5 Too many people eat meals direct from the fridge, which is not always very healthy.
   6 When I visit you, I could cook a food that is from my country.
   7 The cost of your holiday includes two dishes a day: breakfast and dinner.

3 EP Complete these collocations by writing *food, dish* or *meal* in the correct gap. You will need to use one of the words twice. In one case, more than one answer is correct.

Some noun and adjective collocations with *food, dish* and *meal*:
   1 a .... source/supply/shortage
   2 organic/convenience ....
   3 a(n) elaborate/simple .... or ....
   4 a balanced/filling/light/heavy ....

4 EP Complete these sentences by writing the correct form of a collocation from Exercise 3. In some cases, more than one answer may be possible.
   1 At weekends, Santos likes to spend hours in the kitchen carefully cooking *elaborate dishes* containing many ingredients.
   2 Growing populations may lead to .... in some countries.
   3 I wouldn't call yoghurt and a banana a .... – it's more like a snack.
   4 If we continue to overfish, we won't be able to rely on the oceans as a .... in the future.
   5 Many people lead such busy lives that they tend to buy .... from supermarkets to save time.
   6 My mum always tries to provide .... with fresh vegetables, pasta or potatoes and some meat or fish.
   7 The hotel's .... is delivered directly from local markets every morning.
   8 There's little evidence that .... is healthier than other types of food.

5 Work in pairs. Write a list of foods you think might be good for the brain. Swap your list with another pair. Look at their list and decide which two foods you would like to test. Think about the following questions:
   - How you would decide whether or not they had made you more intelligent?
   - How would you conduct the research?
   - How long would it take?
   - How would you measure whether or not your brain power had improved?

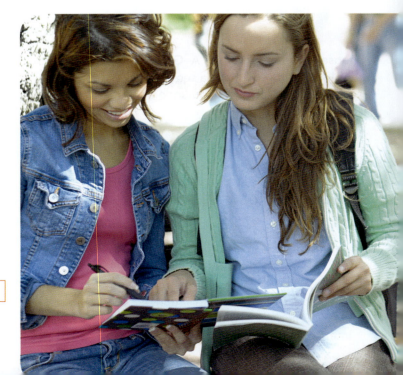

Answers to Starting off, Exercise 1 1 c, 2 b, 3 a, 4 c

Grammar
so and such

1 Complete these sentences from Reading and Use of English Part 6 by writing *so*, *such* or *such a* in the gaps.

1 It isn't actually .... crazy idea.
2 However, given that .... many people don't eat chocolate for various reasons, this means that some of us will have to compensate and do more than our fair share of the work.
3 And although it's .... important work, for the sake of your teeth, you should do it at the end of a meal ...
4 ... they would not fully explain why the link is .... close between chocolate consumption and the number of Nobel Prize winners.

→ page 175 Language reference: *so and such*

2 Write *so*, *such* or *such a(n)* in the gaps in these sentences.

1 I like going to my friend's house because his sister makes .... delicious cakes.
2 There was .... much food on the table that we didn't know where to start.
3 I don't think eating a pizza at your place is .... good idea if your parents are at home.
4 It's difficult not to cook good food when the ingredients are .... fresh.
5 We took .... little to eat on the picnic that we were starving when we got home.
6 It was .... scary film that I couldn't get to sleep when I went to bed.

3 Put the jumbled words in the right order to complete the sentences.

1 I'll always ...
   that / delicious / because / so / meal / remember / was / it
   ....
2 I ...
   in / noisy / can't / place / a / study / such
   ....
3 It was ...
   us / of / for / be / together / all / such / to / fun
   ....
4 My ...
   such / friend / best / jokes / funny / makes
   .... !
5 I'm glad ...
   you / long / such / time / to / after / a / see
   ....
6 What a pity ...
   football / spectators / match / at / few / were / so / the / there
   .... !

4 For questions 1–6, complete the second sentence so that it has a similar meaning to the first sentence, using the word given. Do not change the word given. You must use between two and five words, including the word given.

1 This is the best meal I've ever eaten.
   GOOD
   I have .... meal before.
2 She spoke too quickly for us to understand.
   THAT
   She spoke .... could not understand her.
3 He was given a good grade because he gave an excellent answer to the question.
   ANSWERED
   He .... that he was given a good grade.
4 We all felt hungry because the organisers didn't give us enough food.
   LITTLE
   The organisers provided us .... that everyone felt hungry.
5 It was the most enjoyable party she had ever been to.
   FUN
   She had never .... a party.
6 It's hard to sleep with such noisy neighbours.
   NOISE
   The neighbours .... that it is hard to sleep.

Unit 4

Listening Part 4

EXAM INFORMATION

In Listening Part 4, you:
▶ listen to an interview or a conversation and answer seven questions by choosing A, B or C.
▶ hear the recording twice.

1 Work in pairs. You are going to hear a radio interview with a girl called Lisa, who has done a school project on the subject of using insects as food. Before you listen, discuss these questions.

- Do you enjoy trying food you've never eaten before?
- What new foods have you eaten recently?

2 Quickly read only the questions in 1–7 (do not read options A–C yet) and <u>underline</u> the main idea in each one.

1 What does Lisa say about British people's attitudes towards eating insects?
   A They're unaware of how common it is worldwide.
   B They're surprised how popular it's becoming.
   C They're keen to try anything different.

2 Why did Lisa choose insects as a topic for her school project?
   A She hoped to overcome her fear of them.
   B She wanted to do something different.
   C She read something on the Internet.

3 Lisa says early human beings may have eaten insects because other animals were:
   A less tasty.
   B harder to catch.
   C too difficult to cook.

4 Lisa was surprised that people who eat insects
   A eat the same insects all the time.
   B take time to get used to new kinds of food.
   C find some insects unpleasant.

5 What does Lisa like best about the energy bar made from insect flour?
   A It has a pleasant flavour.
   B It may change attitudes.
   C It is good for people.

6 Lisa says insect farms in the future will increase in
   A size.
   B value.
   C number.

7 What is Lisa's advice about finding insects to eat?
   A Buy them.
   B Go with an expert.
   C Be prepared to experiment.

3 ▶ 14 Now listen, and for questions 1–7, choose the best answer (A, B or C).

4 Work in pairs

- Do you think Lisa chose an interesting topic for her project? Why? / Why not?
- Would you eat food containing insect flour? Why? / Why not?
- Do you think eating insects and insect products is a sensible idea given the difficulty of feeding an increasing world population? What else might help with this global problem?

Grammar
too and enough

1 Read these sentences from Listening Part 4. Write *too*, *too many*, *too much* or *enough* in the gaps.

1 And it's generally recognised now that insects and insect products will play a very important role in ensuring that we have .... food to feed the world's population in the future.
2 I mean, if they could just find .... caterpillars or something and throw them on the fire, then they had an instant meal – lots of protein without .... effort.
3 I'm not brave .... !
4 You wouldn't just go and pick one and eat it without knowing what it was – that would be far .... dangerous ...
5 I'd stick to the ones you can find in shops, though there aren't .... insects on the shelves at the moment.

➡ page 176 Language reference: *too and enough*

Food, glorious food

2 Complete these sentences by writing *too*, *too many*, *too much* or *enough* in the gaps.
1. I really enjoyed the meal, although I thought there were .... chips and not .... fresh vegetables.
2. Few schools spend .... time teaching students about nutrition.
3. A lot of people eat .... quickly to enjoy their food properly.
4. The school canteen is .... small for everyone to eat lunch at the same time.
5. Students don't take .... interest in their diets.

3 👁 Candidates often make mistakes with *too*, *too many*, *too much*, *enough* and *very*. Circle the correct answers in *italics*.

1. I liked the restaurant but *the food wasn't enough / there wasn't enough food*.
2. Experts say that fast food is *not much / not too much* good for you.
3. I don't have *money enough / enough money* to pay for your dinner.
4. We didn't like the hotel because it wasn't *enough comfortable / comfortable enough*.
5. The food takes *too much long / much too long* to prepare, so customers become impatient.
6. The food was not *too much / very* tasty.
7. I'm afraid the meal was *too much / much too* expensive.

4 For questions 1–4, complete the second sentence so that it has a similar meaning to the first sentence, using the word given. Do not change the word given. You must use between two and five words, including the word given.
1. Few people can afford to eat in that restaurant.
   TOO
   That restaurant .... for most people to eat there.
2. We ran out of petrol before we reached our destination.
   ENOUGH
   We did not have .... to our destination.
3. The news surprised her so much that she couldn't speak.
   ASTONISHED
   She .... the news to speak.
4. We did not go swimming because of the cold weather.
   WARM
   The weather .... us to go swimming.

5 Work in pairs. Imagine you have both been to a birthday party at a friend's house, but you didn't really enjoy yourselves. Discuss what was wrong with the party, e.g. *The house was too cold, so we were shivering to start with. There wasn't enough food and I didn't like the music.*

You can talk about:
- the food
- the place
- the other guests
- the music
- how you felt.

45

Unit 4

Speaking Part 4

EXAM INFORMATION

In Speaking Part 4, the examiner:
- asks you questions to find out your opinions on general topics related to Part 3.
- may also ask you to react to ideas and opinions which the other candidate expresses.

This part tests your ability to express and justify opinions, agree and disagree.

1 Martyna and Miguel are answering an examiner's question in Speaking Part 4. Read their answers, ignoring the gaps, and match the words and phrases in bold with the definitions a–g in the next column.

Examiner: Do you think fast food is bad for you?
Martyna: I think it depends. I think the most important thing is to have **a balanced diet**, (1) .... you eat a variety of vegetables, meat, cereals and so on. I'm not sure it matters so much how long it takes to prepare, (2) .... I think fast food is just food which is prepared quickly. (3) .... , if you just **live on**, what's it called, **junk food**, for instance hamburgers and pizzas and things like that, (4) .... you probably need to **cut down** and have a more balanced diet.
Examiner: And Miguel, what do you think?
Miguel: I agree with Martyna. I think it's fine to eat fast food occasionally, (5) .... you have to balance it with other things like fresh fruit and vegetables (6) .... are in season and cut down on **dairy products** and fat. Also, I think that (7) .... you eat is only one part of a healthy **lifestyle**.

a solid or liquid substance obtained from animals or plants and used especially in cooking *fat*
b combination of the correct types and amounts of food
c do less of something
d food that is unhealthy but is quick and easy to eat
e foods made from milk, such as cream, butter and cheese
f only eat a particular type of food
g someone's way of living; the things that a person or particular group of people usually do

2 ▶ 15 Complete Martyna's and Miguel's answers by writing a word or phrase from this box in the gaps. Then listen to check your answers.

> because   but   in other words   on the other hand
> then   what   which

3 Find words or phrases in Martyna's and Miguel's answers where they:
1 explain what they mean using different words
2 give a reason
3 give examples
4 balance one idea or opinion with another.

4 **Pronunciation:** grouping words and pausing (1)

When we speak, we say words in groups which form a meaning together, almost like one word, and we pause slightly between these groups of words.

1 ▶ 16 Listen to Miguel answering the examiner's next question and use a (/) to mark where he pauses.

Examiner: How can families benefit from eating together?
Miguel: Well, / the important thing is not eating, / it's spending time together / so that they can talk about what they have been doing during the day. They get the chance to exchange opinions and make plans as well, because everyone can contribute and that's what makes a rich, meaningful family life. Children learn ideas and attitudes from their parents, while parents keep up to date with their children and what they are thinking and doing.

2 Work in pairs. Read Miguel's answer aloud. While your partner is speaking, check where they pause and if the pause sounds natural.

Food, glorious food

5 Read the questions below and think about how you might answer them. Write a few sentences for one of them and mark where you need to pause when you speak.

- What, for you, is a healthy diet?
- How are the things we eat nowadays different from the things our grandparents used to eat when they were young?
- Do you think young people should learn to cook at school? Why? / Why not?

6 Work in pairs and take turns to ask and answer the questions.

→ page 198 Speaking reference: Speaking Part 4

Reading and Use of English Part 1

EXAM INFORMATION

In Reading and Use of English Part 1, you:
▶ read a text of 150–160 words and fill in the gaps with the best option A, B, C, D.

1 You are going to read a short review of a restaurant in Manchester. Read the review quickly to find out what the writer liked about the restaurant, e.g. *the price*.

2 For questions 1–8, read the review again and decide which answer (A, B, C or D) best fits each gap. There is an example at the beginning (0).

0	A checked	(B tried)	C tested	D proved
1	A revealed	B realised	C spotted	D knew
2	A truth	B case	C matter	D event
3	A achieved	B succeeded	C managed	D reached
4	A plate	B dish	C food	D meal
5	A quality	B level	C condition	D choice
6	A price	B worth	C cost	D value
7	A arrived	B reached	C came	D rose
8	A recommend	B propose	C suggest	D advise

MosoMoso

I **(0)** *tried* Moso Moso for the first time this month with my family for my dad's birthday, and **(1)** ………… that it was easily the best Chinese restaurant we've eaten in.

The surroundings were modern, yet it still felt airy and cosy. The waiters were very welcoming and helpful, and not too rushed, as is often the **(2)** ………… in some popular restaurants.

As I was eating with a group of six, we **(3)** ………… to try a good range of items on the menu, and between us couldn't find a single thing that wasn't satisfying and delicious. Every **(4)** ………… featured wonderful combinations of flavours. All the ingredients were clearly fresh and of the highest **(5)** ………… and I thought the seafood was particularly tasty. My parents felt that we were given very good **(6)** ………… for money, because the meal **(7)** ………… to about £10 per person, which they thought was very reasonable.

All of us would highly **(8)** ………… this restaurant and as it is just a short walk from our house, we will definitely be back for many more dinners!

Adapted from the *Manchester Evening News*

3 Work in groups. Where is the best place in your town for:

- a birthday party with your friends?
- a big family celebration?

Unit 4

Writing Part 2 A review

1 Work in pairs. Read the Exam information box on page 49, then read the writing task below and <u>underline</u> the points you must deal with.

You see this announcement in your local English-language newspaper.

> Do you know a local restaurant, café or snack bar? ... If so, why not write a review for our Food section? Tell our readers what the place and the food are like and say whether you think everyone in the family would enjoy eating there. All reviews published will receive vouchers for a free meal for all the family in a place of your choice.

Write your **review**.

2 Answer these questions with a partner.
   1 Which features below (a–j) do you think a review of a restaurant or snack bar should cover?
   2 Which features does the review in Reading and Use of English Part 1 cover?

   a The type of restaurant, café or snack bar
   b The writer's general opinion of the restaurant, café or snack bar
   c A description of its design and surroundings
   d A description of the food
   e A description of the other customers
   f A description of the service
   g An explanation of how to get there
   h A recommendation
   i An indication of the price
   j The location

Food, glorious food

5 Read this writing task and <u>underline</u> the points you must deal with.

> You see this announcement in your school magazine.
>
> Have you been to a restaurant, café or snack bar in your area? If so, why not write a review for our 'Free Time' section, telling us what it is like and whether you would recommend it to our students.
>
> The three best reviews will receive a prize of €50.
>
> Write your **review**.

6 Write a plan for your review and make notes on what you will put in each paragraph. Here are some things you can cover:

- Introduction: the name and type of place and where it is situated
- Your overall opinion of the place
- Particular dishes the place serves (and your opinion of them)
- The décor, the service, etc.
- Things you particularly like and/or dislike, such as the price or the atmosphere.

7 Work in pairs. Compare your plans.

8 Write your review. Write 140–190 words.

➔ page 192 Writing reference: Writing Part 2 Reviews

EXAM INFORMATION AND ADVICE

► Writing a review tests your ability to describe and give your opinion about something you have experienced (e.g. a restaurant or a concert) and to make a recommendation to the reader.

► When writing a review, you should think about what people want to know when they read the review, e.g. what sort of restaurant is it? What is the food like? Is it expensive?

3 A review is a good opportunity to show your range of vocabulary. Complete the table below by writing each of the adjectives in the box from the review in Reading and Use of English Part 1 in the appropriate row. You can write some adjectives in more than one row.

> airy   cosy   delicious   fresh   helpful   modern
> reasonable   rushed   satisfying   tasty   wonderful
> welcoming

the waiters / the service	
the interior	
the food and menu	
the price	
the restaurant in general	

4 **EP** Now add these adjectives to the table. You can add some of them to more than one row.

> attractive   cheerful   colourful   competitive
> elegant   exceptional   exclusive   expensive
> limited   old-fashioned   original   poor   rude
> satisfactory   (a bit) slow

49

Vocabulary and grammar review Unit 3

Vocabulary

1 Circle the correct word in *italics* in these sentences.
1. The *travel / journey* wasn't as boring as I'd thought it would be.
2. Sarah came back from her shopping *trip / journey* with lots of new clothes.
3. Among Brian's many interests, he lists foreign *journeys / travel* and climbing.
4. Do you know the *way / journey* to the cathedral?
5. It was a long, dangerous *trip / journey* to the South Pole.
6. I often meet my friends on my *journey / way* to school.
7. Are you all prepared for your forthcoming *trip / travel* to Egypt?
8. Many of our students have quite a long *travel / journey* to college each morning.

Grammar

2 For questions 1–6, complete the second sentence so that it has a similar meaning to the first sentence, using the word given. Do not change the word given. You must use between two and five words, including the word given.

1. During my visit to London, I took hundreds of photos.
   WHILE
   I took hundreds of photos .... London.
2. I didn't notice that my passport was missing until I reached the immigration desk.
   LOST
   When I reached the immigration desk, I noticed that .... my passport.
3. I've given up using the bus to go to school.
   USED
   I .... by bus, but I've given it up.
4. She was still at school when she passed her driving test.
   GOING
   She passed her driving test when .... school.
5. Paola and Antonio met for the first time at yesterday's party.
   NEVER
   Paola and Antonio .... before yesterday's party.
6. Pablo is no longer as frightened of spiders as in the past.
   USED
   Pablo .... frightened of spiders than he is now.

Word formation

3 **EP** Read this text. Use the word given in capitals at the end of some of the lines to form a word that fits in the gap in the same line.

Paradise Hotel

We had been promised an (0) ......*exceptional*...... holiday in a three-star hotel, so we made our reservation despite the (1) .... expense this involved. The website said it was an (2) .... three-star hotel which promised outstanding views of (3) .... mountain scenery. Imagine how disappointed we felt when we found that we had been given a room with a view over the kitchens, which was completely (4) .... When we went down for dinner the first evening, we found that the restaurant was so (5) .... that we had to wait for our table even though we had booked it in advance.

When we finally sat down for dinner, the waitress was tired, irritable and generally (6) .... So we decided to spend the (7) .... days of our holiday in a quieter hotel nearby. It wasn't as luxurious as our first hotel, but the view of the mountains and river was certainly (8) .... to a view of the kitchens!

EXCEPT
CONSIDER
EXCLUDE
DRAMA
ACCEPT
ORGANISE
HELP
REMAIN
PREFER

Vocabulary and grammar review Unit 4

Vocabulary

1 Complete this text by writing *food, dish* or *meal* in the correct form in the gaps. In some gaps, more than one answer is possible.

Last week, I went out with my family for a **(1)** .... in a restaurant. The **(2)** .... was not very good though. For my first course, I chose a **(3)** .... called 'Chef's special', which turned out to be a kind of pizza. Generally, I enjoy fast **(4)** .... , but this **(5)** .... was quite disappointing because it wasn't very tasty. The rest of my family didn't enjoy their **(6)** .... very much either. Personally, I think we would have enjoyed ourselves more if we'd cooked a **(7)** .... at home – after all, we always have plenty of **(8)** .... in the fridge.

Grammar

2 For questions 1–6, complete the second sentence so that it has a similar meaning to the first sentence, using the word given. Do not change the word given. You must use between two and five words, including the word given.

1. The food was so hot that we didn't really enjoy it.
   TOO
   The food was .... really enjoy.
2. The waitress spoke so quickly that we had difficulty understanding her.
   ENOUGH
   The waitress didn't speak .... understand her easily.
3. We didn't get a table at the restaurant because it was too full.
   SO
   The restaurant .... we couldn't get a table.
4. I asked for a second helping because the food was so delicious.
   SUCH
   It was .... I asked for a second helping.
5. Julio is not a very good cook, so he won't get a job in that restaurant.
   ENOUGH
   Julio doesn't .... to get a job in that restaurant.
6. We ate very late because Phil spent too much time preparing the meal.
   TIME
   Phil spent .... preparing the meal that we ate very late.

Word formation

3 **EP** Read this text. Use the word given in capitals at the end of some of the lines to form a word that fits in the gap in the same line.

Changing diets

Even in quite **(0)** *traditional* societies, eating habits are changing.	**TRADITION**
In the past, people used to prepare good **(1)** .... meals	**FILL**
from fresh ingredients and what was readily available in markets, but now **(2)** .... food is	**CONVENIENT**
becoming **(3)** .... popular.	**INCREASE**
Research shows that eating some types of food too often may cause health problems, so governments and other **(4)** .... now offer	**ORGANISE**
information about diet and nutrition in the hope that it will **(5)**	**COURAGE**
people from eating too much of the same thing and have a generally more **(6)** .... diet.	**BALANCE**
On the other hand, some people argue that despite the **(7)** .... of	**APPEAR**
many traditional dishes from our menus, in general our diets are not as repetitive as they used to be. There is a much wider **(8)** .... of products available in supermarkets and other shops than there was 20 years ago.	**CHOOSE**

51

5 Study time

Starting off

1 Work in groups.
- What are the people doing in the photos?
- Which of the activities are the most useful?
- Which are most fun?

2 Now talk about the questions.
- What's your favourite subject? Why do you like it?
- Do you think you might like to study it at university in the future?
- Can you study it outside the classroom as well?
- Where could you go to learn more about it?
- Think of two or three activities a school could arrange to help you learn more about this subject.

Listening Part 1

1 🎧 You are going to hear people talking in eight different situations connected with studying. Before you listen, match these words or phrases (1–9) with their definitions (a–i).

1 tutor
2 research (verb)
3 learner
4 mark (verb)
5 admission
6 pass (noun)
7 sit (an exam)
8 course requirement
9 job prospects

a check a piece of work or an exam, showing mistakes and giving a number or a letter to say how good it is
b someone who is getting knowledge or a new skill
c something that is needed or demanded for a course
d study a subject in detail in order to discover new information about it
e successful result in a test or course
f take a test or exam
g the possibility of being successful at finding work
h university teacher who teaches a small group of students
i when someone is given permission to become a member of a club, university, etc.

Study time

2 Now read these questions and underline the main idea in each question (but not the options A, B or C).

1 You overhear a student talking about a course he has been doing. How does he feel about the course now?
 A discouraged
 B nervous
 C satisfied

2 You hear a student complaining about a problem she has had. What was the problem with her essay?
 A It had to be rewritten.
 B It was similar to another essay.
 C It was given a low mark.

3 You hear a student at a language school in Japan. What does she like most about the experience?
 A attending language classes
 B doing other activities after class
 C meeting other language students

4 You hear a boy talking about revising for his exams. What is he finding most difficult at the moment?
 A focusing on geography
 B making time for football
 C getting enough sleep

5 You hear a teacher talking to her class about their school sports day. Why is she talking to them?
 A to tell them how to get information
 B to encourage them to do their best
 C to reassure them about the weather

6 You hear a girl leaving a message about her first day at a new school. What surprised her about the school?
 A the other students
 B the teachers
 C the classrooms

7 You hear two students talking about a lesson. What does the boy think about the lesson?
 A It was too advanced.
 B It was too long.
 C It was too disorganised.

8 You hear a teacher talking to a student. What is he giving her advice about?
 A sitting university exams
 B choosing a university course
 C paying for university fees

3 ▶ **17** Listen and, for questions 1–8, choose the best answer (A, B or C).

EXAM ADVICE

▶ Read the questions carefully and underline important words.
▶ Remember you won't hear exactly the same words as the ones you read in the question. You need to understand what you hear to answer the question.

Vocabulary
Phrasal verbs

1 **EP** Match these phrasal verbs from Listening Part 1 (1–7) with their definitions (a–g).

1	drop	a	be as good as something
2	live up to	b	decide or arrange to delay an event or activity until a later time or date
3	hand back	c	return something to the person who gave it to you
4	get away with		
5	point out	d	to think about something that happened in the past
6	put off		
7	look back	e	succeed in avoiding punishment for something
		f	tell someone about some information, often because you believe they are not aware of it or have forgotten it
		g	to stop doing something before you have completely finished

2 Complete these sentences by writing a phrasal verb from Exercise 1 in the correct form in the gaps.

1 Franz hates writing essays and tries to .... writing them till the last moment.
2 I don't know how Charo .... copying her essays from the Internet, but the teacher never seems to notice.
3 Julia worked really hard for the test, but when the teacher .... it .... she found she'd got a very low mark. I hope she .... the disappointment soon because she's looking really depressed.
4 My mum is very ambitious for me and it's difficult to .... her expectations. I think when she .... at her youth, she feels she didn't study hard enough herself.
5 The exam .... to be easier than I expected and, just as you .... , it was all things we'd studied before.

53

Unit 5

find out, get to know, know, learn, teach and study; attend, join, take part and assist

3 👁 Candidates often confuse the following words: *find out, get to know, know, learn, teach* and *study; attend, join, take part* and *assist*. Circle the correct word in *italics* in these sentences, then check your answers by reading the definitions on page 183.

1 I'm hoping to *study / learn* geography at university.
2 I only *found out / knew* in my class just now when my teacher handed my essay back to me.
3 … I know it's important to *learn / study* about lots of different things.
4 You're expected to *join / attend* all your lessons …
5 … I'm *knowing / getting to know* lots of local people.
6 They also organise lots of other things for us learners to *assist / take part* in after school.
7 There are clubs we can *assist / join* if we're interested …
8 I'm doing a karate course *learned / taught* in Japanese.

Grammar
Zero, first and second conditionals

1 Read the sentences (1–6) below. Which …

a refer to something which the speaker thinks is possible?
b refer to something which the speaker is imagining, thinks is improbable, or thinks is impossible?
c refer to something which is generally true?

1 If you speak a bit of the language, it's much easier to make friends.
2 If I gave up football I'd have more time to study.
3 If you're not sure when your event starts, check the programme.
4 If I could drop some subjects, I'd have more time for geography.
5 If there are any changes to the programme, the teachers will tell you straight away.
6 I won't be able to do that unless I do well in my exams at school.

➡ page 164 Language reference: Conditionals

2 Match the beginning of each sentence (1–8) with its ending (a–h).

1 I won't mention your name
2 If I travelled round the world
3 We don't allow people to do the course
4 I'll have to buy the book
5 I'd get another chocolate bar,
6 If I see her,
7 If I wasn't so busy,
8 If I went to study in Australia,

a I wouldn't see my family for several months.
b I'd go to the cinema with you.
c I wouldn't come back.
d I'll tell her you called.
e unless I can find it in the library.
f unless you want me to.
g if I could afford it.
h unless they have the right qualifications.

54

3 Candidates often make mistakes with first and second conditionals. Read the sentences and write the correct verbs.

1 If I .... (*say*) that technology does not affect the way we study, I would be lying.
2 If I .... (*live*) near my school I .... (*go*) there by bicycle, but unfortunately I live too far away to do that.
3 I agree with you about studying together. I'm sure we can! If we .... (*do*), we .... (*be*) able to test each other at the same time.
4 We can organise a class trip if we .... (*have*) any free time during the term.
5 If you .... (*have*) any problems with your homework, always .... (*ask*) your teacher for advice.
6 If more people in the world .... (*travel*) by bicycle, it .... (*be*) good for the environment.

4 Complete the second sentence so that it has a similar meaning to the first sentence, using the word given. Do not change the word given. You must use between two and five words, including the word given.

1 We will not be able to finish the project without your help.
   ASSIST
   Unless .... project, we will not be able to finish it.
2 You cannot use the swimming pool unless you become a member of the sports club.
   JOIN
   You can only use the swimming pool .... the sports club.
3 Stella will not participate in the concert because she is feeling ill.
   PART
   If Stella was not feeling ill, she .... the concert.
4 It will be necessary for us to postpone the match if the weather does not improve.
   PUT
   Unless the weather gets better, we .... the match.
5 Your English improves because your teacher shows you your mistakes.
   UNLESS
   Your English would not get .... out your mistakes.
6 I will only play in the basketball match if I recover from my cold.
   GET
   Unless .... , I will not play in the basketball match.

5 Work in pairs. Take turns to ask each other these questions.

- If you could study something at school that you don't learn about at the moment, what would it be?
- If you could go on holiday anywhere in the world, where would you like to go?
- How will you celebrate if you pass all your exams this year?
- If you could change one thing in your life, what would it be?
- If, one day, you became famous, what do you think you'd be famous for?

Unit 5

Reading and Use of English Part 7

1. Work in pairs. You are going to read extracts from four reports written by secondary-school students from different countries. Each student has written about a time he/she went to study in another country. Before you read, discuss these questions.

   1. How do you think students benefit from going to school in another country for a term (or even a year)?
   2. What problems do each of the pictures show?
   3. If you were at school in another country, how would you deal with each problem?

2. Now underline the main idea in each question 1–10. Which person …

was surprised by the approach to education?	1
enjoyed cooperating with their host family?	2
believes they are more adult as a result of the experience?	3
says the experience has helped them to make a decision?	4
felt a responsibility to take as much advantage as possible of the experience?	5
had a different attitude to getting up early while abroad?	6
wanted a change from their normal school life?	7
had not expected to be able to go abroad?	8
had mixed feelings about the type of school?	9
changed their opinion of people as a result of the experience?	10

EXAM ADVICE

- Before you read the sections, read the questions carefully, underlining the main ideas.
- Read the first section and find which questions it answers.
- Deal with each section in turn in this way.
- If you have any time left at the end, go back and check what you have written and fill in any questions you missed.

3. For questions 1–10 above, choose the students A–D on page 57 and underline the words which give you the answer. The students may be chosen more than once.

4. Work in groups. Look at this post on an international student forum. Think about the experiences of the students you have just read about and decide what Anna should do.

Anna

I'm 16 years old and I'm interested in coming to your country for a few months to learn the language. I know a little of the language, but I'd like to speak it much better because I might decide to study it at university in the future. What do you think I should do? Should I do an educational exchange and find a family with people my own age to stay with, or would it be better to stay at home and do an online course or go to a language school in my town?

At school abroad

Study time

Have you ever thought of studying abroad? Four students who studied abroad relate their experiences …

A **Divya Singh from Cardiff went on a short language exchange to Chile**

I went to a talk given by a couple of older students at my school who had been on an exchange programme the previous year, and it occurred to me that if I could persuade my mum, this would be just the sort of break from my usual school routine that I needed. I filled in my application while holding out little hope of being selected. However, I got a place, and was soon immersed in a totally different educational culture, which helped me to appreciate many aspects of my school back home. Another great advantage of my month abroad was that I picked up Spanish much more quickly than in classes back home and, because my teachers were pretty demanding, I even feel confident writing it now. As a result, I'd like to do Spanish and Latin American studies at university.

C **Nelson Grace from Boston went to New Zealand for a summer camp on a farm**

I stayed on a farm on South Island, where my host family had a vast flock of about 3,000 sheep. Being a city boy, the experience of farming life was totally novel, but I loved it and took every opportunity to go out and help with the work of the farm. I also got involved in lots of sporting activities, including sailing, rugby and skiing – all firsts for me. I found New Zealanders so enthusiastic about everything that I used to get up with a buzz of excitement and, unusually for me, I didn't mind having breakfast at six every morning. I also think I matured a lot during my summer abroad. I'm not so dependent on my family now, and I've learned to get on with all sorts of different people, even if they're not my type.

B **Bruce Brown from Sydney went to boarding school in England**

Although my parents insisted that I went, I knew what a sacrifice they were making to pay for me to go to school in England, so I was determined to make the most of the opportunity. The students and teachers were really welcoming, but what I found hard to get used to were the seemingly endless days of grey drizzle and the fact that it got dark so early in winter. Even so, I did plenty of sport and made a lot of new friends. At the same time, I was keen to make an impact in the classroom and get good grades, although I found the school work quite challenging. Nevertheless, I learned far more than I expected, and came away with the impression that the British are a lot more interesting than I had been led to expect by people back home.

D **Carmen Echevarria from Bilbao moved to Scotland with her family for a year**

After four years in a state secondary school in Bilbao, it was a huge shock to find myself in a private all-girls school in the Highlands of Scotland, where everyone wore uniforms. Studying there was a complete revelation to me: even though it looked old-fashioned, we weren't expected to spend hours every evening memorising facts. Instead, we spent a lot of time discussing issues, solving problems and writing creatively. I missed my friends back home, but really appreciated learning to think in new ways and seeing that education could be so creative. I missed sharing my classes with boys, but on the other hand, we probably concentrated harder and may have felt more relaxed about the opinions we expressed.

Unit 5

Reading and Use of English Part 3

1 **EP** Form nouns from these verbs.

Verb	Noun
qualify	1 *qualification*
intend	2
respond	3
adjust	4
compare	5
exist	6
demand	7
develop	8
behave	9
advise	10
appear	11
know	12

2 **EP** Each of the nouns below has been formed from a verb. Write the verb next to each noun.

Verb	Noun
1 *agree*	agreement
2	assessment
3	feeling
4	involvement
5	investigation
6	confusion
7	preference
8	approval

➡ page 181 Language reference: Word formation

EXAM ADVICE

Read the text quickly to see what it is about.
▶ Read before and after the gap to decide:
 – what meaning the word has.
 – what type of word you need (noun, verb, adjective or adverb).
▶ Think about how you need to change the word in capitals to form the word you need.
▶ When you have finished, read the completed text to check it makes sense.

3 **EP** Read the text below.
- Decide what type of word (verb, noun, adjective or adverb) you need for each gap.
- Then, use the word given in capitals at the end of some of the lines to form a word that fits in the gap in the same line.

Culture shock for language exchange students

Students going to stay with a host family in another country usually have to make a number of cultural **(0)** *adjustments*. They may find it difficult to form **(1)** .... with the children in the family and they will certainly have to get used to a **(2)** .... of new things, including food, the climate and the language. An extra difficulty may be the different **(3)** .... which the host parents have of them in **(4)** .... with their own parents. They may be **(5)** .... for the fact that they are expected to help with the housework, or come home earlier in the evenings than they ever would at home. They may not have as much **(6)** .... as they are used to, and they may sometimes be surprised by the **(7)** .... of the children in the family who, although usually friendly and **(8)** .... , may sometimes seem a little immature. However, language exchange students generally enjoy themselves and often form lasting friendships.

ADJUST
FRIEND

VARY

EXPECT

COMPARE
PREPARE

DEPEND

BEHAVE

WELCOME

4 Work in groups. How do schools benefit from having visits from exchange students?

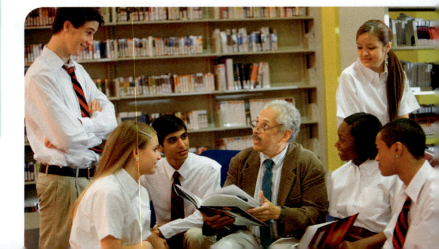

Speaking Part 1

1 ▶ 18 Work in pairs. Complete this extract of two candidates doing Speaking Part 1. Then listen to check your answers.

Teacher: Nikolai, what is your favourite subject at school?
Nikolai: I find biology very interesting. That's (1) .... I enjoy all science subjects a lot and (2) .... I can get good enough marks in my final exams, I'll study medicine (3) .... I go to university. Also, I've got a really excellent biology teacher, (4) .... makes the subject much more fun.
Teacher: And you, Martyna, how do you think you'll use English in the future?
Martyna: Well, I think English is an absolute necessity now and you just can't get by without it. It'll help me to find a job, and (5) .... my work involves travelling, it'll really be essential. I'd like to work in business, (6) .... I think English is really necessary for that too.
Teacher: Thank you. Nikolai, can you …

2 Work in pairs.
1. How many reasons does Nikolai give for his answer?
2. How many situations does Martyna mention for using English?
3. Why is it good to combine ideas and reasons in your answers?
4. Why is it good to sound interested and enthusiastic?

3 Think how you can answer these two questions, combining your ideas and reasons for them. Then work in pairs and take turns to ask and answer the questions.
- What is/was your favourite subject at school? Why?
- How do you think you'll use English in the future?

4 Pronunciation: word stress (2)

With some related words, the stress is different depending on whether it is a noun, a verb or an adjective.

1 ▶ 19 Listen to these words. Which syllable is stressed?

necessary   necessity

2 Decide which syllable is stressed in each of these words.

satisfying / satisfactory   educate / education
exam / examination   explain / explanation
possible / possibility   prefer / preference

3 ▶ 20 Now listen to check your answers. What do you notice about where we stress words ending in
- -tion?
- -ity?

4 Work in pairs. Take turns to read the words aloud.

5 Think about how you can answer these two questions using three or four words from Pronunciation Exercise 2 in your answers.
- What do you particularly like about the school where you study?
- What plans and ambitions do you have for your education in the future?

6 Work in pairs. Take turns to ask and answer the questions above. While you listen to your partner, pay attention to whether they use the correct stress on the words from Pronunciation Exercise 2 that they use. Correct them where necessary.

7 Work in pairs. Decide whether you will be Student A or Student B and take some time to think about how you will answer your questions. Then take turns to ask your partner the questions in their box.

Questions for Student A
- Can you describe the school you go to?
- What would you like to study in the future if you had the chance? Why?
- How much homework do students in your country generally do?
- Can you tell me what you most enjoy about learning English?
- Tell me about the best teacher you have ever had.

Questions for Student B
- Do you prefer studying alone or with other people? Why?
- Can you remember your first day at school? Tell me about it.
- Would you like to study in a different country? Why? / Why not?
- How important are exams in your country?
- How important is learning English to you?

EXAM ADVICE
▶ Listen carefully to the question and make sure your answers are relevant.
▶ Where possible, give reasons for your answer and/or add some extra information.

Unit 5

Writing Part 2 — The set text

EXAM INFORMATION

The 'set text' is a book chosen by Cambridge English for First for Schools candidates to study with their teacher in class. The book changes every two years. In the Writing paper, you have the option of answering a question in Part 2 about this set text. The question is often an essay question, but could be a review, an article or a letter instead. You:
- might want to choose this question if you and your class have studied the set text together.
- should not choose this question if you have not read the book or seen the film adaptation of the book.
- should not write about another book instead. This is very important, because if you write about a different book, you will get a very low mark for this question, or maybe even no marks at all.

1 Read this writing task and look at the essay plan.

Which is the most interesting character in the book you have read? What part does this character play in the story and why is this character interesting?

Introduction: say who the character is

Paragraph 2: brief description of the character's role, giving examples from the story

Paragraph 3: reasons why the character is interesting, giving examples from the story

Conclusion: one or two sentences to sum up your essay

2 Work in groups. Read the two essays below.
- Which essay do you think is best? Why?
- What is wrong with the other essay?

1 Although there are a number of interesting characters in this book, there is one in particular who stands out, in my opinion, and that is the main character: John Grainger.

John definitely plays one of the most important roles in the book. All the other characters can see that he is a reliable person and that is why they are happy to take his advice and follow his example. Right from the start, he stands out compared to the others, and we know he is going to be the hero.

I find him fascinating as a character because I have always been interested in unusual people. It is hard to define what makes someone stand out from the crowd. It may be a certain attitude to life, or the way the person deals with a crisis that they face. I think people can always tell when someone special walks into a room, and if John walked in, everybody would realise they were in the presence of an amazing person.

All in all, John is definitely the most interesting character in the book. The decisions he makes reflect this and engage the reader.

2 The most interesting character in the book is definitely John Grainger. Although several other characters, such as Emma and Harry, are important to the plot, John is the one with the most energy and charm.

John is the hero of the novel, and in the very first chapter, we see how John can't help getting involved in other people's lives. For example, in the café, he tells Harry that he has spilt coffee on his jacket and this is how their unlikely friendship begins. John is always willing to help people, even in tense situations like the boat journey in the storm. As a result, people trust him and he ends up leading everyone to safety at the end of the story.

I find his character interesting because he is so unselfish. He always seems to consider other people's needs and is never afraid of putting himself in danger. This is particularly true when he jumps into the sea and rescues Emma.

John may be just a character in a book, but for all the above reasons, I would love to meet him in real life. He is the kind of person who could teach us all a great deal.

3 Match the teacher's comments (a–b) with the opening paragraph from each example in Exercise 2.

a You start the essay well, identifying the character you have decided to focus on and mentioning other examples of characters in the book who are also central to the plot. You have justified your choice of character by briefly giving reasons why you think he is interesting. This makes your essay interesting and informative right from the start.

b You have said which character you are going to write about, which is good. You could improve your introduction by briefly giving a reason (or examples) why you think the character is interesting, and possibly by mentioning one or two other main characters in the book to make a comparison.

4 Now, think of a book you have read and write your own opening paragraph for the task in Exercise 1.

➜ page 192 Language reference: Set texts

5 Look at how these words and phrases were used in the second essay. Complete Marina's answer by writing the words and phrases from the box (which she uses for linking her ideas together) in the gaps.

> although   as a result   for all the above reasons
> for example   like   such as

My favourite character in the book is Lucy, because (1) .... at first the reader is given the impression that she is shy and a little dull, she actually turns out to be far from boring.

(2) .... , when we first see her, sitting quietly and staring out of the window at the river, Mark and Jane don't even notice that she is there. (3) .... , she hears them talking about their plan to harm Kim, and then the reader realises that 'little' Lucy, as Gavin always calls her, is a brave and intelligent woman.

Throughout the book, the reader is surprised by Lucy, (4) .... when she confronts Gavin about his behaviour towards his sister. Other characters in the book, (5) .... Kim and Mark, soon learn to respect her for her honesty and courage.

(6) .... , Lucy is the most interesting character in the book for me. I still think about her sometimes, even though she is just a fictional character and I read the book a long time ago.

6 Complete the essay you started in Exercise 4. Try to use some of the words and phrases you have practised.

6 My first job

Starting off

Work in pairs.

1 Choose one of the jobs in the pictures that you would most like to do (don't tell your partner which one). Explain why you would like to do this job. Can your partner guess which job you're talking about? Swap and see if you can guess which job your partner has chosen.

2 Which job would suit you least? Why?

Listening Part 3

1 Work in pairs. You are going to hear five young people talking about their holiday job. For each speaker (1–5), you will have to choose from the list of options (A–H) which feelings or opinions they describe. Before you listen, paraphrase each option in your own words.

A I feel people enjoy chatting to me.
   I get the impression people like talking to me.
B I find it surprisingly hard work.
C I'm learning a lot from the people I meet.
D I might have the opportunity to achieve an ambition.
E I feel I'm gaining useful skills.
F I don't talk to my colleagues much.
G I'm hoping to work there again some time.
H I feel frustrated when there are things I can't deal with.

Speaker 1 [1]
Speaker 2 [2]
Speaker 3 [3]
Speaker 4 [4]
Speaker 5 [5]

2 ▶ 21 Now listen. For speakers 1–5 above, choose from the list (A–H) what each speaker says. Use the letters only once. There are three extra letters which you do not need to use.

EXAM ADVICE

▶ Before you listen, read each option carefully and think about what it means.
▶ Listen for the general idea of what each speaker is saying.
▶ Wait until each speaker finishes before you choose an answer.
▶ Remember that the speakers may talk about something connected with other sentences, but there is only one correct option for each speaker.

3 Work in groups.
• Would you be interested in doing any of the jobs the speakers talked about? Why? / Why not?
• What job would be 'a dream come true' for you?

Vocabulary

work or *job*; *possibility*, *occasion* or *opportunity*; *fun* or *funny*

1 👁 Candidates often confuse the following words: *work* or *job*; *possibility*, *occasion* or *opportunity*; *fun* or *funny*. Read these sentences from Listening Part 3 and circle the correct word in *italics*. Then read the definitions on page 183 to check your answers.
  1 This is my first holiday *job / work*, and I'm helping my aunt and uncle in their grocery shop.
  2 It's hard physical *job / work*, but I think I expected that when I started.
  3 It isn't a very well-paid *job / work*, but then lots of holiday *jobs / works* aren't, I suppose.
  4 They like the *possibility / occasion / opportunity* to talk to someone different.
  5 On some *possibilities / occasions / opportunities*, I've even been left on my own in charge of the whole hotel for a short time!
  6 There's always the *possibility / occasion / opportunity* that I'll actually meet a film star.
  7 It's *fun / funny* to chat to all the different people who work in the market.

2 Circle the correct word in *italics* in these sentences.
  1 I know he was trying to be *fun / funny*, but none of his jokes made us laugh.
  2 The trip was *fun / funny* – we should do it again sometime.
  3 I don't think there's much *possibility / opportunity* of him being chosen for the job.
  4 I only wear these smart clothes on special *occasions / opportunities*.
  5 Did you get a(n) *possibility / opportunity* to chat to Matt yesterday?
  6 She's just filled out a form applying for a summer *job / work*.
  7 I'm hoping to study engineering and to find *job / work* in the construction industry when I leave school.
  8 One of my *jobs / works* was to take the children swimming.

3 Work in pairs. Complete the diagram below by grouping these words which form adjective collocations with *job* and *work* according to meaning. In some cases, more than one answer may be possible.

badly paid   challenging   demanding   ~~fascinating~~
~~full-time~~   ~~hard~~   holiday   manual   office   ~~outdoor~~
part-time   permanent   pleasant   responsible
~~skilled~~   temporary   tiring   tough   weekend
~~well-paid~~   worthwhile

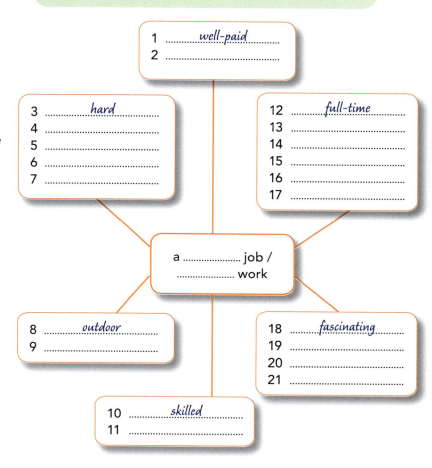

4 Work in pairs. Describe each of these jobs using two or three adjectives from Exercise 3. (Put the adjectives which express your opinion first and the adjectives which express a fact afterwards, e.g. *Being a lifeguard at a swimming pool is a pleasant, outdoor, temporary job.*)
  • waiter
  • doctor
  • taxi driver
  • babysitter
  • actor
  • the job you would like to do in the future

Unit 6

Reading and Use of English Part 5

1 You are going to read an extract from the autobiography of Lucy Irvine, whose first job was in her father's hotel. Before you read, work in groups. What do you think are the advantages and disadvantages of working with your parents?

2 Read the extract quickly to answer these questions.
1 What was Lucy's job?
2 What part of her job involved making things?

Lucy's first job

When I was just 16, my father bought an old guesthouse in the village where we lived and decided to turn it into a luxury hotel. At the early stages of the hotel, he experimented with everything. None of us had ever worked in a hotel before, but my dad had a vision of what guests would like to see. His standards were uncompromisingly high and he believed that in order to achieve those standards the most important thing was work.

For a month that summer, my name was down on the duty roster as waitress at breakfast and dinner, which included laying the tables in the dining room beforehand and hoovering and glass polishing afterwards. This gave me the middle of the day free for studying because, predictably, my school report had not lived up to my father's high expectations.

Like all the other waitresses, I was equipped with a neat little uniform and instructions to treat the guests as though they were special visitors in my own home. Although I did not feel comfortable with this, I did not express my feelings. Instead I concentrated all my attention on doing the job as well as, if not better than, the older girls.

I soon learned how to tackle the two most daunting installations in the kitchen: the dishwasher and the chef, Gordon. He had an impressive chef's hat and a terrifying ability to lose his temper for no clear reason. His breath was strong and fishy, and I avoided him as much as possible and always grabbed the dishes he set down with a forbidding expression on my face which was transformed into a charming smile in the brief space between kitchen and dining room.

Breakfast waitressing was, I found, more enjoyable than the dinner shift. The guests came wandering into the dining room from seven thirty onwards, staring with appreciation at the view of sea and islands through the dining-room window. If the day looked promising, I would note down requests for boats and packed lunches along with their breakfast orders. It was a matter of pride to me that everyone got their order promptly, and I took pleasure in my ability to get on with the people at each table.

It was funny how differently people behaved in the evenings, dressed up and talking with louder, colder voices, not always returning my smile. However, that all changed when Dad, who was keen to make full use of my potential, created a special role for me which made me feel considerably more important.

It began with a few modest trays of cakes for the guests' packed lunches and progressed swiftly to fancy cakes for afternoon teas. I found that recipes were easy to follow and it was amusing to improvise. This led to the climax: a nightly extravaganza known as Lucy's Sweet Trolley. Every evening, I made a grand entrance, wheeling before me a trolley carrying the most extraordinary collection of puddings, cakes and other desserts ever to grace a Scottish hotel. Most were things I had invented myself and I had cooked all of them. Some – Jacobite Grenades, Mocha Genghis Khan and Goat's Milk Bavarios to name a few – were undeniably strange. It was Dad's idea that I should dress smartly and stop at each table and recite the name of each dish.

Adapted from *Runaway* by Lucy Irvine

3 Read these questions and copy out (or <u>underline</u>) the parts of the text which provide the answers.
1. In paragraph 1, what does Lucy say the people working at the hotel had in common?
2. What does the writer mean by *daunting* in line 25?
3. What did Lucy do while she carried food to the dining room?
4. Why did Lucy enjoy serving breakfasts more than dinners?
5. What was special about the food on Lucy's Sweet Trolley?

4 For questions 1–6, choose the answer (A, B, C or D) which you think fits best according to the text. Use the words you underlined in Exercise 3 to help you.
1. What did the people working at the hotel have in common?
   A They all understood the guests' expectations.
   B They all shared the same goals.
   C They all lacked experience.
   D They were all hard-working.

2. What does the writer mean by *daunting* in line 25?
   A disgusting
   B frightening
   C interesting
   D strange

3. What did Lucy do while she carried food to the dining room?
   A She smiled at Gordon in a friendly way.
   B She walked very slowly.
   C She checked the food Gordon gave her.
   D She started to look more friendly.

4. Lucy enjoyed serving breakfasts more than dinners because the guests were
   A more demanding.
   B more friendly.
   C more punctual.
   D more relaxed.

5. What was special about the food on Lucy's Sweet Trolley?
   A It was inspired by traditional recipes.
   B It was prepared along with food for picnics.
   C It was made following her father's instructions.
   D It contained a number of new creations.

6. What impression does Lucy give of her job throughout the passage?
   A She found many opportunities to laugh.
   B She looked for ways of doing it better.
   C She found all aspects of it enjoyable.
   D She could do it with little effort.

EXAM ADVICE
- First read the text quickly to get a general idea of what it is about.
- Read the first question, find where it is answered in the text and read that section carefully more than once before you read the options A, B, C and D.
- Read each of the options A, B, C and D carefully and choose the one which matches what the text says.

5 Work in pairs.
- Would you enjoy doing a job like Lucy's? Why? / Why not?
- Which parts of her job would you enjoy more and which would you enjoy less?
- Do you think being a waiter is a good holiday job for a teenager? Why? / Why not?

65

Unit 6

Speaking Part 2

1 Work in pairs. When you compare photos, you can say what the photos have in common as well as what is different about them. Discuss how you could answer the examiner's instructions below to say:
- which things are similar.
- which things are different.

> I'd like you to compare the photographs and say what you think the people are learning from doing these two types of work.

What are the people learning from doing these two types of work?

2 How could you use these words or phrases to talk about the photos?

> a involve   b deal with   c not well-paid   d coaching
> e full-time   f part-time   g keep somebody in order
> h work under pressure   i keep cool

3 ▶ 22 Listen to Nikolai and Antonia doing this part of the test. Which photo do they use each word or phrase with? Write 1, 2 or B (both) by each word or phrase (a–i).

4 Which of these strategies (a or b) does Nikolai use when doing the task?
- a He describes the first photo and answers the question before moving on to the second photo and doing the same.
- b He points out similarities as well as differences between the two photos and switches between them as he answers.

5 Listen again. Which of these phrases does Nikolai use? Tick ✓ the ones you hear.
- Both photos show … ✓
- Both the jobs in the photos involve … / … neither of them …
- Anyway, the first photo shows …
- While the girl in the first photo …
- … whereas in the second photo … / … whereas the boy's …
- Another thing in the second photo is …
- I think both can …
- On the other hand …
- not just … but also …

6 Pronunciation: sentence stress (2)

We can use stress to contrast ideas or information.

1 Which ideas or information does Nikolai contrast in this sentence?

> Anyway, the first photo shows a girl serving young people in a restaurant, whereas in the second photo a boy is working with children.

2 ▶ 23 Listen to the sentence and underline the stressed words.

My first job

3 Decide which words are stressed in these sentences. Then listen to check your answers.
- The girl's job may be full-time, / whereas the boy's is probably part-time.
- The girl can learn how to keep customers happy, / while the boy has to keep children in order.
- He'll probably learn not just to deal with children, / but also their parents.
- I'd prefer to coach children than work in a restaurant / because really I enjoy being in the fresh air more than being indoors.

7 Work alone.
- Write three sentences to compare the photos and say which job you think is more difficult. Use phrases from Exercise 5 in your sentences.
- When you are ready, work in pairs and take turns to read your sentences aloud using stress to contrast your ideas.

8 Work in pairs.

Student A: Do the speaking task in Exercise 1 on page 66.
Student B: Time your partner and make sure they speak for one minute.

EXAM ADVICE

▶ Compare the general differences between the two photos and also spend time answering the printed question.
▶ You can talk about one photo first and then the other (as you saw in Unit 2), or both at the same time (as in this unit).
▶ Keep speaking till the examiner says 'Thank you'.

9 Work in pairs.

Student B: Follow the examiner's instructions.
Student A: Time your partner and make sure they speak for one minute.

Then change roles.

 Here are your photographs. They show people doing different part-time jobs. I'd like you to compare the photographs and say what you think the people might enjoy or not enjoy about doing these jobs.

What do the people enjoy or not enjoy about doing these jobs?

Unit 6

Grammar
Countable and uncountable nouns

1 Circle the correct word in *italics* in these sentences.
1 Could I have some more *informations / information* about the job?
2 I've done a bit of babysitting, so I can give you *an advice / some advice* if you like.
3 My brother's just found *a work / a job* as a chef.
4 On our school language exchange the *accommodation was / accommodations were* with host families.
5 The *furnitures / furniture* in the office where my dad works is so old-fashioned!
6 The football flew through the open window into the living room, but luckily it didn't do *many damages / any damage*!
7 When we go on holiday, we always take too *many luggages / much luggage*.
8 Everyone loves the band, because they play such fantastic *musics / music*.

→ page 165 Language reference: Countable and uncountable nouns

2 Candidates often make mistakes with countable and uncountable nouns. Circle all the *uncountable* nouns in each list.
1 (accommodation) hotel (luggage) suitcase (scenery)
2 advice information knowledge news suggestion
3 accident bus damage transport
4 bed furniture
5 dish food meal
6 homework job service task work
7 equipment tool
8 instrument music

3 Complete these sentences by writing a word from the box in the gaps. In some cases, more than one answer may be possible.

| piece   bit   deal   number   amount |

1 Can I give you a .... of advice about shopping in this town?
2 During the storm, quite a large .... of trees were blown down.
3 Have you brought that .... of equipment I asked for? The amplifier, I mean.
4 I've just been given a great .... of news – I've passed my exams!
5 Seb put a great .... of effort into organising the party.
6 There were a large .... of guests at the party, judging by the .... of food that was eaten!

Articles

4 Look at the underlined examples from the reading text in extracts 1–6. Then match them with the rules for articles (*a, an, the*) below (a–f).
1 When I was just 16, my father bought <u>an old guesthouse</u> … (lines 1–2) *b*
2 … my father bought an old guesthouse in <u>the village where we lived</u> … (line 2)
3 At the early stages of <u>the hotel</u>, he experimented with everything. (line 4)
4 … but my dad had a vision of what <u>guests</u> would like to see … (lines 6–7)
5 … <u>the most important thing</u> was work. (lines 9–10)
6 … the most important thing was <u>work</u>. (lines 9–10)

a No article is used when using uncountable nouns in the singular.
b *a* and *an* are used with singular countable nouns mentioned for the first time.
c *the* is used when it's clear who or what we are referring to from the context.
d No article is used when talking in general and in the plural.
e *the* is used with superlative adjectives and adverbs.
f *the* is used with things mentioned before.

→ page 163 Language reference: Articles

5 Complete this text by writing *a, an, the* or '–' if no article is needed in the gaps.

> I was 15, and it was **(1)** .... first time I'd ever had a job. I spent a month in **(2)** .... office, helping a friend of my sister's. It was **(3)** .... holidays and I didn't have to go to **(4)** .... school for **(5)** .... couple of months. I thought it would be **(6)** .... good way of earning **(7)** .... bit of money so I had some to spend during **(8)** .... rest of **(9)** .... summer. I spent most of **(10)** .... day keying **(11)** .... information into the company's database. Although I found **(12)** .... job rather boring, I earned **(13)** .... good salary.

Reading and Use of English Part 2

1 Read this article quickly, ignoring the gaps. What activities does the programme include?

A NEW SUMMER PROGRAMME

HOME • NEWS • ENTERTAINMENT

This summer, a group of 16-year-old students are taking **(0)** ..*part*.. in a three-week programme designed to teach them new skills and **(1)** .... them used to working with people they have never met before. **(2)** .... things go according to plan, in two years' time, nearly one in six teenagers will be involved in the programme with **(3)** .... eventual aim of offering it to **(4)** .... young person in the country. **(5)** .... far, our group has spent two weeks living **(6)** .... from home (many for the first time), initially on an outdoor course, with activities **(7)** .... as rock climbing, rafting and trekking, and then spending a week in self-catering accommodation where they are planning and setting up a volunteering project. At the moment, the students are putting their plans into action not **(8)** .... by cooking for themselves, but also by organising a night outside sleeping rough in order to raise money for a local homeless shelter.

2 Read the text again and think of the word which best fits each gap (1–8). Use only one word in each gap. There is an example at the beginning (0).

Unit 6

3 Check or complete your answers using these clues.

1. a verb
2. a conditional
3. an article
4. a synonym of *all*
5. a synonym of *up to now*
6. the opposite of *at home*
7. a synonym of *for example*
8. *not* .... *but also*

4 Work in groups.

1. Do you think all 15–17-year-olds should get experience of:
   - living away from home?
   - doing outdoor activities?
   - cooking for themselves?
   - helping other people?

   Why? / Why not?
2. Which of the experiences above are the most useful for them to have?

EXAMPLE ADVICE

- Read the text quite quickly to get a general idea what it is about.
- Look at the words before and after the gap and decide what type of word you need (an article, pronoun, preposition, etc.).
- When you've chosen a word, read the completed sentence to make sure it makes sense.
- Words may sometimes be part of fixed phrases, e.g. *in order to*, *as far as I know*, etc.

Writing Part 2 — A letter or email

1 Read this writing task and underline the three points you must deal with in your reply.

You have received an email from an English friend, Rosie. Read this part of the email.

> I'm doing a school project on weekend jobs that teenagers all over the world do while they are still at school. Can you help me by describing the sort of weekend jobs teenagers do in your country, any problems they have and how people find part-time jobs?
>
> Thanks,
>
> Rosie

Write your **email**.

2 Work in pairs. Discuss what you can say to answer the three points. Note down your ideas as you speak.

3 Write a brief plan for your reply (in note form).
- How many paragraphs do you need?
- What ideas or information will you include in each paragraph?

My first job

4 Read Pablo's email to Rosie, ignoring the spelling mistakes, and answer these questions.

1. How does Pablo begin and end his email?
2. How do we know the subject of each of the three main paragraphs straight away?

Hi Rosie

It's good to hear from you.

In Spain, it's quite hard for young people to find jobs. Some teenagers have parents who run small businesses like shops or restaurans, and they often help out at the weekend. Others may do baby sitting or earn extra money by washing cars for their neibours or their parents' friends.

Teenagers who work regularly at the weekends have two main problems. First, it can be quite difficult for them to combine part-time work with the large amount of homework and studing for exams wich they have to do. Second, the jobs are often not well payed. On the other hand, the money is usefull becaus they can buy little things for themselves and be a bit more independent.

Finding a weekend job isn't always straightforward, especialy if you don't live in a big city, or in an area which is visited by tourists. Teenagers in my area usually do a bit of work from time to time for family members or people they know, rather than have a regular weekend job!

I hope this helps and good luck with your project.

Cheers,

Pablo

5 Pablo's email contains eight spelling mistakes often made by candidates. Find and correct the mistakes, e.g. ~~restaurans~~ *restaurants*

6 Decide whether these words are spelled correctly or not. Where they are spelled wrongly, write the correct spelling.

accomodation *accommodation*	comunicate
embarassing	excelent
oportunity	foward
confortable	preffer
convenient	recieved
greatful	recomend
believe	wich
enviroment	easely
necesary	course
experience	advertisment
begining	

→ page 176 Language reference: Spelling

7 Read the writing task below and:
- <u>underline</u> the points you must deal with in your answer
- write a short plan.

You have received an email from an American friend, Sam. Read this part of the email.

I'm doing a project on teenagers' part-time jobs. Can you help me by describing a part-time job you've done (or the job of someone you know well), what you (they) learned from it and any problems you (they) had with it?

Thanks

Sam

8 Write your email. You should write between 140 and 190 words.

→ page 189 Writing reference: Emails and letters

EXAM ADVICE AND INFORMATION

When writing a letter or email for Writing Part 2:
▶ read the letter/email in the task carefully and <u>underline</u> the points you must deal with.
▶ use the <u>underlined</u> points to write a plan, dealing with one point in each paragraph.
▶ write following your plan.

Vocabulary and grammar review Unit 5

Vocabulary

1 Complete these sentences by writing a phrasal verb from page 53 in the correct form in the gaps.

1 It's getting harder for students to ……………… copying essays from the Internet, because teachers check up.
2 Our science teacher is ill, so she has ……………… our test until she has ……………… her infection and is back at work.
3 Piotr works hard because he wants to ……………… his parents' ambitions for him.
4 When I ……………… to when I first started secondary school, I realise that I didn't expect to enjoy studying chemistry, but it has ……………… to be quite interesting.
5 When my teacher ……………… my essay, she ……………… that I hadn't answered the question exactly and that there was a lot which was irrelevant.

2 Circle the correct word in *italics* in these sentences.

1 Mario is thinking of taking driving lessons to *know / learn* how to drive.
2 Ludmila wants to *know / study* biology at university.
3 Sven is *teaching / learning* me how to ski.
4 If you *join / assist* this club, you will *know / get to know* people from all over the world.
5 You should *attend / assist* lessons every day if you want to get high marks.
6 Sayed decided to *assist / take part* in the debate on human rights.

Grammar

3 Complete the second sentence so that it has a similar meaning to the first sentence, using the word given. Do not change the word given. You must use between two and five words, including the word given.

1 He won't pass the test because he doesn't work hard enough.
   HARDER
   If he worked ……………………………… pass the test.
2 Cycling to school will make you more independent.
   BECOME
   If you ……………………………… more independent.
3 Sandra only goes to dance classes because she wants to keep fit.
   ATTEND
   If Sandra didn't want to keep fit,
   ……………………………… dance classes.
4 I'll lend you my book if you take care of it.
   AFTER
   If you ……………………………… , you can borrow it.
5 I can't tell you the answer because I don't know.
   WOULD
   If I ……………………………… tell you.
6 He's not very enthusiastic because he's tired.
   SO
   If ……………………………… , he'd be more enthusiastic.

Word formation

4 **EP** For questions 1–8, read this text. Use the word given in capitals at the end of some of the lines to form a word that fits in the gap in the same line. There is an example at the beginning (0).

It is sometimes said that 'Your schooldays are the happiest days of your life', and people often feel that this should be a period of (0) *enjoyment*. However, exams often affect students' happiness, and many students express a (1) ……………… for alternative methods of assessment, where the work they do throughout the year counts towards their final mark. They say that exams test short-term memory and (2) ……………… which is forgotten immediately after the exam. Also, assessing coursework as part of the final mark changes students' (3) ……………… , making them more responsible about studying. There are some students, however, who prefer final examinations, saying that in (4) ……………… they only have to work hard for two months a year and so they have more time for their leisure (5) ……………… . They say that some students receive (6) ……………… with their coursework from their parents, so it is not an accurate (7) ……………… of how hard they have worked or of their real (8) ……………… in the subject they are studying.	ENJOY PREFER KNOW BEHAVE COMPARE ACT ASSIST MEASURE ABLE

72

Vocabulary and grammar review Unit 6

Vocabulary

1 Complete the sentences below by writing a word from the box in the gaps.

> fun funny job occasion occasion opportunity possibility work

1 Andrea's birthday was a great .... – I won't forget it for a long time.
2 Excuse me! I have to get to .... and I'm already late.
3 My sister did an excellent .... arranging the party for us so well!
4 My uncle has lost his temper on only one .... as far as I can remember.
5 I didn't find the gym class much .... because the other people there weren't very friendly.
6 Olga sees the school play as a great .... to show how well she can act.
7 Polly took us to see a very .... film which made us laugh a lot.
8 You have no .... of getting a more responsible job with your qualifications.

Grammar

2 Complete the second sentence so that it has a similar meaning to the first sentence, using the word given. Do not change the word given. You must use between two and five words, including the word given.

1 I found my first day at work so enjoyable.
   FUN
   I .... my first day of work.
2 Were you able to speak to your teacher after class?
   OPPORTUNITY
   Did you .... to your teacher after class?
3 Our class may be able to go on an exchange trip to Canada next year.
   POSSIBILITY
   Sandra may .... on an exchange trip to Canada next year.
4 We didn't expect the news to be nearly so good.
   MUCH
   The news .... we expected.

5 Patricia helped us a lot with her advice.
   DEAL
   Patricia provided us .... helpful advice.
6 William has only spoken to his great uncle once during the year.
   OCCASION
   William has only spoken to his great uncle .... all year.

3 Complete these sentences by writing one word in each gap. In some cases, more than one word may be possible.

1 Careful! This laptop cost my mum a great .... of money.
2 I heard an interesting .... of news at school this morning – we're going to get a new sports hall next year.
3 I'd like to offer you a little .... of advice: don't go up to the castle at midday as it gets very hot.
4 That's a really useless .... of equipment – you should throw it away!
5 There are a large .... of shops in the town centre where you can buy souvenirs.

4 Complete this story by writing *a*, *an*, *the* or '–' if you think no article is needed in the gaps.

I was travelling around Europe by (1) .... train one summer when I was about 18 years old and I arrived in (2) .... city (I can't remember (3) .... name) just as it was getting dark. I went looking for somewhere to stay such as (4) .... youth hostel, but the only one I found was full, and they couldn't recommend anywhere else for (5) .... cheap accommodation. As usual, I had (6) .... problem with (7) .... money: I didn't have enough for (8) .... hotel. I wandered round (9) .... city looking for (10) .... park to sleep in. It was very dark when I came to (11) .... pair of (12) .... imposing gates leading into what looked like (13) .... park. I went inside, and fortunately I had (14) .... excellent sleeping bag, which I unrolled and climbed inside. Then I ate some bread, which was (15) .... only food I had. When I woke up and looked around me, I had (16) .... enormous surprise when I saw I had been sleeping in (17) .... someone's back garden!

73

7 High adventure

Starting off

1 Match these adventure sports with the photos.

canoeing/kayaking   mountain biking   parasailing   rock climbing   snowboarding   windsurfing

2 Work in groups.
1 Which of these activities looks the most fun? Why?
2 Which do you think would be the easiest / most difficult to learn? Why?
3 Are there any activities you wouldn't like to do? Why not?

High adventure

Listening Part 2

1 Work in pairs. You are going to hear Gary giving a talk about adventure racing as part of a school project. Read this text and discuss what type of information you need for each gap.

Adventure racing

Gary participated with his (1) .... in his first adventure race last year.

Adventure racing became popular as a sport in the (2) .... , although there were races before that.

In many adventure races, there must be a balance of (3) .... in each team.

Gary thinks teams which contain (4) .... are more successful.

Although some races take place in urban areas, most happen in (5) ....

Teams are really alone on the race because there are almost no (6) .... in the area where they race.

Gary's ambition is to do a race called the (7) .... Race in New Zealand.

Some races may take up to (8) .... to complete.

Gary thinks (9) .... must be the hardest thing in long races.

Adventure racing is considered (10) .... by many athletes from other sports as well.

2 ▶ 25 Listen and, for questions 1–10, complete the sentences with a word or short phrase.

EXAM ADVICE

Before you listen:
▶ look at the incomplete sentences, including any words which come after the gap.
▶ think about what type of information you need for each gap (a date, a job, etc.).
▶ think about what type of word(s) you need for each gap (a noun (phrase), verb (phrase), etc.).

3 Work in groups.
- What do you think are the advantages of racing in teams?
- What are the main difficulties of adventure racing?

Vocabulary
Verb collocations with sporting activities

1 Complete these extracts from Listening Part 2 by writing an appropriate verb in the correct form in the gaps.
1 Adventure racing is a sport you .... in teams.
2 Anyway, it's not like just .... jogging or running or something like that.
3 The races are .... in all sorts of different places.
4 The majority are .... in mountains or deserts.
5 Many people who are at the top of their sport in other fields are now .... because they find that, rather than .... as individuals … they need to work as a team.

2 Use the table of collocations below to complete these sentences. In some cases, more than one answer may be possible.
1 I think local governments should .... competitions for schools in their area where any student over 15 can ....
2 I would encourage people to .... swimming two or three times a week because I think it's an excellent way of .... exercise.
3 People who enjoy team sports often .... basketball or football, whereas people who enjoy individual sports .... golf or .... windsurfing.

verb	sport
hold / organise / compete in / enter / take part in	a race / a competition / a tournament / a championship
do / take	exercise
go*	jogging / cycling / skiing / swimming / windsurfing
play**	football / golf / basketball
do***	sports / athletics / gymnastics / judo / weightlifting

* for sports that end in -ing and are usually or often done outdoors
** for sports which are considered games
*** for other sports which do not use go or play

3 Work in groups. Plan your own adventure race.
- Where would it be?
- What sports would it involve?
- How long would it last?
- If you were in one of the teams, what would you have to take with you?
- Tell the rest of the class about your race.
- Which one sounds the most fun? Which one sounds the hardest?

Unit 7

Reading and Use of English Part 6

1 Work in pairs. You are going to read an article by an adventure racer. Before you read the whole article, read the title and the subheading in *italics*. What do you expect to find out by reading the article?

2 Read the article quite carefully and make a short note in the margin about the subject of each paragraph. An example has been done for you.

Are you ready for an adventure race?

Rebecca Rusch has competed in several Eco-Challenge races, where teams of four men and women race non-stop over a 500 km course which includes trekking, canoeing, horse riding, scuba diving, mountaineering and mountain biking.

need for experience

Obviously, I did not feel so ready for the early races in my career as the races we have done recently. There is a lot to be said for just gaining experience. Just getting out there and getting your feet wet teaches you the right skills and attitude.

It's often not the most physically prepared or the fittest teams that win. The ones who come first are the teams who race intelligently and adapt to unexpected situations. **1** ☐ The only way to develop those qualities is to get out and race or do long training trips with your team-mates and friends.

Adventure races are such a huge challenge that when you enter a race you always think, "Am I ready? Did I train enough? Did I forget something?" I remember one race in particular, my very first Eco-Challenge and only my second race ever. **2** ☐ A 24-hour race seemed like an eternity to me. My background was cross-country running in high school and college where a two- or three-mile race seemed long. Most of my fear was due to lack of experience and knowledge. I really had no idea what I was getting into because I had never done a 24-hour race before. **3** ☐

In preparation for Australia, I tried to approach my training in a methodical way. Looking back, I wasn't methodical at all. In fact, what I did involved simply running, biking and paddling a kayak as much and as hard as I could. I was also working at the same time. In reality, I was training a couple of hours a day during the week to get fit and at weekends training with the team for perhaps four hours. **4** ☐ I spent the rest of the time worrying about how slow I was.

So, we went to Australia and entered the race. We didn't plan a strategy at all, but just ran as fast as possible from the start. I just tried to keep up with my team-mates, who were more experienced than I was. **5** ☐ It was a furious 36 hours. We arrived at a few of the check points in first place and were among the top five. I knew we didn't belong there.

To cut a long story short, two of my team-mates decided not to continue the race after just a day and a half. One was suffering hallucinations and feeling ill. He was just too tired to carry on. **6** ☐ We had been going so fast that he felt uncomfortable asking us to stop so he could take care of his blisters. The other two of us, feeling fresh still, had to drop out with the rest of our team. Four days later, we watched in disappointment as the winners crossed the finishing line. I knew that our team had not been prepared or realistic about the pace we could keep, but not finishing that race was the most valuable lesson I could have learned.

I promised then to come back one day and finish the race. That was seven years (and thousands of race miles) ago.

Adapted from *Adventure Sports Journal*

High adventure

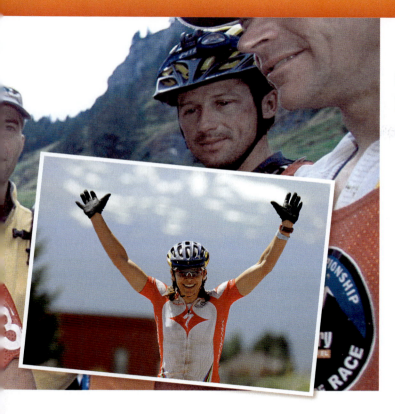

Grammar
Infinitive and verb + -ing

1 These sentences (some of which are from the article you have just read) are examples of when to use the infinitive and when to use the verb + -ing form. Decide which sentence (a–i) is an example (1–10) for each of the rules on this page. You can use some of the sentences as examples for more than one rule.

a **Not finishing** that race was the most valuable lesson I could have learned.
b I promised then **to come back** one day and finish the race.
c In fact, what I did involved simply **running, biking** and **paddling** a kayak as much and as hard as I could.
d There is a lot to be said for just **gaining** experience.
e I was training a couple of hours a day during the week **to get fit**.
f There are medical teams **to take care of** injured runners.
g He was just too tired **to carry on**.
h It's no use **entering** a race if you haven't prepared properly.
i Two of my team-mates decided **not to continue** the race after just a day and a half.

Using the infinitive and verb + -ing

The **infinitive** is used:
1 to say why you do something (sentence ...*e*...)
2 to say why something exists (sentence ....)
3 after *too* and *enough* (sentence ....)
4 after these verbs (there is a more complete list on page 166): *agree, appear, ask, arrange, decide, expect, fail, help, promise* (sentences .... and ....)
5 The negative is formed by placing *not* before the infinitive (sentence ....)

The **verb + -ing** is used:
6 after prepositions (sentence ....)
7 as subjects or objects of a verb (sentence ....)
8 after these verbs (there is a more complete list on page 166): *admit, enjoy, finish, involve, mind, postpone, risk, suggest* (sentence ....)
9 after these expressions: *it's no good, it's not worth, it's no use, it's a waste of time, spend time, can't help* (sentence ....)
10 The negative is formed by placing *not* before the verb + -ing (sentence ....)

➡ page 166 Language reference: Infinitive and verb + -ing forms

3 Six sentences have been removed from the article. Read the sentences below one by one. As you read each sentence:

- <u>underline</u> words and phrases which you think refer to something in the article
- decide which gap (1–6) it fits.
  There is one extra sentence which you do not need to use.

A Another had severe problems with his feet.
B I kept my mouth shut and followed them.
C We won it even so, and were invited to compete in the Eco-Challenge in Australia.
D His encouragement helped me to complete it.
E That was how much I had prepared.
F When I did it, I felt totally afraid and unprepared.
G To achieve this, you have to be flexible and patient.

4 Work in pairs.
- Do you prefer team sports or individual sports? Why?

EXAM ADVICE

▶ Pay attention to pronouns (*we, that, it*, etc.), adverbs (*however, even so*, etc.) and other reference words/phrases in the sentences which have been removed. Decide what they refer to before you place the sentence in a gap.

Unit 7

2 Complete these sentences by writing the verb in brackets in the correct form in the gaps.

1 Carlos has suggested ......*starting*...... (*start*) a five-a-side football team. What do you think?
2 I don't think the weather is good enough .... (*go*) sailing this afternoon.
3 We've decided .... (*hold*) the race early in the morning before it gets too hot.
4 .... (*train*) is essential if you want to perform well.
5 I've joined a gym .... (*get*) myself fitter.
6 If you train too hard, you risk .... (*injure*) yourself before the race.
7 It's no good .... (*run*) in a marathon if you're not wearing the right shoes.
8 She was disqualified from the race for .... (*push*) an opponent.

3 Circle the correct form in *italics* in each of these questions.

1 What sport would you advise someone *to do / doing* in order to make friends?
2 What sport would you choose *to learn / learning* if you had plenty of time and money?
3 If someone needed to get fit, what sport would you suggest *to do / doing*?
4 What sports do you avoid *to take part in / taking part in* and why?

4 Work in pairs. Ask and answer the questions in Exercise 3, giving your opinions.

5 👁 Candidates often make mistakes with the infinitive and verb + -ing. Some of these sentences are correct. Find and correct the mistakes.

1 Students are not allowed running along school corridors.
2 Few people choose spending their time taking exercise.
3 The Internet means that we spend more time sitting at home, but we cannot imagine to live without it.
4 Being fit and healthy does not mean to run 20 km a day.
5 Many students would prefer to cycle to school than go by school bus.
6 Many people only think about take exercise when they are overweight.
7 Unless they try to compete as a team, they will not succeed to win the competition.
8 Doing a sport is a good alternative if you are bored to sit and read a book.
9 It may be good to use a bicycle instead of going by public transport.
10 There are several good reasons for ride a bike.

Reading and Use of English Part 4

1 Work in pairs. For questions 1 and 2, choose the correct answer A–D. Why are the other answers incorrect?

1 Why don't we start jogging if we want some exercise?
   TAKING
   He suggested .... in order to get some exercise.
   A that they should take up jogging
   B taking up jogging
   C to take up jogging
   D going jogging

2 She won the match without difficulty.
   EASY
   She found .... the match.
   A it easy to win
   B that it was easy to win
   C she could easily win
   D it simple to win

High adventure

2 Now do these Part 4 questions. Use the clues below each question to help you.

1 Marianne prepared for the race by training every evening.
READY
Marianne trained every evening ……………………… for the race.
- Can you think of an expression with *ready* which means *prepare*?
- Why did Marianne train every evening?
- Do you use the verb + *-ing* or an infinitive to say why she trained every evening?

2 I found it impossible not to laugh at his efforts.
HELP
I ……………………… at his efforts.
- You need an expression with *help* which means 'find it impossible'.
- Your answer needs to be in the same tense.

3 Cycling on the pavement is prohibited.
USE
Cyclists ……………………… the pavement.
- How do you use *allowed* to mean it's prohibited?
- Do you use the verb + *-ing* or an infinitive after *allowed*?

3 Now do these Part 4 questions.

1 We'd like all our students to participate in the sports programme.
PART
We are keen on all our students ……………………… the sports programme.

2 Buying the equipment for this sport is cheaper than hiring it.
MORE
It's ……………………… the equipment for this sport than to buy it.

3 You should have phoned her to tell her the game was cancelled.
GIVE
You were supposed ……………………… to tell her the game was cancelled.

4 Mateo managed to win the race.
SUCCEEDED
Mateo ……………………… the race.

5 'I'll never get angry with the referee again,' said Martin.
TEMPER
Martin promised never ……………………… the referee again.

6 Tanya found windsurfing easy to learn.
DIFFICULTY
Tanya ……………………… to windsurf.

> **EXAM ADVICE**
> - Use the word in **CAPITALS** without changing it.
> - Count the words. Contractions (*isn't, don't*, etc.) count as two words.
> - Read both sentences again at the end to check that they mean the same.

4 Check your answers by looking at these clues for each of the questions in Exercise 3.

1 Did you use a fixed phrase which means *participate*?
2 Have you used an opposite of *cheap*? Did you use an infinitive or a verb + *-ing*?
3 Did you use an expression which means *phone* (*give her a …*)?
4 *Managed* is followed by an infinitive. Is *succeeded* also followed by an infinitive? Do you also need a preposition?
5 Can you remember an expression with *temper* which means *become angry*?
6 You cannot write *did not have any difficulty in learning* because it's seven words.

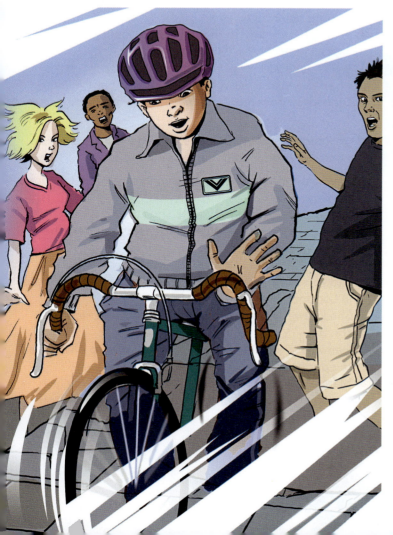

Unit 7

Listening Part 4

1 Work in pairs. You will hear an interview with someone who went on a paragliding course. Before you listen, look at the photo.
- Do you think paragliding is a risky sport?
- Would you like to try it? Why? / Why not?

2 Read these questions and <u>underline</u> the main idea in each one.

1 Why did Hannah want to try paragliding?
   A She had seen other people doing it.
   B She wanted to write an article about it.
   C She was bored with the sport she was doing.
2 Why did Hannah choose to do a paragliding course in France?
   A The location was safer.
   B The course was cheaper.
   C The weather was better.
3 Hannah says that the advantage of learning to paraglide from a sand dune is that
   A you are unlikely to fall in the sea.
   B you can land comfortably on the sand.
   C you cannot fall too far.
4 How did Hannah spend the first morning of her course?
   A She learned to lift her paraglider.
   B She flew to the bottom of the dune.
   C She watched other people paragliding.
5 When she started flying, her instructor
   A shouted at her from the ground.
   B talked to her over the radio.
   C flew next to her.
6 When you land after paragliding, it feels like
   A jumping from a seat.
   B falling from a horse.
   C falling from a bicycle.
7 What, for Hannah, is the best reason to go paragliding?
   A It's exciting.
   B It's unusual.
   C It's quiet.

3 ▶ 26 For questions 1–7, listen and choose the best answer (A, B or C).

EXAM ADVICE
► When you listen, wait until the speaker has finished talking about an idea before you choose your answer.
► Listen for the same idea to be expressed, not the same words.

Vocabulary
look, see, watch, listen and *hear*

1 👁 Candidates often confuse the following words: *look*, *see* and *watch*, and *listen* and *hear*. Complete these sentences from Listening Part 4 by writing *look*, *see*, *watch*, *listen* or *hear* in the correct form in the gaps.

1 I spend my life .... people doing different sports.
2 I was .... down the course, planning my next shot or something, when I .... these paragliders floating down.
3 In fact, I .... to my instructor, Chantalle, through an earphone.
4 It was generally very quiet, calm and civilised, except when she raised her voice to shout at other flyers to keep away from me. And then you really .... her!

2 👁 Read the two definitions on page 183. Then circle the correct word in *italics* in these sentences.

1 I *looked at / watched* my watch and saw that it was time to leave.
2 I really enjoy *looking at / watching* cartoons.
3 We live near a motorway and can *listen to / hear* the traffic non-stop.
4 I've been *looking at / watching* our holiday photos.
5 Did you *watch / see* Buckingham Palace when you were in London?
6 She knew the policeman was *looking / watching* what she did.
7 Ivan was in the kitchen, so he didn't *listen to / hear* the telephone when it rang.
8 Marisa looks so relaxed when she's *listening to / hearing* music on her MP3 player.

80

High adventure

Speaking Part 3

1 Before you start this speaking section, look at the work you did on Speaking Part 3 on pages 37–38. Work in pairs. Read the examiner's instructions and the speaking task below. Then take about two minutes to do the task together.

> I'd like you to imagine that the director of your school is interested in getting students to do more sport. Here are some ideas. Talk to each other about how each of them might encourage students to do more sport.

- A visit to the national athletics championships
- A talk by a professional footballer
- A weekend doing adventure sports
- Free membership of a sports club
- A school sports day

How could these activities encourage students to do more sport?

2 Look at this checklist. Which things did you do?

		Yes	No
1	Talk about all of the activities.		
2	Listen to each other and respond to what the other person says.		
3	Ask each other's opinion.		
4	Interrupt each other.		
5	One student tried to speak much more than the other.		

3 Now listen to Miguel and Irene doing this speaking task from Exercise 1. Which of the things on the checklist in Exercise 2 did they do?

4 Listen to Miguel and Irene again and write each of these phrases in the correct column in the table below.

> How do you think …?   Well, perhaps …   Yes, and …
> I imagine students would see …   Maybe, but …
> What about …?   I suppose that might be …
> I suppose so, but …   Yes, I see what you mean.
> That's a good point, and …   Do you really think …?
> That's true.   Yes, good idea.   You're right.
> Yes, but …

suggesting ideas	asking your partner's opinion	agreeing	disagreeing
	How do you think …?		

5 **Pronunciation:** intonation (2)

You will make a good impression in the exam if you sound interested and enthusiastic about what you discuss. You can use intonation to show your interest.

1 **28** Listen to how the voices rise and fall on the highlighted words.

Speaker 1: Well, perhaps this could be organised in a more adult **way**, you know, with some **serious** sports for people who were **interested** and **less serious** activities for **other** people. That way **everyone** could get **involved**.

Speaker 2: Yes, good **idea**, and people could be organised into **teams** and it could all be made quite **competitive** and **enjoyable** at the same **time**. When I **think** about it, it could be **really successful**.

2 Now work in pairs and read the extract aloud. Take turns as Miguel and Irene.

6 Work in pairs. Follow the examiner's instructions for the second part of Speaking Part 3.

> Now you have a minute to decide which idea the head of your school should choose.

Unit 7

7 Work in pairs.

1 Take about two minutes to do the first part of the speaking task below.

> I'd like you to imagine that a town wants young people to spend their free time in ways which are useful for them. Here are some ideas that they are thinking about and a question for you to discuss. Talk to each other about how these ideas would provide useful ways for young people to spend their free time.

- Building a sports centre and gym
- Organising trips abroad
- How would these ideas provide useful ways for young people to spend their free time?
- Running adventure-sports weekends
- Starting a cinema and theatre club
- Providing a library

2 Now follow the examiner's instructions for the second part of Speaking Part 3.

> Now you have a minute to decide which two facilities the town should build.

EXAM ADVICE

When you discuss the first part of the task, you needn't talk about all of the options, but you should make suggestions, ask your partner's opinion and respond to your partner's ideas.

When you discuss the second part of the task, it's not necessary to reach agreement, but you should:
▶ discuss which option(s) to choose and give reasons for choice(s)
▶ listen and respond to what your partner says. Don't be afraid to disagree politely – this can lead to a good discussion.

Writing Part 2 An article

1 Read this writing task and <u>underline</u> the points you must deal with in your answer.

You see this notice on your school noticeboard.

The editors of the school magazine would like contributions to the magazine on the following subject:

A great way to keep fit.

Describe a sporting activity or form of exercise you enjoy, how you started and why you would recommend it to other people.

The writer of the best article will receive ten tickets to the local cinema.

Write your **article**.

2 Work in pairs.
- Discuss the ideas each of you could express to deal with the points you have <u>underlined</u> in the task.
- Which ideas would you use in your article?

3 Read the article on page 83.
- What does the writer enjoy about his way of taking exercise? Why?

Cycling: tough but fun

I love cycling. I got my first bicycle when I was just nine years old and loved going for long bike rides with my parents, *despite* not enjoying sport much at school. It was compulsory for us to play football twice a week, and I never enjoyed it, mainly because I was smaller than most of the other boys my age and our opponents were often quite rough! *However*, I was quite athletic and fit, so I was delighted to find a sporting activity that I really enjoyed.

Although cycling is something anyone can do just for fun, it's also a competitive sport and if you start to take part in races and join a team, you'll find you have to train several times a week and you'll need someone to coach you. And if you and your team want to win a trophy, you'll all have to work extremely hard.

Although it's a tough sport, I would recommend cycling to anyone who loves being outdoors and keeping fit. *However*, if you don't want to cycle in competitions, it's a great sport for spectators as well, and it's often on TV!

4 Look at the structure of the article. In which paragraph does the writer deal with these points?

1 Describing an activity.
2 How he started.
3 Why he would recommend it.

5 Study how the words in *italics* in the article are used. Then complete these sentences by writing *although*, *however* or *despite* in the gaps.

1 .... the swimming pool is quite far from where I live, I try to go there three times a week.
2 .... being given tickets to the football match, we decided to watch it on TV.
3 I'd love to be a professional footballer, ... I don't think I'm talented enough.
4 He was very easy to talk to .... being a famous tennis star.
5 .... feeling very tired, she managed to finish the race.
6 I didn't enjoy the match. .... , our opponents played very well.

→ page 168 Language reference: Linking words for contrast

High adventure

6 Study how the writer used the words in the box in his article. Then use them in the correct form to complete the sentences below.

athletic   opponents   competitive   rough   trophy
coach   spectators

1 Although Valerie enjoys .... sports, she prefers exercising on her own.
2 Ice hockey is a .... game where players often get hurt.
3 If I was more .... , I might be able to win a few more races.
4 Our .... for the next match are last year's champions.
5 We need someone to .... our team so that we learn to play better.
6 Few .... watch adventure sports because they take place in areas that are hard to get to.
7 We're rated as one of the top teams despite never having won a single ....

7 Now write your own answer to the writing task in Exercise 1.

- Before you start writing, make a brief plan.
- Try to use structures and vocabulary you have studied in this writing section and this unit.
- Write between 140 and 190 words.
- Read through your article when you have finished to improve it and to check it for mistakes.

EXAM ADVICE

▶ Write a plan before you start writing the article.
▶ Organise your ideas into paragraphs, and use linking words such as: *however, despite, in addition, for example* and *on the other hand.*

Before you write:
▶ think about what the people reading the article will find interesting, enjoyable or useful.
▶ write a plan by:
  - underlining all the points you must deal with.
  - organising your ideas into paragraphs so that you cover everything you've been asked to do.

8 Dream of the stars

Starting off

1 Work in groups. Look at the photos. Do you recognise the people? Talk about:
- what they are doing
- the advantages/disadvantages of being famous
- your favourite star.

2 If you could be a star, what sort of star would you like to be? Why?

Reading and Use of English Part 7

1 You are going to read an article from a school magazine about four teenage actors. Before you read, discuss this question in pairs.
- What are the advantages and disadvantages of being an actor?

2 Read questions 1–10 and underline the main idea in each question.

Which teenager

believes actors must be ready to accept negative comments?	1
has learned a lot from people who work in the theatre and TV?	2
says that listening to other people's suggestions improves their acting?	3
comments on the variety that performing in the theatre offers?	4
is prepared to be disappointed initially?	5
found that acting satisfied their need to impress other people?	6
isn't sure exactly what type of acting they'd like to do in the future?	7
won't mind doing different sorts of work to begin with?	8
wasn't originally so interested in acting in the theatre?	9
is worried about performing in front of some important people?	10

3 Now read the school magazine article. For questions 1–10, choose from the people A–D.

EXAM ADVICE

▶ Many of the sections may say quite similar things. You will have to read carefully to decide which section answers the question exactly.
▶ If you see a word you don't understand, and you think you need to understand it to answer a question, try to guess what it means by reading the text around the word.
▶ Underline phrases in the texts which give you the answers and check them against the questions.

4 Work in groups.
- Have you ever performed in public (e.g. acting, speaking in public, dancing, doing a sport)?
- How did you feel about the experience? What did you enjoy about it? What did you dislike?

Four young actors

Dream of the stars

A Jenna Bell, 15

I got my first taste of performing when I was just six, at primary school. I loved being up on stage and I've been hooked ever since. I just found it so exciting to perform in front of an audience. That's when I decided I wanted to be an actor. At first I wanted to get into TV as I really liked the idea of being a celebrity in a soap. Nowadays, I think performing in plays is just as good – more exciting really, because in the theatre you have a live audience in front of you and every performance is slightly different. I've done some ballet too but I prefer stage acting. At my drama club we all dream of being discovered by someone from theatre or TV and being offered a contract – that would be a huge opportunity!

B Roland Green, 13

I joined an after-school youth theatre company when I was ten years old and I'd say it was the best thing for me at that age because I'd always been a bit of a show-off. I still go twice a week and I feel it's given me a great introduction to acting as a profession. When I leave school, I definitely want to pursue a career as an actor on stage, TV, film or radio. I've had the chance to try out all sorts of different things, so I've gained some really useful experience. When you're involved in a production, it can get a bit intense and people give you all sorts of advice about your acting, which helps get rid of any bad habits you may have developed, like looking at the audience too much. Some of the criticism you get can be pretty brutal but that's the nature of the acting profession so you might as well be prepared for it.

C Chloe Desmond, 13

A group of us from our school theatre club have been working in a professional production at our local theatre for the past three months. It's been a fantastic opportunity and has brought us into contact with actors and other people who have told us all about the industry – not just about working in theatre but in TV as well. It's been useful because, to achieve your ambitions as an actor, the more you know about the profession the better. When I finish school, I'm planning to apply to drama school in London. If I'm rejected first time round, which happens to a lot of people, I'd like to take a year out and go travelling. Then I'd come back and give it another go.

D Frank Lee, 14

I've been going to a drama school every Saturday since I was eight and it's great. I've actually had the chance to do some film and TV work. Film and theatre directors often come to our end-of-year productions to look for new talent. They're coming to one of our performances next week, which is nerve-wracking, but if you want to be a TV actor, like I do, then you have to be able to deal with nerves. My brother used to be into acting too but now he's gone to university and has given it up completely. He was never as keen as I am though. I don't yet know whether I'll go for TV, film or theatre work – I think they're all interesting. One thing I'm sure of is that no matter what job I'm offered when I first start out, I'll be very unlikely to turn it down. Any acting job would be amazing, even if it's not my dream role.

Unit 8

Vocabulary

Verb collocations with *ambition*, *career*, *experience* and *job*

1 Complete these extracts from Reading and Use of English Part 7 by writing a word or phrase from the box, in the correct form, in the gaps.

> achieve   gain   offer   pursue   turn it down

> When I leave school I definitely want to (1) .... a career as an actor ...
>
> ... to (2) .... your ambitions as an actor, the more you know about the profession, the better.
>
> ... no matter what job I'm (3) .... when I first start out, I'll be very unlikely to (4) ....
>
> I've had the chance to try out all sorts of different things, so I've (5) .... some really useful experience.

2 **EP** Complete these groups of collocations by writing *an ambition, a career, experience* or *a job* in the gaps.

1 *gain / get / have / lack* ....
2 *apply for / find / leave / look for / offer / turn down*
 ....
3 *abandon / build / launch / make / pursue / start out on*
 ....
4 *abandon / achieve / fulfill / have / realise* ....

3 Complete Dean's story by writing a verb from Exercise 2 in the correct form in the gaps. For some gaps, more than one answer may be possible.

> I've always enjoyed performing in front of people and I'd like to (1) .... a career as an actor. If I could (2) .... my first ambition of going to drama school, I'd (3) .... the knowledge and experience which is needed if I'm going to (4) .... a job in the theatre. Acting is a very competitive profession, and you have to (5) .... your career step by step until, hopefully, a well-known director recognises your talent and (6) .... you a job which really (7) .... your career on the stage.

4 Work in pairs. Tell each other about your ambitions and the careers each of you would like to follow.

play, performance and acting; audience, (the) public and spectators; scene and stage

5 👁 Candidates often confuse these words: *play, performance* and *acting; audience, public* and *spectators; scene* and *stage*. Circle the correct word in *italics* in each of these sentences. Then check by looking at the text in Reading and Use of English Part 7 again.

I loved being up on (1) *stage / scene* ...
I think performing in (2) *plays / performances* is just as good – more exciting really, because in the theatre you have a live (3) *public / audience* in front of you and every (4) *acting / performance* is slightly different.
I've done some ballet too but I prefer stage (5) *acting / playing*.

86

Dream of the stars

6 Read the definitions on page 184 and look at the photos. Then complete each of these sentences by writing one of the words or phrases in the gaps in the correct form. Use each word only once.

1 The garden in all its glory is now open to ..*the public*.. .
2 He wrote his latest .... in under six weeks.
3 The thing I enjoy most about .... is the chance to work in films on location.
4 She gave a superb .... as Lady Macbeth.
5 The .... were clearly delighted with the performance.
6 The actor forgot what he was supposed to say in the final .... of the play.
7 The show ended with all the performers singing on .... together.
8 He broke the world 400-metres record in front of over 40,000 cheering ....

audience

spectators

the public

Grammar
at, in and on in phrases expressing location

1 👁 Candidates often confuse *at*, *in* and *on* when saying where something is located. Complete these sentences from Reading and Use of English Part 7 by writing the correct preposition in the gaps.

1 I got my first taste of performing when I was just six, ... primary school.
2 ... because .... the theatre you have a live audience in front of you.
3 When I leave school, I definitely want to pursue a career as an actor .... stage, TV, film or radio.
4 I'm planning to apply to drama school .... London.
5 My brother used to be into acting too, but now he's .... university and has given it up completely.

➡ page 172 Language reference: Prepositions – *at*, *in* and *on* to express location

2 👁 Write the correct preposition in the gaps in these sentences written by candidates in the exam.

1 Every morning, we got up early and went to walk .... the mountains.
2 Every year, many people are injured .... the roads because of bad driving.
3 I am studying English .... school, and a spell in your country would be a great chance for me to improve.
4 I think that your cinema is the best .... the city.
5 I was alone .... home, my parents were .... a party and my sister was .... a friend's house.
6 Despite spending two hours a day commuting, I prefer living .... the outskirts of London.
7 The seaside is the ideal place for a family holiday because children can swim .... the sea as well as play .... the beach.
8 Our next destination was Italy, where we spent one week .... the seaside.
9 The journey was a good one, and I met an old friend .... the train.
10 You can waste a lot of time .... a car .... traffic jams.

Unit 8

Listening Part 2

1 Work in pairs. You are going to hear a student called Julie giving a talk to students in her year about the time her father was on a television quiz show. Before you listen, read the sentences and decide:
- what sort of information you need in each gap (a person, a number, type of transport, etc.)
- what sort of word(s) could go in each gap (noun, adjective, verb, etc.).

Ten minutes of fame

A TV producer invited Julie's aunt to the quiz show while she was working in the (1) .... belonging to the family.

She didn't go because she was worried that she would be too (2) .... to answer any questions.

Julie's father used a (3) .... to travel to the show.

When he went to the show, he forgot to wear a (4) ....

He prepared for the show by learning large numbers of (5) .... from the newspapers.

The contestants were asked to wait in (6) .... for the show to begin.

He competed against a (7) .... , a bus driver and a bank employee.

The contestants were asked questions on (8) .... during the show.

The show was broadcast almost (9) .... after it was recorded.

Julie's father won a (10) .... and a toy elephant.

2 ▶ 29 Listen and, for questions 1–10, complete the sentences with a short word or phrase.

EXAM ADVICE

▶ Be careful to choose the right information from what you hear, e.g. if you need to write a type of animal in the gap, the speaker will probably mention other animals which are not the correct answer.
▶ Write exactly the word(s) you hear without changing them in any way.
▶ Read the completed sentences to make sure the words fit grammatically and match what the speaker said.
▶ Answer every question, even if you're not sure.

3 Work in groups.
- How would you feel if you were invited to take part in a quiz programme?
- What would you like to win?
- Have you ever won anything in a competition?

Grammar
Reported speech

1 Look at these two sentences from Listening Part 2. What do you think Julie's aunt's and sister's exact words were?
1 She said she was afraid she'd get too nervous and be unable to speak when they asked her questions!
   a 'I'm afraid I'll get too nervous and be unable to speak when they ask me questions!'
   b 'I'm afraid I got too nervous and was unable to speak when they asked me questions!'
2 My elder sister, who was only 11 at the time, told her she should go because it was the chance of a lifetime.
   a 'You'll go because it's the chance of a lifetime.'
   b 'You should go because it's the chance of a lifetime.'

➡ page 173 Language reference: Reported speech

88

Dream of the stars

2 For questions 1–6, complete the second sentence so that it has a similar meaning to the first sentence, using the word given. Do not change the word given. You must use between two and five words, including the word given.

1 'Last night I saw a fantastic film,' said Phil.
  PREVIOUS
  Phil told me that the .... a fantastic film.
2 'I'll return quite late from the theatre tonight,' said Elena.
  BACK
  Elena warned me that .... quite late from the theatre that night.
3 'I won't be late for the show,' said Lucy.
  ARRIVE
  Lucy promised she .... time for the show.
4 'You can't borrow my camera, Mike,' said his father.
  ALLOWED
  Mike's father told him he .... his camera.
5 'I know I got several answers wrong in this exercise,' Hannah said.
  MISTAKES
  Hannah admitted that she .... in the exercise.
6 'I really enjoyed the play,' Katie told George.
  FOUND
  Katie told George that she .... very enjoyable.

3 Circle the correct form of the verb in *italics* in each of these sentences from Listening Part 2.
1 Anyway, when she was asked, she just refused *to even consider / even considering* it.
2 Well, he saw his opportunity and offered *to go / going* on the show himself.
3 He had to ask the producer *do you have / if they'd got* a spare one at the studio he could borrow.
4 In fact, I don't think we've ever had an encyclopedia in the house, though I suggested *to buy / buying* one for the occasion.

➡ page 174 Language reference: Reported speech – reporting verbs

4 Complete these sentences by writing the verb in brackets in the correct form in the gaps.
1 She admitted .... (*steal*) the watch.
2 Susan accused Brian of .... (*lie*).
3 Mark's mother agreed .... (*buy*) him a new mobile phone.
4 The children apologised for .... (*break*) the window.
5 Peter has invited me .... (*visit*) him in Switzerland this summer.
6 Ewan persuaded his mother .... (*buy*) him a new bike.
7 Karen has promised .... (*visit*) me after the summer.
8 I would recommend .... (*install*) new computers in the school.
9 Can I remind you to .... (*send*) your grandmother a birthday card?
10 Martin warned me .... (*not use*) the machine.

89

Unit 8

Reading and Use of English Part 1

1 Work in pairs. You are going to read an article about how people make money from YouTube. Before you read, discuss these questions.

- What things do you most enjoy on YouTube?
- Why do many people prefer YouTube to watching television?

2 Read the article quickly. How do people make money on YouTube?

Back 111

YouTube millionaire celebrities

Geeks, musicians, teenage boys in their bedrooms – (0) ..*anyone*.. can now become a global internet sensation and a millionaire in the (1) .... In between the amusing videos of animals doing strange things and skateboarding accidents, people are building (2) .... by uploading videos.
In (3) .... years, there have been many success stories of people who started at home with just a webcam and have now huge followings. With over 100 million visitors to YouTube every month, advertisers have started (4) .... on the most popular video makers to take advantage of their loyal (5) .... Last year, 'YouTuber' Michael Buckley (6) .... that he was making over $100,000 a year from YouTube advertisements alone.
The YouTube payment system works on a pay-per-click basis. Effectively, the amount of money you (7) .... is determined by the number of views you get. A video of around a million views, which is (8) .... for popular YouTubers, may bring in about a thousand dollars.

adapted from the *Daily Mail*

3 For questions 1–8, read the article again and decide which answer (A, B, C or D) best fits each gap.

0	A someone	B anyone	C everyone	D all
1	A way	B process	C method	D manner
2	A work	B jobs	C careers	D occupations
3	A recent	B last	C past	D latest
4	A aiming	B directing	C focusing	D pointing
5	A public	B people	C watchers	D spectators
6	A informed	B told	C reminded	D announced
7	A gain	B pay	C win	D earn
8	A conventional	B typical	C traditional	D everyday

4 Now check your answers to Exercise 3 by using these clues.

1 This phrase means 'one thing happens as a result of the other'.
2 This will be a part of their whole working life.
3 Notice the sentence uses the present perfect.
4 Only one option is followed by this preposition.
5 Look back to the vocabulary section in this unit.
6 This means he has said it publicly. The wrong options all need an object.
7 The correct answer is a collocation with *money*.
8 This is normal for popular YouTubers.

EXAM ADVICE

▶ Read the title and the text quickly to get a general idea of what it's about.
▶ Deal with the gaps one by one. Read carefully before and after the gap. The words in each option will be similar in meaning, but only one will fit correctly into the gap.
▶ Check that the word fits into the sentence grammatically by looking at prepositions and other grammatical structures.
▶ If you are not sure which option is correct, reject the options you think are wrong and choose from the others.
▶ When you have finished, read the whole text quickly again to check your answers.

5 Discuss one of these questions in groups.

1 Have you ever uploaded something onto a video-sharing website such as YouTube? If so, what?
2 What would you like to upload onto YouTube? Why? / Why not?

Speaking Part 4

Dream of the stars

1 ▶ 30 In Speaking Part 4, the examiner will ask you questions which encourage you to give your opinions on topics related to Part 3. Read and listen to Antonia and Peter answering the examiner's question. Underline the words or phrases they use to speak in general.

Examiner: Do you think schools should teach subjects such as dance, drama or music?

Antonia: Well, I think generally speaking / schools should teach these subjects to small children so that they can find out if they like them. I think these subjects help children to learn how to express themselves. But I don't think generally it's so important for older children or teenagers to do these subjects because they tend to have lots of other things to study. So, on the whole, I guess these subjects should be voluntary, not compulsory as children get older.

Examiner: Peter, do you agree with Antonia?

Peter: Generally, yes, but I feel it's a pity when students don't have time for the subjects they enjoy.

2 Look at the answer again.

1 How does Antonia give a balanced answer?
2 What reasons does she give?
3 Which of these things does Peter do?
a He just says he agrees.
b He says he agrees, but adds his own opinion.
c He says he agrees and gives a reason.

3 Work alone. Think of general things you can say to give a balanced answer to this question. Then in pairs take turns to ask and answer this question.

• Do you think that schools should teach subjects such as painting and photography? Why? / Why not?

4 Pronunciation: grouping words and pausing (2)

We tend to pause between groups of words which form a meaning together, for example: *The family had a small shop / just round the corner from where we live, / and one day my aunt was working there on her own.*

1 Look back to Exercise 4 in the speaking section on page 46. Then use a (/) to mark where you think Antonia and Peter pause in their answers in (Speaking) Exercise 1.

2 ▶ 30 Now listen again and check your answers.

3 Work in pairs. Take the part of Antonia or Peter and read their answers aloud.

4 Note down your own ideas to answer the examiner's question in (Speaking) Exercise 1 and think where you will pause as you speak. Then take turns to answer the question.

91

Unit 8

5 **EP** Read these questions. Then decide which phrases in the box you could use in your answer to each question. Some phrases can be used for more than one answer.

1. Do you think that all young people should learn to play a musical instrument? Why? / Why not?
2. What things do young people learn from acting in plays?
3. What are the advantages of seeing a film in the cinema instead of on television?
4. Should newspapers and magazines pay so much attention to singers' and actors' lives and relationships? Why? / Why not?
5. Which do you think is the purpose of television: to entertain or to educate people? Why?

> a celebrity ....
> a compulsory/voluntary activity ....
> avoid/cause a scandal ....
> develop their acting/musical abilities ....
> develop their artistic expression ....
> develop their musical knowledge ....
> help society develop ....
> disturb/protect someone's privacy ....
> interrupt a film with advertisements ....
> make people aware of problems ....
> the media ....
> when the film is released ....
> a tabloid (newspaper) ....
> work in a team ....

6 Work alone and think how you can give balanced, general answers to each question in Exercise 5. Then work in pairs and take turns to ask and answer the questions.

EXAM ADVICE

▶ Many of the questions will be general questions of opinion; give your opinion and support it with reasons and or examples.
▶ Listen carefully to what your partner says: you may be asked if you agree.

Writing Part 1 — An essay

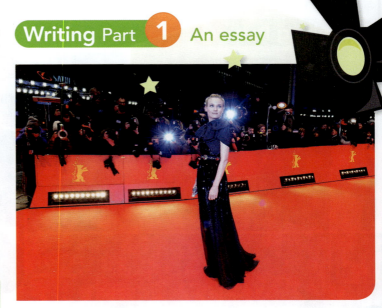

1 Read this writing task and underline the key points you must deal with.

In your English class, you have been talking about the advantages of being famous as a film star.
Now your English teacher has asked you to write an essay. Write an essay using **all** the notes and give reasons for your point of view.

Essay question
Being famous as a film star has both advantages and disadvantages. Do you agree?

Notes
Write about:
  1. media attention
  2. lifestyle
  3. .... (your own idea)

Write your **essay**.

2 Work in groups. Discuss the advantages and disadvantages of being famous as an actor or film star. While you discuss, you should:
- note down the main points of your discussion
- cover all three notes in the essay task in Exercise 1.

3 Work alone and write a brief plan for your essay. In your plan, you should have:
- the number of paragraphs
- the main idea of each paragraph.

4 Look back to page 61, Exercises 4 and 5. Then write your own opening paragraph. When you have finished, work in pairs and compare your paragraphs.

5 Work in pairs. Read this opening paragraph.
- How does it compare with yours?

> Many young people dream of achieving fame as actors or film stars. However, it is a life which has both advantages and disadvantages.

6 Javier wrote a balanced essay to answer the question in the writing task. Read the essay. Then work in pairs to answer questions 1–6 below.

a Many young people dream of achieving fame as film stars. <mark>However</mark>, it is a life which has both advantages and disadvantages.

b <u>There are three main advantages</u>. Firstly, if actors are well-known, people will want to watch their films and if their films are popular, they will be offered more jobs in the future. Also, they live exciting and glamorous lives with plenty of foreign travel and luxury. There is no doubt that most actors find this very enjoyable. Finally, fame and success go together.

c <u>On the other hand, fame brings disadvantages for actors too.</u> First, many film stars have little privacy or time to themselves because they are always being followed by reporters and photographers. Next, people with glamorous lifestyles meet other glamorous people and this can sometimes cause problems with, for example, their family relationships. Finally, they have to work very hard to be successful and this may lead to considerable stress.

d <u>To conclude,</u> I think for film stars the advantages of being famous outweigh the disadvantages because being well-known is a result of their professional success. However, they need common sense to deal with the disadvantages.

1 Are Javier's ideas about being famous similar to yours?
2 How does he balance his arguments in the essay?
3 What is the purpose of the <u>underlined</u> phrases in the essay?
4 <mark>Highlight</mark> words and phrases he uses to link ideas together throughout the essay.
5 In which paragraph (a–d) does Javier give his own opinion?
6 Why is it important to make your opinion clear?

7 Work alone.
1 Write a second paragraph where you outline the advantages you discussed in Exercise 2. Start it using an introductory sentence.
2 Write a third paragraph where you balance the advantages of the second paragraph with the disadvantages. Start it with an introductory sentence as well.

8 Write your answer to the writing task below.
- Follow the stages of <u>underlining</u>, thinking of ideas and planning that you have practised.
- Use Javier's answer in Exercise 6 as a model.
- You should write between 140 and 190 words.

In your English class, you have been talking about the advantages and disadvantages of a career in music or acting.
Now your English teacher has asked you to write an essay. Write an essay using **all** the notes and give reasons for your point of view.

Essay question
There are both advantages and disadvantages to a career as a musician or an actor. Do you agree?

Notes
Write about:
 1. doing something you enjoy
 2. becoming well-known
 3. .... (your own idea)

Write your **essay**.

EXAM ADVICE

▶ To make your argument easy to follow, you can start paragraphs with a short sentence which says what the paragraph is about.
▶ If you decide to write a 'balanced essay', try to have the same number of points in favour as against, or advantages as disadvantages.
▶ The writing task will not be complete unless you express your personal opinion clearly.

Vocabulary and grammar review Unit 7

Word formation

1 EP Read this text. Use the word given in capitals at the end of each line to form a word that fits in the gap in the same line.

Adventure racing

The teams that come first are the ones who race **(0)** *intelligently* and adapt to the sort of **(1)** .... situations which arise in these races. The teams who do well show both flexibility and **(2)** .... Unfortunately, our **(3)** .... for the race in Australia weren't methodical in any way. In fact, as a beginner, I was so **(4)** .... that the training I actually did was **(5)** .... to run and cycle as much and as hard as I could. When we actually did the race, one of my team-mates became just too tired to continue. We had been going really fast without taking any rests, and he had been **(6)** .... to ask us to take a break. I knew that our team had not been **(7)** .... about the pace we could keep. Not finishing that race was the most **(8)** .... lesson I could have learned.

INTELLIGENT
PREDICT

PATIENT
PREPARE

EXPERIENCE
SIMPLE

WILL

REAL

VALUE

Grammar

2 Complete the sentences by writing the verb in brackets in the infinitive or verb + *-ing* form in the gaps.

1 Can I suggest .... (*take*) a break in about ten minutes?
2 Did you manage .... (*get*) in touch with her?
3 Do you want me .... (*invite*) her?
4 My cousin's considering .... (*change*) his car.
5 He absolutely refuses .... (*wear*) any other make of trainers.
6 He admitted .... (*finish*) all the cake.
7 He persuaded them .... (*finish*) the job.
8 I expect .... (*become*) very rich one day.
9 I really don't mind .... (*help*) my little sister with her homework.
10 It's no good .... (*ask*) him anything. He's really unhelpful.
11 My brother enjoys .... (*work*) in an internet café.
12 You know it's not worth .... (*spend*) so much money on one computer game.

3 Complete the second sentence in each question so that it has a similar meaning to the first sentence, using the word given in capitals. Do not change the word given. You must use between two and five words, including the word given.

1 You can't go skydiving until you're 18 years old.
ALLOWED
People under 18 .... skydiving.
2 He didn't want to get sunburnt, so he stayed in the shade.
AVOID
He stayed in the shade .... sunburnt.
3 Paola hates windsurfing when the weather is cold.
BEAR
Paola .... when the weather is cold.
4 Could you please turn your mobile phone off?
MIND
Would .... your mobile phone off?
5 You might have an accident if you don't take all the safety precautions.
RISK
If you don't take all the safety precautions, ... an accident.
6 The weather is so wet that it's not worth going for a walk today.
POINT
The weather is so wet that there's .... for a walk today.

Vocabulary and grammar review Unit 8

Vocabulary

1 Choose the best word, A, B, C or D, for each gap.

1 The flying display attracted about 50,000 ..... despite the rain.
   A public   B assistants   C spectators   D audience
2 As a police officer, I get a lot of questions from members of the ..... asking how to get to one place or another.
   A people   B public   C audience   D spectators
3 During the musical, the ..... clapped at the end of every single song.
   A audience   B spectators   C public   D attendants
4 British actress Amanda Haslett gave a superb ..... as Lady Macbeth at the Globe Theatre last night.
   A play   B act   C performance   D acting
5 I'd love to be able to have a career in ... one day!
   A acting   B playing   C performance   D stage
6 That play is much better on the ..... than in the film version.
   A theatre   B play   C scene   D stage
7 My sister is thinking of pursuing a .... in the music industry.
   A work   B job   C career   D position
8 My uncle always says it's more important to do a job you enjoy than one where you ... a lot of money.
   A win   B earn   C gain   D pay

Grammar

2 Complete each of the sentences below by writing a word or phrase from the box. In some cases, more than one answer may be possible. You can use the words and phrases more than once.

> although   despite   even though   however
> in spite of   whereas   while

1 .... Eva wanted to pursue a career in acting, she couldn't find a job.
2 Max gave a wonderful performance in the school concert .... his headache.
3 .... Jason dreams of being a footballer, Eva wants to work in the theatre.
4 .... not being very talented, she became a highly successful Hollywood star.
5 They spent millions on the film. .... , not many people were interested in going to see it.
6 I enjoy watching documentaries .... my brother prefers soap operas.
7 He insisted on playing loud music .... it was nearly two o'clock in the morning.
8 People of all ages go to rock concerts, ... classical music concerts are mainly attended by people over 50.

3 For questions 1–6, complete the second sentence so that it has a similar meaning to the first sentence, using the word given. Do not change the word given. You must use between two and five words, including the word given.

1 Although it was dangerous, she went swimming.
   THE
   In spite .... she went swimming.
2 The concert was sold out, despite the high price of the tickets.
   EXPENSIVE
   Although .... , the concert was sold out.
3 Although he felt ill, he went to school.
   DESPITE
   He went to school .... well.
4 She enjoys her Saturday job in spite of her low pay.
   EVEN
   She finds her Saturday job enjoyable .... low.
5 'I've been asleep all the way through the film.'
   HAD
   Helen admitted that .... whole film.
6 'I'll phone when the concert finishes.'
   CALL
   Martin said he .... end of the concert.

9 Secrets of the mind

Starting off

1 Work in pairs. Find eight things which might make people happy by matching these words and phrases.

1 being admired
2 being part of
3 doing really well
4 having enough money to
5 having lots of
6 having lots of time to spend
7 living
8 not having to

a a loving family
b in your studies or work
c by the people around you
d live well
e friends
f in a nice neighbourhood
g on the things you enjoy doing
h work too hard

2 Which of the things in Exercise 1 do you think are essential for happiness? Which do you think are not so important?
Are there any other important things which make people happy?

3 Work in pairs. Take turns to do the task below.
- Student A should look at photos 1 and 2.
- Student B should look at photos 3 and 4.

The photos show people who are happy. Compare the photos and say why you think the people might be happy.

Why might the people be happy?

Reading and Use of English Part 5

1 You are going to read an article about a teenager who went to classes to become happier. Read the article quickly to find out what she learned in these classes.

| Article | Video | Picture gallery |

Happiness or Harvard?
How one teenager redefined her attitudes to success

Gathering her backpack for school, 14-year-old Carolyn Milander, from Houston, Texas, burst into tears for the second time that week. 'Not again, Carolyn!' her mother said, worriedly, 'When you get perfect grades, you're on a
5 high. But when you pull all-nighters and don't get enough sleep, you get so tired and depressed! This terrible cycle has got to end!' Blurting back in anger, Carolyn screamed, 'I'm fine, just leave me alone!' Carolyn had just started at a new secondary school and was having trouble coping
10 with the increased expectations and pressures to perform. This type of angry interchange is all too familiar for today's teens and their parents, and it's no surprise. The stress of getting good grades and trying to get into the best universities doesn't encourage happy family dynamics.

15 Instead of watching and hoping things would improve, Carolyn's mother recognized the potential damage to family relationships and demanded change. She carried out a bit of personal research to find out what sort of help was available. She discovered that there was a special
20 stress-reduction class at Carolyn's school, affectionately known as the 'Happy Class', and she insisted that Carolyn should attend it. That was four years ago. Recently, Carolyn told her story to a magazine for young people.

'I remember angrily climbing into the car and sitting
25 silently as my mum drove me to my first Happy Class,' Carolyn said. 'Then I shyly walked into the classroom and took a seat. With the lights off, the leaders and students sat facing each other in a circle. I felt awkward and embarrassed, hoping no one would see me when
30 they walked by the classroom. We started by closing our eyes, focusing on our breathing. The goal was to trace our breath like a roller coaster – in, down, back up, like a loop.' As Carolyn began to notice her breath, she said, 'I quit thinking about people in the hallway. I felt really

Secrets of the mind

35 relaxed and focused on that moment in time.' <u>This was a feeling she liked and she could tell she would benefit from what the classes could offer.</u>

Happy Class was a significant turning point for Carolyn. She learned how to meditate and still does so every
40 day. She began to explore deeper life issues, defining what gave her feelings of happiness and fulfilment. She also learned to accept herself for who she was, instead of striving to live up to other people's notions of success. Many of her friends and family expected
45 her to attend Harvard or another top university, but Carolyn created her own version of happiness instead. She stopped pulling all-nighters, organized her time better so she was able to relax and do things she enjoyed, and tried to eat more healthily, while not
50 skimping on hard work. She realized that she could achieve happiness close to home, rather than by going to an elite university. In fact, Carolyn decided to become a nurse and to apply to just one college – a 20-minute drive away. 'I didn't want to be tempted by a
55 top university, even if I received a scholarship. I wanted to remain true to the goals I set for myself.'

Adolescence is a time when young people should be able to discover their own identities. When Carolyn devoted some time to discovering what was
60 meaningful to her, personal success followed. This is what all teens should be able to do. 'I feel good about myself for sticking to what I believe in,' Carolyn affirmed. 'I would encourage other teens to make the choices that are best for them and to discover
65 what makes them happy. If what makes you happy is attending one of the best universities, then that is the path you should take.' In fact, it's the path many of Carolyn's friends chose and she says she is happy for them. 'My goal in becoming a nurse is to spend my life
70 helping others in meaningful ways,' said Carolyn. What she may not realize is just how impressive she already is. That scene with her mother feels like a very long time ago.

EXAM ADVICE

When a question asks what a word or phrase refers to:
▶ read carefully what is said in the preceding sentence.
▶ make sure you understand the reference before you read the options.

2 For questions 1 and 2, the sentences in the article which give you the answers have been <u>underlined</u>. Read the questions and the underlined sentences. Then choose the answer (A, B, C or D) which you think fits best according to the underlined sentences.

1 What does the writer suggest about Carolyn in the first paragraph?
  A She had always got on badly with her mother.
  B Her mother's expectations of her were too high.
  C She was different from other people her age.
  D It was hard for her to control her behaviour.
2 What point does Carolyn make about her first Happy Class?
  A She realised the techniques being taught were effective.
  B She wished there weren't so many other people there.
  C She found discussing her problems made her feel better.
  D She would have learned more if she hadn't felt so negative.

3 Now, for questions 3–6, choose the answer (A, B, C or D) which you think fits best according to the text.

3 What does *striving* mean in line 43?
  A often demanding   C working hard
  B agreeing enthusiastically   D seriously intending
4 Why did Carolyn decide not to apply to one of the top universities?
  A She hadn't spent enough time on her studies.
  B They were all too close to her home town.
  C Her parents couldn't afford to pay the expensive fees.
  D She had already made up her mind to do something else.
5 What does *this* refer to in line 60?
  A becoming successful at school
  B finding out what matters to them
  C spending time on what they enjoy
  D improving their personalities
6 In the final paragraph, Carolyn says that
  A she is proud to be doing what she thinks is right.
  B she would like her friends to choose a career like hers.
  C she appreciates the good advice she has been given.
  D she is attempting to understand her friends' decisions.

4 Work in groups.
  • Do you think it's normal for teenagers to argue with their parents? Why? / Why not?
  • How much do you think parents should put pressure on their children to get good results at school?
  • Do you think success and happiness go together? Why? / Why not?

Unit 9

Vocabulary

achieve, carry out and devote

1 Complete these sentences from Reading and Use of English Part 5 by writing the correct form of *achieve*, *carry out* or *devote* in each gap.

1 She realized that she could .... happiness close to home ...
2 She .... a bit of personal research to find out what sort of help was available.
3 ... Carolyn .... some time to discovering what was meaningful to her ...

2 👁 Write the nouns in the box by each verb they can form collocations with.

> ~~an aim~~   an ambition   energy   an improvement
> an instruction   an objective   an order   one's life
> research   success   a test   a threat   time

1 achieve   *an aim, ...*
2 carry out
3 devote ... (to)

3 Complete these sentences by writing collocations from Exercise 2 in the correct form in each gap. In some cases, more than one answer may be possible.

1 Last year, my uncle .... a lifelong .... to visit New York.
2 Scientists have been .... to discover the cause of the disease.
3 The exercise is quite easy, so you won't need to .... very much .... to doing it.
4 Igor felt very tired because he had .... a lot of time and .... to the project.
5 My mum said she'd stop my pocket money if I was home late, but I don't think she'll .... her ....
6 In the army, you have to be obedient and .... immediately.

stay, spend and pass; make, cause and have

4 👁 Candidates often confuse the following words: *stay*, *spend* and *pass*; *make*, *cause* and *have*. Read these sentences and circle the correct word in *italics*. Then check your answers by reading the definitions on page 184.

1 Remember, your behaviour will *have / cause* an effect on other people.
2 I'm very sorry if I've *made / caused* you any problems.
3 I have *passed / spent* my life studying happiness.
4 Yesterday, I *spent / stayed* two hours listening to the radio.
5 I really enjoy late-night films on TV when I can *stay / be* awake.
6 The news that her sister had had a baby *made / had* her very happy.

5 Now complete each of these sentences using *stay*, *spend*, *pass*, *make*, *cause* or *have* in the correct form.

1 I decided to .... the afternoon in the park.
2 Colin played a game on his phone to .... the time while he was waiting for the train.
3 We should be able to go camping because they say the weather is going to .... like this for the rest of the week.
4 Your talk was excellent and .... a powerful impact on the other students.
5 How did you .... the weekend? Did you enjoy yourself?
6 I .... two hours today trying to finish my homework.
7 The bus strike has been .... problems for students trying to get to school.
8 The bad sound quality .... the film very difficult to understand.
9 Using up-to-date materials can .... a dramatic effect on the amount students learn.
10 Our maths teacher .... the whole lesson explaining algebra to us.

6 Which verb – *make*, *cause* or *have* – forms a collocation with each of these nouns? In some cases, more than one verb–noun collocation is possible.

> an accident   a change   an effect   an impact
> an impression   a problem   trouble

7 Complete these sentences by writing a collocation from Exercise 6 in each of the gaps. In some cases, more than one answer may be possible.

1 A dog ran onto the road and would have .... if I hadn't reacted quickly.
2 Amalia obviously .... a good .... on the examiners because they gave her a Grade A.
3 I hope I haven't .... you .... by coming to stay unexpectedly.
4 I .... that she's not very organised. Otherwise, she'd hand her work in on time.
5 Living in the country .... a nice .... after spending the last three years living in a city.
6 Your choice of subjects at university will .... a big .... on your future career.

Secrets of the mind

Listening Part 1

1 You are going to hear people talking in eight different situations. Before you listen, work in groups. Discuss whether you agree with these statements or not.

- Your first impression of a person is usually formed by what they say, not how they look.
- In general, people choose friends who are quite similar to them rather than someone very different.
- Young people nowadays are generally more intelligent than their grandparents were.
- Few people are afraid of flying in planes and getting in lifts. More people are afraid of heights.
- Everyone sometimes has a dream where they're flying, falling or running.

2 Now work in pairs. Read questions 1 and 2 and match the words and phrases in the box with each of the options A, B and C in the two questions. (For some options there may be more than one word or phrase.)

> actual words   body language   character
> things in common   gestures   hobbies   intonation
> people we like   appearance   mirror

1 You hear an expert giving advice about meeting people for the first time. What has the most impact?
 A how you sound
 B how you look
 C what you say

2 You hear two girls talking about their friendship. They agree that the most important factor in a successful friendship is having
 A similar personalities.
 B being part of the same social group.
 C similar interests.

3 ▶ 02 Now listen and for questions 1 and 2, choose the best answer (A, B or C). Then say which words and phrases you heard from the box in Exercise 2.

4 ▶ 03 Listen and, for questions 3–8, choose the best answer (A, B or C).

3 You hear a psychologist in the UK talking about intelligence. What does she say?
 A The human brain is changing.
 B Scores in intelligence tests are rising.
 C Exams are getting harder.

4 You overhear a boy calling a friend on his mobile phone. Why is he calling his friend?
 A to complain about her behaviour
 B to explain a problem
 C to change an arrangement

5 You overhear a man talking about things which frighten people. What frightens him?
 A using an escalator
 B taking a flight
 C using a lift

6 You hear a girl talking to a boy about a dream. She has read that the dream means
 A she's worried about lack of success.
 B her life is in danger.
 C she has to escape from something.

7 You overhear two students talking about a classmate. Why are they discussing her?
 A To organise something for her.
 B To see if they can help her.
 C To point out her faults.

8 You hear a boy and a girl talking about the boy's free-time activities. What do they agree about his personality?
 A He's friendly and sociable.
 B He prefers his own company.
 C He's creative and adventurous.

EXAM ADVICE

▶ Listen to the whole piece before you choose: the answer may depend on the general idea rather than a few words.
▶ If you are not sure about the answer after listening the first time, try to decide which answers you think are wrong before you listen the second time.

5 Work in pairs.
- When you feel stressed, what do you do to relax?
- Talk about someone in your family. What do you think their free-time activities might show about their personality?

Unit 9

Grammar
Modal verbs to express certainty and possibility

1 Read these extracts from Listening Part 1 and look at the underlined modal verbs. Then answer the questions below.

- That's right! I think I <u>must have</u> got the problem when I was trapped in one as a kid. I <u>can't have</u> been there for more than ten minutes, but I was trembling when I came out.
- Well, the interpretation I've heard is that you <u>may</u> be afraid of failing in some way. You know, there are all sorts of interpretations for other dreams, for example that you <u>could</u> find something subconsciously threatening and your dream <u>might</u> be sort of pointing that out to you.

1 Which of the underlined verbs do we use when we:
- are certain something is true? (1) ....
- are certain something is not true? (2) ....
- think something is possibly true? (3) .... , (4) .... and (5) ....

2 Which of the underlined verbs refers to
a the present?
b the past?

➡ page 170 Language reference: Modal verbs – expressing certainty and possibility

2 👁 Candidates often make mistakes with modal verbs. Four of these sentences contain mistakes with modal verbs. However, one is correct. Find and correct the mistakes.

1 I think the school play was lovely. You may have really enjoyed acting in it!
2 He's had a really good sleep, so he mustn't be tired any more.
3 The road is very busy, so cross it carefully or you can have an accident.
4 I have a lot of homework to do, so I may go to bed late.
5 She lives in a really nice house, so her mum and dad can be earning a lot of money.

3 Complete these sentences by writing a suitable modal verb and the verb in brackets in the correct form (present or past) in the gaps. In some cases, more than one answer may be possible.

1 Everyone in the class .... (work) incredibly hard because you have all passed the exam!
2 I think she .... (be) a really happy person because she's always smiling and laughing.
3 Jamie woke up in the night screaming. He .... (have) a nightmare.
4 I don't know why Irina hasn't arrived yet. She .... (have to) stay on late at school, or she .... (stop) on the way home to see some friends.
5 I don't know how old the teacher is, but he looks quite young, so he .... (be) more than 25.
6 They say it .... (rain) at the weekend, so we won't be able to play football on Saturday.

4 Work in pairs. Look at these two pictures and, using *may*, *might*, *must*, *could* and *can't*, say what you think
- has happened or is happening in each picture
- the people are feeling and why.

Reading and Use of English Part 4

1 Work in pairs. In Reading and Use of English Part 4, you have to complete a sentence so that it has a similar meaning to the first sentence, using the word given. You must write between two and five words. Look at questions 1–6 and the different answers students wrote (a–c).

- Decide which is the correct answer.
- Say why the other answers are wrong.

1 'I spoke to Maria yesterday,' Paola said.
  HAD
  Paola said she ………………………………… day before.
  a had had a conversation with Maria the
  b had spoken to Maria the
  c spoke to Maria the

2 Although the music outside was loud, we managed to sleep.
  DESPITE
  We managed to sleep ………………………………… outside.
  a despite of the loud music
  b despite the loud music
  c despite they played loud music

3 I'll forget the number if I don't write it down.
  NOT
  I will ………………………………… I write it down.
  a remember the number if
  b not remind the number unless
  c not remember the number unless

4 You needn't give me your homework tomorrow.
  HAND
  It is ………………………………… your homework to me tomorrow.
  a not necessary for you to hand
  b not needed handing in
  c not necessary to hand in

5 It is possible that Eva collected the parcel from the post office.
  MAY
  Eva ………………………………… up the parcel from the post office.
  a may have collected
  b could have taken
  c may have picked

6 'You should try harder at maths,' my teacher said.
  MORE
  My teacher advised ………………………………… an effort at maths.
  a that I do more
  b me to make more of
  c making more of

EXAM ADVICE

Read the original sentence, the word given and the sentence with the gap. Think about:
▶ whether you need an expression, e.g. *he changed his mind*.
▶ whether you need a phrasal verb, e.g. *give up*.
▶ what grammar you will need, e.g. do you need to change from active to passive or put something into reported speech?

You should try to spell your answers correctly.

2 For questions 1–6, complete the second sentence so that it has a similar meaning to the first sentence, using the word given. Do not change the word given. You must use between two and five words, including the word given.

1 My grandma hates it when people make a noise in her house.
  STAND
  My grandma can't ………………………………… in her house.

2 'Don't forget to lock the front door, Karl,' said his wife.
  REMINDED
  Karl's wife ………………………………… the front door.

3 Sven enjoyed the film despite missing the beginning.
  MANAGE
  Although Sven ………………………………… the beginning of the film, he enjoyed it.

4 I'm sure Annabel wasn't in London all weekend.
  HAVE
  Annabel ………………………………… in London the whole weekend.

5 How long did it take you to write the essay?
  SPEND
  How long ………………………………… the essay?

6 It's possible that my brother has discovered that I have borrowed his bike.
  MAY
  My brother ………………………………… out that I have borrowed his bike.

Unit 9

Speaking Part 2

1 Look at this speaking task. Then complete Peter's answer below with words or phrases from the box which he uses to compare or speculate about what he can see.

Why have the people decided to do these activities?

could be   exactly what   looks as if   may
have decided   must   perhaps   seem   unlike
different   who appears

Examiner: Here are your photographs. They show young people doing difficult activities. I'd like you to compare the photographs and say why you think the people have decided to do these activities. All right?

Peter: The first photo shows young people walking up a mountain. They **(1)** .... to be tied together with ropes and they **(2)** .... be resting, or **(3)** .... they've been waiting for one of the group to catch them up. They may be part of an adventure activity which they're doing from their school or college and they may have been climbing for quite a long time. The second photo shows a **(4)** .... situation. The girl seems to be working with equipment in a factory. I'm not sure **(5)** .... she's doing, but she **(6)** .... building a machine or something. There's a man **(7)** .... to be supervising her. The girl in the first photo **(8)** .... to climb the mountain because she wants a new experience, or she just enjoys being in the mountains even though she looks a bit tired. The girl in the second photo **(9)** .... she's starting a new job and learning to do something. She looks as if she's quite warm from her work, **(10)** .... the girl in the first photo.

2 **04** Now listen to check your answers.

→ page 168 Language reference: *look, seem* and *appear*

3 Work in pairs. Look at the examiner's instructions and the photos. Then complete the sentences on page 103 with your own ideas.

> Here are your photographs. They show people celebrating at different events. I'd like you to compare the photos and say what you think the people are enjoying about the different situations.

What are the people enjoying about the different situations?

Speculating about photos
1 In the first photo, the people look as if …
2 The old man seems to be …
3 They are probably going to …
4 In the second photo, the people appear to be …
5 They could be …
6 Unlike the first photo, …
7 In both photos, the people seem …

4 Pronunciation: sentence stress (3)

We can use sentence stress to emphasise certain words in a sentence.

1 ▶ 05 Look at this sentence from Peter's answer in Exercise 1 and listen to it.
  - Underline the words emphasised in **a** and the words emphasised in **b**.
  - How does the different emphasis change the meaning of what he says?

  a The girl seems to be working with equipment in a factory. I'm not sure exactly what she's doing, but she could be building a machine or something.
  b The girl seems to be working with equipment in a factory. I'm not sure exactly what she's doing, but she could be building a machine or something.

2 Work in pairs. Take turns to read either sentence **a** or sentence **b** aloud to your partner. Your partner should listen and say which sentence you are reading.

3 ▶ 06 Work in pairs. Decide which words you would like to emphasise in the extract. Take turns to read the extract aloud. While you listen to your partner, underline the words he/she emphasises.

The girl in the first photo may have decided to climb the mountain because she wants a new experience, or perhaps she just enjoys being in the mountains even though she looks a bit tired. The girl in the second photo looks as if she's starting a new job and learning to do something. She looks as if she's quite warm from her work, unlike the girl in the first photo.

4 Look at the sentences you completed for Speaking Part 2 Exercise 3 and decide which words you would like to emphasise when you speak. Then work in pairs and take turns to read your sentences aloud.

Secrets of the mind

5 Look again at the answer in Pronunciation Exercise 3. How many words or phrases can you find which mean *a little*?

6 Now take turns to do the task in Speaking Part 2 Exercise 3. When talking about people's feelings, use words or phrases which mean *a little* where appropriate.

7 Work in pairs. Take turns to do the speaking tasks on page 104.
  - While you listen to your partner doing the speaking task, think about the things he/she is doing well and the things he/she could do better.
  - When he/she has finished, give feedback and suggestions. If necessary, look at the checklist in Exercise 3 on page 24 to give you ideas.

EXAM ADVICE

▶ When you're not sure how to answer the question in the task, use phrases which allow you to speculate. Practise these before you go to the exam.
▶ Spend about half the time comparing the photos and half the time answering the question.

Unit 9

Task 1

> Here are your photographs. They show people who have just done something special. I'd like you to compare the two photographs and say how you think the people feel about what they have just done.

How are the people feeling about what they have just done?

Task 2

> Here are your photographs. They show people in frightening situations. I'd like you to compare the two photographs and say why you think the people are frightened in these situations.

Why are the people frightened in these situations?

Writing Part 2 — A story

1 Look at the writing task on the right and think about a special day in your life. What made it special? Here are some suggestions:

- you met someone interesting
- you were successful at something (passing an important exam, winning a competition, etc.)
- you spent the day somewhere unusual
- you did something really enjoyable

You see the following announcement on an English-language website for teenagers.

Short story competition

Write a story for our short story competition for teenagers!

Your story must begin with this sentence:

When David read the email, he realised it was going to be a very special day.

Your story must include:
- some tickets
- a friend

Write your **story**.

Secrets of the mind

2 Work in pairs. Decide what happened to David that day. Think about:
- what the email was about and why it meant the day was going to be special
- events before the email
- what the tickets were for and who the friend was
- what happened on the day

3 Read the following answer to the writing task. It should be divided into three paragraphs. Where do you think each new paragraph should begin?

> When David read the email, he realised it was going to be a very special day. It said, 'Congratulations, you have won two tickets to tonight's concert!' A month ago, he **(1)** *'d entered / was entering* a competition to win tickets to a concert, but **(2)** *didn't hear / hadn't heard* anything since then. His favourite band was going to play in his town, but the tickets **(3)** *had been selling out / had sold out* immediately and he'd been unable to get one. He **(4)** *'d been listening / was listening* to them and downloading all their songs for two years, so he'd felt very disappointed. Now, however, he **(5)** *'d received / been receiving* this incredibly exciting email. He called his best friend Marco straight away. Marco **(6)** *listened / was listening* to one of the band's songs when David called and at first he couldn't believe it. 'That's just so incredible!' he exclaimed. The tickets were VIP tickets, which **(7)** *had included / included* a meeting with the band before the concert started. David and Marco **(8)** *were walking / walked* straight through security at the concert hall and then **(9)** *spent / had been spending* an hour sitting on comfortable sofas chatting to the band. They also got to watch the concert from right in front of the stage, which **(10)** *made / was making* it the best concert ever!

4 You can make a story more interesting for your reader by using a variety of tenses. Read the sample answer again and choose the correct verb tenses.

➡ page 178 Language reference: Verb tenses

5 Read the writing task below and think about what you can write about.
- Why was Barbara smiling?
- What or who was in the photograph?
- Who did Barbara meet?

You see this announcement in an English-language magazine for teenagers.

Stories wanted! Write a short story for our magazine. The best story will win a prize!

Your story must begin with this sentence:

Barbara just couldn't stop smiling.

Your story must include:
- a photograph
- a journey

Write your **story**.

6 Work in pairs. Take turns to make up a story. When you tell your story:
- describe the photograph
- say why Barbara was smiling
- say who Barbara met and describe the meeting.

7 Do the writing task following the steps below. Write between 140–190 words.
- Think about what you will say and make notes.
- Plan your story: how many paragraphs do you need and what will you put in each paragraph?
- Write your story following your plan.
- Check what you have written for mistakes.

EXAM ADVICE

When you have finished writing, follow these tips:
▶ Read your story again and make sure it follows on from the prompt sentence.
▶ Check your work carefully for mistakes. If you often make certain spelling mistakes, check that you haven't made them again. Have you used the right verb tenses?

105

10 On the money

Starting off

Work in groups.

1 Look at the pictures. Which of these things do you enjoy buying? Where would you buy each of them? Would you buy any of them online?

2 Are you given a regular amount of money by people in your family to spend on whatever you like?
- Do you think children should have to help their parents around the house if they want a bit of 'pocket money'?
- Have you ever saved up to buy something? If so, what was it? How long did it take you to save up the money you needed?

Reading and Use of English Part 2

1 Work in groups. You are going to read an article by a teenager about her shopping habits. Before you read, discuss these questions.
- What are the advantages and disadvantages of shopping online?
- Which do you prefer: online shopping or going to shops? Why?

On the money

2 Read this article in one minute ignoring the gaps. How does the writer say she prefers to shop? Why does she prefer it?

Online shopping? No thanks!

Some adults think that because teenagers do so (0) ...*much*... else online, we probably do most of our shopping on the internet too. That isn't actually true, at (1) .... not for me and my friends. First of all, (2) .... a thirteen-year-old, I don't have a credit card. So if I want to buy anything online I have to ask my mum to carry (3) .... the transaction for me. You can probably imagine (4) .... well that works if she doesn't think I'm making a 'wise decision'!

There's also the social aspect of shopping. I'd (5) .... go out shopping with a group of friends than sit at home on my own. And some shops are (6) .... a pirate's treasure chest: you never know (7) .... you might find!

We don't necessarily buy very much, but we do spend a lot of time looking. Sometimes we choose things online, then go and look for them in the shops. And we love trying (8) .... clothes together!

3 Work alone. Decide which word best fits each gap. Where you are not sure, think of the type of word (preposition, article, etc.) you need. When you have finished, compare your ideas with the rest of the group.

4 Work in pairs.
- Do you or members of your family ever buy things online? If so, what are your favourite websites for online shopping? What are your favourite shops in town?

EXAMS ADVICE
▶ Answer the questions you find easy first. Go back to the more difficult questions later.
▶ Pay careful attention to the meaning of the text to help you think of the right word.
▶ Answer all the questions. If you can't decide what word to write, think what type of word you need (preposition, pronoun, etc.) and guess.
▶ When you have finished, check your answers by reading the completed text again.

Grammar
as and like

1 Look at these sentences (a–d) and answer the question below.
a My dad has two jobs: he's a teacher and a football referee. As a teacher he's very easy-going, but as a referee he's really strict.
b My aunt is really nice, but sometimes she is rather strict with us and then she sounds like a teacher!
c ... as a thirteen-year-old, I don't have a credit card.
d ... some shops are like treasure chests.

Which, *as* or *like*, means ...
1 he is / they are (a teacher / a thirteen-year-old, etc.)?
2 he is similar to / they are similar to (a teacher / treasure chests, etc.)?

➡ page 163 Language reference: *as* and *like*

2 Complete these sentences by writing *as* or *like* in the gaps.
1 He has a weekend job .... a shop assistant.
2 He was regarded by his teachers .... one of the most brilliant students they had ever taught.
3 Tanya's father gave her a car for her 18th birthday .... she'd done so well in her exams.
4 I find subjects .... physics and chemistry very difficult.
5 I shall be on holiday next week, ... you know.
6 I'm afraid I don't study .... much .... I should.
7 I'm speaking to you .... a friend.
8 My English teacher is lovely. She's .... a mother to me!
9 Some Swiss cities, such .... Zurich and Berne, have earned a reputation .... excellent places to live.
10 How embarrassing! Donna came to the party wearing exactly the same clothes .... me!

Unit 10

Reading and Use of English Part 5

1 Work in groups. You will read a story called 'My greatest influence' written by a teenager from Texas. Before you read, discuss these questions.

- Who or what has had the greatest influence on you?
- How have they / has it influenced you?

2 Read the story quite quickly to find out what happens.

My greatest influence
By Rachel S., Colleyville, Texas

Sundays, I walk to the supermarket. Mother hands me the grocery list and puts money in my pocket, hoping it will be enough. She's had a hard day, and I've had a hard week. Nothing out of the ordinary happens when I get to the store. I grab the bread, some milk, and other things on the list. As I turn to head out, I see it, all pinks and yellows. It looks gorgeous in the window, and I'm sure if I were to try it on, it would be a perfect fit. I smile for a moment and turn away, bitter that I could never own such a dress as that. Instead, I grab the last item and check out.

Outside, traffic zooms by, an artificial breeze across my face. The sun beats down, making me sweat. These paper sacks in my arms are not the easiest things to carry. Yet, even with all these distractions, I cannot stop thinking about that pretty sundress in the window of the market. It is not fair that I can never have what I want. I work so hard to help my family and yet I get nothing in return, just another grocery list or errand to do.

In my anger, I fail to realize the tear that had been growing along the bottom of one of the sacks. Its contents spill out everywhere so that I must drop everything else just to chase after the soup cans and apples rolling across the sidewalk. Suddenly, I see a pair of hands that do not belong to me. They hold out to me a can of green beans. I follow them up the forearms, from the shoulders, and to the face of this stranger. His skin is tanned and wrinkled from so many years in the sun. His clothes are mismatched, borrowed or stolen. But his eyes are soft and kind.

I pause in silence, only able to stare at him. "Huh ... thanks," I say, coming to my senses, and I take the can from him. No other words are spoken as he continues to help me recover my purchases and get back on my feet. There is an awkward silence between us. Not knowing what else to say in this sort of situation, I tell him "thank you" one more time and am on my way because I have many other chores to finish. Suddenly, he speaks for the first time, and all he says is "Have a good day, ma'am." And then he gives me the biggest, most gap-toothed smile I have ever seen. Right then, he looks years younger—and I feel a fool.

Look at me, feeling sorry for myself because I do not get what I want! Do I not think others are in the same boat, or worse? I am but one person out of the billions that exist on this earth, so who am I to think that I deserve more than I already have?

To say that I try to follow the example of just one person would be to oversimplify things. The human character is much more complex than that. Just as our world is shaped by many different outside sources, so, too, have I been influenced by many familiar and unfamiliar faces.

It is not a matter of who, but what, has been the greatest influence in my life. I do not wish to be that homeless man on the street, for he has taught me with one genuine smile that my life is enough, and that there are worse things out there than not having a pink and yellow sundress. But it is his selfless character that continues to mold me.

My mother will hand me the grocery list today. I will make the same journey to the supermarket, and most likely, I will get the same items as last time. And I will probably see something I want but cannot have. But before I start to feel sorry for myself, I will remember the kind stranger with the gap-toothed grin, I'll grab the last item, and check out.

Source: www.teenink.com 'My Greatest Influence'

On the money

3 For questions 1–6, choose the answer (A, B, C or D) which you think fits best according to the text.

1. What impression do we have of Rachel in the first paragraph?
   A She enjoys doing the family shopping.
   B She comes from a family with not much money.
   C She never buys herself new clothes.
   D She is in a hurry to get home.

2. Rachel feels angry as she walks home because
   A she is expected to do too much.
   B she dislikes the area where she lives.
   C her family pay little attention to her.
   D she is not rewarded for her effort.

3. Rachel only speaks briefly to the man who helps her because
   A she thinks he has a criminal past.
   B she has never met him before.
   C she doesn't like the way he's dressed.
   D she's in a hurry to do other work.

4. What does Rachel mean by 'others are in the same boat' in line 43?
   A She has similar ambitions to other people.
   B She deserves to be treated the same as other people.
   C She lives in similar circumstances to other people.
   D She can share her problems with other people.

5. Who, according to Rachel, has had the greatest influence on her?
   A the homeless man
   B her mother
   C many different people
   D her family as a whole

6. Which of these phrases best summarises the lesson Rachel has learned?
   A She shouldn't complain about her situation.
   B She shouldn't envy other people.
   C She can be poor but happy.
   D She should value her family more.

4 To understand a text, you often need to understand exactly what the writer is referring to at different points in the text. Which noun phrase (a or b) does each of these words/phrases refer to?

1. it (line 2)
   a the grocery list
   b the money

2. it (line 6)
   a the list b the dress

3. these distractions (line 14)
   a the traffic, the sun, the sacks
   b the dress, the window, the supermarket

4. everything else (line 21)
   a the other sacks b the spilled contents

5. them (line 25)
   a the soup cans and apples b the hands

6. him (line 30)
   a the stranger b a friend

7. others (line 43)
   a other people b other strangers

8. that (line 49)
   a following the example of just one person
   b oversimplifying things

9. what (line 52)
   a a familiar face b one genuine smile

EXAM ADVICE

► The answers to the questions come in the same order in the text, so, for example, you will locate the answer to question 2 after question 1.
► The final question may refer to the whole passage: in this case, consider the general message, but also skim the text for words which support your choice.

5 Work in groups.

- Do you think Rachel was right to feel angry that she couldn't have the dress? Why? / Why not?
- If they can afford it, how much pocket money should parents give their children at these ages: 13, 15 and 18? Why?
- What is the best age for young people to have their own bank account? When should they have their own credit card?
- Should young people be encouraged to save? Why? What for?
- Do you think teenagers should earn some of the money they need by doing housework or taking a part-time job? Why? / Why not?

Unit 10

Vocabulary
arrive, *get* and *reach*

1 Candidates often confuse *arrive*, *get* and *reach*. Circle the correct word in *italics* in each of these sentences. Then check your answers by reading the definitions on page 185.

1 Nothing out of the ordinary happens when I *arrive / get / reach* to the store. I grab the bread, some milk, and other things on the list.
2 The plane was late taking off and has only just *arrived / got / reached*.
3 When they *arrived / got / reached* the top of the mountain, they were unable to see anything due to the thick cloud.

2 Complete these sentences with *arrive*, *get* or *reach* in the correct form. In some cases, more than one answer may be possible.

1 Stop writing when you have ……………… 190 words.
2 The traffic was so bad that they didn't ……………… to the concert till after it had started.
3 She's driving home and she'll phone me when she ……………… there.
4 What time do you normally ……………… to school in the morning?
5 When they ……………… at the hotel, they went straight to their rooms.
6 When you ……………… the end of the road, turn left.

3 Complete the sentences below with an adverb / adverbial phrase from the box to form collocations with *arrive*.

> finally   in time   on time   safe and sound   shortly
> unannounced

1 Mum was worried that we might have an accident because of the snow, but we arrived home ……………… , much to her relief.
2 Sandy was late for the refreshments, but he arrived ……………… to hear the speeches.
3 The airline has a great reputation for punctuality, with 90% of flights arriving ……………… .
4 The train that will be arriving ……………… at Platform 13, just two minutes after its scheduled time, is the Orient Express from Paris.
5 Uncle Kamal arrived ………… in the middle of lunch, so we had to set an extra place for him at the table.
6 We were very late because of the traffic and when we ………… arrived, the shop was closed.

Listening Part 4

1 Work in pairs. You are going to hear a student interviewing two teenagers about a new shopping centre they've been researching for a school project. Before you listen, why do many people prefer shopping centres? Make a list of your ideas.

2 07 Listen to the interview once. How many of your ideas from Exercise 1 do they mention?

3 Read questions 1–7. How many can you answer already?

1 Where is the shopping centre situated?
   A in the city centre
   B on the edge of the city
   C in the countryside
2 The location was chosen because
   A it would not harm the environment.
   B it was easy to get permission to build there.
   C it was easy for people to reach.
3 What is the main attraction of the shopping centre?
   A It's a convenient place to do the shopping.
   B It's attractive to the whole family.
   C It offers high-quality goods at low prices.
4 Kerry particularly enjoys the shopping centre's
   A feeling of luxury.
   B good security.
   C friendly atmosphere.
5 Salim says families argue when they go shopping because
   A they don't enjoy the same things.
   B they can't agree on what to buy.
   C they find each other's company stressful.
6 How are the shops organised?
   A Each shop in the centre chooses its own location.
   B Each section of the centre has a variety of shops.
   C Similar shops in the centre are located near each other.
7 What innovation does Salim describe for making shopping easier?
   A electric vehicles
   B moving walkways
   C automatic delivery systems

4 Listen again. For questions 1–7, choose the best answer (A, B or C).

On the money

5 Work in pairs. Do you have shopping centres like this one in your country? Do you / Would you enjoy shopping in places like this?

EXAM ADVICE

You have one minute to read the questions before you listen.
► Read the main part of each question carefully first.
► If you have time, go back and read the options for each question.

Vocabulary
Phrasal verbs

1 Match the phrasal verbs (1–12) from Listening Part 4 with their definitions (a–l).

1 take over
2 pull in
3 cater for
4 hang around with
5 chill out
6 be up to
7 pop into
8 cut down (on)
9 wear out
10 come up against
11 come up with
12 pick up

a attract
b collect, or to go and get, someone or something
c do less of something or use something in smaller amounts
d go into a place or visit for a short time
e have to deal with a problem
f make someone extremely tired
g provide what is wanted or needed by someone or something
h spend time with someone
i suggest or think of an idea or plan
j take control of / occupy
k be doing something
l relax completely

2 Use one of the phrasal verbs from Exercise 1 in the correct form in each of these sentences.

1 Chantal .... the brilliant idea of selling her old clothes in the market on Saturday.
2 I'm spending far more than I can afford. I'll really have to .... the amount of shopping I do.
3 My dad asked me to .... the post office and post a parcel for him.
4 It's an enormous music shop which .... all musical tastes from classical music to heavy metal.
5 Melanie doesn't like .... her parents, so she's gone shopping on her own.
6 Shopping in Oxford Street .... us .... , so we decided to take a taxi back to the hotel.
7 This new film is so popular that it has been .... huge audiences.
8 They've .... an old building in the city centre for their new shop.
9 I never expected to .... so many problems trying to get my mobile phone fixed.
10 Do you want to come shopping with me? I'm going to .... those red shoes I ordered.
11 What have you .... ? You should have finished the shopping by now.
12 It's a great little café to .... in after a hard day at school.

111

Unit 10

Grammar
Modals expressing ability

1 Look at these sentences and answer the questions below (four sentences come from Listening Part 4).

a They <u>could have</u> put the shopping centre out in the country ... but they chose an area with an underground station that's also close to the motorway.
b They <u>were able to</u> get permission in the end.
c Everyone had to get there by car, but at least they <u>could</u> park easily.
d From where I'm standing I <u>can</u> see trees ...
e You shouldn't have jumped off the wall. You were lucky – you <u>could have</u> broken a leg.
f I <u>can</u> drive really well, even though I haven't passed my test yet.
g My mum started teaching me letters when I was very small and I <u>could</u> read by the age of four.
h We <u>were able to</u> complete the project because there was plenty of info available on the Internet.

In which sentence do the <u>underlined</u> words or phrases mean ... ?

1 It is possible (for me) to do something: ..d.. and .....
2 It was generally possible to do something: ..... and .....
3 It was possible but it didn't happen: ..... and .....
4 We managed to do / We succeeded in doing something: ..... and .....

➔ page 170 Language reference: Modal verbs – expressing ability

2 Circle the correct form of the verb in *italics* in each of these sentences.

1 We walked all day, and at five o'clock we *could / were able to* reach the top of the mountain.
2 I was so worried that I *couldn't sleep / couldn't have slept* and I lay awake all night.
3 When I was a small child, I *could / was able to* sing beautifully, but my voice isn't so good now.
4 *Can you / Are you able to* hear the neighbours' television? It's far too loud!
5 I *could play / could have played* tennis with Luis yesterday, but I wasn't feeling well so I stayed at home.
6 Although the shop was very crowded, we *could / were able to* get the shopping done quite quickly.

3 Candidates often confuse *can*, *could* and *able to*. Write eight sentences about yourself, your family or a friend. Use each of the words or phrases in the box twice.

> could   was/were able to   could have   can

4 For questions 1–5, complete the second sentence so that it has a similar meaning to the first sentence, using the word given. Do not change the word given. You must use between two and five words, including the word given.

1 Mara has not succeeded in reducing the amount she spends.
   CUT
   Mara has not been .... on the amount she spends.
2 You were lucky that you did not have an accident – you were driving so fast.
   COULD
   You were lucky because .... an accident – you were driving so fast.
3 Did you manage to collect my books from the library?
   PICK
   Were .... my books from the library?
4 The shop is not able to deal with so many customers at the same time.
   CATER
   The shop .... a large number of customers at the same time.

112

On the money

Speaking Part 1

1 Read these Speaking Part 1 questions and note down a few ideas you could use to answer each of them (do not write complete sentences).

   1 Are you ever given money by people in your family? (Are you given money regularly, or on special occasions?)
   2 What do teenagers in your country typically spend their money on?
   3 Do you have a favourite shop? (Can you describe it to us?)
   4 Is there anything you'd like to buy but can't afford?

2 ▶ 08 Look at these descriptions of how some candidates answer Part 1 questions. Then listen to Thomas and Anna answering questions 1–4 from Exercise 1 and match the candidates with the descriptions by writing T (for Thomas), A (for Anna) or B (for both) by each one.

   1 This person is not sure how to answer at first, but then gives quite a long, complete answer. ☐
   2 This person gives lots of other information about themselves while they give reasons for their answer. ☐
   3 This person gives other information about themselves as background before they answer a question. ☐
   4 This person gives two alternative answers as well as a combined answer. ☐

3 Work alone. Choose three questions from Exercise 1 and three strategies for answering them from Exercise 2. Then think how you will answer the questions you have chosen using the strategies.

   - When you are ready, work with a partner and take turns to ask and answer the questions you have chosen.
   - While you are listening to your partner, for each answer, decide which strategy they are using and how successfully they are able to use it.

4 Pronunciation: linking (1)

To speak fluently, speakers often
- do not pronounce the last consonant of a word. In the example, many speakers would not pronounce the final 't' in *but*.
- link the last consonant of the word to the word which follows when it begins with a vowel. In the example, many speakers would link the final 't' of *didn't* to *answer* so that the 't' sounds as if it begins the word *answer*.

1 ▶ 09 Listen to these example sentences.

He understood but didn't answer.
I like eating and talking.
I don't often buy clothes and shoes.

2 ▶ 10 Look at and listen to the answer to question 2 and notice how the speaker:
   1 does not pronounce the crossed out letters
   2 joins the words indicated with ‿.

   I think it really depends, because teenagers are all different and so they spend their money in all sorts of ways. I guess some people spend more money on clothes and magazines, while others spend more on music and things like sports equipment. In general though, I think most teenagers spend money on things like going out to cafés or cinema tickets.

3 When can we:
   1 not pronounce the final letter of a word?
   2 link a word to the following word?

4 Work in pairs. Take turns to read the answer in Exercise 2 aloud, sentence by sentence, in the same way.

5 ▶ 11 Look at the answer to question 3 and:
   - underline the final consonants you think the speaker won't pronounce
   - mark with a ‿ the words you think the speaker will link.

   Then listen to check your answers.

   Hmm, I'm not sure, because I don't go shopping much really. Umm, but there is one shop I really like. It's one of a chain of sports shops and what's cool about it is I can just wander round and see all the clothes and equipment and stuff they sell. I look at clothes and equipment I'd like to buy – when I can afford it I mean.

6 Write your own answer to one of the questions in Exercise 1 and cross out the final consonants you shouldn't pronounce and indicate the words you should link with a ‿. Then work with a partner and take turns to read your answers.

113

Unit 10

5 Listen to Anna and Thomas each answering the examiner's question below.

Which strategy (1–4) from Exercise 2 do Anna and Thomas use?

> What sort of shops do you go to regularly?

6 Work in pairs. Look at the questions below and the words in the box. Which words could you use to help you answer the questions?

> a bargain   a brand   competitive   a consumer
> to purchase   the sales   in stock / out of stock
> unavailable

- What sort of shops do you go to regularly?
- Tell us about a shop you've visited recently. Why did you go there?
- Which shops in your area are the most attractive? Why?
- What's the best time of year to go shopping in your town?
- Tell us about something you really enjoyed buying.
- If you won a lot of money in a competition, how would you spend it?

7 Now take turns to ask and answer the questions.

EXAM ADVICE

▶ Practise by working in small groups, asking and answering questions about your personal life and interests. Make sure you choose topics that involve using a range of phrases.
▶ Don't go to the exam with memorised answers, as you will lose marks for not responding naturally. However, you can prepare by thinking about the vocabulary to describe your life, your studies or work, the neighbourhood where you live, etc.
▶ Look at the examiner while you're speaking and try to sound confident.

Writing Part 2 — A review

1 Look at this writing task and underline the key points you must deal with.

You've seen this announcement on an English-language website for teenagers.

Reviews wanted!

We are looking for reviews of something our readers have been given or bought recently. It could be a gadget, a piece of clothing, or something else. Write a review describing it. Tell us whether you like it and why, and if you would recommend it to other people.

Write your **review**.

2 Work in groups.
- Discuss what you could review and what information and ideas you could use to deal with the points you've underlined in Exercise 1.

On the money

3 Work alone and write a plan for your review. Then compare your plan with a partner's.

4 Read Eva's answer and write notes to complete her plan below.

My new bicycle

I was given a new bicycle for my birthday. I went to choose it with my mother in *Jones' Bikes*, our local bicycle shop. I chose a red *Abacus cruiser* and it cost my mother £200. All the other bicycles I've ever had were second-hand, so I'm still getting used to how shiny and amazing it looks. Apart from looking cool, my new bike is great to ride.

It's a road bike and although it isn't as high-tech as the ones in the Tour de France, it still goes pretty fast. I love the fact that it's so comfortable to ride and very light. It has three gears, which are all I need because I live in such a flat part of the country that I wouldn't use more if I had them. However, don't worry if you live somewhere hilly, the nine-gear models are not very expensive either.

The *Abacus cruiser* is light and really comfortable. In fact, the saddle is the most comfortable I've ever had as it is made of leather. What's more, you can ride it easily in the rain as the tyres are made of good thick rubber that doesn't slip on wet roads.

Go to your local shop or have a look online and see if you can find it! It's one of the cheapest models out there and is available in a range of colours.

I recommend it to anyone because it's cheap and great to ride. It's probably the best bike you can buy at the moment.

Plan

Para. 1: .... *what the thing is: a bike* ....

Paras. 2 and 3: ....

Para. 4: ....

Para. 5: ....

5 Study how Eva uses the highlighted words or phrases. Then join these sentences using the words in brackets and making any other changes which are necessary.

1 I've always wanted a new camera. This was the perfect present. (*so*)
   I've always wanted a new camera, so this was the perfect present.
2 This camera is very easy to use. It takes excellent pictures. (*apart from*)
3 It's blue, which isn't my favourite colour. The camera looks very smart. (*although, still*)
4 It has a strong case. This is very important. I am a clumsy person. I would soon damage it while carrying it around. (*which, because, such, that*)
5 My brother showed me how to use all the different functions. Don't worry if you have to work it out yourself. It comes with a very good instruction manual and DVD. (*but, as*)

6 Write your own answer to the writing task in Exercise 1.
 • Before you write, think how you can use the highlighted words in Eva's answer in your own writing.
 • Use as many as possible.
 • Write between 140 and 190 words.

> ### EXAM ADVICE
> ▶ Think about who will read your review and what information they want to know.
> ▶ Write a plan thinking about each of the things you want to describe and in what order.
> ▶ Decide what recommendation you are going to make and include it in your answer.

Vocabulary and grammar review Unit 9

Vocabulary

1 Circle the best word from the words in *italics*.

1 Sheila *spent / passed* most of her holiday at her cousins' house.
2 I think the bad weather might *cause / have* an impact on the plans for the class trip.
3 Air travel *causes / makes* a lot of pollution.
4 People play with their mobile phones to *spend / pass* the time when there's nothing more interesting to do.
5 Patricia studied really hard all weekend, but it *had / caused* no effect on her final result in the exam.
6 Hearing my brother's good news *caused / made* me very happy.
7 I *stayed / spent* six hours doing homework for my English class last weekend.

Grammar

2 Look at the photos and question for Speaking Part 2. Then complete the sentences in the next column from Patricia's answer by writing words and phrases from the box above them.

What do the people enjoy about these free-time activities?

> appear to   both   could just   look   look as if
> may be   might be doing it   perhaps   very different

The first photo shows two young people doing archery. They **(1)** .... taking part in a competition, or they **(2)** .... be practising, I'm not sure. They **(3)** .... as part of a traditional activity in their country or because they enjoy the sport.

The second photo shows a **(4)** .... situation. In this photo, there are two middle-aged or older people playing the piano together. They **(5)** .... very happy and relaxed.

The teenagers in the first photo **(6)** .... be enjoying themselves because they're having to concentrate hard in order to hit the target or win the competition. On the other hand, in the second photo, the people **(7)** .... they're just enjoying each other's company and **(8)** .... they're not taking the music too seriously. In **(9)** .... photos, the people are enjoying doing things which need a lot of practice to do well.

3 Complete this dialogue between two friends by putting the verbs in brackets into the correct form.

Andy: Why won't Stephen answer his mobile phone?

Nigel: He **(1)** .... (*must / switch*) it off while he was playing football and forgotten to turn it back on again.

Andy: He **(2)** .... (*can't / turn*) it off because he didn't have football training today – it was cancelled.

Nigel: Well, he **(3)** .... (*may not / hear*) it, or he **(4)** .... (*could / leave*) it at home. Try ringing again. He **(5)** .... (*might / answer*) this time. Anyway, why do you want to call him?

Andy: I want to remind him that he's coming round to my house tomorrow afternoon after school. He **(6)** .... (*might / forget*) – you know what he's like.

Nigel: He **(7)** .... (*can't / forget*) – he was talking about it yesterday and he was looking forward to it.

Vocabulary and grammar review Unit 10

Vocabulary

1 Read the text and decide which answer (A, B, C or D) best fits each gap.

I think that we, as teenage shoppers, are naturally very **(0)** ...B.... to price. We're always hunting for **(1)** .... and many of us plan our shopping and do not just **(2)** .... into shops and buy on impulse.

Funnily enough, many of my friends say their parents have a lot of **(3)** .... both over how much they spend on clothes and what they buy, even if they have **(4)** .... the money themselves from a part-time job; in short, despite what many older people might think, we worry about our parents' reaction to the clothes we **(5)** ....

The shops in my area operate in a highly **(6)** .... environment, so they have to make sure they **(7)** .... for young people's tastes by having a wide range of fashion clothes in **(8)** .... at any one time.

0	A sensible	B (sensitive)	C affected	D considerate
1	A values	B cheapness	C bargains	D decreases
2	A jump	B pop	C enter	D pass
3	A impact	B importance	C pressure	D influence
4	A earned	B won	C gained	D acquired
5	A invest	B achieve	C purchase	D obtain
6	A competent	B competitive	C contested	D combative
7	A offer	B cater	C sell	D supply
8	A stock	B shelf	C place	D existence

Grammar

2 Complete the second sentence so that it has a similar meaning to the first sentence, using the word given. Do not change the word given. You must use between two and five words, including the word given.

1 Manu didn't succeed in completing the crossword.
   ABLE
   Manu .... off the crossword.
2 We need to use less paper.
   AMOUNT
   We need to cut .... paper we use.
3 Katya found the climb so tiring that she fell asleep at the top.
   WORN
   Katya .... the climb that she fell asleep at the top.
4 Pierre was unable to suggest an answer to the problem.
   COME
   Pierre .... an answer to the problem.
5 Did you manage to collect Paz from the station?
   PICK
   Were you .... from the station?
6 When Alexis reached the cinema, the film had finished.
   GET
   Alexis did not .... the film was over.

3 Write *as* or *like* in each of the gaps.

When my grandfather left school at the age of 14, he got his first job **(1)** .... an office assistant. In those days, he was extremely thin, **(2)** .... he wasn't paid very much and couldn't afford to eat a lot. But he was in the same situation **(3)** .... a lot of boys at that time, **(4)** .... most children left school at that age and had to look for a job. I have one or two photos of him from that time, and he looks just **(5)** .... me, but thinner! When he grew older, he worked at all sorts of things, such **(6)** .... reporting for a local newspaper and working **(7)** .... a part-time mechanic. **(8)** .... many people of his generation, he worked hard all his life, but he always found time for the things he enjoyed, **(9)** .... walking in the country or spending time with his grandchildren. I hope I'll be **(10)** .... him when I'm an old man!

117

11 Medical matters

Starting off

1 Here I am, in my 80s and still quite .... – I mean I go shopping, visit my friends and go to the cinema when I want to. What more can you ask for?

2 I do an hour's .... in the morning before school, and in the evening I usually have time for a couple of hours' football, so I really think I'm very fit.

3 I do .... the occasional cold or other .... I'm a doctor, so I can't really avoid them, but I .... them pretty quickly and they don't usually stop me going to work.

4 I visit the doctor regularly once a year for a .... Once or twice I've needed .... for something she's found, but it's never been anything very serious.

5 I never go to the doctor and in fact I don't even know my doctor's name. I'm lucky, I've never had a day's .... in my life.

6 I'm very careful to eat a .... – only a little meat and plenty of fresh fruit and vegetables – and I'm careful about not .... weight, so I do a reasonable amount of exercise as well.

1 Work in pairs. Complete what each of the people says about their health by writing the words or phrases from the box in the gaps.

> active   balanced diet   catch   check-up   get over
> illness   infection   putting on   treatment   workout

- Do you ever think about your health?
- Do you think you and your friends have a healthy lifestyle?

2 ▶13 Work in pairs. Listen to the first part of what each speaker (A–F) says about their health and, when you hear the 'beep', predict which extract (1–6) from Exercise 1 comes next.

Example: *A2*

3 ▶14 Now listen to the complete extracts to check your answers to Exercises 1 and 2.

4 Work in pairs.
- Which speaker do you think has the healthiest lifestyle?
- Which speakers say something you agree with? Why?

Medical matters

Listening Part 3

1 You are going to hear five people talking about a visit to the doctor. Before you listen, answer the questions in the Exam round-up box.

EXAM ROUND-UP

How much do you remember about Listening Part 3? Circle the correct option in *italics* in these sentences.
1 You listen to *four / five* speakers and you must choose the statement which best summarises what they say from *seven / eight* options.
2 Before you listen, you should *read and think about the meaning of each option / read through the options, then wait patiently for the listening to begin.*

2 Match the words and phrases (1–8) with their definitions (a–h).

1	cure	a	piece of paper on which a doctor writes that a patient is ill and has permission not to go to school or work
2	diagnose	b	say what medical treatment someone should have
3	examination	c	recognise and name the exact character of a disease or a problem, by making an examination
4	heal	d	use drugs, exercises, etc. to cure a person of a disease or heal an injury
5	prescribe	e	when a doctor looks at a patient carefully in order to discover the problem
6	sick note	f	make someone with an illness healthy again
7	surgery	g	make or become well again, especially after a cut or other injury
8	treat	h	a place where you can go to ask advice from or receive treatment from a doctor or dentist

3 ▶ 15 Now listen and tick ✓ the words and phrases from Exercise 2 as you hear them.

4 Listen again. For speakers 1–5, choose from the list (A–H) what each speaker says about their visit. Use the letters only once. There are three extra letters which you do not need to use.

A I wasn't given enough attention at first.
B I was told that I needed to relax.
C I was irritated by what was said to me.
D I wish I hadn't gone at all.
E I felt better afterwards.
F I asked for a specialist to deal with my problem.
G I agreed with the diagnosis.
H I arrived late for my appointment.

Speaker 1 ☐
Speaker 2 ☐
Speaker 3 ☐
Speaker 4 ☐
Speaker 5 ☐

5 Work in pairs.
- How often do you go to the doctor?
- Do you feel nervous before you go to the doctor? Why? / Why not?

Unit 11

Vocabulary
Idiomatic expressions

It's important to be able to guess the meanings of idiomatic expressions from the context.

Match the highlighted expressions 1–5 in these extracts from Listening Part 3 with their definitions a–e below.

- I've been **(1) feeling a bit off-colour** for some time now and my dad's taken me to the doctor several times to try to **(2) get to the bottom of it**.
- I'd been coughing and sneezing all week and **(3) feeling very under the weather**.
- I must say he looked a bit **(4) taken aback**, but then he got up from his desk and came and gave me a really thorough check-up.
- … he'd been up all night on duty in the local hospital, where he'd been **(5) rushed off his feet**.

a be very busy
b feel slightly ill
c discover the truth about a situation
d feel really ill
e surprise or shock someone so much that they do not know how to behave for some time

Reading and Use of English Part 4
Saying things in different ways

1 Read the email below from an English teenager called Jack to his friend Ahmed.

- What job does Jack want to do in the future?

Subject: What would you like to do?

Hi Ahmed,

How are you doing? Do you remember that time we talked about what jobs and careers we might do in the future? **(1)** I'm finding it almost impossible to make up my mind.

My parents tell me I'm too young to be expected to know what I want to do and that **(2)** as long as I keep working hard at school for the next few years, I'll be able to choose whatever I want to do in the end. I'm not sure I agree – sometimes, in my class, I feel as if **(3)** I'm the only person who hasn't got a career in mind! It's a big decision to make, but even so **(4)** I hadn't expected it to be nearly so hard.

Sometimes I think I'd like to go into medicine, or maybe into biochemistry. My biology teacher is really interested in genetic medicine and he thinks **(5)** they'll make major advances over the next few years. That sounds really fascinating! **(6)** As a result, cures to many diseases could be found and only a few years ago, people **(7)** didn't think it was possible. It would be great to be involved in that.

Then again, I'd also love to be a racing driver. That's a very interesting field too and it would be really exciting! When I've finally **(8)** managed to make up my mind, I'll let you know! In the meantime, I'd love to hear what you think – have you decided what you want to do? Do let me know if you have!

All the best,

Jack

Medical matters

2 Read the text carefully and replace the underlined words with one of the options below. There are five options you do not need to use. You may need to use a capital letter if the option is used at the beginning of a sentence.

a everyone apart from me has
b provided I continue to work
c major advances are being made
d it's far harder than I'd thought
e it's extremely hard for me
f got ready to make
g there may be cures to many diseases
h succeeded in making
i if I manage to work
j much progress is likely to be made
k thought it was impossible
l it was almost as hard as I'd expected
m it could lead to cures to many medical problems being

3 For questions 1–6, complete the second sentence so that it has a similar meaning to the first sentence, using the word given. Do not change the word given. You must use between two and five words, including the word given.

1 Last winter Jane was the only person in our class who didn't catch a cold.
APART
Last winter everybody in our class .... Jane.

2 I hadn't expected to wait for nearly so long to see the doctor.
FAR
The wait to see the doctor .... I'd expected.

3 The nurse finally managed to persuade my little sister to have the injection.
SUCCEEDED
The nurse finally .... my little sister to have the injection.

4 I don't think they'll ever find a cure for the common cold.
UNLIKELY
I think a cure for the common cold .... found.

5 As a result of the mistake some patients were misdiagnosed.
LED
The mistake .... misdiagnosed.

6 The doctor says I'll get better provided I continue to take these pills for four weeks.
KEEP
The doctor says I'll get better as .... these pills for four weeks.

4 Write sentences about yourself and your friends using the words and phrases in the box.

apart from   far ... than   succeeded   unlikely
led to   as long as

Unit 11

Grammar
Relative pronouns and relative clauses

1 Complete these sentences from Listening Part 3 by writing one word in the gaps. In some cases, more than one answer may be possible.

1 ... when I finally saw the doctor he said I'd just got a slight infection, ... is what I was expecting ...
2 The doctor .... normally sees me was on holiday.
3 ... this time I saw a different doctor .... was just so sympathetic!
4 ... he'd been up all night on duty in the local hospital .... he'd been rushed off his feet.

➡ page 172 Language reference: Relative pronouns and relative clauses

2 Read these sentences. Which contain defining relative clauses? Which contain non-defining relative clauses? Write D for defining or ND for non-defining after each sentence.

1 The village where I go for my holidays has a very healthy climate. .....
2 Mrs Altmeyer, who you met on the train, is a nurse. .....
3 The children who you've been talking to all go to the same school. .....
4 Have you still got the book which I lent you? .....
5 My physical education teacher, who was an Olympic champion, says that exercise is essential for good health. .....
6 Students who eat a good breakfast often do better at school. .....

3 In which of sentences 1–6 above could you use *that* instead of *which* or *who*?

4 In which sentences could you omit *who* or *which*? Why?

5 Join these sentences using a relative clause.
1 Did you see the film? They broadcast it on television last night.
Did you see the film (– / that / which) they broadcast on television last night?
2 He studied hard for his maths exam. He found it quite easy.
3 The man is a taxi driver. They sold the car to him.
4 Could you give me the newspaper? You were reading it earlier.
5 That white house over there is the house. He was born there.
6 Where's the envelope? I put the money in it.
7 Every morning, I go running in the park with Patricia. You know her brother.
8 Karen and Teresa are on holiday in the Caribbean at the moment. We're looking after their dog.

Reading and Use of English Part 3

1 Read this sentence from Reading and Use of English Part 4 and choose the best answer to the question below.

> As a result of the mistake, some patients were misdiagnosed.

What does *misdiagnosed* mean?
a diagnosed badly or wrongly
b not diagnosed at all

2 Now read these two sentences and answer the questions below them.

He unlocked the front door and walked in.

1 What does *unlock* mean?
a lock something wrongly
b open something which was locked

The football competition was so disorganised that no one knew what time their team had to play.

2 What does *disorganised* mean?
a not organised
b organised wrongly

3 Which prefix, *mis-*, *un-* or *dis-*, has a different meaning from the other two?

4 Complete these sentences using the negative form of the verb given in capitals. Remember to use the correct form of the verb.

1 Could you help my little brother .... his seatbelt, please? **DO**
2 I know the news will .... you, but we are unable to offer you the job. **APPOINT**
3 If you .... the equipment, it will probably break. **USE**
4 The knot was so tight that he couldn't .... it. **TIE**
5 *Accommodation* is a word which many students .... **SPELL**
6 I can't find my keys anywhere. They seem to have just .... **APPEAR**
7 This isn't a complete check-up, so you needn't get .... – just take off your shirt. **DRESS**
8 I'm afraid you must have been .... ; there's no concert here tonight. **INFORM**

5 **EP** Add a prefix *un-*, *dis-*, *in-*, *im-* or *mis-* to form opposites of these words. In some cases, more than one answer may be possible.

> ability   agreement   appear   aware   certain
> experienced   formal   happiness   helpful   honest
> like   patient   predictable   reliable   satisfied
> understand

6 **EP** For questions 1–8, read this text. Use the word given in capitals at the end of some of the lines to form a word that fits in the gap in the same line. Before you decide which word, decide what type of word you need (adjective, noun, etc.), whether you need a negative form, a plural form or the correct form of a verb.

Is there a doctor on board?

You're on a plane in mid-air. You
(0) ....*undo*........ your seatbelt and begin   **DO**
to relax when you hear an **(1)** ....   **EXPECT**
announcement: 'Is there a doctor on board?'

As we all know, air travel can be an extremely
stressful experience, especially after going
through airport **(2)** .... checks.   **SECURE**
Studies of airline passengers reveal that we all
(3) .... worry that we or another   **OCCASION**
passenger may have a **(4)** ....   **MEDICINE**
problem far from a hospital at a
(5) .... of 10,000 metres.   **HIGH**

Well, now Lufthansa, the German airline,
has made the **(6)** .... that on   **CALCULATE**
80% of its flights, there is in fact a doctor
amongst the passengers. Having previously
obtained the doctor's agreement, when there's
a medical emergency on board, one of the
cabin staff will discreetly ask for his or her
(7) .... It is hoped that in the   **ASSIST**
future, this system will avoid making the other
passengers **(8)** .... when these   **EASY**
situations arise.

EXAM ADVICE

Check:
▶ whether nouns need to be singular or plural.
▶ whether a prefix – positive or negative – is needed
▶ that verbs are in the correct form.
Be careful to spell your answers correctly.

Unit 11

Speaking Part 2

1 Complete the table below with these phrases for getting out of difficulties in the Speaking paper. (You can use them in any part of the Speaking paper.)

Phrases for getting out of difficulties
I can't think of the word, but it's a type of …
I'm not sure how to say it, but it's used for …
I'm sorry, what I meant was …
Let me think …
No, I mean …
What I want to say is that …
What's the word?
Sorry, I mean …

When you need time to think	When you can't think of the word	When you've made a mistake

2 ▶ 16 Work in pairs. Listen to Antonia doing Speaking Part 2 and then complete the checklist on the right.

How important is each activity for staying healthy?

The candidate …	yes	no
1 spoke for the complete minute or until the examiner said, 'Thank you'		
2 compared the photos and spent roughly equal time on each		
3 answered the examiner's question clearly with his/her opinion		
4 gave (a) reason(s) for his/her opinion		
5 found ways of explaining things when he/she didn't know a word		
6 corrected his/her mistakes		
7 sounded interested and enthusiastic about what he/she was saying.		

3 Work in pairs. Look at the examiner's follow-up question to different candidates and their answers. Then answer the questions below.

Examiner: Now, which activity would you prefer to do?
Miguel: I'd prefer to go cycling, because I'm not very good at cooking and I really enjoy making— I mean doing physical exercise. I find cycling in the city quite exciting, but if I can, I'd rather cycle in the country because it's less polluted.
Peter: Making salad is better because the other is dangerous.
Nikolai: Oh, I think cycling is very good for the health, even in the city, and also it's important to have a healthy diet because you know what they say: we are what we eat!

1 Who do you think gave the best answer: Miguel, Peter or Nikolai? Why?
2 Match what the examiner might be thinking with each candidate's answer:

a 'Did he listen to my question? He isn't answering it at all!'
b 'This is a good answer: two or three sentences, he corrects himself and he uses a variety of vocabulary.'
c 'Too short! He hasn't used much language and he's not really answering the question!'

Medical matters

EXAM ADVICE

▶ If you can't think of a word, explain what the thing is used for or what it looks like.

4 Pronunciation: intonation (3)

We tend to use more intonation on stressed words than on unstressed words.

1 ▶ 17 Work in pairs. Look at this extract from Antonia's answer. <u>Underline</u> the words you think she stresses. Then listen to check your answers.

OK, so both photographs show people doing things which might be good for their sanity, sorry, I mean their health. In the first photo I can see someone who looks as if he's, um, what's the word, he's commuting by bicycle in busy traffic.

2 ▶ 18 Listen to the extract with two different intonations.
- In which version, a or b, does the speaker sound more certain and confident?
- Does the voice rise or fall on the final stressed word in each sentence? What does this show?

3 Take turns to read the extract in Exercise 1 aloud. Your partner should say whether your intonation is more like version a or b.

4 ▶ 19 Decide which words will be stressed in these two extracts. Then listen to check your answers.
  a I'd say there are some problems with the idea of health in the first photo because of the danger from the traffic, especially because he's cycling in the night, I mean the dark, and the um, I can't think of the word, but it's a type of smoke which comes from the cars.
  b On the other hand, if you live in the city, it's a good way of getting exercise. In the second photo, the kids should remember that they need to eat a mixed, sorry, a balanced diet, not just salad and fruit.

5 Does the speaker sound more certain and more confident in extract a or b? Why? Take turns to read these extracts aloud.

5 ▶ 20 Work in pairs.
- Student A: Listen to the examiner's instructions and do the Speaking Part 2 task in Exercise 2.
- Student B: Listen and complete the checklist in Exercise 2 for your partner. When your partner has finished, give feedback.

6 ▶ 21 Now, Student B should listen to the examiner's follow-up question and answer it.

7 ▶ 22 Work in pairs. Student B should listen to the examiner's instructions and do this task. Student A should complete the checklist in (Speaking) Exercise 2 and give feedback at the end.

Why is it important for these people to deal with their problems?

8 ▶ 23 Now, Student A should listen to the examiner's follow-up question and answer it.

Unit 11

Writing Part 1 — An essay

1 Work in groups. Look at this discussion question. Discuss and note down at least three healthy or unhealthy aspects for each discussion point (a–e). When you have finished, change groups and report what your group decided.

Do you think modern lifestyles are healthy or not?
Talk about:
a the environment and health
b diet
c work activities
d information, e.g. about exercise, diet
e free-time activities.

2 Work in pairs. Read the writing task below.
- <u>Underline</u> the main ideas in the task.
- Decide which points from your discussion you would include in your answer and write a plan.

In your English class, you have been talking about whether modern lifestyles are healthy or not.

Now your English teacher has asked you to write an essay.

Write an essay using **all** the notes and give reasons for your point of view.

Essay question
Modern lifestyles can seriously endanger our health. Do you agree?

Notes
Write about:
1. food
2. physical activity
3. … (your own idea)

Write your **essay**.

3 Work in pairs. Discuss what the strong points and weak points of this essay are. Then say what comments you would write at the end if you were this student's teacher.

It seems strange that although we know a lot about how to live healthily, many people continue to do things which may be harmful to their health.

There are many parts of our lifestyles which enable us to live healthily. For instance, we all know about the importance of eating a balanced diet and taking regular exercise. Moreover, in rich countries we have easy access to good-quality fresh food and suitable sports facilities, so it should be easy to adopt healthy living habits.

However, there are things which prevent people from having a healthy lifestyle. For example, industry and traffic have led to serious environmental pollution. What is more, we spend a lot of time sitting down, and this often means we have less time for activities which keep us fit. For example, there are many people who spend many hours sitting in front of computers working, studying, or playing computer games. In addition, many people do not eat the right sort of food.

Medical matters

4 Work in pairs. Read these concluding paragraphs and decide which one is most suitable for the essay in Exercise 3. Why?

> 1 All in all, I believe that we have to find ways of living which are as healthy as possible. Also, I think people should try to drive more carefully.

> 2 In conclusion, I would agree with the statement because although we have plenty of opportunities to follow a healthy lifestyle, in practice we often choose a less healthy alternative.

> 3 To summarise, modern lifestyles have good and bad aspects, but the lifestyle we choose depends on us. However, often our health depends on factors which we cannot control.

5 Match each of these teacher's comments (a–c) to one of the concluding paragraphs in Exercise 4.

> a A good brief final paragraph where your opinion is clearly stated and you summarise the main arguments of your essay.
>
> b This concluding paragraph doesn't seem to sum up the arguments you expressed in the main part of the essay, but it sums up other arguments. What a pity, because it's well written!
>
> c You're giving an opinion which is not exactly connected with the essay question. Also, your final sentence introduces a new argument which hasn't been dealt with in the main part of the essay, so it's not really a conclusion.

6 If you're not sure how to begin a paragraph, you can begin with a sentence which:

- says what the paragraph will contain
- relates the paragraph to the previous paragraph.

Look at the opening sentences (a and b) from the sample answer in Exercise 3.

1 What will each paragraph contain?
2 Which word relates one of the paragraphs to the previous paragraph?

a There are many parts of our lifestyles which enable us to live healthily.
b However, there are things which prevent people from having a healthy lifestyle.

7 Write opening sentences for paragraphs which will contain:
1 three advantages of living in the country
2 some disadvantages of living in the country
3 reasons exercise is important
4 dangers of taking too much exercise.

8 Work in groups. Discuss whether you agree or disagree with the essay question in Exercise 9. You can talk about:
- diet
- sport and exercise
- free-time activities.

9 Do this writing task. Write between 140 and 190 words. Before you write, make a plan. When you write, you can use the essay in Exercise 3 as a model.

In your English class, you have been talking about how interested young people are in health and fitness.

Now your English teacher has asked you to write an essay.

Write an essay using **all** the notes and give reasons for your point of view.

Essay question
Young people generally don't pay enough attention to their health and fitness. Do you agree?

Notes
Things to write about
1. physical exercise
2. other habits which affect health
3. .... (your own idea)

Write your **essay**.

EXAM ADVICE

▶ Your concluding paragraph should summarise your opinion and the reasons for it.
▶ Don't include new arguments or ideas in your final sentence because you won't be able to support them with reasons or examples.
▶ Be careful not to spend too long on Part 1, or you won't have time to do Part 2 well.

12 Animal kingdom

Starting off

Work in pairs.

What is the relationship between the people and the animals in each photograph? Are animals important in your life? If so, why are they important?

Here are some words and phrases that may help you with your discussion:

pet   owner   working animal   competitive sport
farming   leisure

Listening Part 1

1 Work in pairs. Before you listen, answer the questions in the Exam round-up box.

EXAM ROUND-UP

How much do you remember about Listening Part 1? Circle the correct option in *italics* in each of these sentences.

In Listening Part 1:
1 you hear *six / eight* extracts; the extracts are on *the same subject / different* subjects.
2 you hear each extract *once / twice*.
3 you *read and hear / read but don't hear* the question before the extract.
4 you should underline the main idea *in the question only / in the question and each of the options*.
5 you should answer *while you listen / after you have heard the whole of each piece*.

Animal kingdom

2 🔊 **24** You are going to hear people talking in eight different situations. For questions 1–8, choose the best answer (A, B or C). As you hear the question, <u>underline</u> the main idea.

1 You overhear a conversation between two women about animals. Which animal does she think her family will choose?
  A a cat
  B a dog
  C a horse

2 You hear part of a television programme about zebras. What does the presenter say about their appearance?
  A All members of a family of zebras have the same stripes.
  B Zebras can recognise each other by their stripes.
  C Male and female zebras have similar stripes.

3 You overhear a conversation between a boy and a girl about birds in the girl's garden. How does the girl's mother feel about birds?
  A She enjoys watching them.
  B She likes feeding them.
  C She worries about them.

4 You overhear part of a conversation in which a girl and a boy are talking about dogs. What is the boy doing?
  A recommending having a dog
  B complaining about his dog
  C suggesting where to keep a dog

5 You hear a woman giving part of a lecture about animal rights. She says zoos
  A are no longer necessary in modern times.
  B should only be for endangered species.
  C should be closely supervised.

6 You hear a girl talking about some animals she worked with. When she was with them, she felt
  A frightened.
  B relaxed.
  C strange.

7 You hear a boy talking about hippos. What does he say about them?
  A They are more dangerous than people think.
  B They often attack people for no reason.
  C They are easily frightened.

8 You hear a woman talking to her husband about a circus. She is talking to him in order to
  A make a suggestion.
  B make a complaint.
  C remind him of something.

Vocabulary

avoid, prevent and *protect; check, control, keep an eye on* and *supervise*

1 👁 Candidates often confuse the following words: *avoid, prevent* and *protect; check, control, keep an eye on* and *supervise*. Circle the correct word in *italics* in these extracts from Listening Part 1.

1 … my mum and dad got him to *avoid / prevent / protect* us from burglars. Mine only seems to bark at other dogs.
2 … you never know: all that barking might *avoid / prevent / protect* a burglary.
3 … the more modern zoos need to be strictly inspected to make sure that the animals are kept in the best conditions possible. That way diseases and other problems can be *avoided / prevented / protected*.
4 I had to *check / control / keep an eye on* them as well because they could be quite rough when playing with each other …
5 I mean, we'd have to *check / control / supervise* her quite closely to start with to make sure she was safe. At least until we know she can *check / control / keep an eye on / supervise* it.

2 Read the definitions on page 185. Then complete these sentences (1–8) by writing one of the words in the correct form in the gaps. In some cases, more than one answer may be possible.

1 This cream is perfect for …................ you from insect bites.
2 The new law …................ people from building houses near the National Park.
3 There was a man who was …................ the tickets as people walked into the stadium.
4 I think we should set out early to …................ the worst of the traffic.
5 You ought to be wearing a hat to …................ your head from the sun.
6 It's the chemistry teacher's responsibility to …................ students when they're doing experiments to make sure nothing explodes!
7 Make sure you …................ your answer for mistakes before you hand it in.
8 We should always respect the forces of nature because we will never be able to …................ them.

129

Unit 12

3 Complete each of the sentences below with an adverb/verb collocation from the box in the correct form.

> avoid … at all costs   check … carefully
> closely supervise   heavily protect
> narrowly avoid   properly protect   strictly control
> successfully prevent

1 Ben ………………… the bear from attacking them by making a lot of noise.
2 Juan ………………… an accident when a dog ran in front of the car.
3 Rhinos are an endangered species and need to be ………………… by game wardens.

4 The number of visitors to the game reserve is ………………… to avoid upsetting the animals.
5 Tourists visiting the park need to be ………………… to make sure they don't go near the wild animals.
6 When it rains heavily, you should ………………… crossing the river ………………… , as the current can be very strong.
7 You need to ………………… your route ………………… on the map before you start, as you could easily get lost.
8 The camp is ………………… with a high fence and an alarm to prevent dangerous animals from getting in.

Grammar
Third conditional and mixed conditionals

1 Look at this sentence from Listening Part 1 (extract 7) and then decide whether the statements (1–3) are true (T) or false (F).

If he hadn't reacted quickly, the hippo would have killed him.

1 The man reacted quickly.
2 The hippo killed him.
3 The speaker is talking about the past.

2 Now look at these sentences and answer the questions below.

a *I think if they'd had more acrobats, we'd have enjoyed the circus more.*
b *I think if they had more acrobats, we'd enjoy the circus more.*

Which sentence (a or b) … ?
1 means: *They don't have enough acrobats, so we don't enjoy the circus very much.* …………
2 means: *They didn't have enough acrobats, so we didn't enjoy the circus very much.* …………
3 has this form: *if* + past simple, *would* + infinitive …………
4 has this form: *if* + past perfect, *would have* (been/done/enjoyed, etc.) …………
5 is second conditional (see pages 54–55) …………
6 is third conditional …………
7 has the same form as *If he hadn't reacted quickly, the hippo would have killed him* in Exercise 1 …………

➔ page 165 Language reference: Conditionals – third conditional

Animal kingdom

3 👁 Candidates often make mistakes with tenses in third conditional sentences. Complete each of these sentences by writing the verb in brackets in the correct form.

1 If Martin had concentrated on his work, he .... (*finish*) it earlier.
2 If I .... (*know*) that the train was going to be so late, I .... (*catch*) an earlier one.
3 If there had been a swimming pool in the garden I .... (*go*) swimming in it.
4 John could have spoken to Emma if the phone .... (*not be*) broken.
5 We wouldn't have become friends unless you .... (*sit*) next to me on the school bus.
6 If you had been there, you .... (*enjoy*) yourself, too!
7 Sorry! I .... (*not make*) so much noise if I'd known you were asleep.
8 We .... (*not hear*) the burglar downstairs unless the dog had barked.

4 Work in pairs. Answer these questions in any way you like.

- What would have happened if you'd got up an hour later this morning?
- Where was the last place you went on holiday? What would you have done if you hadn't gone on holiday there?
- What was the last exam you passed? What would have happened if you'd failed the exam?

5 If you want to talk about past and present time in the same conditional sentence, you can combine second conditional with third conditional. Look at these two extracts from Listening Part 1. Which part of each sentence (a or b):

- is second conditional, and which part is third conditional?
- refers to present time and which part refers to past time?

1 Probably, if we lived in a safer area,ᵃ they wouldn't have bought a dog.ᵇ
2 I'd be happier,ᵃ if my parents had bought a house in the country.ᵇ

➡ page 165 Language reference: Conditionals – mixed conditionals

6 Complete these sentences by writing the verb in brackets in the correct form (second or third conditional) in the gaps.

1 My dad doesn't have a car, so he didn't drive me to my dancing lesson yesterday. If my dad .... (*have*) a car, he .... (*drive*) me to my dancing lesson yesterday.
2 Katie feels nervous about the test because she didn't study last weekend. If she .... (*study*), she .... (*not feel*) nervous about the test.
3 Our dog barks too much, so we didn't take him on holiday with us. If our dog .... (*not bark*) so much, we .... (*take*) him on holiday with us.
4 Karl was very rude to me, so we are no longer friends. If Karl .... (*not be*) so rude to me, we .... (*still be*) friends.

131

Unit 12

Reading and Use of English Part 1

1 Work in pairs. You will read a short article by someone who worked in a circus. Before you read, discuss these questions.
- Are circuses popular in your country? Why? / Why not?
- What other traditional forms of entertainment are popular in your country? Why?

2 Before doing Reading and Use of English Part 1, answer the questions in the Exam round-up box.

3 Read the article quickly without paying attention to the gaps. What animals do Nell and Toti have in their circus?

My sister's circus

My aunt and uncle, Nell and Toti, (0) ...*own*... a circus. It is (1) .... Gifford's Circus, and it tours some of the loveliest parts of south-west England. Circuses have always been a part of Nell's life, even when she was a child. When she (2) .... Toti, she had already worked in (3) .... circuses in Britain and Europe. She had ridden elephants, but what she really (4) .... for was a circus of her own. If the word 'circus' (5) .... you of clowns and lions, think again. The show is (6) .... on traditional travelling circuses and aimed at a rural (7) ....
There are no wild animals, but horses play a leading role in performances, which are a mixture of theatre, dance, traditional circus acts and clowns. I had visited Nell at the circus a lot, but this time I was going to (8) .... the summer there.

Adapted from the Daily Telegraph

EXAM ROUND-UP

How much do you remember about Reading and Use of English Part 1? Complete the information below with these words and phrases.

eight   after   all the questions   the text quickly
you have finished   the options

1 There are .... questions in this part. You must choose A, B, C or D.
2 Read .... before attempting the questions.
3 Read the words before and .... the gaps carefully.
4 Try all .... in the gaps before deciding.
5 Read the text again carefully when ....
6 Answer ....

4 For questions 1–8, read the text again and decide which answer (A, B, C or D) best fits each gap. There is an example at the beginning (0).

0	A belong	B keep	C (own)	D possess
1	A called	B known	C named	D titled
2	A encountered	B knew	C met	D saw
3	A few	B number	C plenty	D several
4	A desired	B longed	C wanted	D needed
5	A recalls	B recollects	C remembers	D reminds
6	A based	B built	C put	D set
7	A spectator	B public	C viewer	D audience
8	A be	B pass	C spend	D stay

5 Work in pairs.
- Many people think it's cruel to use animals in circuses. Do you agree?
- Do you think it's cruel to keep animals in zoos? Why? / Why not?

Grammar
wish, if only and *hope*

1 Read these sentences (a–f) and answer the questions (1–8) below.

a My aunt has a white cat, and I wish I had one too.
b I wish the dog next door wouldn't bark, especially at night.
c I wish it had made some kind of scratch on my skin to show my friends.
d If only I was back in Italy!
e We get quite a variety of birds at this time of year. I always hope the cats don't get them.
f I hope you enjoy your holiday and have good weather!

1 In which sentences is the speaker talking about something in the present?
2 In which three sentences is the speaker saying he/she would like the present situation to be different?
3 In which sentence is the speaker complaining about an activity which is annoying?
4 What tenses are possible after *wish* and *if only* when referring to present time?
5 In which sentence is the speaker talking about something which happened in the past?
6 What tense is used after *wish* (and *if only*) when referring to past time?
7 In which sentence is the speaker talking about something in the future?
8 What tense can be used with the verb after *hope* when we talk about the future?

➔ page 180 Language reference: *wish, if only* and *hope*

2 Candidates often confuse *wish* and *hope*. Read these sentences and decide when *wish* is used correctly and when you should use *hope*. If you think a sentence is correct, write *correct*.

1 It was lovely seeing you and I wish to see you again very soon in my house.
2 Going to the theme park together was great and I wish you enjoyed the experience.
3 I wish I'd visited you last summer when I had the chance.
4 I'm looking forward to having news from you soon and I wish you have a good time in New York.
5 My neighbour's children are always shouting; I wish they wouldn't be so noisy.
6 The performance was really good but I wish more people will come next time.
7 I don't get many letters from you and I wish you'd write to me more often.
8 We wish you enjoy your stay at our hotel while you're here in Tokyo.

3 For questions 1–5, complete the second sentence so that it has a similar meaning to the first sentence, using the word given. Do not change the word given. You must use between two and five words, including the word given.

1 It's a pity I can't cook well.
  BETTER
  I wish I ………………………………… cook.
2 I regret not studying harder when I was at school.
  STUDIED
  If only ………………………………… when I was at school.
3 I want the neighbours to stop making so much noise.
  MAKE
  I wish the neighbours ………………………………… noise.
4 What a pity that they cancelled the match!
  CALLED
  If only they ………………………………… the match.
5 I'm sorry you didn't meet my brother.
  WISH
  I ………………………………… my brother.

Unit 12

Reading and Use of English Part 7

1 Work in pairs. Before you read, answer the questions in the Exam round-up box.

EXAM ROUND-UP

How much do you remember about Reading and Use of English Part 7? Say whether the following statements are true (T) or false (F). If a statement is false, correct it.

1 In this part, there are 12 questions.
2 You have to match the questions with different texts or different parts of a text.
3 You should read the text(s) carefully before you read the questions.
4 You should underline the main ideas in the questions.
5 If you can't find an answer, leave the gap blank.

2 Work in groups. You are going to read a newspaper article about people who have been attacked by animals. Before you read, discuss these questions.

- Are there any dangerous wild animals in your country?
- What do you think you should do if you see a dangerous animal?

3 Now read questions 1–10 carefully and underline the main idea in each.

Which person

didn't immediately react to their injury?	1
was unwilling to injure the animal?	2
believes his behaviour caused the attack?	3
gave advice which was ignored?	4
was helped by someone else's quick reaction?	5
felt no pain despite their injury?	6
regrets the result of his encounter?	7
thinks that the animal's behaviour was unusual?	8
was happy at first to see the animal which later attacked him?	9
was surprised to eventually escape?	10

4 Now read the article and, for questions 1–10, choose from the people (A–D). Each person may be chosen more than once.

5 Work in pairs. What should people do to protect themselves when they are in places where there are dangerous animals?

Surviving an animal attack

No matter how well prepared you are as a traveller, animals can still attack you. Our advice? Keep your distance!

A Colin Bristow

I was working as a safari guide in Botswana with four American clients. There was a sudden movement to my left, and a charging elephant crashed through some small trees less than 20 feet away. I always brief my clients that you should never take your eyes off a dangerous animal or show signs of fear or panic. I turned to face it and was immediately knocked over by one of the clients screaming 'run, run' at the top of his voice. I landed on my back between the exposed roots of a large acacia tree. My backpack tangled with one of the roots so that I couldn't move. The elephant was kneeling over me smashing his thick trunk into the roots on either side of my body. Elephants have poor eyesight and this may have been what saved me. I managed to free myself from my backpack and I ran for my life hardly daring to believe that the elephant wasn't chasing me.

B Charlotte Hunt-Grubbe

I was working as a guide in Botswana. One day, I saw four workmen who'd been digging out an old drain, carrying what looked like a log. Except it wasn't a log, it was a 4.5 metre-long snake, a rock python, which had found a cool and comfortable spot deep in the drains to rest in. I was a bit scared but I helped my boss and a couple of other guides to hold it up to be photographed for our records. This may sound like a silly thing to do, but it would normally be quite safe. This time, however, I was unlucky. I had the head end and unfortunately, the snake suddenly woke up, and bit my arm. Everyone froze in terror. Then my boss threw his hat over the snake's head and it reared away.

Curiously, the bite didn't hurt at all, and the whole thing happened so quickly that I didn't have time to be shocked. Luckily, pythons aren't poisonous and I didn't need any medical treatment. So both the snake and I survived: me to tell the story about how I was bitten by a 4.5 metre rock python; the python to find another place where it wouldn't be disturbed.

C Baz Roberts

On our penultimate night on the Arctic ice as we were returning from the Pole, I was just falling asleep when Paul's voice woke me: 'Guys, there's a bear in the camp. I'm serious!' I leant forward on my knees to unzip the tent door. Directly in front was a polar bear about ten metres away. It heard the sound of my tent zip and turned to face me, all 600 kilos or so of him.

Due to melting ice, the polar bear's habitat is under threat and may one day disappear. As an intruder in their fragile world, I wanted to avoid causing it any harm. I started screaming and waving my arms. When he got about one metre away, I threw a large jar of coffee powder into the bear's face. If he hadn't turned and walked off at that moment, we wouldn't have survived.

D Zebedee Ellis (aged six)

I was at a zoo and dinosaur park with Mummy and Daddy two years ago. I had eaten about 400 tons of ice cream and now I wanted to see more animals. In a large open area next to a pond, Daddy saw some big fat pelicans, all full of fish. 'There you are!' he said. 'Some animals for you to annoy.'

I was very pleased and danced up and down in front of them. Then one big pelican tried to eat my T-shirt. I think it went for me because I was moving around so much and that made it nervous, but I really wish it had made some kind of scratch on my skin to show my friends.

Adapted from the *Sunday Times*

Animal kingdom

Speaking | Parts 3 and 4

1 ▶ 25 Work in pairs. Look at the speaking task below and listen to Miguel and Irene doing the task.
   1 What is going wrong?
   2 What can Irene do to put things right?

- choosing a pet
- protecting animals in danger
- working with animals
- **What would students find interesting and useful about each of these subjects?**
- how animals communicate
- strange and amazing animals

2 ▶ 26 Now listen to Miguel and Irene doing the task again. What phrases does Irene use to interrupt?

3 Work in pairs. Do the speaking task in Exercise 2, but take turns playing the role of a very talkative student and a student who wants to interrupt.

4 ▶ 27 Now listen to the examiner and do the second part of Speaking Part 3.

Unit 12

5 ▶ 28 Part 4 questions are on topics related to Part 3. Listen to Irene answering two Part 4 questions.

1 Which of these strategies does she use?
   a She just gives her opinion.
   b She expresses a range of ideas, but doesn't say which she agrees with.
   c She summarises other people's opinions, then gives her own.

2 Complete the table below by writing these phrases from Irene's answer in the correct column.

> I'm not sure that I agree   People often suggest that
> Some people say that   That's a difficult question
> I think that's true   That's quite interesting

comment on the question	introduce other people's opinions	say whether you agree or disagree with the other people's opinions
		I think that's true

3 Work in pairs. Think of two more phrases you can add to each column of the table.

6 Pronunciation: word stress (3)

We sometimes pronounce individual words differently, depending on whether we stress them or not.

1 ▶ 29 Listen to these phrases from Irene's answers again and underline the highlighted words which are stressed.

> That's a difficult question. Some people say that it's cruel to keep animals in zoos where they don't have the freedom that they'd have in their natural habitat.
>
> They say that animals get stressed and can't relax, but I'm not sure that I agree. I think they can. If animals have some space, they can have a nice relaxed life in a zoo.
>
> That's quite interesting. People often suggest that children learn to be responsible because they have to look after the animal.
>
> I think that's true and also, from my experience, I think that it's an extra relationship which develops children's ability to love and care about the animals and the people around them.

2 Listen again and notice how the pronunciation of the highlighted words changes depending on whether they are stressed or not.

3 Work in pairs. Take turns to read the sentences in Exercise 1 aloud.

7 Work in pairs and take turns to ask and answer these Part 4 questions.

1 What pet do you think is most suitable for young children? Why?
2 How can children benefit from having an animal to look after?
3 Which is better: to live in the country or to live in a large town? Why?
4 Why is it important to protect animals and other wildlife?
5 Do you think animals should be kept in zoos? Why? / Why not?

EXAMR ADVICE

▶ Answer the questions in Speaking Part 4 with your opinion backed up with an example from your own experience if possible.
▶ Be prepared to discuss with your partner – you will gain marks if you have a conversation rather than just speaking one at a time.

Writing Part 2 A letter or email

1 Work in pairs. Read this exam task and discuss the questions below.

> You have received a letter from your British friend, Les. Read this part of the letter.
>
> My family is thinking of visiting your country this summer. We'd be interested in seeing some beautiful scenery. Also, we'd like to see some wildlife. Can you advise me on where to go, what to see and the best way of getting around?
>
> Best wishes,
>
> Les

Write your **letter**.

1 What three things must you deal with in your letter?
2 What advice would you give Les about your country?
3 What style would you use: formal or informal? Why?

2 Work in pairs. Write a plan for your letter.

3 Read Manolo's reply to Les's letter and answer these questions.

1 How does Manolo show that he has read Les's letter?
2 Has he answered all three things from the question? What advice did he give about each?
3 Does he give reasons for his advice?
4 What style does he use: formal or informal?

4 Find and underline these ways of giving advice in Manolo's letter.

1 *I'd advise you* + infinitive
2 *You should* + infinitive (without *to*)
3 *If I were you, I'd / I would …*
4 *The best idea would be* + infinitive
5 *Make sure that …*

5 Write five similar sentences using each of the five phrases in Exercise 4 once to give advice to Les for visiting your country.

6 Write your own answer to the question.
- Use Manolo's letter as a model.
- Write between 140 and 190 words.

EXAMADVICE

▶ If you're writing a letter/email to a friend, use an informal style with contractions.
▶ Start in a friendly way with a phrase like *It's good to hear from you* or *I'm glad you're thinking of coming*, etc.
▶ Finish with something friendly like *I hope you enjoy yourself* or *Looking forward to seeing you*.

Dear Les,

I'm very glad to hear that you're thinking of visiting my country this summer. You can see beautiful countryside and scenery all over the country, although it varies a lot, depending on the region.

If you want somewhere that's not usually too hot in summer, I'd advise you to go to Asturias, in the north of Spain. It's a region which has some fantastic mountains as well as green countryside and beautiful rivers. You should visit the 'Picos de Europa', which are really spectacular mountains and canyons. All the paths are clearly marked, which makes walking quite safe, and you're sure to see a lot of wildlife while you're there. You may even see bears and wolves if you're lucky!

If I were you, I'd hire a car to get around. The best idea would be to hire it online before you leave home. Make sure that you take warm clothes and a raincoat as we can have heavy rain, even in summer.

I hope you enjoy your holiday and have good weather!

Best wishes,

Manolo

Vocabulary and grammar review Unit 11

Vocabulary

1 Complete sentences 1–10 below with a word from the box in the correct form in the gaps.

> check-up   cure   diagnose   fit   get over   heal
> infection   prescription   put on   treatment

1 After a brief examination, my doctor ……………… that I was suffering from a slight infection.
2 As long as you keep the cut clean, it should ……………… on its own quite soon.
3 Farouk has been having ……………… in hospital following an accident he had last month.
4 She's spent the last two or three days in bed because of a minor ……………… she picked up at school.
5 I have to be quite careful what I eat so that I don't ……………… too much weight.
6 It's a good idea to keep ……………… by doing regular exercise – at least 40 minutes a day.
7 Rana's doctor has given her a ……………… for antibiotics to treat her illness.
8 Take this medicine. It should ……………… you in a couple of days.
9 You may not be very ill, but it's still worth going to the doctor for a ……………… to make sure it's nothing serious.
10 It took her several weeks to ……………… her illness, and she missed a lot of classes in that time.

Word formation

2 **EP** Complete each of these sentences by using the word given in capitals at the end of the sentences to form a word that fits in the gap.

1 I'm sorry about the mistake. The trouble is I ……………… the instructions. **UNDERSTAND**
2 My mum and dad ……………… of some of my friends because they make a lot of noise when they come round to our house. **APPROVE**
3 My dad said he felt very ……………… with the quality of the food at that restaurant and he complained to the waiter, which was rather embarrassing. **SATISFY**
4 My friend's joined our hockey team, and although she's a little ……………… , she's very keen and tries hard. **EXPERIENCE**
5 Luis goes to school even when he's feeling ill because he ……………… missing lessons. **LIKE**
6 Even though Sandra offered to lend her favourite book to her brother, he was ……………… to help Sandra with her essay. **WILL**
7 It would feel a bit strange and ……………… to chat with my teachers online. **NATURE**
8 We got the answers wrong because we were given ……………… information by the teacher. **LEAD**
9 My cousin always wears ……………… clothes, even when she's just watching TV at home. **FASHION**
10 My friend was told that his behaviour was ……………… in the classroom. **ACCEPT**
11 Teresa is quite ……………… , so I'm not sure if she'll turn up to dance practice every week. **RELY**
12 I want to know the truth, so don't be ……………… with me. **HONEST**

Grammar

3 Complete the second sentence in each question so that it has a similar meaning to the first sentence, using the word given in capitals. Do not change the word given. You must use between two and five words, including the word given.

1 The boy with the broken arm is still in hospital.
   IS
   The boy ……………………………………… not left hospital yet.
2 Did the doctor treat this injury?
   ONE
   Is this ……………………………………… doctor treated?
3 Everyone who lives in the town Paola comes from is very friendly.
   INHABITANTS
   Paola comes from a town ……………………………………… very friendly.
4 The teacher liked how Jan had answered the questions.
   WAY
   Jan answered the questions ……………………………………… the teacher liked.
5 His email left us in no doubt about his opinion.
   WHAT
   It was clear to us ……………………………………… his opinion was.
6 No one finds Chiaro's jokes amusing.
   TELLS
   The jokes ……………………………………… amuse anyone.

Vocabulary and grammar review Unit 12

Vocabulary

1 For questions 1–6, read this text and decide which answer (A, B, C or D) best fits each gap.

Due to the destruction of their natural habitats, more and more animals need to be **(1)** .... by creating nature reserves and passing laws. The laws are often designed to **(2)** .... farmers from using land where rare species live. The idea is that humans and animals **(3)** .... coming into conflict by not competing for the same land. Sometimes local people complain about losing farm land to nature reserves. However, jobs are often created for game wardens, whose job is to **(4)** .... the nature reserves to make sure everything functions correctly. Other people get jobs selling tickets to visitors, and there are also jobs for people to **(5)** .... the tickets as the visitors pass the entrance. In nature reserves containing dangerous animals, it may only be possible to visit them by car, and wardens need to **(6)** .... the number of cars entering the reserve to make sure they keep within reasonable limits.

1	A prevented	B protected	C avoided	D defended
2	A avoid	B stop	C prevent	D disallow
3	A avoid	B prevent	C miss	D fail
4	A check	B control	C prevent	D supervise
5	A check	B control	C look	D supervise
6	A check	B control	C prevent	D supervise

Grammar

2 Complete these sentences with the correct form of the verb in brackets. In some sentences more than one answer is possible.

1 The lions wouldn't have attacked us if they .... (*not be*) so hungry.
2 I wish it .... (*be*) summer – then we could go to the beach!
3 If my maths teacher .... (*be*) ill at the moment, we .... (*have*) a maths test yesterday.
4 If only you .... (*not make*) so much noise! I can't concentrate on my studies, and it's really annoying me!
5 I wish I .... (*live*) near the city centre. It's such a long bus ride from here.
6 Where's Candice? I hope she .... (*not miss*) the train.
7 I wish you .... (*speak*) more clearly so I could understand you better.
8 I think this soup .... (*be*) nicer if I'd used a bit less salt, don't you?
9 I hope you .... (*change*) your shirt before we go out to the restaurant.
10 I know my mother wishes she .... (*study*) harder when she was my age.
11 We .... (*get*) to the cinema in time if there hadn't been so much traffic.
12 If you .... (*eat*) more breakfast this morning, you wouldn't be feeling hungry now.

3 Complete the second sentence in each question so that it has a similar meaning to the first sentence, using the word given in capitals. Do not change the word given. You must use between two and five words, including the word given.

1 We are lost because we did not bring the map with us.
   LEFT
   If we .... the map behind, we would not be lost now.
2 My sister only did the work in our neighbour's garden because they gave her some money for helping them.
   PAID
   My sister would not have done the work in our neighbour's garden unless they .... for helping them.
3 Even if he had worked harder, the result would have been the same.
   DIFFERENCE
   It would not .... if he had worked harder.
4 It is a pity I do not get on better with my brother.
   RELATIONSHIP
   I wish I .... my brother.
5 Sasha would like Irina to help him from time to time.
   ONCE
   Sasha wishes Irina .... a while.
6 Sergei is disappointed because the youth orchestra rejected him.
   TURNED
   If the youth orchestra .... , Sergei would not be disappointed.

139

13 House space

Starting off

1. Work in pairs. Match each of these types of place to live with the photos.

   a a villa
   b a chalet in the mountains
   c a block of flats with several storeys
   d a house in a village
   e a housing estate
   f a mobile home

2. Which of these things do you think are important when choosing somewhere to live? Why? / Why not?

   > a quiet neighbourhood   a good view
   > shops within walking distance   a garden
   > parking space   public parks or gardens
   > good public transport   a good local school

3. Look at the pictures, Which of these places would you like to live in? What would you like about living there? Is there anywhere in the pictures you wouldn't like to live? Why not?

Reading and Use of English Part 5

1. Work in pairs. You are going to read an extract from a historical novel about a house in Venice. Before you read, look at the painting. Do you think you would have enjoyed life in 18th-century Venice? Why? / Why not?

2. Before doing Reading and Use of English Part 5, answer the questions in the Exam round-up box.

EXAM ROUND-UP

How much do you remember about Reading and Use of English Part 5? Circle the correct option in *italics* in each of these sentences.

In Reading and Use of English Part 5:
1. there are *six / eight* questions; you must choose the best option: A, B, C or D.
2. you should read *the text quickly before reading the questions / the questions quickly before reading the text*.
3. you should read the options *before / after* reading the section of text where a question is answered.

3. Read the extract quite quickly to find out why the writer thinks the house is in a good location.

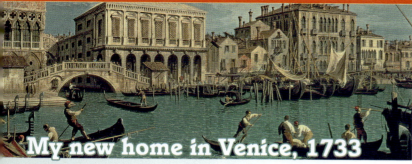

My new home in Venice, 1733

Uncle Leo gives me a suspicious look when I call this place the 'Scacchi Palace'. It is really a house, called Ca'Scacchi in Venetian. Anywhere else in the world, this would surely be regarded as a palace, although it is one in need of a little care and attention.

Our house is by the side of the little San Cassian canal and a small square of the same name. We have a door which leads onto the street and two entrances from the water. One runs under a grand, rounded arch into the ground floor of the house, which, as is customary in the city, is used instead of a cellar for storing
10 things. The second is used for our commercial activities and *it* is situated in another building, which is three storeys high, attached to the north side, towards the Grand Canal.

Finally, there is yet another exit: a wooden bridge, with handrails, runs from the first floor of the house between the two river entrances straight over the canal and into the square itself. Consequently I can wander over it in the morning and find fresh water from the well in the centre of the square while still rubbing the sleep from my eyes. Or I may call a gondola from my bedroom window, find it waiting for me by the time I get
20 downstairs and, just one minute later, be in the middle of the greatest waterway on Earth: the Grand Canal of Venice.

The house is almost 200 years old, I am told, and built of bricks of a rich dark brown colour. It has elegant arched windows and green-painted shutters to keep out the cruel summer heat. I live on the third floor in the third room on the right with a view over the canal and the square. When I lie in bed at night, I can hear the chatter and songs of the passing gondoliers and the conversations in the square nearby. I understand why Uncle runs his business here. The prices are not too steep. The location of the house is
30 near the city centre and easy for our clients to find. Furthermore, the printing trade has many roots in this area of Venice, even if some of the old publishers from the area no longer exist.

Oh sister! I long for the day when I can show you these things instead of struggling to describe them in a letter which may take a long time to reach you in Spain! Venice is like a vast imitation of our old library at home, full of dark corners and unexpected surprises, some very close to me. Last night, while searching in the jumbled corners of the warehouse cellar, I found a single copy of *Aristotle's Poetics*, published in the city in 1502. I raced
40 to Uncle Leo with my discovery and – now here's a victory – a smile almost appeared on his face. 'A find, boy! This'll fetch good money when I sell it down in the market.'

'May I read a little first, sir?' I asked, and felt some anxiety when I made the request. Leo has a frightening manner at times.

'Books are for selling, not reading,' he replied immediately. But at least I had it for the night, since the dealers were by that time closed.

Adapted from *The Cemetery of Secrets* by David Hewson

House space

4 For questions 1–8, choose the answer (A, B, C or D) which you think fits best according to the text.

1 In what way is the house typical of Venice, according to the writer?
 A There are several ways of entering it.
 B People live and work in the same building.
 C The storage area is not below ground.
 D It consists of two separate buildings.

2 What does *it* refer to in line 10?
 A the family business
 B an entrance
 C a floor
 D a building

3 What does the writer say about his uncle's printing business in the fourth paragraph?
 A His printing business is less expensive than others.
 B The business has plenty of customers.
 C There are other similar businesses in the district.
 D It's the only printing business left in the district.

4 What do we understand about the writer and his sister in the fifth paragraph?
 A They both enjoy reading.
 B They both used to live in Venice.
 C They write to each other often.
 D They don't expect to see each other soon.

5 What does the incident with the book show about Uncle Leo?
 A He dislikes having the writer in his house.
 B He has a good sense of humour.
 C He has problems with money.
 D His main interest is making money.

6 In the text as a whole, the writer regards Venice as
 A a strange and special place to live in.
 B somewhere that could never be home.
 C a city it's easy to get lost in.
 D a place dominated by money.

5 Work in pairs. Take turns to describe a house which you have really enjoyed living in or visiting. You should each speak for about one minute.
- Before you speak, spend a few minutes planning what you are going to say.
- When your partner speaks, listen and think of one or two questions to ask at the end.

Unit 13

Vocabulary

space, place, room, area, location and *square*

1 Candidates often confuse the following words: *space, place, room, area, location* and *square*. Circle the correct word in *italics* in these sentences from Reading and Use of English Part 5.

1 Uncle Leo gives me a suspicious look when I call this *place / area* the 'Scacchi Palace'.
2 When I lie in bed at night, I can hear the chatter and songs of the passing gondoliers and the conversations in the *square / place* nearby.
3 The *place / location* of the house is near the city centre and easy for our clients to find.
4 Furthermore, the printing trade has many roots in this *area / place* of Venice.

2 Look at the extracts on page 185. Then circle the correct word in *italics* in these sentences.

1 We don't have enough *area / space* in our garden to hold the party.
2 I hope I will have enough *place / room* for all the things I am bringing.
3 I'm enclosing a map which shows the *location / place* of my school.
4 It's dangerous to go walking in a mountainous *area / place* without the correct equipment.
5 The animals in this zoo have a lot of *area / space* to move around.
6 The concert will take place in the main *square / place* in front of the cathedral.
7 There isn't enough *place / space* to build more houses in this neighbourhood.
8 It's fine for you to stay at our place, as we've got loads of *room / place*.

3 Work in pairs. Write *area, place, room* or *space* in the gaps to form collocations, e.g. *hiding place*. Then discuss what each of them means, e.g. *A hiding place is a place to hide or to hide something.*

1 hiding / market / meeting ....
2 floor / green / office / parking / personal / public ....
3 head / leg / standing ....
4 dining / penalty / picnic / play / reception ....

4 Complete these sentences by writing one of the collocations from Exercise 3 in the gaps.

1 If someone makes you feel uncomfortable by standing too close to you, we say that they have entered your ....
2 I love my school. It's surrounded by .... with lots of trees and lawns.
3 I'm tall, and the seats on the plane didn't have enough ....
4 There are lots of stalls in the .... selling fresh fruit and vegetables.
5 When you go to the country, it's good to find a .... where you can sit and eat a sandwich.

Listening Part 2

1 Work in pairs. You are going to hear a student giving a talk to his classmates about his house, which he claims is haunted. Before you listen, do you think it's possible for houses to be haunted? Why? / Why not?

2 Answer the questions in the Exam round-up box.

EXAM ROUND-UP

How much do you remember about Listening Part 2? Say whether these statements are true (T) or false (F). If a statement is false, correct it.

1 In Listening Part 2, you hear a conversation.
2 There are eight questions.
3 You will need just one or two words for each gap.
4 You hear the actual words you need to write.
5 You must spell your answers correctly.
6 Before you listen, read the questions as quickly as possible.
7 When you finish, make sure your answers form grammatical sentences.

3 Now read these sentences and predict what type of information or what type of words you need for each gap, e.g. question 1 is probably *a length of time*.

Haunted House

Jeff has lived in the house for **(1)** ....
He thinks his house is haunted because of the **(2)** .... which people have had there.
His **(3)** .... saw medieval soldiers.
Another guest saw furniture moving in the **(4)** ....
When doing homework, Jeff has felt a person **(5)** .... him.
His mother decided to convert the **(6)** .... into a study.
An expert told them the house was built on the site of a **(7)** ....
His father recently had a **(8)** .... installed.
One of the workers saw a man with **(9)** .... on his clothes.
His father is normally at home **(10)** ....

4 ▶ 30 For questions 1–10, listen and complete the sentences with a word or a phrase.

5 Work in groups. Would you be happy to live in a house with a reputation for being haunted? Do you know of any haunted houses?

Grammar
Causative *have* and *get*

1 In Listening Part 2, Jeff describes two changes to the house. What were they? Listen again if necessary.

2 Look at these sentences and answer the questions in the next column.

1. a She turned the old garage at the back of the house into a study.
   b She had the old garage at the back of the house turned into a study.
2. a Then my dad checked the whole house.
   b Then my dad got the whole house checked by a specialist.

1 Which sentences (a or b) did you hear in Listening Part 2?
2 Which sentences (a or b) mean … ?
 • he/she did it himself/herself?
 • he/she asked someone else to do it for them?
3 In the b sentences, who do you think did these things?

➡ page 164 Language reference: Causative *have* and *get*

3 Complete the sentences below by writing the correct form of *have* or *get* and the correct form of one of the verbs in the box in the gaps.

> cut down   deliver   pull out   extend   paint   renew

1 We'll need .... your passport .... before we go to America next autumn.
2 She went to the dentist yesterday and .... a tooth .... , so she's not feeling too well today.
3 We're thinking of .... the house .... blue. What do you think?
4 I love the old tree in the park near my house, so I'm sorry the council have decided to .... it ....
5 My parents are planning to .... the house .... Then I'll get a room of my own!
6 When my parents go out for the evening, they arrange for us to .... pizzas .... from a local restaurant.

4 For questions 1–4, complete the second sentence so that it has a similar meaning to the first sentence, using the word given. Do not change the word given. You must use between two and five words, including the word given.

1 Someone stole my bag during the bus journey.
   HAD
   I .... I was on the bus.
2 A professional photographer is taking a photo of Stephan.
   PICTURE
   Stephan .... by a professional photographer.
3 Marianne wants the hairdresser to change the colour of her hair.
   DYED
   Marianne wants to .... at the hairdresser's.
4 The college rejected Pascual's application.
   TURNED
   Pascual had .... by the college.

Unit 13

Reading and Use of English Part 2

1 Work in pairs. Look at the photo. Would you like to live here? Why? / Why not?

2 Before doing Reading and Use of English Part 2, answer the questions in the Exam round-up box.

EXAM ROUND-UP

How much do you remember about Reading and Use of English Part 2? Complete the following sentences with the words and phrases in *italics*.

eight   before and after   one word ONLY   general idea   grammar   the completed text

1 There are .... questions in this part.
2 The words you need are .... words: articles, pronouns, auxiliary verbs, etc. and parts of fixed phrases (e.g. *take part in*) or phrasal verbs (e.g. *make up*).
3 First, read the text quickly to get a .... of what it's about.
4 Read .... the gaps to decide what type of word you need.
5 Answer every question with .... , and check your spelling.
6 When you have finished, quickly read .... to check.

3 Read this article quickly, ignoring the gaps. Do you think you'd enjoy living on a houseboat?

Living on a houseboat

When we first moved onto our houseboat on the River Crouch, there **(0)** ...*was*... a big storm. The lights swung backwards and forwards **(1)** .... though we were at sea, but in **(2)** .... of the bad weather, not a single cup fell off the shelves. In fact, in the four years **(3)** .... we moved from our small house in the town nearby, **(4)** .... anything has been broken.

The boat is huge: 20 metres long and 4 metres wide. **(5)** .... to my dad, it is about four times the size of the house we had before. The kitchen **(6)** .... up about half of the main living space and it is not separated from the rest of it, so that whoever is cooking doesn't feel left **(7)** .... Our friends often **(8)** .... round to see us after we have been to school. In the living area, there is even room for a ping-pong table.

Adapted from *The Observer*

4 Now think of the word which best fits each gap. Use only one word in each gap.

5 Work in pairs.
- Do you think it's important for a house to have plenty of space? Why? / Why not?
- What things would you like to have room for in your house? Why?
- Would you like to live in a different place? If so, where? If not, why not?

House space

Speaking Part 2

1 Work in pairs. Before doing Speaking Part 2, answer the questions in the Exam round-up box.

EXAM ROUND-UP

How much do you remember about Speaking Part 2? Say whether the following statements are true (T) or false (F). If a statement is false, correct it.
1 Each candidate must speak alone for about one minute.
2 You have to compare four photos and answer a more general question about them.
3 You should compare the photos in detail.
4 You should spend about half the time on the photos and half the time on the printed question.
5 After your partner has spoken, you will be asked a question about the same photos.

2 Work in pairs. Look at the speaking task on the right and the examiner's instructions. Then brainstorm words and phrases you could use to talk about each photo.

> Here are your photographs. They show two different places to live. I'd like you to compare the photographs and say what you think it is like for the people to live in each of these places.

3 Look at these words and phrases. Which could you use with the first photo (1), which with the second photo (2) and which with both (B)?

close to nature .... environment ....
fresh air .... hi-tech ....
maintain a lifestyle .... occupants ....
organic food .... a rural setting ....
spend quality time .... social life ....
sophisticated entertainment .... pollution ....

4 Work in pairs. Take turns to speak for a minute about the photographs following the examiner's instructions.

What is it like for the people to live in each of these places?

5 ▶ 31 Work in pairs. Listen to Peter and Martyna doing the task, then say whether the statements on this checklist are true (T) or false (F).

	Checklist	T	F
1	Peter spends a lot of time describing what he sees in each photo.		
2	He outlines the main idea of each photo.		
3	He concentrates on answering the question more than comparing the details of the photos.		
4	He compares what it would be like to live in each place.		
5	He mentions things which he thinks are similar about the people in both photos.		
6	He uses language which shows he is imagining the lifestyle in each photo.		
7	He uses a good range of vocabulary to express his ideas.		
8	He uses short, simple sentences.		
9	Martyna gives a long, detailed answer to her question.		

145

Unit 13

6 Pronunciation: linking (2)

In order to speak more fluently, you sometimes put a consonant between the first and the second word when the second word begins with a vowel.

1 ▶32 Listen to these extracts from Peter's answer. In the highlighted phrases, what consonant is used in the extracts to link:

a the yellow highlighted words?
- with the occupants, a family standing in the garden
- On the other hand, living in the city flat might be quite exciting

b the green highlighted words?
- where they grow their own vegetables
- Money and success in your career are not so important as being close to nature and the countryside
- which is probably busier and more stressful

c the blue highlighted words?
- Money and success in your career are not so important
- The family in the second photo must need to earn quite a lot of money

2 Work in pairs. Take turns to read Peter's phrases in Exercise 1 aloud.

3 ▶33 In the gaps in these sentences, write the consonant which you think can link the two words. Then listen to check your answers.

1 We live further........away from the........old town.
2 Does he........ever........answer your questions?
3 Our........aunt comes to stay........at our house just now........and then.
4 Fewer........and fewer shops in our........area are........open at weekends.

4 Work in pairs. Take turns to read sentences 1–6 in Exercise 3 aloud.

7 Work in pairs. Choose either Task A or Task B. Then discuss what you can say to do the task in a similar way to Peter (see questions 2–7 from the checklist in (Speaking) Exercise 5).

8 Change partners and work with someone who chose the other task.
- Take turns to do your tasks.
- While you are listening to your partner, use questions 2–7 from the checklist in (Speaking) Exercise 5 as a checklist.
- When your partner has finished, use all the questions from the checklist in Exercise 5 to give him/her feedback.

Task A

" Here are your photographs. They show people on holiday in different places. I'd like you to compare the photographs and say what you think the people are enjoying about having a holiday in these places. "

What are the people enjoying about having a holiday in these places?

146

House space

Task B

 Here are your photographs. They show old people living in two different types of place. I'd like you to compare the photographs and say which place you think is better for old people to live.

Which place is better for old people to live?

Grammar
Expressing obligation and permission

1 Work in pairs. You will hear five English teenagers who are staying with host families while on a school exchange visit to Germany. Before you listen, make a list of things students who stay with a host family in your country should and shouldn't do, e.g. *You should keep your room tidy. You shouldn't stay up too late.*

2 Look at these sentences and then answer the questions below.

A *I can* use their phone to call my parents.
B *I have to* help with the housework.
C *I can't* take food from the fridge.
D *I'm supposed to* go to bed quite early.
E *They let me* invite a friend round.
F *They won't let me* do any cooking.

1 Which phrases in *italics* have a similar meaning to
 a I must? ....
 b I'm not allowed to? ....
 c I'm allowed to? ....
2 Which phrase below has a similar meaning to *I'm supposed to* in D?
 a I must be.
 b I should, but sometimes I don't.

3 ▶ 34 Listen and, for questions 1–5, choose which sentence in Exercise 2 (A–F) best summarises what each student says. There is one extra letter which you do not need to use.

1 Michael ☐   4 Luke ☐
2 Irene ☐   5 Laura ☐
3 Mary ☐

147

Unit 13

4 Which speaker said each of these sentences? If necessary, listen again to check.
1 *I don't have to* do anything around the house.
2 *I had to* make conversation in German.
3 *They don't allow me to* spend much time online talking to my English friends.
4 Apparently, *I was supposed to* phone to say I was going to be late back.
5 ... *they didn't let me* go to a party in the evening the other day.

5 Work in pairs. Copy this table into your notebook. Complete it using the phrases from Exercises 2 and 4.

	obligation	prohibition	permission	no obligation
present				
past				

➡ page 171 Language reference: Modal verbs – expressing obligation, prohibition and permission

Writing Part 2 An article

1 Work in pairs. Before working on Writing Part 2, answer the questions in the Exam round-up box.

EXAM ROUND-UP

How much do you remember about how to do Writing Part 2? Put these tasks in the correct order by writing a number 1–6 by each.
a Check what you have written, looking for specific mistakes you know you make. ☐
b Organise your notes into a plan. ☐
c Read all the questions and quickly choose the one you think you will find easiest. ☐
d Think and make notes. ☐
e Underline the things you must deal with in your answer. ☐
f Write your answer (140–190 words) following your plan. ☐

2 Work in groups of three. Read this writing task and discuss the questions below.

You see this announcement in your school magazine.

My ideal home
If you could choose the type of house you would like to live in and its location, where would you live, what sort of house would it be and what features would it have?

The best articles will be published in the next issue of our magazine.

Write your **article**.

1 What would be the ideal location for your house?
2 What sort of house would you choose?
3 What features would your ideal house have?

148

House space

3 Work in pairs with someone from another group.
- Take turns to give a short talk describing your ideal house.
- When your partner finishes speaking, ask a few questions to find out more details.

4 Look at the writing task again and discuss these questions.
1. Who will read your article?
2. What style would be suitable for this article?
3. Which of these should your article particularly use: present simple, *going to / will*, conditional? Why?
4. What information must it contain?
5. How can you make the article interesting for your readers?

5 Read the sample answer below to the writing task, ignoring the gaps.
1. How does this ideal home compare with your own?
2. Has the writer answered the question completely?

6 Complete this plan for the sample answer in Exercise 5 by writing the notes in *italics* below beside the correct paragraphs.
Para. 1: ....
Para. 2: ....
Para. 3: ....

Advantages of ideal flat
Characteristics of flat
Conclusion: room for my friends
My present accommodation
Type of flat and location

7 Complete the sample answer by writing one word in each of the gaps.

8 Work in pairs. Discuss whether these statements are true (T) or false (F).

		T	F
1	The article uses plenty of adjectives.		
2	It uses conditionals.		
3	The writer mentions all the furniture she would need.		
4	You can tell something about the writer's personality and tastes from the article.		
5	There are plenty of relative clauses.		
6	The writer doesn't say where she lives now.		

9 Write your own article.
- Before you write, decide what features of the sample answer on the left you could also use. Then think and write a plan.
- When you write, follow your plan.
- Write 140–190 words.

My space, my place

I dream of living in a small, stylish modern flat in a historic old building near the centre of a large city **(0)** *such* as Barcelona, where my aunt lives. What a change that would be **(1)** .... the ordinary suburban house **(2)** .... I live now! I could enjoy all the things a big city has to offer, going to cool shops, trendy cafés, seeing the latest films at modern cinemas or going bowling with my friends – who would naturally all live nearby!

What would the flat be like? Well, for a start, I'd live on my **(3)** .... , so I'd be able to do **(4)** .... I wanted whenever I wanted. The flat would be hi-tech, with the heating and lighting controlled automatically. There would be a light, airy sitting room with an enormous comfortable sofa in it, a huge TV screen and all the latest gadgets, of course. Ideally, it would **(5)** .... big windows in all the rooms.

I wouldn't need much space, as **(6)** .... as I had room to have a **(7)** .... friends round too. **(8)** .... I had all these things, I'd be happy for years.

14 Fiesta!

Starting off

1 Work in pairs. Write one of the verbs from the box in the correct form in each of the gaps below to complete the descriptions of festivals and celebrations. Use each verb once only.

> celebrate   commemorate   dress up   gather round
> hold   let off   march   perform   play   wearing

1 We hold a festival every March to .... the arrival of spring.
2 People in our region .... in **traditional costumes** and then they .... one of our **traditional dances**.
3 People .... through the town in a spectacular **parade** to .... a famous battle.
4 In many parts of the town, residents .... **street parties**.
5 **Bands** .... dance music all night long.
6 Crowds .... **street performers**.
7 During the festival, we .... **fireworks**.
8 People from the town go out in the streets .... **disguises**.

2 Find the words and phrases in bold in Exercise 1 illustrated in the photos on this page and the next.

3 Look at the photos again. They show different events which take place during festivals.

1 Why do people do these different things at festivals?
2 Which type of activity is most enjoyable for people to watch?
3 Which country do you think each of the photos was taken in?

4 Work in pairs. Tell each other about a festival you have been to or one you have seen on TV.

- What kind of festival was it?
- Did you enjoy it? / Would you like to go to this festival? Why? / Why not?
- Would you recommend it to other teenagers? Why? / Why not?

Fiesta!

Listening Part 4

1 Work in pairs. You are going to hear an interview with a street performer at festivals, including one called the Hat Fair. Before you listen discuss these questions.
- Have you ever seen any street performers?
- Where were they and what were they doing?
- Did you enjoy watching them? Why? / Why not?

2 Answer the questions in the Exam round-up box.

EXAM ROUND-UP

How much do you remember about Listening Part 4? Complete the following sentences with the words and phrases in *italics*.

seven   general ideas   an interview   underline   different words

1 Listening Part 4 is .... or a conversation between two or more speakers.
2 There are .... questions; you must choose A, B or C.
3 Read the questions carefully and .... the main ideas. These will be expressed using .... from the question.
4 Listen for .... as well as specific information.

3 ▶ 35 Now listen, and for questions 1–7, choose the best answer (A, B or C).

1 Why is the festival called the Hat Fair?
  A It was started by local hat-makers.
  B Many participants wear hats.
  C Street performers collect money in hats.
2 What does Max most enjoy about the Hat Fair?
  A the type of audiences he gets
  B the other street performers he meets
  C the shows he can do
3 How did Max start in street theatre?
  A He lost his job in a circus.
  B He did it while he was at university.
  C He learned it from his father.
4 What do audiences enjoy most about Max's act?
  A the jokes
  B the acrobatics
  C the danger
5 According to Max, what makes street performers perform well?
  A They earn a lot of money.
  B They are paid by results.
  C They enjoy their work.
6 What does he say is usually the main problem with street theatre?
  A the weather
  B the location
  C the police
7 According to Max, how does the Hat Fair help the city?
  A It attracts visitors to the town.
  B It encourages people to work together.
  C It helps people to relax together.

4 Work in pairs. Sometimes towns and cities discourage street theatre. Why do you think this is?

151

Unit 14

Grammar
The passive

1 The passive is formed by the verbs *be* or *get* + a past participle (*eaten, done, played*, etc.). Read the following extracts from the recording script and underline the verbs in the passive.

  a I've been told the fair was only started in 1974, as a way of encouraging street performers like myself.
  b A hat's passed around so that the performers can earn a living.
  c They really seem to love it when they're being made a fool of by other people in the crowd.
  d I actually went to quite a famous circus school in Canada as a teenager where I was taught juggling and acrobatics.
  e Here we're given the main shopping street, which is fine. In other places, if you haven't got permission, you'll get moved on by the police.

2 Work in pairs. In which extracts (a–e) does the speaker do the following? (You can use the extracts for more than one answer.)

  1 He tells us who or what does/did the action.
    In extract c and part of extract e (the police)
  2 He uses the passive because he doesn't know who or what does/did something.
  3 He uses the passive because he doesn't need to say who or what does/did something because it's obvious from the situation or context.
  4 He uses the passive because what happens is more important than who does it.

➡ page 177 Language reference: The passive

3 Rewrite these sentences in the passive, starting with the words given.

  1 They founded our school in 1904.
    Our school ....
  2 Someone has stolen my wallet!
    My wallet .... !
  3 You won't be able to email me while they are repairing my laptop.
    You won't be able to email me while my laptop ....
  4 Have you heard? They've given me second prize!
    Have you heard? I ....
  5 If you hadn't done the work, your teacher would have told you off.
    If you hadn't done the work, you ....

4 Read this text quickly to find out what happens at the Egyptian festival of Sham el Nessím.

5 For questions 1–10, read the text again and think of the word which best fits each gap. Use only one word in each gap.

6 Look at this sentence from the text about Sham el Nessím and answer the questions below.

It is thought to have been the first festival to celebrate the beginning of spring.

  1 What does the sentence mean?
    a People think that this was the first festival that celebrated the beginning of spring.
    b It used to be the first festival to celebrate spring.
  2 It follows the pattern 'subject + passive verb + infinitive'. Other verbs which can be used in this way include: *believe, report, say, consider, expect*. Which other two sentences in the text follow the same pattern?
  3 The sentence could also be expressed as follows: *It is thought that this was the first festival to celebrate the beginning of spring.* How would the other two sentences be expressed using this pattern instead?

Sham el Nessím

A large number of contemporary Egyptian traditions (1) .... said to have their origins in very ancient times. These include the holiday which is known (2) .... Sham el Nessím. This holiday may have (3) .... celebrated as early as 4,500 years ago. It is thought (4) .... have been the first festival to celebrate the beginning of the spring.

Nowadays, in the early morning of Sham el Nessím millions of Egyptians come out to crowded public parks and other open areas. Young men swim in the Nile and families generally enjoy the cool breeze of spring.

Sham el Nessím (5) .... also celebrated by eating traditional foods and these include salted fish, coloured eggs, sunflower seeds and raw onions. The reason for each of these foods (6) .... eaten is supported (7) .... a different myth. For example, offerings of fish are believed to (8) .... been made to the ancient gods and by (9) .... this a good harvest was ensured. Salted fish symbolised welfare to the ancient Egyptians and in ancient times fish (10) .... easily caught by being trapped in natural pools created by the movement of the Nile.

Fiesta!

→ page 177 Language reference: The passive with reporting verbs

7 Rewrite the following sentences beginning with the words given.

1. Sham el Nessím is thought to have marked the start of the spring festival in ancient Egypt.
   It is thought …
2. Eating salted fish is known to have been a custom of the ancient Egyptians.
   It is known …
3. It is reported that five thousand people joined in the festivities.
   Five thousand people are reported …
4. It is said that our festival has the best fireworks in the world.
   Our festival is said …

8 For questions 1–6, complete the second sentence so that it has a similar meaning to the first sentence, using the word given. Do not change the word given. You must use between two and five words, including the word given.

1. People believe that the festival originated in the 18th century.
   HAVE
   The festival ………………………………… in the 18th century.
2. People expect that she will be chosen as carnival queen.
   BE
   She is ………………………………… as carnival queen.
3. The festival is said to be more popular than ever.
   THAT
   It is ………………………………… more popular than ever.
4. They think Channel 4 is the only channel which will broadcast the opening ceremony.
   THOUGHT
   Channel 4 ………………………………… the only channel which will broadcast the opening ceremony.
5. People think that Carnival is the best festival of the year.
   CONSIDERED
   Carnival ………………………………… the best festival of the year.
6. We know the festival started more than three thousand years ago.
   BACK
   The festival is known ………………………………… three thousand years.

Unit 14

Reading and Use of English Part 6

1 Answer the questions in the Exam round-up box.

EXAM ROUND-UP

How much do you remember about Reading and Use of English Part 6?

Say whether the following statements are true (T) or false (F). If a statement is false, correct it.

1 This part of the exam will contain eight questions, including the example.
2 You should first read the whole text carefully to form an idea of how it develops.
3 <u>Underline</u> clues in the text while you read, such as pronouns (e.g. *this, he,* etc.), adverbs which suggest something mentioned before (e.g. *the second point, however,* etc.), relationships of meaning (e.g. *it was* **expected** to be **huge** ... **in fact** it was **tiny** ..., etc.).
4 Read each sentence carefully, thinking about where it could fit and looking for clues.
5 When you've finished, quickly go to the next part of the paper.

2 Work in groups. You will read an article about a Peruvian festival. Before you read, look at the festival in the photos.

- What do you think is happening?
- Would you enjoy a festival like this? Why? / Why not?

3 Six sentences have been removed from the article. Read the article (but not the missing sentences) quite carefully. As you read:

- think about and perhaps quickly note down the subject of each paragraph.
- <u>underline</u> any words and phrases before and after the gaps which may refer to the missing sentences (one has been done for you as an example).

The world's highest festival?

It felt as if we had been climbing for hours. I stopped to catch my breath as a wave of dizziness swept over me in the thin mountain air. I stood to one side of the path to let the mass of travellers with us pass. I was on an amazing trip with my family, following Marco, our guide to experience the festival of Qoyllur Rit'i which takes place at 4,300 metres in the southern Andes of Peru, a festival which few foreign tourists ever get to see.

Where the writer was going

As I looked back down the trail we had climbed and up towards where we had to go, I marvelled at the colourful sight. Entire families wearing local costumes were travelling to this unique festival from all over Peru. Among them there were old men, mothers with small babies and children all following the same route. Many of them had horses and donkeys to carry their food, blankets, cooking pots and tents. **1**☐ Others had made their way on foot through the mountains for days to attend this remarkable event.

We continued our upward ascent for another hour and a half before reaching the Sinakara valley. There we looked down on a flat plain of open grassland crossed with streams from the glaciers and overlooked by snow-topped mountain peaks. Right across this flat piece of ground people were putting up shelters and tents of blue plastic to protect themselves from the freezing mist and rain. **2**☐ The air of excitement, even from our vantage point more than a mile away, was palpable.

Marco chose a spot between two icy streams to put up our tent. While thus occupied, one of the many women dressed in the traditional costume of a wide-brimmed hat, woolly jacket, skirt and stockings came to sell us some very welcome hot soup and fish. **3**☐

Not far away in another open market, people were buying tiny houses, cars or small pictures showing a baby or a wedding. Marco explained that these represented something the pilgrims desired. **4**☐ This, they believed, would ensure that what they wished for would come true in the year ahead.

After dining in a makeshift restaurant we went to bed fully clothed inside our sleeping bags. **5**☐ The ukukus, men wearing black masks and costumes, had left the encampment in the early hours to climb the nearest mountain by the light of the full moon. **6**☐ In the dawn light, we watched them winding their way back down like a great black serpent. As they descended, they were joined by groups of dancers in bright traditional costumes. They performed wherever there was a space. Although there did not seem to be anyone organising them or any timetable, the whole festival had become a huge harmonious celebration.

154

Fiesta!

4 Now choose from the sentences A–G the one which fits each gap (1–6) in the text. There is one extra sentence which you do not need to use. As you do this,

- think about how the sentence matches the subject of the paragraph
- <u>underline</u> words in the sentences which refer to things in the paragraph.

A From time to time during the procession, they stopped to dance on the glaciers, believing this would bring luck to their villages for the year to come.

B We were up early the next morning, the main day of the festival, despite having slept badly on the frozen ground.

C It was clear, however, from the sound of drums and singing rising from this improvised camp that the weather was not going to dampen the festival spirit.

D But just as the celebrations were reaching their climax, it began to rain and everyone ran for shelter.

E Others, meanwhile, were offering goods for purchase such as warm clothes, food, torches and trinkets by spreading them on blankets on the ground.

F Some, like us, had come by bus to Mahuayani, the nearest town, and were walking up from there.

G They would take them and bury them in the mountain.

5 Quickly read the article again with your answers to check that it makes sense.

6 Work in pairs.
- Would you be interested in visiting this festival? Why? / Why not?
- Do you think festivals in your country are more for tourists or more for local people?

Reading and Use of English Part 3

1 Look at these extracts from Reading and Use of English Part 6 and use the word given in capitals at the end to form a word that fits in the gap. Then check your answer by looking at the text again.

1 … a festival which few ………………………… see. **TOUR**
2 They were joined by groups of ………………………… in bright traditional costumes. **DANCE**

➡ page 181 Language reference: Word formation – forming personal nouns

2 **EP** Form personal nouns from the noun or verb given.

noun/verb	person	noun/verb	person
1 design		7 motor	
2 novel		8 comedy	
3 research		9 sales	
4 collect		10 special	
5 survive		11 refuge	
6 consult			

3 Answer the questions in the Exam round-up box.

EXAM ROUND-UP

How much do you remember about Reading and Use of English Part 3?

Circle the correct option in *italics* in these sentences.

1 This part contains *eight / ten* questions.
2 *Write an answer as soon as you see a gap / Read the whole text quickly before answering the questions.*
3 If you can't think what to write, *leave the gap blank / think what type of word you need.*
4 *Make sure you have spelled the word correctly (look at the base word you have been given) / Correct spelling is not important in this part.*
5 When you have finished, *go to Part 4 / read the completed text again.*

Unit 14

4 EP For questions 1–8, read this text. Use the word given in capitals at the end of some of the lines to form a word that fits in the gap in the same line.

My local festival

The (0) ...preparations... for the festival in my town are an extremely exciting time. Months before, the (1) .... who work together on the committee start making all the necessary (2) .... and finalising the details of the processions and other (3) .... that are going to take place. They also keep the main (4) .... up to date with what is going on so that everyone knows when and where things will happen. When the festival finally arrives, it becomes virtually impossible to drive around the town because the streets are full of local people, visitors from (5) .... towns, and tourists. Everyone in the town seems to become more (6) .... as the excitement grows. They dress up in traditional costumes, stay out all night with their friends and behave in an (7) .... noisy way for our normally quiet, respectable town. For me, however, the most (8) .... part of the town's festivities is the firework display.

PREPARE

ORGANISE

ARRANGE

ACT

PARTICIPATE

SURROUND

ENERGY

USUAL

IMPRESS

Speaking Parts 3 and 4

1 Before doing Speaking Parts 3 and 4, answer the questions in the Exam round-up box.

EXAM ROUND-UP

How much do you remember about Speaking Parts 3 and 4? Say whether the following statements are true (T) or false (F). If a statement is false, correct it.

Speaking Part 3
1 There are two parts: the first part takes two minutes and the second part one minute.
2 In the first part, you needn't discuss all five prompts – it's better to discuss a few in more detail.
3 You should ask your partner to express his/her ideas.
4 In the second part, you must reach a decision together.

Speaking Part 4
5 You are asked your opinions on a new subject.
6 You and your partner may be asked the same questions or different questions.
7 You should try to give your opinion plus an explanation, reason or example.
8 In both Speaking Parts 3 and 4, you should listen carefully to what your partner says and be ready to say something about it or comment on it.

2 ▶ 36 Work in pairs. Listen to the examiner's instructions and then spend two minutes doing the first part of this Part 3 task.

- learning about history
- having fun as a community
- Are festivals important in the modern world?
- keeping traditions alive
- hearing different types of music
- suitable for people of all ages

3 ▶ 37 Listen to the examiner's next instruction and spend a minute doing the second part of the Speaking Part 3 task.

156

Fiesta!

4 ▶ 38 Now listen to Noelia and Denis doing the first part of Speaking Part 3. Were their ideas different from yours?

5 Listen again. Noelia and Denis help each other to do this part of the exam.
1 How is it clear that they are listening carefully to each other, and why is this important?
2 What phrases do they use to:
 a encourage each other?
 b help their partner to express an idea?
 c take over when their partner gets into trouble?

6 ▶ 39 Work in pairs. Listen to the examiner's instructions and do the first part of this Part 3 task. Try to use phrases you noted down in Exercise 5 to help the discussion along.

- a new baby in the family
- passing exams
- a first car
- moving into a new home
- winning at a sport

How should we celebrate each of these occasions?

7 ▶ 40 Listen to the examiner's instructions and do the second part of the Part 3 task.

8 ▶ 41 Work in pairs. Listen to Antonia and Nikolai answering this Part 4 question. Who do you agree with more? Why?

How do towns and cities benefit from having festivals and other celebrations?

9 Pronunciation: improving fluency

1 ▶ 42 Work in pairs. Read and listen to Antonia's answer and underline the words she stresses.

Hmm, ↗that's a good ↘question. / Some people say that it's good for, what's it called, community spirit, but I think the main benefit is for local businesses because tourists and visitors are attracted to the town to spend their money in shops and restaurants.

2 Listen again and mark with a ↗ or a ↘ to show where her voice rises or falls on stressed words.

3 Use a (/) to mark where you think she pauses. Then listen again to check your answers.

4 ▶ 43 Now read and listen to Nikolai's answer and follow steps 1–3 above.

Yes, I partly agree with her. I think in many places people spend a lot of time during the year preparing for their festival and I think it really encourages a feeling of cooperation and a community feeling.

5 Take turns to read both answers aloud.

6 Think for a moment how you will answer this question. Then take turns to answer the question using stress, intonation and pauses suitably.

Do you think festivals should be organised more for tourists or more for local people?

10 Work in groups of three. One student should take the role of the examiner and ask these questions to the others. When you have finished, change roles and ask and answer the questions again.
1 What can tourists learn from visiting a festival in another country?
2 Do you think that some towns and cities spend too much time and money on organising festivals?
3 How important is it for people to remember their traditions?
4 Do you think there should be a limit to noise at festivals or other celebrations?

Unit 14

Writing Part 1 — An essay

1 Before doing Writing Part 1, answer the questions in the Exam round-up box.

EXAM ROUND-UP

How much do you remember about Writing Part 1? Choose the best option in *italics* in these sentences.

In Writing Part 1:
1. you must write an essay of between *120–180 words / 140–190 words* in *40 / 60* minutes.
2. you *can write whatever you want / you must deal with three points, one of which is your own idea.*
3. you should *write a plan first / just start writing your answer.*
4. you should *check your answer carefully when you finish / you won't have time to check your answer.*

2 Work in pairs. Read the writing task below.
- <u>Underline</u> the key points in the task.
- Make a list of the advantages and disadvantages of going to music festivals and concerts to listen to live music instead of listening to recorded music.
- Discuss: Which do you prefer? Why?

In your English class, you have been talking about the advantages and disadvantages of going to music festivals and concerts to listen to live music instead of recorded music.
Now your English teacher has asked you to write an essay. Write an essay using **all** your notes and give reasons for your point of view.

Essay question
Is it better to listen to live music or recorded music?

Notes
Write about:
1. quality
2. convenience
3. …………… (your own idea)

Write your **essay**.

3 Decide which of the ideas you discussed you can use in this essay and write a brief plan.

When you have finished, work in pairs and compare your plans.

4 Read Ulli's essay and answer these questions.
1. Which of her ideas are the same as yours?
2. Which is her own idea?
3. Do you agree with her opinion?

Although people can listen to recorded music on their music players when they[1] are travelling working or studying music festivals and concerts are becoming more and more popular. This[2] is because I believe they[3] offer two main advantages.

The first advantage is that the quality of the sound is much better at live concerts where the music and voices come directly from the performers. This[4] makes it[5] a much more emotional experience because you have direct contact with the musicians and you react to them[6] and they react to you.

The second advantage is the atmosphere. Instead of listening to a recording alone on your personal music player you are listening with a huge crowd of people and enjoying the music together. This[7] means it is a social as well as an artistic experience.

The main disadvantage is that you cannot listen to live music whenever you want like you can on a personal device. Apart from that[8], the noise from the audience sometimes spoils the quality of the sound.

In my opinion however the best way to enjoy music is the spontaneous atmosphere of a live concert. It[9] is more exciting because you are surrounded by other enthusiastic fans who are dancing with you.

Fiesta!

5 👁 Candidates often make mistakes with punctuation. Ulli's answer in Exercise 4 is missing ten commas. Punctuate it correctly by placing the ten commas.

➡ page 177 Language reference: Using commas

6 Work in pairs. Ulli connects her ideas by using words which refer to other parts of her essay. What does each of the underlined words in her essay refer to? *1 'they' refers to people.*

➡ page 178 Language reference: Using *it*, *this*, *that* or *they*

7 👁 Candidates often make mistakes with *it*, *this*, *that* and *they* when referring to other parts of their writing. Complete these sentences by writing *it*, *this*, *that* or *they* in the gaps. In some cases, more than one answer may be possible.

1 In my opinion, going to live concerts is better. .... gives you the chance to really connect with the band.
2 Listening to live music is better, but on the other hand .... is more expensive.
3 A further disadvantage is that when young people want to go to a concert, ... cannot always afford the ticket price.
4 During the tour, the band performed in Paris and Berlin, but .... had played in Amsterdam before ....
5 The band's tour had various problems: the bus broke down and some of their equipment was stolen. On top of all .... , there was a storm on the night of the concert.
6 Many live concerts are held late at night. .... leads to complaints from people living nearby who cannot sleep.
7 The sound quality of the recording is not very good, and in addition to .... it is quite expensive.
8 I am not very keen on being in large crowds. In spite of .... , I would never miss a concert by my favourite band.

8 Work alone. Do this writing task.

In your English class, you have been talking about the advantages and disadvantages of going to the cinema rather than watching films on DVD or television.
Now your English teacher has asked you to write an essay. Write an essay using **all** your notes and give reasons for your point of view.

Essay question
Is it better to watch films at the cinema or at home?

Notes
Write about:
   1. quality
   2. cost
   3. .... (your own idea)

Write your **essay**.

Vocabulary and grammar review Unit 13

Vocabulary

1 Circle the correct word in *italics* in these sentences 1–10.

1. I never seem to have enough *space / place* for everything on my desk!
2. Bring your family to stay with us! We've got plenty of *room / place* for all of you.
3. He loves travelling and the first thing he does when he arrives in a new *location / place* is take a photo.
4. The teacher said he'd found an excellent *location / space* for our class picnic this year.
5. There aren't really many sports facilities in this *area / location*.
6. There's an empty *place / room* at that table if you want to sit there.
7. We may have to take two taxis because I don't think there's *space / place* in one for all of us.
8. You can buy international newspapers at the newsagent's in the main *square / place*, just behind the station.
9. I found the flight uncomfortable because there wasn't enough leg *place / room*.
10. She's got a good hiding *place / room* for the money she keeps in her bedroom.

Grammar

2 For questions 1–8, read this text and think of the word which best fits each gap. Use only one word in each gap.

3 For questions 1–6, complete the second sentence so that it has a similar meaning to the first sentence, using the word given. Do not change the word given. You must use between two and five words.

1. My grandparents are hoping to employ someone to paint their house soon.
   HAVE
   My grandparents are hoping to .... soon.
2. Make sure that someone checks the bike for you before your parents buy it.
   HAVE
   Make sure that you .... before your parents buy it.
3. Magda must tidy her room each morning.
   CLEAR
   Magda has .... her room each morning.
4. They make us do three hours of homework a day in this school.
   HAVE
   We .... three hours of homework a day in this school.
5. In this restaurant, you should pay for your food when you order it.
   SUPPOSED
   In this restaurant, you .... for your food when you order it.
6. Speaking is forbidden during the exam.
   ALLOWED
   You .... during the exam.

| home | news | search | living green | stories | advice | contact |

LIVING IN CAVES

Wherever people live, they need to protect themselves (0) ...*from*... the weather, and ever (1) .... humans started to walk the Earth, they have lived in caves. To start with, they (2) .... use of natural caves, but they soon ran (3) .... of these. It then became simpler for them to create their own caves (4) .... to build shelters using other materials or techniques. On volcanic islands, for example, people found the rock was soft (5) .... to dig into, and (6) .... are places in the world where these artificial caves are still inhabited.

Modern-day caves have some unexpected advantages. For anyone who has ever visited (7) .... , the benefits are immediately apparent: they will have found that the cave is isolated from noise and has a generally pleasant temperature. It is not too hot in the summer, while it stays warm in the winter. (8) .... is more, a modern cave is likely to contain all the modern household gadgets that make life comfortable.

Vocabulary and grammar review Unit 14

Word formation

1 **EP** Read the text. Use the word given in capitals at the end of the lines to form a word that fits in the gap in the same line.

Getting work experience is a good way for young people who are still at school to see whether they will enjoy a particular career. Future (0) ...employers... like to see work experience on CVs and it can be a good way to see whether, for example, someone will enjoy being a (1) .... before they start on a law degree. They get the chance to consider various (2) .... for a future career with working professionals whose advice they will find (3) .... helpful when thinking about the different choices they will have to make. Work experience often involves uncomfortable situations but people who do it learn how to behave (4) .... in front of clients and how to take (5) .... for things in the workplace. Appearance is important and they need to dress (6) .... whether they are going for a job as an air-traffic controller or an IT specialist or a job which is perhaps less technical but equally (7) .... such as a sales (8) .... or teacher.	EMPLOY LAW POSSIBLE SPECIAL SUIT RESPOND APPROPRIATE DEMAND REPRESENT

2 Complete each of the following sentences by using the word given in capitals at the end of each question to form a word that fits in the gap.

1 Tanya has a .... as a very hard-working student. **REPUTE**
2 In this airline, we make sure that we follow all the .... procedures in order to avoid accidents. **SAFE**
3 My teacher just looked at me in .... when I answered all the questions perfectly. **AMAZE**
4 My mother expressed her .... with the work, which was very badly done. **SATISFY**
5 Visitors are often confused to find the .... of two streets with similar names in the town. **EXIST**
6 If only Maria would tell us the .... instead of trying to deceive us with obvious lies! **TRUE**
7 Pierre swam the .... of the river in five minutes. **WIDE**
8 The .... of a swimming pool has made the hotel much more popular. **ADD**
9 Can you tell the .... between this fake Rolex and the original one made in Switzerland? **DIFFER**
10 I have several other .... in July, so I won't be able to go on holiday then. **OBLIGE**

Grammar

3 For questions 1–6, complete the second sentence so that it has a similar meaning to the first sentence, using the word given. Do not change the word given. You must use between two and five words, including the word given.

1 It is almost certain that the flight will arrive on time.
 EXPECTED
 The flight .... on time.
2 Thieves entered our school at the weekend.
 BROKEN
 Our school .... thieves at the weekend.
3 According to reports, seven firefighters were injured in the fire.
 REPORTED
 Seven firefighters .... been injured in the fire.
4 It's two months since I last tidied my room!
 BEEN
 My room .... two months!
5 According to many people, elephants' memories are excellent.
 SAID
 Elephants' memories ....
 excellent.
6 There were very few cakes left by the end of yesterday's party.
 EATEN
 Almost every .... by the end of yesterday's party.

161

Language reference

Contents

Adjectives with *-ed* and *-ing*	163
Articles	163
as and *like*	163
Causative *have* and *get*	164
Conditionals	164
Countable and uncountable nouns	165
Infinitive and verb + *-ing* forms	166
Linking words and phrases: *when, if, in case, even if* and *even though*	167
Linking words for contrast	168
look, seem and *appear*	168
Making comparisons	169
Modal verbs	170
Prepositions	172
Relative pronouns and relative clauses	172
Reported speech	173
so and *such, too* and *enough*	175
Spelling	176
The passive	177
Using commas	177
Using *it, this, that* or *they*	178
Verb tenses	178
wish, if only and *hope*	180
Word formation	181
Words which are often confused	183

Adjectives with -ed and -ing

There are many adjectives which are formed with -ed or -ing. Some adjectives do not have both forms, e.g. *living* but not *lived*.

- Adjectives with *-ed* express how the person feels about something:
  *I was **fascinated** by the photos of her trip to Australia on her Facebook page.*
- Adjectives with *-ing* are used to describe the person or thing which produces the feeling:
  *Have you seen that **amazing** video on YouTube?*
  (I felt amazed when I saw it.)

 See also page 176: Spelling

Articles
The indefinite article

We use *a* or *an*:
- with singular, countable nouns mentioned for the first time:
  ***A blue car** came round the corner.*
  *We have **a new chemistry teacher**.*
- to talk about jobs:
  *His mother's **a doctor**.*

We do not use *a* or *an* with uncountable nouns or plural countable nouns:
  ***Knowledge** makes people **powerful**.*
  *More girls go to **university** in this country than **boys**.*
- Use *an* before words which begin with a vowel sound: ***an** app*, ***an** email* (but not when the letters 'u' or 'e' produce a 'y' sound: ***a** useful tool*, ***a** European student*, ***a** university*).
- When 'h' is silent, use *an*: ***an** hour*, ***an** honest man*.

The definite article

The is used:
- with things we have mentioned before or when it's clear who or what we are referring to from the context:
  *I've got two new teachers. **The** maths teacher is from California and **the** English teacher is from Ireland.*
  *Could you go to **the** shop for me, please?* (i.e. the shop we always use)
- when referring to particular things:
  *I love music, but I don't like **the** music my sister listens to.*
- with things which are unique: ***the** Internet*, ***the** moon*
- with adjectives to express groups:
  *In this country, **the** rich are growing richer and **the** poor are growing poorer.*
- with nationalities: ***the** French*, ***the** Spanish*, ***the** Italians*
- with superlative adjectives: ***the** best*, ***the** longest*
- with ordinal numbers (e.g. ***the** first*, ***the** second*, ***the** third*) used as adjectives:
  *Manolo won **the first prize** and Igor won **the second**.*
- with names of countries which include the words *Republic*, *Kingdom*, *States* or *Emirates*:
  The** Czech **Republic, ***The** United **Kingdom***, ***The** United **States***, ***The** United Arab **Emirates***
- with names of rivers, mountain ranges, seas and oceans:
  ***the** Nile*, ***the** Alps*, ***the** Mediterranean*, ***the** Pacific*
- with many common expressions:
  *at **the** moment*, *at **the** age of 15*, *in **the** end*, *on **the** one hand … on **the** other hand*

Do not use *the*, *a* or *an*:
- when talking in general and in the plural:
  Teachers are not paid enough.
  I can't imagine life without computers.
- with many common expressions:
  in bed/hospital/prison/school: He's in bed.
  at home/university/school: I'm at school.
  (go) to bed/hospital/university/school: What time do you go to school?

as and like
as

We use *as*:
- to say someone or something is that thing, or has that function:
  *He works **as a nurse**.*
  *She uses email **as a way of** keeping in touch with **friends**.*
  *Can I give you some advice **as a friend**?*
- to mean *the same as* before a subject + verb or a past participle:
  *Things happened exactly **as I had predicted**.*
  *The exam was **as expected** – very difficult!*
- to mean 'because':
  ***As** tomorrow is a public holiday, I will not be giving you any homework to do.*
  ***As** a 15-year-old, I'm not allowed to drive.*
- after certain verbs including *describe* and *regard*:
  *The teachers **regard** you **as the best group of students in the school**.*
  *The police **are describing** him **as extremely dangerous**.*
- with adjectives and adverbs to make comparisons:
  *Mike is **not as clever as** his sister.*
- to mean 'for example' in the phrase *such as*:
  *My family spent the summer travelling round Europe and visiting lots of places **such as Venice, Florence and Barcelona**.*
- with *the same … as*:
  *You're wearing **the same colour shirt as me**!*

- in the phrases *as far as I know* (I think it's true but I don't know all the facts), *as far as I'm concerned* (this is my personal opinion), *as far as I can see/tell* (this is what I've noticed or understood):
  As far as I know, my grandparents have always lived in the same house.
  You can spend all your time playing football *as far as I'm concerned*.
  Arsenal aren't going to win the cup this year *as far as I can see*.

like

We use *like*:
- to mean 'similar to' (especially after the verbs *be, seem, feel, look, sound, smell* and *taste*):
  He's eating what **looks like a hamburger**.
  This swimming pool is fantastic – the artificial waves mean it's **like swimming in the sea**.
- to mean 'for example':
  He enjoys all sorts of adventure sports **like paragliding, windsurfing and canoeing**.

Causative *have* and *get*

We use *have/get* + something + *done* (cleaned/fixed/made, etc.) when we ask someone else to do something for us:
I've just **had my bike mended**. (i.e. Someone has mended my bike.)

- *get* is less formal than *have*:
  My dad **has just got some new furniture delivered**.
- It's not usually necessary to say who did it for us, but it is possible:
  I'm going to **have my hair dyed blonde** this afternoon **by my sister**. (i.e. My sister is going to dye my hair for me.)
- *have/get* + something + *done* can be used in any tense or form:
  I'm going to **get** my suit dry-cleaned for the wedding.
- We can also use this structure to say we have been the victim of something:
  Tim had his wallet stolen while he was waiting for the bus.

➔ See also page 177: The passive

Conditionals

Conditional sentences express a condition (*If* …) and the consequence of the condition. The consequence can be expressed before or after the condition:
If you come to Canada, we can visit Vancouver.
We can visit Vancouver *if you come to Canada*.

Note: If the condition comes first, a comma is used. If the consequence comes first, no comma is used.

Zero conditional

We use a zero conditional to express:
- things which are always or generally true:
  If the teacher **is** late, it **sets** a bad example to the class.
  People **tend to get** annoyed if/when you **shout** at them.
- scientific facts: When/If water **boils**, it **evaporates**.

Note: In zero conditionals, *when* and *if* often mean the same.

First conditional

We use a first conditional to express a future condition we think is possible or likely:
If I **pass** the exam, my parents **will buy** me a bike.
If you **wash** the car, it **will look** much smarter.
I **won't phone** you **unless** it's urgent.
We can **go** to the cinema if you **finish** your homework.
You **shouldn't go** swimming **unless** you **think** it's safe.
If he **phones, tell** him I'm busy.

Note: *unless* means 'except if'. We can often use *unless* instead of *if not*:
I can't watch the football with you **unless I finish my school work** beforehand. (If I don't finish my school work before the game begins, I can't watch the football with you.)

Second conditional

We use a second conditional to express a present or future condition which is imaginary, contrary to the facts, impossible or improbable:
I **would go** for a walk **if** it **wasn't** so cold.
If I **was** as rich as Bill Gates, I **wouldn't work**. (Being as rich as Bill Gates is imaginary.)
I **wouldn't fly** in a helicopter **unless** I **was** sure it **was** completely safe. (This is how I would feel in this situation.)
We'd win more matches **if** we **trained** harder. (This is contrary to the facts – we don't train hard enough.)

Third conditional

We use a third conditional to talk about:
- something which did not happen in the past and
- its results, which are imaginary.

*If you **had gone** to the concert, you **would have enjoyed** it.*
*If you **hadn't phoned** me this morning, I **would not have been** late for school.*
*If I **had lived** in the 19th century, I **would have gone** to school by horse.* (If I had lived in the 19th century (something which did not happen – I am alive now), I would have gone to school by horse (an imaginary consequence because I didn't live in the 19th century).)
*If he **hadn't reacted** quickly, the hippo **would have killed** him.* (He reacted quickly, so the hippo didn't kill him.)

Note: We can contract the third conditional as follows: *If **I'd** lived in the 19th century, **I'd have gone** to school by horse. If he **hadn't** been in such a hurry, he **wouldn't** have had an accident.*

We can use *could* and *might* instead of *would*:
*If our team had played harder, they **could have won** the match.* (They had the ability to win the match, but they didn't, because they didn't play hard enough.)
*If our team had played harder, they **would have won** the match.* (They were sure to win, but they didn't because they didn't play hard enough.)
*If the weather had been better, we **might have gone** swimming.* (Swimming was a possibility.)
*If the weather had been better, we **would have gone** swimming.* (Swimming was a certainty.)

Mixed conditionals

When we want to use a conditional sentence to talk about both the past and the present, we can use second conditional in one part of the sentence and third conditional in the other:

If tickets weren't so expensive, [2nd conditional (present time)] *I'd have gone to the cinema last night.* [3rd conditional (past time)]

- The tickets are expensive and that is why the speaker didn't go to the cinema.

If Mar hadn't fallen off her bike, [3rd conditional (past time)] *she'd be champion now.* [2nd conditional (present time)]

- Mar fell off her bike and that is why she isn't champion.

Note: You cannot use zero or first conditionals in mixed conditionals.

Countable and uncountable nouns

Nouns can be either countable [C] or uncountable [U]. However, some nouns can be both countable [C] and uncountable [U], but with a difference in meaning:
*They say it's healthy to drink **tea**.* (tea in general, uncountable)
*Would you like **a tea**?* (a cup of tea, countable)
*Studying for exams **is a lot of work**.* (work in general, uncountable)
*That picture is **a work of art**.* (a particular work, countable)

The grammar for countable nouns is different from the grammar for uncountable nouns.

countable nouns	uncountable nouns
• use *a* or *an* in the singular: ***a** job, **an** animal*	• do not use *a* or *an*
• can be made plural: *cars, books*	• cannot be made plural: *work, music*
• use *some* and *any* in the plural: ***some** friends, **any** answers*	• use verbs in the singular: *The news **is** good, Music **helps** me relax.*
• use *few* and *many* in the plural: ***few** students, **many** years*	• use *some* and *any* in the singular: ***some** food, **any** advice*
	• use *little* and *much* in the singular: ***little** information, **much** homework*
	• use other words to refer to a quantity: ***a piece of** advice, **a small amount of** money*

👁 *Some common uncountable nouns in English*
accommodation   advice   behaviour   countryside
damage   equipment   experience   food   furniture
homework   housework   information   knowledge
luggage   media   music   news   paper   pollution
research   scenery   smoke   software   stuff
transport   work

Infinitive and verb + -ing forms
Infinitive

We use the infinitive:
- to say why we do something:
  I've just gone running **to get some exercise**.
  He's taken up tennis **to make friends**.
- to say why something exists:
  There's an example **to help you**.
- after *too* and *enough*:
  It's **too cold to go** swimming today.
  He isn't good **enough to make** the national team.
- We use the infinitive in the following verb patterns:

verb + to infinitive	agree appear bother decide demand fail hope learn manage offer plan refuse seem be supposed threaten	She **agreed to meet** him after work.
verb + (somebody/something) + to infinitive	ask choose expect help intend promise want	She **expected to win** the race. I **expect you to play** in the match.
verb + somebody/something + to infinitive	advise allow enable encourage forbid force invite order permit persuade recommend remind teach tell warn	My parents **encouraged me to learn** the guitar.

- We use these verbs from the lists above to report speech:

advise agree allow ask decide encourage forbid invite offer order permit persuade promise recommend refuse remind tell threaten warn

➔ See also page 173: Reported speech

Verb + -ing

We use a verb + -ing:
- after prepositions:
  He's made a lot of friends **by joining** the tennis club.
  We watched a film **about climbing** in the mountains.

Note: We also use a verb + -ing after *to* when *to* is a preposition:
I'm **looking forward to going** on holiday.
She's **used to studying** everything in English.

- as subjects or objects of a sentence:
  Climbing is safer than it looks.
  He decided to take up **running**.

We use a verb + -ing after these verbs:

admit appreciate avoid celebrate consider delay deny dislike enjoy finish imagine involve keep mind miss postpone practise regret risk stop suggest

I really **enjoyed winning** that match.
She **suggested playing** a game of squash after school.

We can use these verbs from the list above in reported speech:

admit deny regret suggest

➔ See also page 174: Reported **speech**: reporting verbs

We use a verb + -ing after these expressions:

it's no good   it's not worth   it's no use
it's a waste of time   can't stand   can't bear   can't help

It's **not worth joining** that sports club.
It's a **waste of time entering** the competition unless you're really fit.
I **can't bear watching** my team when they play badly.

Verbs followed by either an infinitive or a verb + -ing with almost the same meaning:

love begin continue hate prefer like start

I **love playing** tennis. I **love to play** tennis.
It **continued raining** all day. It **continued to rain** all day.

Note: When *love*, *hate*, *prefer* and *like* are used with *would*, they are always followed by the infinitive:
I **wouldn't like to do** an adventure race.
I'd **prefer to watch** it on television.

Verbs followed by either an infinitive or a verb + -ing with a difference in meaning

	verb + infinitive	verb + -ing
remember	*Did you remember to bring your running shoes?* (an action you have to do)	*I remember feeling very tired at the end of the race.* (a memory of something in the past)
forget	*Don't forget to bring your tennis racket.* (an action you have to do)	*I'll never forget winning my first tennis championship.* (a memory of something in the past)
regret	*I regret to tell you the race has been cancelled.* (I'm sorry to give you this information.)	*I regret not training harder before the race.* (I'm sorry I didn't do this.)
try	*I'm running every day because I'm trying to get fit.* (My objective is to get fit.)	*If you want to get fit, why don't you try swimming?* (Swimming is a method to reach your objective.)
mean	*Mario means to win the championship.* (This is his intention.)	*I wanted to be a swimming champion, but it meant going to the pool every day at 5.30.* (it involved)
stop	*Halfway through the race, he stopped to drink some water.* (in order to drink some water)	*When he realised he couldn't win, he stopped running.* (He didn't continue.)

Note: The form *forget* + verb + *-ing* is unusual. It is more normal to use (*not*) *remember*:
*I **don't remember riding** a bike the first time.* (~~I forget riding a bike the first time~~.)

Linking words and phrases: *when, if, in case, even if* and *even though*

We use *when* to talk about:
- a situation: *I feel very uncomfortable **when** the weather is so hot.*
- something we know will happen at some point in time: *I'm writing an essay at the moment. **When** I finish, I'll phone you back.*

We use *if*:
- when we are not sure something will happen. *We'll miss the beginning of the film **if** the bus is late.*
- Compare:
  ***If** I go to college, my parents will buy me a new scooter.* (I'm not sure if I'll get a place at college.)
  ***When** I get a place at university, my parents will buy me a new car.* (I'm confident I'll get a place at university.)

We use *in case* with the:
- present tense to talk about something which might happen in the future:
  *I'll take a book to read **in case** I have to wait a long time for the train.*
  *Take a bottle of water with you **in case** you get thirsty.*
- past simple to explain why someone did something:
  *Clara turned off her mobile phone **in case** it rang during the exam.* (She thought it might ring during the exam, so she turned it off.)

in case and *if* are different. Compare:
- *I'll take my swimming costume **in case** we go to the beach.* (I'll take it now because we might go to the beach later.)
- *I'll take my swimming costume **if** we go to the beach.* (I won't take my swimming costume now, because I don't know if we'll go to the beach – we might not go.)

We use *even though* as a stronger way of saying *although* when we are certain about something:
- *He bought a new computer, **even though** his old one was working perfectly.* (The speaker is certain the old one was working perfectly.)
- *I'm really looking forward to my holiday, **even though** the weather forecast is for rain.* (The speaker knows the weather forecast is for rain.)

We use *even if* as a stronger way of saying *if*, when we are not certain about something:
- *I'm going on holiday in the USA this summer **even if** I fail all my exams.* (I'm not sure if I'm going to fail my exams – but I'm going to have the holiday anyway.)
- *I'll come to your party **even if** I have to walk there.* (I don't know if I'll have to walk there, but I'll make sure I come to your party.)

Linking words for contrast

We use these linking words to show contrast:

| although   even though   while   whereas   but |
| however   despite   in spite of |
| on the one hand, … (on the other hand,) |

although, even though, while and whereas

- We use *although, even though, while* and *whereas* to put two contrasting ideas in one sentence:
  *I didn't buy the dress **although** I thought it was beautiful.*
- They can be placed at the beginning of the sentence or in the middle, between the two contrasting ideas:
  It was late. She decided to phone him. → ***Although** it was late, she decided to phone him.* OR *She decided to phone him **although** it was late.*
- When the sentence begins with *although, even though, while* or *whereas*, we separate the two parts with a comma. When these words are placed in the middle, the comma is optional:
  Berlin is a noisy city. My home village is quite peaceful. → ***While** Berlin is a noisy city, my home village is quite peaceful.* OR *Berlin is a noisy city **whereas** my home village is quite peaceful.*
- *even though* is stronger than *although*:
  *I didn't buy the book, **even though** I had the money in my pocket.*

but

- *but* can be used to join two sentences. In this case, it is used in the middle of the sentence and it often follows a comma:
  *We warned her, **but** she didn't pay any attention.*
- *but* can sometimes be used at the beginning of a new sentence:
  *He likes romantic films. **But** don't tell anybody!*

 See also page 177: Using commas

however

- *however* normally starts a new sentence and refers to the sentence before.
- It is usually followed by a comma:
  *He decided to go out to the cinema. **However**, he didn't tell his family where he was going.*

despite and in spite of

- *despite* and *in spite of* mean 'without taking any notice of or being influenced by'; 'not prevented by':
  *He got into the basketball team **despite** being quite short.*
  *She went swimming **in spite of** the cold weather.*
- They can be placed at the beginning of the sentence or in the middle. They are followed by a noun or a verb + *-ing*.
- When used at the beginning of a sentence, a comma is also used to separate the two parts of the sentence:
  ***Despite** working all day, Teresa didn't feel at all tired.*
  *We got to school on time **in spite of** the heavy traffic.*

on the one hand, … (on the other hand,)

- *on the one hand … (on the other hand)* normally start new sentences and can be used to balance two contrasting ideas or points of view:
  *I'm not sure whether to go to the seaside for my holidays this year. **On the one hand**, most of my friends are going. **On the other hand**, it's time to have a change and go somewhere different.*
- *on the other hand* can be used to introduce a contrasting idea even if you haven't used *on the one hand*:
  *Doing sport can be a great way to relax. **On the other hand**, it can cause quite serious injuries.*

look, seem and appear

We use these verbs to express our impressions of something or someone:
*I haven't talked to him very much, but he **seems** very intelligent.*
*You still **look** tired, even if you have slept all night.*

We use these with the following patterns:

look/seem/appear + adjective	She **looks** very *old*. He **seems** *hungry*. Marga **appeared** *tired*.
subject + look + as if	The car **looks as if** it needs washing. You **look as if** you've had a bad day.
it looks/seems/appears + as if	It **looks as if** the car needs washing. It **seems as if** you've had a bad day.
seem/appear + infinitive	The weather **seems to have** changed. She **appeared to be** crying.
look/seem + like + noun	He **looks like** my uncle. It **may seem like** an impossible task, but it isn't really.

Making comparisons

Comparative and superlative forms of adjectives and adverbs

comparative forms	adjective/adverb + -er + than	Tennis is **cheaper than** golf. Marina works **harder than** before.
	more + adjective/ adverb + than	Golf is **more expensive than** tennis. It rains **more often than** in the past.
superlative forms	the + adjective/ adverb + -est the most + adjective/adverb	Chess is one of **the cheapest** hobbies. Playing team sports is **the most sociable** free-time activity.

Comparison of adjectives

Add -er and -est with:	• one-syllable adjectives: Fiona is **fitter** than last year. • two-syllable adjectives ending in -y and -ly, e.g. happy, friendly: My brother's **the friendliest** person in my family.
Use more and most with:	• adjectives of two syllables or more (except two-syllable adjectives ending in -y and -ly): Biking is **the most dangerous** activity.

→ See also page 176: Spelling

These form irregular comparisons:

good – better – best   bad – worse – worst
well – better – best   badly – worse – worst
much – more – most   many – more – most
little – less – least   far – farther/further – farthest/furthest

To say two things are the same, use *as* + adjective + *as*:
She finds doing zumba **as tiring as** playing team sports (this means 'She finds doing zumba and playing team sports equally tiring').

To say that one thing is less than another, use:
- *not so/as* + adjective + *as*:
  Window shopping is **not so/as enjoyable as** watching films.
- *less/least* + adjective:
  Playing chess is **less healthy than** playing team sports. Watching TV is **the least healthy** activity you can do.

Comparison of adverbs

Add -er and -est with:	• one-syllable adverbs, e.g. hard, fast, straight: My mum works **harder** than my dad.
Use more and most with:	• two-syllable adverbs including adverbs ending in -ly: Maria read the text **more quickly** than Susanna. She visits me **more often** than in the past.

These adverbs form irregular comparisons:

well – better – best   badly – worse – worst

To say two things are the same, use *as* + adverb + *as*:
Julia finished the exercise **as quickly as** Mark. (Julia and Mark finished the exercise equally quickly.)

To say that we do one thing differently from another, use:
- *not so/as* + adverb + *as*:
  Sophie **doesn't** speak Spanish **so/as well as** Gordon.

We can use words and phrases with comparative forms to express large and small differences. These are some ways of expressing a large difference:
- *much / far / a lot / considerably* + adjective/adverb + *-er/ more* + adjective/adverb:
  Playing team sports is **much riskier** than many people imagine.
- *not nearly as* + adjective/adverb + *as*:
  Some apps are **not nearly as fun** to play **as** computer games.

These are some ways of expressing a small difference:
- *slightly / a bit / a little* + adjective/adverb + *-er/more* + adjective/adverb:
  People drive **slightly slower** than they did in the past.
- *not quite as* + adjective/adverb + *as*:
  I **don't** find running **quite as enjoyable as** cycling.

Modals and other verbs

We use modal verbs to express the speaker's view of ability, certainty and possibility, obligation, prohibition and permission.
- These modal verbs are always followed by the infinitive without *to*: *can, could, may, might, must, shall, should, will, would*
- These modal verbs are always followed by the infinitive with *to*: *have to, ought to*

Note: Modal verbs always have the same form, i.e. no 's' in the third person singular (*He can come*) or -ed in the past. *Have to* changes in the same way as the verb *have*.

Expressing ability

To say someone has an ability, we use *can, can't, could, couldn't,* and *be able to*.

In the present, we use:
- *can* or *am/is/are able to* to express ability
- *can't* or *am not / isn't / aren't able to* for things which are not possible.

Francesca **can speak** *five languages, but she* **can't speak** *Russian.*
The dentist **isn't able to see** *you today, but* **is able to see** *you on Friday next week.*

Note: We usually use *can* and *can't* when speaking because they are shorter and less formal than *able to*.

In the past, we use:
- *could*, but only when speaking in general:
When I was younger, I **could read** *without glasses.* (not *I was able to read without glasses.*)
- *was/were able to* when speaking about something someone succeeded in doing on one particular occasion:
Dad didn't have any money on him, but fortunately he **was able to use** *his credit card to pay the bill.* (not *He could use his credit card to pay the bill.*)
- *couldn't* and *wasn't/weren't able to* when speaking in general and also when speaking about one particular occasion:
Pascual **wasn't able to / couldn't do** *all the questions in the maths exam.*
Olga **couldn't / wasn't able to ride** *a bike till she was 18.*

When talking about ability, we use *can* only in the present and *could* only in the past. For perfect and future tenses, we use *able to*:
I've been very busy so I **haven't been able to finish** *reading the novel.* (present perfect)
*When you finish the course, you'***ll be able to speak** *English really well.* (future simple)

Note: We do not use *be able to* in continuous forms.
- We use *be able to* after an infinitive:
She **hopes to be able to study** *medicine when she goes to university.*
- We use *be able to* after modal verbs (*might, should, may,* etc.):
If I'm free this weekend, I **might be able to help** *you paint your house. When you've finished this course, you* **should be able to speak** *English very well.*
- We usually use *can* and *could* with *see, hear, smell, feel* and *taste*:
From the top of the mountain we **could see** *for miles. I* **can hear** *a strange noise coming from upstairs.*
- However, we use *manage* when we succeed in doing something quite difficult to do:
I know you've been busy, but **did** *you* **manage to phone** *my mum?*
He **managed to pass** *the exam, although he was feeling ill when he did it.*

Note: *could* is not possible in this example:
He could pass the exam, although he was feeling ill when he did it.

Expressing certainty and possibility

To express certainty about the present, we use:
- *must*:
She's been in over 15 films, so she **must be** *very well-known.*

Note: We usually have a good reason for expressing this certainty, e.g. *She's been in over 15 films*.

- *can't* or *couldn't* in negative sentences (not *mustn't*):
You **can't be** *tired. You've just got out of bed!*
Mark **couldn't be** *in London – he's on holiday in America at the moment.*

To express certainty about the past, we use:
- *must have* + past participle:
You have a very big part in the play. It **must have taken** *you ages to learn all the lines.*
- *can't have* and *couldn't have* + past participle in negative sentences:
She **can't have left** *her glasses at home – I saw her wearing them on the bus.*
She **couldn't have stolen** *the money because she's far too honest!*

To express possibility about the present or future, we use:
- *may, might* or *could*:
I **may come** *and visit you next summer.*
We **might go** *to the cinema if we finish all our work in time.*
We'd better go for a walk now because it **could rain** *later.*

- *may not* and *might not* (or *mightn't*) in negative sentences (not *can't* or *couldn't*):
  Frankie is looking very pale. He **may not be** very well.
  Don't wait for me because I **might not be** back in time.

To express possibility about the past, we use:
- *may have, might have, could have, may not have, might not have* + past participle:
  It's **unusual for** Sally to be late. She **may have overslept**, or she **might not have remembered** the appointment.

Expressing obligation, prohibition and permission

Obligation – *must* and *have to*

We can often use *must* and *have to* without any difference in meaning:
Teachers **must / have to** try to make their lessons as interesting as possible.

However, we use:
- *must* + infinitive without *to* in the present tense. For other tenses, we use *have to* + infinitive:
  I'd like to go camping, but **I'll have to ask** my parents.
  In order to get the holiday job I **had to fill in** an application form and **go to** an interview.
- *have to* more often in questions:
  Do we **have to answer** all the questions?
- *must* for a goal (or an obligation) that we give ourselves:
  I **must go** to the supermarket later.
- *have to* when the obligation comes from someone else:
  My teacher has given me a lot of homework which I **have to do** for Monday.
- *must* for strong advice:
  You **must be** careful if you go paragliding.

Other ways of expressing obligation:
- We use *be supposed to* + infinitive to talk about an obligation which is different from what really happens:
  We're **supposed to do** five writing tasks each term. (But most people only do two or three.)
  Aren't you **supposed to be** in class right now? (i.e. not in the park playing football)
- We use *should* + infinitive without *to* to talk about the right thing to do, but which is different from what really happens:
  You **should answer** using your own ideas, not things you have memorised beforehand.
- The past of *should* is *should have* + past participle:
  You **shouldn't have tried** to answer three questions in Writing Part 2!
- We can use *ought to* to mean 'should':
  You **ought to be** polite to the people you meet.

Prohibition

We use these modal verbs and phrases to express prohibition: *can't, mustn't, not let, not allowed to, don't allow (somebody) to*.
You **can't go** in there – it says 'No entry!'
You **mustn't speak** during the exam – it's forbidden.
My sister **won't let** me **listen** to her CDs.
I'm **not allowed to use** the computer in my host family's house.
My parents **didn't allow** me **to play** computer games when I was small.

We do not use *don't have to* to express prohibition:
You **mustn't use** your mobile phone in class. (It's not allowed.)

Compare this with:
You **don't have to use** your mobile phone to speak to Fayed. Look! He's over there. (i.e. It's not necessary.)

In the past we use: *couldn't, didn't let, not allowed to, didn't allow (somebody) to*:
I **couldn't leave** the room until the end of the meeting.
She **wasn't allowed to invite** her friend to the party.

We don't use *mustn't* to talk about the past:
I ~~mustn't~~ **couldn't ride** my bike to school because my mum thought it was dangerous.
We ~~mustn't~~ **weren't allowed to** use our dictionary in the exam last week.

Permission

To express permission, we use: *can* (past *could*), *let, allowed to* and *may* (past *was/were allowed to*).
You **can** only **use** your phone during the break, not in class.
Are we **allowed to use** calculators in the maths exam?
She **let** him **borrow** her bicycle to get to the station.

We only use *may* in formal situations:
When you have answered all the questions, you **may leave** the room.

To say that there is no obligation, or it's not necessary, we use: *don't have to, don't need to* and *needn't*:
This is a really good exercise on phrasal verbs for anyone who's interested, but it's not for homework, so you **don't have to do** it if you don't want to.
You **needn't learn** all the vocabulary on this page – only the words you think are useful.

I didn't need to means 'It wasn't necessary and I didn't do it'; *I needn't have* means 'It wasn't necessary but I did it':
I **didn't need to buy** a newspaper to find out the story because I'd already heard it on the radio.
What lovely flowers! You **needn't have bought** me so many, but it was very generous of you.

Prepositions

at, in and on in time expressions

We use *at* with:
- points of time:
  at three o'clock, at the end of the lesson, at midnight
- mealtimes:
  *We can meet **at breakfast**.*
- the weekend, Christmas and Easter:
  *Why don't we go to the cinema **at the weekend**?*
- *night* when talking about nights in general:
  *I prefer to study **at night** because it's quieter.*

Note: *on the weekend* is common in American English.

We use *in*:
- for periods of time:
  in 2014, in April, in the summer, in the 19th century
- for parts of the day:
  *Paola often has a short sleep **in the afternoon**.*
- to say the period of time before something happens or how long something takes:
  *I'll be going to university **in six weeks' time**.*
  *He did the writing task **in just 13 minutes**.*

We use *on*:
- for particular dates, days, parts of days or types of days:
  *He was born **on July 13th**.*
  *What are you doing **on Sunday night**?*
  *I remember getting my first pet dog **on a sunny day** in August.*

at, in and on to express location

We use *at*:
- when we think of a place as a point, not an area (including *at home, at school, at work, at university*):
  *The postman is **at the front door**.*
- to talk about an event with a number of people:
  *I'll see you **at the party** tonight!*
- for addresses:
  *The party is **at 367 Wood Avenue**.*

We use *in*:
- when we think of a place as an area or space:
  *Olga lives **in St Petersburg**. Sonia lives **in a large house in the country**.*
- for cars and taxis:
  *I love listening to music when I'm **in the car**.*
- normally with *in class, in hospital, in prison, in court*:
  *Patrick is **in hospital** with a broken leg.*
- with people or things which form lines:
  *We stood **in the ticket queue** for four hours.*
- for *the world*:
  *He's reputed to be one of the richest men **in the world**.*

We use *on*:
- to talk about a position in contact with a surface:
  *There's an insect **on your forehead**.*
  *She lay **on the beach** all day.*
- with *coast, road to, the outskirts of, the edge of, border, the way to/from*, etc:
  *We can stop at my village, which is **on the way** to Madrid.*
- with means of transport apart from cars and taxis:
  *I always get frightened **on planes**.*
- for technology:
  *He's been **on the phone** for hours.*
  *I found out about it **on Facebook**.*
- with *left* and *right*:
  *Talk to the student **on your right**.*
- with *premises, farm, floor, island* and *list*:
  *It's **on the fifth floor**.*
  *You're not **on my list** of students for this class.*

at	in	on
at your/my house	in the world	on the beach
at the festival	in the city	on the/a train
at the party	in the mountains	on the island
at the theatre	in the country	on the/a farm
at the/your hotel	in the town	on the outskirts
at the concert	in the sky	on the floor
at my school	in the hotel	on the stage
at the camp	in a car	on the bus
at the university	in this area	on the road(s)
at the beach	in the countryside	on the plane
at the airport	in the street	
at the seaside	in the sea	
	in traffic jams	

Relative pronouns and relative clauses

A clause is a group of words containing a subject and a verb in a tense which form a sentence or part of a sentence. Relative clauses start with these relative pronouns: *who, which, that, whose, where, when* and *why*.

relative clause ↓
The man **who phoned you** is my doctor.

Defining relative clauses

Relative clauses which tell us which particular person or thing the speaker is talking about are called defining relative clauses. They give essential information:
*The doctor **who treated me** is my aunt.*

The relative clause tells us which doctor we are talking about.

Non-defining relative clauses

Relative clauses which give us extra information are called non-defining relative clauses:
*My aunt **is a doctor** who plays at the same tennis club as you.*

We already know which doctor (it's my aunt); *who plays at the same tennis club as you* does not tell us which doctor we are talking about; it just adds extra information.

There are differences in grammar:

defining relative clauses	non-defining relative clauses
• Don't have commas. • Use the following relative pronouns: *who, which, whose, where, when* and *why*. • Can use *that* instead of *who* or *which*. • *who, which* or *that* can be omitted when they are the object of the clause: *The medicine (–/which/that) the doctor gave me should be taken twice a day.*	• Use commas (or pauses in spoken English). • Use the following relative pronouns: *who, which, whose, where* and *when*. • Don't use *that*. • The relative pronoun cannot be omitted.

Reported speech
Tense changes in reported speech

If the reporting verb (*said, told, admitted, warned*, etc.) is in the past, we tend to change the original verb to a past form as well. Here are some changes we make:

present simple → past simple	'I live in Berlin.'	She said she **lived** in Berlin.
present continuous → past continuous	'I'm watching TV.'	He said he **was watching** TV.
present perfect → past perfect	'I've seen the film already.'	She said she **had seen** the film already.
past simple → past perfect	'I missed the concert.'	He told me he **had missed** the concert.
will → would	'I'll phone you soon.'	She promised she **would phone** me soon.

We also change these modal verbs:

can → could	'I **can understand** German, but I **can't speak** it.'	She said she **could understand** German but she **couldn't speak** it.
may → might	'I **may give** the book to John.'	The teacher suggested he **might give** the book to John.
must → had to	'I **must cook** dinner.'	Tanya said she **had to cook** dinner.

We do not change these modal verbs in reported speech: *could, would, should, might, ought to* and *used to*:
'I **would prefer to study** in London.' → She said that she **would prefer to study** in London.

must can change to *had to*:
'You **must read** this text for the next lesson.' → My teacher told me I **had to read** the text for the following lesson.

But we don't change *must* when:
• it's negative:
'You **mustn't tell** Katya our secret.'
→ Ana told Stefan he **mustn't tell** Katya their secret.
• it expresses a deduction:
'Arturo **must** still **be** asleep.'
→ She said that Arturo **must** still **be** asleep.

Note: If the reporting verb is in a present tense, no tense changes are necessary: 'I**'ll help** you with your homework.'
→ She says she**'ll help** me with my homework.

Questions in reported speech

To report a question, we make the following changes.
• We change the word order in the question to the same as a normal sentence.
• We make the same tense changes as in reported speech (see above).
• We use the same question words (*when, how*, etc.).
• We use a full stop (.), not a question mark (?):
'How long have you been living in London?' → She asked me how long I had been living in London.
'When can I phone you?' → Abdullah asked Magdi when he could phone him.
• We do not use the auxiliary verbs *do, does* and *did*; the question has the same form as a normal sentence:
'**What time does the lesson start**?' → Ludmila asked what time **the lesson started**.
• We use *if* or *whether* with Yes/No questions:
'Can I come to your party?' → Aniela wanted to know **whether** she could come to our party.

We often use these verbs and phrases to introduce reported questions: *ask, wonder, want to know, enquire*.

Pronoun, adjective and adverb changes in reported speech

We usually make the following changes:

you → he/she/they	'I spoke to you earlier.'	He said he had spoken to her earlier.
• your → his/her/their • our → their	'I saw your brother earlier.'	He mentioned that he had seen her brother earlier.
this/that (as pronouns) → it	'You should give this to Joan.'	She told him he should give it to Joan.
this/that/these/those + noun → the + noun	'This work is very good.'	She told him the work was very good.

Remember that references to times also need to change in reported speech:
'I saw Adam this morning.' → She said she had seen Adam that morning.

Other changes include:

present reference	• today • this week / this month / this year	• that day • that week / that month / that year
future reference	• tomorrow • next month / next year	• the next / the following day • the next / the following month/year
past reference	• yesterday • last week/ month/year	• the day before OR the previous day • the previous week/month/year OR the week/month/year before

Descriptions of place also frequently change: 'Did I leave my book here?' He asked if he'd left his book there.

Imperatives in reported speech

We use verb + infinitive to report orders and commands:
'**Fetch** that book!' → She asked him **to fetch** the book.
'**Don't look** out of the window!' → She told him **not to look** out of the window.

Reporting verbs

There are many verbs which we can use to introduce reported speech, each followed by different grammatical patterns. You will see that most verbs can be followed by more than one grammatical pattern.

verb + infinitive
- agree: Magda **agreed to look after** the children.
- offer: She **offered to take** the children to the zoo.
- promise: She **promised to phone** me later.

verb + object + infinitive
- advise: The doctor **advised Mrs Carter to take** a long holiday.
- ask: The neighbours **asked us to turn** our music down.
- invite: Patsy **has invited me to go** to the party with her.
- order: The police **ordered everyone to leave** the building.
- persuade: I **persuaded my mother to take** a holiday.
- remind: Can you **remind me to phone** Stephen?
- tell: Carl **told Jane to close** all the windows.
- warn: They **warned us not to walk** on the ice.

verb + preposition + noun or verb + -ing
- accuse of: Sophie **accused Marcel of stealing** her books.
- admit to: Bill **admitted to the mistake**.
  Sally **admitted to taking** the money.
- apologise for: Tommy **apologised for the accident**.
  Mandy **apologised for being** late.
- complain about: The neighbours **have been complaining about the noise**.
  We **complained about being** given too much homework to do.

verb + noun or verb + -ing
- admit: Danny **admitted the theft**.
  Sue **admitted stealing** the money.
- deny: Silvia **denied the crime**.
  Sean **denied causing** the accident.
- recommend: I can really **recommend this book**.
  I **recommend cycling** as a way of getting fit.
- suggest*: Jasmine **suggested the solution** to the problem.
  Mike **suggested going** climbing at the weekend.

verb + (that)
- admit: Sally **admitted (that)** she had taken the money.
- agree: The headteacher **agreed (that)** the exam had been too difficult.
- complain: We **complained that** we had been given too much homework.
- deny: Pablo **denied that** he had caused the accident.
- explain: She **explained that** she wasn't feeling very well.
- promise: Mandy **promised (that)** she would phone later.
- recommend: The doctor **recommended (that)** I do more exercise.
- say: Robin **said (that)** he was going swimming later.
- suggest*: Liz **suggested (that)** I should try the shopping centre on the edge of town

verb + object + (that)

- **persuade:** *I* **persuaded my mother that** *she should take a holiday.*
- **promise:** *Lynn* **promised Charlie (that)** *she would phone him later.*
- **remind:** **Can I remind you (that)** *you've got to phone Stephen?*
- **tell:** *The school* **told the students (that)** *they had the rest of the day free.*
- **warn:** *Nobody* **warned me (that)** *my grandmother was visiting us today.*

*****Note:** *suggest* is never followed by the infinitive. The following patterns are possible:

- *suggest* + verb + *-ing*: *Maria* **suggested buying** *a new computer.*
- *suggest* + noun: *Phil* **suggested the idea.**
- *suggest* + *(that)*:
  Tony **suggested that** *they played football that afternoon.*
- *suggest* + *(that)* + *should*: *Chantal* **suggested (that)** *I* **should** *write a letter.*

Other common patterns are:

- *ask* + *if/what*, etc. + sentence:
  She **asked** *me* **what** *I was doing.*
  He **asked** *me* **if** *I was free.*
- *invite* + object + *to* + noun: *Patsy* **has invited me to the party.**

➡ **See also page 166:** Infinitives and verb + *-ing* forms

➡ **See also page 177:** The passive – the passive with reporting verbs

Language reference

so and *such*, *too* and *enough*
so and *such*

so and *such* (*a/an*) mean 'very', 'extremely':
That was **so** *kind of you!*
I've had **such a** *nice time.*

We use *so* and *such* (*a/an*) to talk about cause and effect:
He was **so** *late that he missed the beginning of the exam.*
She gave **such a** *good performance that she won an Oscar.*

so + adjective or adverb (+ *that*):	*such* + adjective + uncountable noun / plural noun (+ *that*)
• He was **so nervous** before the exam **that** he couldn't sleep at all. • That remark was just **so silly**! • He cooks **so well that** I think he'll win the competition.	• She tells **such good jokes**. • Switzerland has **such spectacular scenery that** we always choose it for our holidays.

so + *much/many/few/little* + noun (+ *that*)	*such a/an* + adjective + singular countable noun (+ *that*); *such a lot of …*
• We had **so little money** left at the end of our holiday that we had to buy food in supermarkets. • Marta makes **so many mistakes** when she's speaking!	• Why did you come in **such an old pair of jeans**? • It was **such a beautiful day** that we decided to go for a picnic. • Elena's got **such a lot of friends** that her phone never stops ringing.

We also use *such* (+ noun) to mean 'of a similar type':
When children commit crimes, adults are often shocked. Fortunately **such behaviour** *is not as common as newspapers make us believe.*

175

too and enough

- *too* means 'more than is needed or wanted':
  She's **too young** to drive.
- *enough* means 'as much as is necessary or needed':
  Have we got **enough eggs** to make a cake?

too + adjective (+ noun) + (for somebody) (+ infinitive)	adjective/adverb + *enough* + (for somebody) (+ infinitive)
He's **too young** to drive. That suitcase is **too heavy** for me to lift.	This coffee is **not warm enough**! Please heat it up again. Franz didn't play **well enough** to win. That hotel is **not clean enough** for her.
too + adverb + (for somebody) (+ infinitive); *too much / too many* + noun + (for somebody) (+ infinitive)	*enough* + noun + (for somebody) (+ infinitive)
You're driving **too quickly**. Please slow down. They brought **too much food** for us to eat. I've received **too many emails** to answer.	Have you got **enough money to get** to London? There isn't **enough cake for me to give** some to everyone.

Spelling

Spelling changes when adding -ed, -ing, -er and -est to words

We double the final consonant when we add -ed, -ing, -er or -est to words:
- which are one syllable and end in a consonant–vowel–consonant:
  stop – stopped, hit – hitting, flat – flatter
- which have two or more syllables which end in consonant–vowel–consonant and the final syllable is stressed:
  admit – admitted, occur – occurring

Note: In British English, we double a final 'l' after a single vowel: travel – travelling, cancel – cancelled

We don't double the final consonant when:
- there are two final consonants:
  send – sending, hard – hardest
- there are two vowels before the final consonant:
  appeal – appealed, mean – meanest
- the word ends in a vowel:
  strike – striking, safe – safest
- for a verb, the stress is not on the final syllable:
  open – opening

- the word ends in -w, -x or -y:
  slow – slower, relax – relaxing, display – displayed

When adding -ed, a final 'y' after a consonant becomes 'i':
study – studied, lovely – loveliest
When adding -ing, a final 'y' after a consonant does not change: study – studying

Note: Notice how the spelling of these words changes:
lie – lying – lied; die – dying – died; lay – laying – laid; try – trying – tried

Spelling changes when adding prefixes and other suffixes

We normally do not change the spelling of the base word when we add a prefix or a suffix:
arrange – **arrange**ment

However:
- we drop the final 'e' when there is a consonant before it and the suffix begins with a vowel (-er, -ed, -ing, -ance, -ation, etc.): irritate – irrita**ting**, fame – fam**ous**
- we do not drop the final 'e' when the suffix begins with a consonant: safe – safe**ty**, manage – manage**ment**
- a final 'y' becomes 'i': industry – industrial

Adding prefixes

When we add a syllable like *un-*, *dis-*, or *in-* before the word to make it negative, we do not change the spelling, e.g. with *dis-* and *un-*: appoint – **dis**appoint, satisfied – **dis**satisfied, like – **un**like, necessary – **un**necessary

Note: Before words beginning with 'r', we use *ir-*: **ir**relevant; before words beginning with 'm' or 'p', we use *im-*: **im**mature, **im**patient; before words beginning with 'l', we use *il-*: **il**logical, **il**literate.

These words are frequently misspelled by exam candidates:

Common spelling errors

accommodation advertisement beautiful because
beginning believe between children
comfortable communicate convenient
country/countries course different
embarrassed/embarrassing environment excellent
experience government loose lose necessary
nowadays opinion opportunity/opportunities
prefer receive recommend restaurant society
their until wealthy which

The passive

The passive is formed from the verb *to be* + past participle (*done/eaten/cleaned*, etc.).

active	passive
• **They ate** all the food very quickly.	• All the food **was eaten** very quickly.
• **We've sold** the car.	• The car **has been sold**.
• It's nice when **people invite** me to dinner.	• It's nice when **I'm invited** to dinner.
• On a clear day, **you can see** Ibiza from the mainland.	• On a clear day, Ibiza **can be seen** from the mainland.

We use the passive when:
- what happens is more important than who does it:
  The car **has been repaired**, so we can go away this weekend.
- we don't know who or what does/did something:
  My mobile phone **has been stolen**!
- we don't need to say who or what does/did something because it's obvious from the situation or context:
  The law **was passed** earlier this year (obviously by a government).
- when writing in an official style:
  Your ticket **has been booked** and **can be collected** from our office.

The passive with *get*

- We can use *get* instead of *be* to form the passive, especially when we want to say that something happened to someone or something:
  He **got hurt** playing football yesterday. (He was hurt.)
  I'm afraid we were playing football and one of your windows **got broken**. (One of your windows was broken.)
- *get* is used mainly in informal spoken English.
- We only use *get* when something happens or changes:
  He **got arrested** by the police.
- It is not possible with state verbs:
  ~~The car got owned by a film star.~~ The car **was owned** by a film star.

The passive with reporting verbs

We often use the passive to report what people say or think, etc., especially when we don't know who said it or thought it, or it's not important:
The Queen **is thought to be suffering** from a heavy cold.
Fernando Alonso **is considered to be** the best Spanish Formula One driver of all time.
This use of the passive is common in news reports.

We use three possible forms:
- He/She is said/thought/considered, + infinitive:
  Lions **are known to hunt** in this area.
  Elena **is thought to be** highly intelligent.
- Verbs that we can use with this pattern are:

  consider   expect   feel   know   say   suppose   think   understand

- To talk about the past, we can use:
  She is said to have played/eaten/been:
  The Prime Minister **is understood to have spoken** to the rebels on the phone.
- It is said/thought/considered, etc. + that:
  It is thought that Elena is highly intelligent.
  It is known that lions hunt in this area.
- Verbs that we can use with this pattern are:

  agree   consider   decide   expect   feel   find   know   propose   recommend   say   suggest   suppose   think   understand

- It is agreed/planned + infinitive:
  It has been agreed to change the dates of the meeting.
- Verbs that we can use with this pattern are:

  agree   decide   forbid   hope   plan   propose

Using commas

We use commas (,):
- when we make lists:
  I like playing tennis, listening to music, chatting with friends **and** watching TV.

Note: We don't use a comma with the final item on the list; we use *and*.

- to separate adjectives when there are a number of adjectives before the noun:
  He's an enthusiastic, hard-working student.

Note: With short common adjectives, commas are not necessary: *My village is quite a friendly little place.*

- after an adverb or a short introductory phrase at the beginning of a sentence such as *first, as a result, consequently, for this reason, all in all, generally, finally, however, in my opinion*, etc.:
  Generally, people in my country start university aged 19.
  In my opinion, young people should help their parents to do the housework.
- after a time phrase at the beginning of a sentence:
  In 2014, he left school and started work.

- after clauses at the beginning of sentences starting with *if*, *unless*, *when*, *while*, *after*, *before*, *although*, *even though*, *whereas*, *as*, etc.:
  When everyone in a family helps with the housework, they have a better relationship.
- when we join two sentences with *but*, we often put a comma before *but*:
  He got quite good marks in his exams, **but** he wasn't happy with his results.

Using *it*, *this*, *that* or *they*

We use *it*, *this* and *that* (in the plural *they*, *these* and *those*) to refer to something we have already mentioned. Often more than one of them is correct in the context. However:
- we use *it* when we are not making any emphasis:
  I prefer listening to live music. **It's** more spontaneous.
- *this* and *that* are more emphatic in drawing attention to the thing just mentioned:
  People usually **listen to music through headphones**. There's some evidence that **this** damages their hearing.
- we often use *this* when:
  – we still have something more to say about the thing we are referring to:
    File sharing has become a common activity. **This** is having serious effects on the music industry.
  – we refer to the second of two things mentioned in the previous sentence. Compare:
    1 While many festivals are welcomed by local people, they are usually very **noisy**. **This** means that people living in the district find it hard to sleep. (This = the noise)
    2 While many *festivals* are welcomed by local people, **they** are usually very noisy. Also, they are normally held in the summer. (they = the festivals)
- we often use *that* in conditional sentences:
  I think that every town and village should have a festival if **that** is what local people want.

Verb tenses

Simple and continuous forms

- Present simple describes a situation which is permanent, or happens regularly:
  Paul **lives** in London.
  He **catches** the bus at eight every morning.
- Present continuous describes a temporary situation or one in progress:
  I'**m staying** with my aunt while Mum and Dad are away.
  He'**s playing** tennis at the moment.

State verbs

We do not usually use verbs which describe states, rather than actions, in the continuous. State verbs describe:

- thoughts: *believe*, *know*, *remember*, *think* (meaning 'believe'), *feel* (meaning 'believe'), *suppose*, etc.
- feelings: *love*, *like*, *hate*, *want*, *prefer*, etc.
- senses: *smell*, *hear*, *taste*, *see*, *feel*, *touch*
- possession: *have*, *belong*, *own*, etc.

Note:
- When *think* means 'to use your brain to plan something, solve a problem or make a decision', it can be used in the continuous:
  I'**m thinking** about what to do today. (I'm planning.)
- When *feel* means 'to experience something physical or emotional', it can be used in the continuous:
  I don't want to come to the party because I'**m feeling** tired.

Candidates often spell these verb forms wrong:

~~writting~~ writing   ~~studing~~ studying   ~~comming~~ coming

➡ See also page 176: Spelling

Present perfect simple and continuous

Both the present perfect simple and present perfect continuous talk about something which started in the past and:
- either has a result in the present:
  He'**s twisted** his ankle, so he can't play football with us this afternoon.
- or is still happening now:
  We'**ve been building** an extension to our house (and we haven't finished yet).

Often they are interchangeable. However:

The present perfect simple	The present perfect continuous
emphasises the result: I'**ve phoned** all my friends and they're coming to the party.	emphasises the action: I'**ve been phoning** my friends (and that's why I haven't done my homework).
says how much of an activity is complete: I'**ve written** two essays.	says how long the activity has been in progress: I'**ve been studying** all afternoon.

may give the idea that something is permanent (and may be accompanied by a time expression which shows this): My dad **has worked** in the same shop all his life. I've always **lived** here.	may give the idea that something is temporary (and may be accompanied by a time expression which shows this): **I've been working** here for the last two months. **We've been eating** dinner in the garden during the warm weather.
is used when we want to say how many times an action has been repeated: **I've invited** her two or three times, but she always says she's busy.	when we want to emphasise the process of change over a period of time and that these changes are not finished: My teacher says my English **has been improving** since I started doing my homework!

Remember! State verbs are not normally used in the continuous.

 See also page 178: Verb tenses – state verbs

Past simple, past continuous and *used to*
Past simple

We use the past simple to talk about:
- actions or events in the past: I **visited** Egypt last year.
- actions or events which happened one after another: I **saw** the Pyramids, then I **went** round the Cairo Museum and later I **went** to a traditional restaurant.
- things which happened for a long time in the past: She **lived** in Zurich for ten years from 2003 to 2013.

Past continuous

We use the past continuous to talk about:
- an activity which started before and continued until an event in the past:
  He **was riding** to school when his motorbike broke down. (The activity of riding was interrupted by the problem with the motorbike.)
- an activity which started before and continued after an event in the past:
  I **was watching** television when the news was announced. (I continued to watch television afterwards.)

Remember! State verbs are not normally used in the continuous.

 See also page 178: Verb tenses – state verbs

used to

We use *used to* to talk about:
- situations or states in the past which are not true now: My maths teacher **used to be** in the army.
- repeated activities or habits in the past which do not happen now:
  She **used to run** a marathon every year until she injured her leg.

Note: We only use *used to* in the past:
She **used to run** in marathons.
Did you **use to** run in marathons?
I **didn't use to** run in marathons.

- When we want to talk about habits in the present, we use the present simple with an adverb like *usually*, *every day*, etc.:
  I **usually drink** water with my lunch. He **catches** the same train **every day**.

Past perfect simple and continuous
Past perfect simple

We use the past perfect simple:
- to indicate that we are talking about something which happened before something which is described in the past simple:
  When he **got** to the station, his train **had** already **left**.
  Compare this with:
  When he **got** to the station, his train **left**.
  This indicates that the train left at the time he arrived.
- typically with time expressions such as *when, as soon as, after, before*, etc.:
  She started driving **before** he'd **fastened** his seatbelt.
- often with these adverbs: *already, just, never*: He'd **never eaten** steak and kidney pie until he came to England.

Past perfect continuous

We use the past perfect continuous to show that we are talking about something which happened before something which is described in the past simple, but it:
- focuses on the length of time:
  Mandy needed a walk because she'**d been sitting down all day**.
- says how long something happened up to a point in the past:
  It was **two months before** the teachers noticed that Paula **hadn't been coming** to school.
  He'**d been playing** for Arsenal **for only two games** when he scored his first goal.

 See also page 176: Spelling

wish, if only and hope

We use *wish / if only* + past simple to say we would like a present situation to be different:
*I **wish** I **had** a warmer jacket.* (This one doesn't keep me warm.)
*If only it **was** the summer holidays!* (But it isn't – I'm still at school.)

Note: This use of *wish / if only* is similar to second conditional as it uses a past tense to refer to something which is contrary to the facts in the present.

We use *wish / if only* + *would* to say:
- we want something to happen:
  *I **wish** the concert **would start**.* (I can't make it start and I want it to start.)
- we want someone to start doing something they don't do:
  If only you'd listen to me!
- or we want someone to stop doing something which annoys us:
  *If only my mum **wouldn't** phone every five minutes!*

We use *wish / if only* + past perfect to talk about things which we are unhappy about which happened in the past:
*He **wishes** he **had studied** harder when he was at school.* (He didn't study hard enough – perhaps if he had studied harder he would have passed his exam.)

Note: This use of *wish / if only* is similar to third conditional, i.e. it uses a past perfect tense to refer to something which is contrary to the facts in the past.

If only means 'I wish'. When talking about other people, we use *he wishes, they wish*, etc. We use *if only* when we feel something very strongly. Otherwise we use *I wish*.

We use *hope* when we want something to happen or to be true, and usually have a good reason to think that it might:
*I **hope** you have a good holiday.*
*She **hopes** her students will get a high grade in their exams.*

Note: We use *hope* + present/future tense with a future meaning, especially when the subject of the two clauses is different, i.e. *I* and *you* in *I hope you have a good holiday*. We often use *hope* + infinitive when there is only one subject to the sentence:
*He **hopes to go** into politics in the future.* (He hopes he'll become a politician in the future.)

We can use *hope* when we want something to be true about the past, but we don't know if it is true:
*I **hope** you had a good flight.* (But I don't know if you had a good flight.)

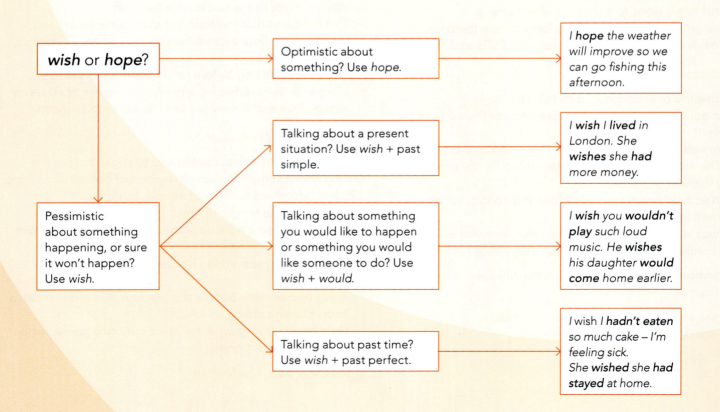

Word formation

Forming personal nouns

You can form personal nouns (nouns which describe people who do particular activities) by adding:
- *-er, -or, -ant, -ee* to a verb, e.g. *entertain – entertain**er**, operate – operat**or**, inhabit – inhabit**ant**, refer – refer**ee***
- *-ist, -ian, -man/-woman/-person* to a noun, e.g. *motor – motor**ist**, electricity – electric**ian**, post – post**man***

Adding prefixes
Prefixes to give negative meanings

You can give some words the negative meaning by adding a prefix (e.g. *dis-* + *like* = *dislike*) to the beginning of a word. Here are some common prefixes which give a negative meaning:
- *dis-*: ***dis**courage*
- *in-*: ***in**experienced*
- *un-*: ***un**believable*

Before many words beginning with:
- 'l' we add the prefix *il-*: ***il**legal*
- 'm' and 'p' we add the prefix *im-*: ***im**patient*
- 'r' we add the prefix *ir-*: ***ir**responsible*

Other prefixes and their meanings:
- *mis-* usually means 'wrongly' or 'badly': ***mis**understand* (= understand wrongly or badly)
- *re-* usually means 'do again' and is often added to verbs: ***re**write* (= write again)
- *inter-* means 'between or among': ***inter**act*

Note: When you add a prefix to a word, the spelling of the original word does not change: *dis* + *satisfied* = *dis**satisfied***

Adding suffixes

You can form verbs, nouns, adjectives and adverbs from other related or base words by adding a suffix (e.g. *appear* + *-ance* = *appearance*) to the end of the word. There are no clear rules – each word and the words which can be formed from it must be learned individually.

➡ See also page 176: Spelling – spelling changes when adding prefixes and other suffixes

Some of the most common suffixes and their usual meanings are listed below.

EP verb ➡ noun

suffix	verb	noun
-ment	adjust	adjust**ment**
-ation/-ition/-tion/-sion	combine	combin**ation**
	define	defin**ition**
	create	crea**tion**
	divide	divi**sion**
-er/-or	publish	publish**er**
	survive	surviv**or**
-ance/-ence	guide	guid**ance**
	exist	exist**ence**
-ant	inhabit	inhabit**ant**
-al	approve	approv**al**
-ee	employ	employ**ee**

EP adjective ➡ noun

suffix	adjective	noun
-ance/-ence	relevant	relev**ance**
	patient	pati**ence**
-ness	friendly	friendli**ness**
-ity	popular	popular**ity**
	available	availab**ility**

EP noun ➡ adjective

suffix	noun	adjective
-y	boss	boss**y**
-ful	meaning	meaning**ful**
-ous	fury	furi**ous**
-less	hope	hope**less**
-al	emotion	emotion**al**
-ic	optimist	optimist**ic**
-ish	child	child**ish**

EP noun ➡ noun

suffix	noun	noun
-ism	critic	critic**ism**
-ist	motor	motor**ist**
-ship	partner	partner**ship**

EP adjective/noun → adjective/noun

suffix	adjective / noun	verb
-ify	simple class	simpl**ify** class**ify**
-ise/-ize	special critic	special**ise**/special**ize** critic**ise**/critic**ize**

EP verb → adjective

suffix	verb	adjective
-ed	educate	educat**ed**
-ing	mislead	mislead**ing**
-able/-ible	rely respond	reli**able** respons**ible**
-ent	confide	confid**ent**
-ive	compete	competit**ive**

EP adjective → adverb

Adverbs are almost always formed by adding -ly. If the adjective ends in -ic, you change it to an adverb by adding -ally.

suffix	adjective	adverb
-ly / -ally	simple organic	simp**ly** organic**ally**

Words which are often confused

👁 These words are often confused by candidates at Cambridge English: First for Schools.

Unit 4, Vocabulary, Exercise 1 (page 42)

food noun [U] something that people and animals eat, or plants absorb, to keep them alive: *baby food. There was lots of food and drink at the party.*

dish FOOD noun [C] food prepared in a particular way as part of a meal: *a chicken/vegetarian dish.*

meal FOOD noun [C] an occasion when food is eaten, or the food which is eaten on such an occasion: *I have my main meal at midday. You must come round for a meal sometime.*

Unit 6, Vocabulary, Exercise 1 (page 63)

fun or **funny**?

If something is **fun**, you enjoy doing it.
I really liked the skating – it was such fun.

1 If something is **funny**, it makes you laugh.
It's a very funny film.

2 If something is **funny**, it is strange, surprising, unexpected or difficult to explain or understand.
The washing machine is making a funny noise again.

possibility, occasion or **opportunity**?

A **possibility** is a chance that something may happen or be true. Possibility cannot be followed by an infinitive.
Is there a possibility of getting a job in your organisation?

An **occasion** is an event, or a time when something happens. Occasion does not mean 'chance' or 'opportunity'.
Birthdays are always special occasions.

An **opportunity** is a possibility of doing something, or a situation which gives you the possibility of doing something.
*The trip to Paris gave me an opportunity to speak French.
I have more opportunity to travel than my parents did.*

work or **job**?

Work is something you do to earn money. This noun is uncountable.
She enjoys her work in the hospital.

Job is used to talk about the particular type of work activity which you do. This noun is countable.
He's looking for a job in computer programming.

Unit 5, Vocabulary, Exercise 3 (page 54)

assist verb [I or T] *formal*: to help: *You will be expected to assist the editor with the selection of illustrations for the book.*

attend BE PRESENT verb [I or T] *slightly formal*: to go to an event, place, etc.: *The meeting is on the fifth and we're hoping everyone will attend.*

get to know sb/sth: to spend time with somebody or something so that you gradually learn more about them: *The first couple of meetings are for the doctor and patient to get to know each other.*

join BECOME A MEMBER verb [I or T]: to become a member of an organisation: *I felt so unfit after Christmas that I decided to join a gym.*

take part: to be involved in an activity with other people: *She doesn't usually take part in any of the class activities.*

know or **find out**?

If you **know** something, you already have the information.
Andy knows what time the train leaves.

If you **find** something **out**, you learn new information for the first time.
I'll ring the station to find out what time the train leaves.

learn, teach or **study**?

To **learn** is to get new knowledge or skills.
I want to learn how to drive.

When you **teach** someone, you give them new knowledge or skills.
My dad taught me how to drive.

When you **study**, you go to classes, read books, etc. to try to understand new ideas and facts.
He is studying biology at university.

Unit 7, Vocabulary, Exercise 2 (page 80)

look, **see** or **watch**?

See means to notice people and things with your eyes.
She saw a big spider and screamed.

Look (**at**) is used when you are trying to see something or someone. If **look** is followed by an object, you must use a preposition. The usual preposition is **at**.
I've looked everywhere, but can't find my keys.
I looked at the map to find the road.

Watch means to look at something for a period of time, usually something which moves or changes.
He watched television all evening.

listen, **listen to** or **hear**?
Use **hear** when you want to say that sounds, music, etc. come to your ears. You can hear something without wanting to.
I could hear his music through the wall.

Use **listen** to say that you pay attention to sounds or try to hear something.
The audience listened carefully.

Use **listen to** when you want to say what it is that you are trying to hear.
The audience listened to the speaker.

Unit 8, Vocabulary, Exercise 6 (page 87)

acting *noun* [U] the job of performing in films or plays:
He wants to get into acting.

audience *group noun* [C] the group of people gathered in one place to watch or listen to a play, film, someone speaking, etc., or the (number of) people watching or listening to a particular television or radio programme, or reading a particular book

performance *noun* [C] the action of entertaining other people by dancing, singing, acting or playing music

play *noun* [C] a piece of writing that is intended to be acted in a theatre or on radio or television

(the) public *noun* [U + singular or plural verb] all ordinary people

scene *noun* [C] a part of a play or film in which the action stays in one place for a continuous period of time

spectator *noun* [C] a person who watches an activity, especially a sports event, without taking part

stage *noun* [C] the area in a theatre which is often raised above ground level and on which actors or entertainers perform

Unit 9, Vocabulary, Exercise 4 (page 98)

stay *verb* to continue doing something, or to continue to be in a particular state:
He's decided not to stay in teaching.
The shops stay open until nine o'clock.

spend *verb* to use time doing something or being somewhere:
My sister always spends ages in the bathroom.

pass *verb* If you **pass** time, you do something to stop yourself being bored during that period:
The visitors pass their days swimming, windsurfing and playing volleyball.

make *verb* (+ *noun/adjective*) to cause to be, to become or to appear as:
It's the good weather that makes Spain such a popular tourist destination.
Don't stand over me all the time – it makes me nervous.

cause *verb* to make something happen, especially something bad:
The difficult driving conditions caused several accidents.

Some common collocations with **cause**: *cause trouble, cause problems, cause damage, cause traffic jams, cause stress, cause pollution.*

Note, however, these collocations:
have an effect (on): *The good weather has had a beneficial effect on his health and happiness.*
have/make an impact (on): *The anti-smoking campaign had/made quite an impact on young people.*

Unit 10, Vocabulary, Exercise 1 (page 110)

arrive (+ *at*) *verb* to reach a place, especially at the end of a journey:
It was dark by the time we arrived at the station.
You **arrive at** a building or part of a building:
We arrived at the theatre just as the play was starting.
You **arrive in** a town, city or country:
When did you arrive in London?
You **arrive home/here/there**: *We arrived home yesterday.*

get (+ *to*) *verb* to reach or arrive at a place:
If you get to the hotel before us, just wait at reception.
You **get home/here/there:**
What time does he normally get home?

reach *verb* to arrive at a place, especially after spending a long time or a lot of effort travelling:
We finally reached the hotel just after midnight.
It is not normally followed by a preposition. It is not normally used with *here* or *there*.

Unit 12, Vocabulary, Exercise 2 (page 129)

prevent *verb* to stop something from happening or someone from doing something:
Label your suitcases to prevent confusion.

avoid *verb* to stay away from someone or something:
We left early to avoid the traffic.

protect *verb* to keep someone or something safe from injury, damage or loss:
It's important to protect your skin from the harmful effects of the sun.

check *verb* to make certain that something or someone is correct, safe or suitable by examining it or them quickly:
You should always check your oil, water and tyres before taking your car on a long trip.
After I'd finished the exam, I checked my answers for mistakes.

supervise *verb* to watch a person or activity to make certain that everything is done correctly, safely, etc.:
The UN is supervising the distribution of aid by local agencies in the disaster area.

control *verb* to order, limit, instruct or rule something, or someone's actions or behaviour:
If you can't control your dog, put it on a lead!
The temperature is controlled by a thermostat.

keep an eye on to watch or look after something or someone:
Will you keep your eye on my suitcase while I go to get the tickets?

Unit 13, Vocabulary, Exercise 2 (page 142)

space EMPTY PLACE *noun* [C or U] an empty area which is available to be used:
Is there any space for my clothes in that cupboard?

place AREA *noun* [C] an area, town, building, etc.:
Her garden was a cool, pleasant place to sit.
[U] a suitable area, building, situation or occasion:
University is a great place for making new friends.

room SPACE *noun* [C or U] the amount of space that someone or something needs:
That sofa would take up too much room in the flat.

area PLACE *noun* [C or U] a particular part of a place, piece of land or country:
All areas of the country will have some rain tonight.

location POSITION *noun* [C or U] SLIGHTLY FORMAL a place or position:
The hotel is in a lovely location overlooking the lake.
A map showing the location of the property will be sent to you.

square SHAPE *noun* [C] an area of approximately square-shaped land in a city or a town, often including the buildings that surround it:
A band were playing in the town square.

Writing reference

What to expect in the exam

The Writing paper is Paper 2. It lasts 1 hour and 20 minutes. You do two tasks.

- In Part 1, there is one task (an essay) which you must do.
- In Part 2, you choose one of three tasks.

Part 1: Essays

You write an essay. The purpose of an essay is for you to discuss a subject, express your opinion and give reasons for your opinion.
You are given an essay title and some notes.

- You must write an essay answering the essay question and using all the notes. The task will tell you: *In your English class, you have been talking about / discussing … Now your English teacher has asked you to write an essay.*

The notes outline three areas you must cover. The final note will always be your own idea.

- Your essay must be between 140 and 190 words.

The title will ask you to write one of **two** types of essay:
1. An essay in which you are asked to discuss a statement and give your opinion, e.g. *School holidays should be shorter. Do you agree?*
2. An essay in which you are asked to discuss which of two things is better, e.g. *Is it better for students to study subjects they really enjoy or subjects which will be useful when they leave school?*

You should:
- cover the two points you are given in the notes as well as your own idea in the third point
- organise your answer in a logical way using paragraphs and linking sentences and paragraphs appropriately
- express your opinion clearly on the subject of the essay
- give reasons and examples to support your ideas
- use a style appropriate for the situation (this should be quite formal, as it is an essay for your teacher)
- write grammatically correct sentences
- use accurate spelling and punctuation.

You have 40 minutes to do this part (the Writing paper lasts 1 hour 20 minutes, so if you spend more time on this part, you will have less time for the other part).

You studied and practised writing essays for Part 1 in Units 1, 5, 8, 11 and 14.

How to do Part 1

1. Read the task very carefully.
2. Underline the parts of the task you need to write about. You'll lose marks if you don't discuss everything.
3. Think about what your opinion really is. Why do you think this?
4. Make notes about all the things you've underlined.
5. Now think about putting your notes in a good order to make a plan. How many paragraphs do you need? What will go in each paragraph? Don't forget your introduction and conclusion (see Units 5 and 11).
6. Before you start to write check that your plan covers all three points in the question.
7. Keep checking your plan as you write.
8. Make your points clearly and explain your opinions.
9. When you've finished, read your answer carefully. Look for mistakes and correct them.
    Make sure you know what 140–190 words of your writing looks like on a page so you don't waste time counting words in the test. You need all the time for writing, not counting words.
10. Think carefully about why you are writing and who you are writing for. (You will be given a context, a target reader and a purpose for writing.)

Note:
You'll lose marks
- if you haven't written enough because you probably haven't answered the question
- if you've written too much because if you write a lot of words very quickly you'll make mistakes. Also, the examiner will stop reading after about 200 words and she may not read important things you've written.

Writing reference

Exercise 1

1. Read this writing task, which asks you to discuss an opinion, and <u>underline</u> the areas you must deal with.
2. Decide what your position or opinion is and why.
3. Think how you can cover notes 1 and 2 to support your position/opinion.
4. Think what your own idea is and how you can use this to support your position/opinion.

In your English class, you have been talking about the best age to leave school.
Now your English teacher has asked you to write an essay.
Write an essay using **all** the notes and give reasons for your point of view.

Essay question
All young people should stay at school until they're 18. Do you agree?

Notes
Write about:
1. why it's good to study at school
2. why some people don't like school
3. .... *(your own idea)*

Write your **essay**.

Exercise 2
Read the essay in the next column and complete this plan for it.

Para. 1: Introduction: the situation now + ...
Para. 2: Why stay at school:
1st reason ....
2nd reason ....
Para. 3: Why leave school:
1st reason ....
2nd reason ....
Para. 4: My own idea: .... + solution: ....
Para. 5: My opinion .... + reason(s) ....

Write a brief introductory paragraph where you:
- *explain the present situation*
- *explain your position/ opinion.*

An essay for your teacher has quite a formal style, so don't use contractions.

Use linking words and phrases to help your readers follow the ideas.

In my country people are allowed to leave school at the age of 16. However, I believe it would be better if they stayed at school until they are 18.

There are two good reasons for encouraging all young peole to stay at school. Firstly, it is really important these days to study hard. If students leave school before the age of 16, they may not have good qualifications. Students need these if they intend to study at college or for getting jobs.

On the other hand, many students would like to leave school at 16. This is because they find school difficult or they do not enjoy studying. They would prefer to be working and earning money.

A further point is that if students are not happy to be at school they can make things difficult for other students who do want to study. This can prevent good students from working hard and doing well. Therefore, many people think that after the age of 16 they should study practical subjects that interest them or leave school and find a job.

In conclusion, I believe it is a mistake for people to leave school too soon, because they will miss opportunities and may regret this in the future.

Exercise 3
Read this writing task and <u>underline</u> the areas you must write about.

In your English class, you have been talking about going on holiday.
Now your English teacher has asked you to write an essay. Write an essay using **all** the notes and give reasons for your point of view.

Essay question
Is it better to visit places in your own country or a foreign country when you go on holiday?

Notes
Write about:
1. advantages of holidays in your country
2. why people visit other countries
3. .... *(your own idea)*

Write your **essay**.

Exercise 4

Read this essay. It shows a different way of organising an essay from the sample answer in Exercise 2. How is this essay organised differently?

> There are strong arguments in favour of both staying in your own country and travelling abroad. I personally think that people should do both.
>
> There are several reasons for staying in your own country. Firstly, I think it's important to know, enjoy and feel proud of your country and there is usually a lot which is fascinating about its history and culture, which is important to learn and experience. Secondly, it's easier to get to places in your country. You don't have to travel long distances by plane or boat. Finally, because you speak the language, you will avoid many of the problems you might have when travelling abroad.
>
> On the other hand, when you go abroad, you can learn from the way other people live. If you choose the right destination you can have wonderful new experiences, try different food and see sights you've only seen on television or in books. Finally, it gives you an opportunity to learn and practise other languages, which is good for your education.
>
> For these reasons, I think that people should travel abroad from time to time, but also spend time visiting their own country to appreciate what is good and interesting in both.

You don't have to choose one option or the other if you think both have advantages.

It helps the reader if you have a short sentence or phrase at the beginning of the paragraph stating the topic.

Use a variety of grammatical structures, e.g. conditionals and relative clauses.

Introducing a personal opinion
- In my opinion, …
- I think …
- I feel …
- I believe …
- From my point of view, …

Introducing other people's opinions (often ones you don't agree with)
- Some people think/say …
- Many people argue that …
- It is sometimes/often argued/suggested/said that …

Putting your ideas in order
- There are two good reasons for …
- On the other hand, there are a number of reasons against …
- Firstly … / Secondly … / Finally …
- Also … / Furthermore … / What is more …

Giving reasons for your point of view
- … because/since …
- Because of this, …
- For this reason, …
- That is why …
- One of the main reasons is that …

Expressing results
- As a result/consequence, …

Expressing consequences
- In consequence, …
- Consequently, …
- … which means that …

Introducing your conclusion
- In conclusion, …
- To conclude, / sum up, / summarise, …

Ways of expressing contrasts
- However, …
- On the one hand, … On the other hand, …

➡ page 168 Language reference: Linking words for contrast

Part 2

In Part 2, you must choose from one of four questions.

- The tasks you choose from will be: an article, an email/letter, a review or a story. It is important to know how to write all of these things so you can make the best choice in the exam.
- You must answer the task with your own ideas.
- You must write between 140 and 190 words.

This part tests your ability to:
- deal with the type of task you have chosen
- use the correct style for the task you have chosen
- organise and plan your writing
- express opinions, describe, explain, make recommendations, make suggestions, etc.
- use a range of vocabulary and grammatical structures.

How to do Part 2

1. Quickly read the questions and choose the task you think you can do best. Don't spend too long deciding.
2. Read the task you choose carefully and underline:
   - who will read what you write
   - the points you must deal with
   - anything else you think is important.
3. Decide if you need a formal or informal style.
4. Think of ideas you can use to deal with the question and note them down while you're thinking.
5. Decide which ideas are the most useful and write a plan. When writing your plan, decide how many paragraphs you need and what to say in each paragraph.
6. Think of useful vocabulary you can include in your answer and note it down in your plan.
7. Write your answer following your plan.
8. When you have finished, read your answer carefully. Check you have written between 140 and 190 words and correct any mistakes you find.

Emails and letters

You studied and practised writing an email/letter in Units 6 and 12.

Exercise 1

Read the writing task below and underline:
1. who the reader(s) will be
2. what points you must deal with
3. anything else you think is important.

You have received this letter from an English friend, Pat. Read this part of the letter.

> I'm doing a project on family life in different countries and I'd like to know what a typical family is like in your country and what families do together when they have free time.

Write your **letter**.

Exercise 2

Read Teresa's answer below.
1. What details does she give of a typical family in Spain?
2. What do families do together in their free time in Spain?

Dear Pat,

Thanks for your letter asking for information. In Spain family life is very important. We get together in big family groups with our grandparents and cousins. Everyone knows each other and we gather in one house or another to have a chat.

Spain is a really hot country and as a consequence many people come home from work during the afternoon to escape from the heat of the day and have a long lunch with their families. They sometimes sleep too and this afternoon sleep is called a siesta.

At weekends in summer, people often walk outside together with their families. Families living in big cities like Barcelona often go to street celebrations together to watch large floats going past full of people wearing traditional costumes.

However, family life is changing. More and more young people are leaving their families to find work in other cities.

I hope that answers your questions. Please write to me if you need any more information. I'd love to see your finished project and read what you say about family life in other countries too.

Love,
Teresa

Write a natural introduction and conclusion.

Use linking words and phrases, e.g. As a result, However, As a consequence ...

Starting and finishing emails and letters

You know the person well

	emails	letters
start with	Dear/Hello/Hi + name: Hi Magda, **Hello** Francesco	Dear Barbara,
finish with	Best wishes, / All the best,	Best wishes, / Love, / With love,

You don't know the person well

	emails	letters
start with	Dear + first name: Dear Barbara Dear + surname: Dear Mr Hatton (if you don't feel comfortable using their first name)	Dear Mr Hatton, (if you know the person's name) Dear Sir or Madam, (if you don't know the person's name)
finish with	Best wishes, / Kind regards,	Yours sincerely, Yours, (if you know the person's name) Yours faithfully, (if you don't know the person's name)

Starting the first paragraph of a letter or email
- Thanks for your email …
- Thank you for your letter about …
- I am writing to request information about / complain about / apologise for / explain, etc.

Referring to something in a letter or email which you're replying to
- Your project on the history of Italy sounds good.
- As for the books you need, …
- With reference to the book you asked about, …
- You mentioned/asked about visiting …

Making suggestions
- How about + verb + -ing:
How about going to the cinema on Friday evening?
- What about + verb + -ing:
What about having a meal in a restaurant afterwards?
- It might also be a good idea to …:
It might also be a good idea to visit the museum.
- Can I suggest that …?:
Can I suggest that you give your talk on 5th November?
- I suggest + verb + -ing:
I suggest going to the museum at the end of the week.

Asking for information
- Could you tell me …
- I would / I'd like to know if …
- I would / I'd like information on …
- Do you know if/whether/when/what, etc.

Complaining
- I'm not very happy about + noun/verb + -ing:
I'm not very happy about the price. I'm not very happy about paying so much.
- I would like to complain about + noun/verb + -ing:
I would like to complain about the books you sent me.
I would like to complain about teachers giving students too much homework.
- I am writing to complain about + noun/verb + -ing:
I am writing to complain about the meal I had at your restaurant last week.

Apologising
- Sorry about + noun / verb + -ing
(informal): *Sorry about being* late for the concert.
- I would like to apologise for + noun / verb + -ing:
I would like to apologise for arriving late for the concert.

Inviting
- How about …?:
How about coming windsurfing with me next weekend?
- Would you like to …?:
Would you like to come to my party?
- I would like to invite you to … + noun/infinitive:
I would like to invite you to visit our town next summer.
I would like to invite you to my house next weekend.

Giving advice
- You should …
- If I were you, I would / I'd …
- It would be a good idea to … + infinitive

Stories

You studied and practised writing stories in Units 3 and 9.

Exercise 1
Read this story writing task and answer the questions below.

> You have seen this announcement in an international magazine for schools.
>
> We are looking for stories for our new English-language magazine for teenagers.
>
> Your story must begin with this sentence:
>
> *Sally looked through the window and watched her parents putting suitcases into the car.*
>
> Your story must include:
> - a photograph
> - a meeting

1. Do you think you should use formal or informal language for the story?
2. Read Christine's story on the right.
   - Which parts of the story are formal?
   - Which parts are informal?
   - Does the story answer the question completely?

Sally looked through the window and watched her parents putting suitcases into the car. Next to the car in the busy street, was a huge van full of boxes. Their life had been packed up inside this van and the boxes were off with them to a new life somewhere else. Sally looked at a photo which was still stuck to the wall of her empty bedroom. All her friends were waving at her. 'Good luck! Have a great life!' read the message underneath it.

During the long journey which took her away from everything she knew, Sally was silent. Finally, the car pulled up outside a pretty cottage in a tiny village. What on earth would she do here?

Sally sat in her new bedroom and looked out at a different scene: a park, a few trees, and … a girl about her age was walking up the path towards the cottage. The doorbell rang. Sally felt shy but she answered it.

'Hi, I'm Ellen – I live next door. We're going to be neighbours! Do you want to come over?'

The girl smiled at Sally and Sally smiled back. Maybe life would be just fine!

Writing reference

> Try to use a range of tenses – don't just use the past simple.

> Use adjectives to make your story more interesting.

> You can use direct speech to bring your characters to life – but don't do this too much.

> Use some shorter sentences. They can be effective too.

> **Think about how you lay out your story**
> Notice the story is laid out in paragraphs – when the story moves, for example, from the bedroom to the journey, Christine uses a new paragraph.

Reviews

You studied and practised writing reviews in Units 4 and 10.

Exercise 1
Read the writing task below.
1 Underline the points you must deal with.
2 Underline anything else you think is important.
3 Who will the reader(s) be, and where will your answer appear?

You see this announcement in your school's English-language magazine.

> Have you seen a film or read a book recently that you think everyone would enjoy? We want to know about it! Write a review of the film or book saying what it's about and why we would all enjoy it.

Write your **review**.

Set texts

You saw possible approaches to the set text in Unit 5.

It is possible to answer a question in Part 2 about a book. Your teacher will tell you which books you can answer questions about (there are two books to choose from). Your teacher may decide to study one of these books with the class. If you decide to answer a question about a set text:

- Make sure you read the correct version of the text because this has been chosen to be suitable for your level of English.
- It's a good idea to find out if there is a film of the book you are studying because it is fine to answer questions about the film version, or even to compare the two.
- It's important to know the story and characters really well and to study vocabulary to help you answer questions.
- You should not choose the question about the book unless you feel you know the book very well and you have good ideas about how to answer the question.

Exercise 2
Read Franz's review below. Which paragraphs say:
1 what the book is about?
2 why we would all enjoy it?

> **'The Time Traveler's Wife' by Audrey Niffenegger**
>
> This is an original and moving love story told from the point of view of the two main characters, Henry and Clare. Henry is a librarian who has a genetic problem which causes him to move backwards and forwards in time. Without warning, he disappears leaving everything behind and arrives at another time in his life. He can't control when or where he's going.
>
> When he travels, he often meets the same girl, Clare, at different times in her life. Eventually they fall in love even though sometimes when they meet he is much older than her and at other times they are the same age.
>
> I think everyone will enjoy this unusual story because it combines a little science fiction with a wonderful romantic story. Henry's problem causes situations which are funny, sometimes frightening, usually awkward and often very strange. The novel is fascinating because it makes you think about the nature of time. At the same time, you see how the characters and their relationships change during their lives but how their love grows stronger.

- The idea in Part 2 is to show your range of grammar, expressions and vocabulary. Choose whichever Part 2 question you think will best enable you to do this. It might be the set book question, or it might be one of the other questions. Read the questions through carefully before you decide.

Remember reading a set book is not just about taking the test. It gives you the opportunity to enjoy reading English and to discuss ideas with friends. It also gives you a larger choice of questions in Part 2 of the test.

Give your review a title.

Mention:
- the type of book/film
- the characters
- some of the story
- what makes the book/film different.

Use plenty of adjectives to describe:
- the book/film
- how you feel about it.

Ways of praising
- I think everyone will enjoy this ... (book/film/restaurant, etc.) because ...
  The ... (book/film/restaurant, etc.) is fascinating/wonderful/marvellous because ...
- This ... (book/film/restaurant, etc.) is really worth (reading/seeing/visiting, etc.) because ...

Articles

You studied and practised writing articles in Units 2, 7 and 13.

Exercise 1

Read this writing task.

> You see the following announcement on your college noticeboard.
>
> **My Best Friend**
>
> Tell us about your best friend for the college newspaper. We want to know:
> - how you met this person
> - why he or she is so special to you.
>
> We will publish the most interesting articles next week.
>
> Write your **article**.

Match the beginnings (1–9) and endings (a–i) of these sentences to make advice about how to write articles.

1 Before writing, identify
2 You can identify the readers by
3 Decide what style
4 Write things you think your readers
5 Before writing the article,
6 In your plan, decide what you will put
7 Make sure that the plan
8 Write the article following
9 While you are writing, think about

a answers the question.
b in each paragraph.
c make a plan.
d looking at the type of newspaper or magazine you are writing for.
e is suitable for your readers.
f the effect on your readers.
g who will read the article.
h will find interesting.
i your plan.

Exercise 2

Read Luis's article below and match the notes for his plan (a–d) with the paragraph numbers.

Para. 1 ....
Para. 2 ....
Para. 3 ....
Para. 4 ....

a How we became friends – same table at school, playground, visit each other's houses
b My first impressions of Thea – contrast with other kids
c When I met Thea – on school bus
d Why so special – share secrets, help each other, spend time together, sit together

> An article should have a title.

> Notice the adverbs. You will get higher marks if you use a range of vocabulary.

> Instead of using the same word again, use different words with similar meanings, e.g. *shy – timidly*.

> Good to have a small joke at the end!

An inseparable friend

Thea has been my best friend from that day when, aged seven, I climbed onto the school bus to go to my new primary school.

I wandered nervously down the bus, which was full of noisy kids shouting and laughing excitedly, and found a place beside a quiet girl with fair hair and friendly green eyes.

We were both very shy, so we didn't talk much to each other on the way to school, although we smiled at each other timidly. And when we went into class we naturally sat down together at the same table. Gradually we got to know each other, we played together in the playground, we visited each other's houses and our parents soon became firm friends as well.

We still share each other's secrets and we have complete confidence in each other. When either of us has a problem, the other is always ready to help. We have so much in common that we spend most of our free time together. We've even been on holiday together sometimes. And we still share the same table at school ten years later!

Speaking reference

What to expect in the exam

The Speaking paper is Paper 4.
- It lasts approximately 14 minutes.
- You do the Speaking paper in pairs. (Certain test centres may allow you to take the test with a friend, otherwise you will be partnered with someone you don't know.)
- There are two examiners in the room; one gives you instructions and asks you questions, the other listens but does not speak.
- You may do the Speaking paper on a different day from the other parts of the exam.
- The Speaking paper has four parts.

How to do Part 1

1 **Don't** prepare detailed answers before you go to the exam and **don't** memorise answers to possible questions: examiners will recognise this.
2 Do make sure that you know the vocabulary you need to talk about your studies, your job, your family, your town and your free-time activities.
3 Listen to the examiner's questions carefully.
4 Look confidently at the examiner and perhaps smile a little when you answer the questions.
5 Don't give one-word answers. Try to give a reason as well.
6 Be ready to offer extra information about yourself and try to speak fluently and confidently.

1 Read the advice and the example questions (1–9) below. Then match the answers (a–i) with the questions.

Advice and example questions

1 Don't just answer the question – give some extra details if you can.
   Question: *Where are you from?* ...b....
2 You can offer several ideas or answers to the same question.
   Question: *What do young people do in their free time in your town?* ....
3 Avoid giving simple Yes/No answers which end the conversation.
   Question: *Do you like doing sports?* ....
4 A question which starts, 'Tell us a little about …' gives you an opportunity to say quite a lot. Two or three sentences is a good amount.
   Question: *Tell us a little about your family.* ....
5 When you speak about things you like or enjoy, sound enthusiastic. Be ready to use past tenses and time adverbs.
   Question: *Tell us about something you really enjoyed doing recently.* ....
6 Be ready to talk about the future and use different tenses to do so.
   Question: *What are you looking forward to doing in the next school holidays?* ....
7 If you don't understand or don't hear the question, ask the examiner to repeat it.
   Question: *Which do you prefer: reading books or watching TV?* ....
8 When appropriate, use a range of grammar and vocabulary. The examiners want to hear how well you can speak English.
   Question: *Do you enjoy travelling?* ....
9 When appropriate, give reasons for your answers.
   Question: *Tell me about a place you'd like to visit.* ....

Good answers

a I'd really like to visit Venice. I've seen photos of it and I've read about it, but it must be an amazing place to actually be in and explore. I'd really like to go there at carnival time because it looks such a colourful festival.
b I'm from Ostrava. It's a large industrial town in the east of the Czech Republic, not far from the Polish border. It's a good place to live, especially in spring and summer.
c Yes, I do, especially ones which are competitive like basketball or tennis, because I like to win. Actually, I play in my school basketball team and at the moment we're at the top of our regional league.
d Sorry, could you say that again, please?

e They go to the cinema, they go out with friends, they go to parties. You know, basically, they do the normal things which I think young people do everywhere.

f Well, two weeks ago we had what in England I think is called a half-term holiday, so I went skiing with my class in the mountains. It was great because we stayed in a hostel with other young people, and the weather and the snow were excellent.

g Well, next summer I'm going to go to Crete with my family. I'm really looking forward to it because my parents told me the weather's always hot and there are lots of lovely beaches too. We're going to stay in a big hotel with two pools and there's entertainment in the evenings, so it should be really good.

h Well, there's just my mother, my father and myself, so I'm an only child. Both my parents have full-time jobs: my mother's a lawyer and my father manages a restaurant.

i Yes, I love it. I really love visiting new and unusual places, meeting new people and trying to understand them and their cultures. But I don't get the chance to travel to other countries very often, so I'm hoping I'll do it more when I'm older.

Part 2

In Part 2, you work alone.
- The examiner gives you two photos on the same topic to speak about.
- He/She asks you to speak for one minute, compare the photos and answer a question about the topic of the two photos.
- The question is also printed above the photos.
- When your partner speaks about his/her photos, you should listen carefully. After your partner has finished, the examiner asks you a short question about the topic of your partner's photos.

Part 2 takes four minutes in total including the examiner's instructions, each candidate's one-minute answer and the short questions.

You studied and practised Part 2 in Units 2, 6, 9, 11 and 13.

How to do Part 2

1 Talk about what the people are doing in each photo, where they are and why. Don't try to describe them in detail.

2 Firstly, compare the photos. Say what's happening in each photograph and how the photos are similar and how they're different. Then look at the question. Answer the question for each photograph.

3 Use your imagination when you're talking about your photographs. Why are the people eating in a restaurant? Maybe it's someone's birthday? Have they been to the restaurant before? There is no 'right answer' and it's good to use your imagination to help you to keep talking for the full minute. (*She seems to be …*, *He might be …* – see **Speculating** on page 196 and in Unit 9.)

4 When you compare the photos, you can say what is similar about them as well as what is different. Give a balanced answer, so: – spend about the same amount of time on each photo – spend some time comparing the photos, but perhaps more time answering the question (see Unit 13).

5 Remember to give reasons for your answers.

6 Use some of the strategies you have practised in this book. Instead of talking about one photo and then the other, you could compare both of them at the same time (see Unit 6).

7 Keep speaking for a full minute. You'll know when to stop because the examiner will say, 'Thank you'.

8 When it's your partner's turn to talk about the photos, listen but don't say anything yourself. The examiner will ask you a question after your partner has spoken. You should answer by giving a brief reason in one or two sentences.

I'd like you to compare photographs, and say what you think is enjoyable about communicating in these ways.

Comparing the photos
- In the first photo, there's a girl who looks as if she's chatting on the Internet or sending an email, **whereas/while** in the second photo a group of teenagers are sitting having a meal and talking together.
- I think that the girl in the first photo is really enjoying keeping in touch with her friends all over the world. The second photo shows a group of friends – they're having a meal together and laughing at each other's news. Maybe they haven't seen each other for a long time and have lots to talk about. They're enjoying seeing each other face to face and joking together
- I think the girl might be talking to a friend about school work, which is always more fun than doing school work on your own, or she may be gossiping about her teachers. **On the other hand**, the group of friends are probably talking about what they've been doing at school all week or maybe planning what they're going to do together at the weekend.
- **In both photos,** the people are probably communicating with friends, and that's usually fun. **However, in the first photo,** the girl may feel a little distant from her friends, which is a pity, **whereas in the second photo** the friends clearly have a close, warm relationship.

What is enjoyable about communicating in these ways?

Referring to the photos
- In the first photo, a girl is …
- In the second photo, there are three young people who are …
- The first photo shows …

Speculating
- In the first photo, I can see a girl who **looks as if** she's chatting on the Internet whereas/while in the second photo a group of teenagers are eating together and gossiping.
- While the girl seems to be concentrating hard, **perhaps** because she's writing, the teenagers **seem** to be relaxed and enjoying themselves. I think this is because they're together and can see each other.
- **I think** the girl **might** be talking to a friend about school work or friends. On the other hand, the teenagers are probably joking or talking about things they have done together.

➡ page 168 Language reference: *look, seem* and *appear*

➡ page 170 Language reference: Modal verbs – expressing certainty and possibility

Part 3

In Part 3, you work with the other candidate.

This part of the Speaking paper is divided into two parts.

In the first part, which takes two minutes:
- The examiner gives you a page with a question and five prompts.
- You have 15 seconds to look at the questions and options before you start speaking.
- You should discuss each of the options in turn.

In the second part, the examiner will ask you another question to summarise your thoughts, for example, by choosing the option that you think is best and saying why. You have one minute for this.

You studied and practised Part 3 in Units 3, 7, 12 and 14.

How to do Part 3

For the first part:
1. Listen carefully to the question, which is also printed next to the options to help you. It will be in a mind map opposite, with the question in the middle and ideas to help you around it.
2. You have 15 seconds to think about the task before you start speaking:
   Think about:
   - the options and how you can express them in your own words and discuss their relative merits in relation to the question
   - how you can start the discussion, perhaps with a suggestion and a reason for your idea.
3. To start the conversation, you can give a brief opinion about one of the options or make a suggestion and ask your partner what he/she thinks.
4. When you discuss, deal with each option in turn. Talk to your partner and share your ideas about one option before going on to the next.
5. When your partner says something, react to his/her ideas. Listen carefully to what he/she is saying. Try to make the discussion like a natural conversation. Don't try to dominate the conversation.
6. Keep the discussion moving by saying things like *What about this option? What do you think?* or *Shall we move on to the next option?*
7. Don't spend too long talking about one particular option.
8. Continue your discussion until the examiner says, 'Thank you'.
9. Don't worry if you don't have time to talk about all the options – you won't lose marks for this.

For the second part:
1. Don't discuss each option again, but just the ones you need in order to summarise your opinions.
2. Try to reach a decision, but remember that you don't have to.
3. Remember you should discuss the question for a minute, so if you agree with your partner's first idea, say so, but suggest discussing other options (see Unit 3).
4. Continue your discussion until the examiner says, 'Thank you'.

Example task: First part

 I'd like you to imagine that a teacher is thinking about the advantages and disadvantages of taking students on a school trip. Here are some things the teacher is thinking about, and a question for you to discuss. You now have some time to look at the task.

Example task: Second part

 Now you have a minute to decide what would be a really good school trip.

Involving your partner
- What do you think?
- Do you agree?
- What about (travelling with a lot of students)? What do you think?
- I think … What about you?

Keeping the discussion moving
- What about (the cost of going on school trips? Should students pay?) What do you think?
- Let's move on to the next option.
- Shall we move on to the next option?

Part 4

In Part 4, you continue to work together.
- The examiner asks you questions which are linked to the Part 3 topic.
- The examiner may ask you to answer questions on your own or may ask you to discuss questions with your partner. Most examiners will ask some questions to one candidate and then go on to ask questions which both candidates discuss together towards the end of the test.
- You may be asked the same question as your partner, if you agree with your partner's answer, or a completely different question.

Part 4 lasts about four minutes.
You studied and practised Part 4 in Units 4, 8, 12 and 14.

How to do Part 4

1. Listen carefully to the questions. If you don't understand a question, don't feel afraid to ask the examiner to repeat (*Sorry could you say that again, please?*). You won't lose any marks if you ask the examiner to repeat a question.
2. The questions will ask you for your opinions on general topics. There are no right or wrong answers. Give your opinions.
3. Answer the questions giving a reason or an explanation. You can give examples from your own experience to explain what you think.
4. Listen carefully to what your partner says, because you may be asked to give your opinion on what he/she has said.
5. If you don't know the answer to a question, don't just say *I don't know*. Say *I don't know a lot about this subject, but I think …* and then give some ideas.

Example questions
- Some people think school trips are a waste of time. What do you think?
- What would be a good place for a school trip in the area where you live? (Why?)
- Some people say that school is just for learning and getting qualifications. Do you agree? (Why? / Why not?)
- Do you think it's true that the best way to learn is in a class with a teacher? (Why? / Why not?)
- What else can schools do to make school life interesting for students? (Why?)
- What do you think makes someone a good teacher? (Why?)

Introducing an opinion and giving a reason
- I think …
- Well, in my opinion, … because …
- I feel …
- I'm not sure. I think …
- No, I don't think so …

Introducing an explanation
- I mean …
- You see …

Giving an example
- For example …
- For instance …
- … such as …

Speaking in general
- In general, …
- Generally, …
- As a rule, …
- … tend to …

Answer key

> **Note**
> You can use contractions to answer the questions,
> e.g. *I am working.* → *I'm working.*
> *She has done it!* → *She's done it!*

1 A family affair

Listening Part 1

1 *Suggested underlining*
2 doing to the house   3 How often, do sporting activities, father   4 family celebrations, feel
5 sister, annoyed   6 tired   7 message, mother
8 chose, trumpet

2 1 A   2 B   3 C   4 A   5 A   6 B   7 C   8 C

▶ **CD 1 Track 02**

Presenter: One. You hear part of a conversation with a boy called Patrick.

Friend: Do you help much around the house then, Patrick?

Patrick: Not much. I make my bed and occasionally do the washing-up, but I'm studying pretty hard for my exams at the moment, so my mum ends up doing most of the housework while I get on with my studying. Even so, she still finds time to give me a hand with my studies from time to time. She used to be a maths teacher and she knows I'm getting a bit nervous about the maths exam. I suspect she finds explaining algebra and things quite fun, and actually she's pretty good at it, too.

Presenter: Two. You hear a girl called Tracey talking to a friend.

Friend: So, how often do you all do things together as a family then, Tracey?

Tracey: Oh, all the time, I mean at least once a week, at weekends. You see, we live in this really old house which we've been working on together. In fact, we've just finished doing up the kitchen. It's been great fun because we've all been doing it together. We made a lot of mess, of course, which we had to clear up, and now we're decorating it, so it's looking nicer and nicer. We had lots of really big arguments about the colour, but in the end, I got my way.

Presenter: Three. You hear a girl called Vicky taking part in a class discussion.

Teacher: Does anyone ever do sports with other people in their family? Yes, Vicky …

Vicky: Well, my dad's a fitness fanatic, so he's always running or cycling or doing something energetic. I do sporty things with him now and again, more often in the summer, though occasionally at other times of the year as well. He's always asking me to go out cycling with him, but I prefer watching music videos and things with my best friend when I don't have schoolwork to get on with, so recently I've been spending more time with her and not so much with my dad.

Presenter: Four. You hear a boy called Kostas talking about family celebrations.

Friend: I take it you don't enjoy family celebrations then, Kostas?

Kostas: Not much, to be honest. I just feel they go on for too long and I'd prefer to be out doing other things with my mates, not sitting around listening to my uncles and aunts and that. Everyone's always telling the same old jokes or singing the same old songs and I've heard them all millions of times, so I guess I've just lost interest. I try not to show it, but, you know, I just wait for things to end and then, when I get the chance, I go out with my friends. That's what I really like.

Presenter: Five. You hear a boy called Rajiv talking to his sister on the phone.

Lina: Hiya!

Rajiv: Are you still at Jasvinder's house?

Lina: Yeah, why? We're just playing some games.

Rajiv: Computer games? I've been looking for my laptop – you wouldn't have any idea what's happened to it, would you?

Lina: Oh, I've just borrowed it for the evening. Hope you don't mind.

Rajiv: Oh, honestly! You're always using my stuff without asking me, and I've got this really important homework project! Now what am I going to do?

Lina: Use Dad's computer instead. He won't mind.

Rajiv: Look, I can't do that – I've got everything saved on mine and you've just walked off with it.

199

Answer key: Unit 1

Presenter: Six. You hear a boy called Marco talking to a friend.

Friend: Hi, Marco. What's the matter? You look exhausted!

Marco: I am! You see, we went on this family outing yesterday. My mum said it'd be good for me to have a break from all my school work – she says I've been working too hard. Anyway, we went down to the seaside, which is quite a long way, as you know, and then my dad and I spent ages swimming and playing in the sea. Mum had to drive us home, we were both so worn out by the time we came out!

Presenter: Seven. You hear a girl called Samin leaving a telephone message for her mother.

Samin: Hi, Mum! It's Julia's birthday today. Anyway, she's having a party, and I've been with Susana and Clare to buy her a present. We got her a really nice bag, but it was a bit expensive. Anyway, the reason I'm phoning you's because she's invited us to spend the night at her place. Is that all right, Mum? It is Friday night, so I don't have to get up early tomorrow or anything. I'll give you a call when I want you to come and pick me up.

Presenter: Eight. You hear an interview with a young musician called Pau.

Interviewer: Pau, you play the trumpet in the town band. Why did you go for that particular instrument?

Pau: Well, I don't think I really had a choice. There've always been trumpeters in the band from my family, and my granddad gave me his when he stopped playing, so I think he'd have been shocked if I'd chosen something else. I quite like it, but I think I'd prefer the guitar because then I could play in a rock band instead. Perhaps I'll learn that as well – you don't have to just choose one instrument. You can play others as well.

3 2 How often **do** you all **do** things together as a family? 3 **Do you (ever) do/play** sports with other people in your family? 4 **Do** you enjoy family celebrations? 5 How **do** other members of the family annoy you? 6 **Do** you have / **Have** you **got** any family traditions?

Vocabulary
Phrasal verbs

1 2 f   3 d   4 b   5 e   6 a

2 2 worn out; clearing up   3 went on
4 pick up; do up

Reading and Use of English Part 6

1 usually positive: concerned, enthusiastic, hard-working, mature, organised, reasonable, responsible, self-confident, understanding
usually negative: aggressive, anxious, bad-tempered, critical, impatient, impolite, unreliable
could be either: sensitive, strict

2 concerned – unconcerned
enthusiastic – unenthusiastic
mature – immature
organised – disorganised
reasonable – unreasonable
responsible – irresponsible
sensitive – insensitive

3 Student's own answers. These may depend very much on local culture.

5 Para. 2: the relationship with your parents changes as you grow up
Para. 3: it's important to try and see both points of view
Para. 4: it's great if you can discuss things with parents reasonably
Para. 5: ways to approach a discussion with parents
Para. 6: it isn't an impossible situation

6 1 D   2 A   3 C   4 G   5 F   6 E
B is not needed.

Grammar
Present perfect simple and continuous

1 1 1 a, 2 b   2 1 b, 2 a   3 1 a, 2 b

2 2 has asked   3 have cleaned   4 has been playing
5 have passed   6 has only been living
7 have spent   8 have been cooking

3 2 have learned / have been learning
3 have fixed   4 have been playing
5 have been doing   6 have been   7 have been talking
8 have been dancing

Reading and Use of English Part 2

1 1 e   2 h   3 d   4 b   5 g   6 f   7 a   8 c

3 For pocket money, preparation for adult life, duty to parents, because it's fair, their parents make them

Answer key: Unit 2

4 1 as 2 at 3 do 4 their 5 There 6 to 7 not
8 rather

Vocabulary
Collocations with *make* and *do*

1 **make:** an appointment, an arrangement, the bed, a change, a choice, a decision, an effort, an excuse, friends, an impression, a mistake, money, a noise, a phone call, a plan, progress, a promise
do: an activity, business, the cleaning, a course, (an) exercise, a favour, homework, housework, a job, the shopping, (a) sport, work

2 1 do 2 make; do 3 make; make 4 made; making
5 do; make 6 doing; do

Speaking Part 1

1 1 *What do you like about the place where you live?* asks for a personal opinion; *Where are you from?* asks for personal information.
2 *Where are you from?* can be answered with a short phrase; *What do you like about the place where you live?* needs a longer answer.

2 *Suggested answer*
Irene: she answers in sentences, not single words; she gives some extra details.

▶ **CD 1 Track 03**

Examiner: So, Irene, where are you from?
Irene: I'm from Llanes. It's a small town on the north coast of Spain, which becomes quite a busy tourist resort in the summer.
Examiner: And what do you like about Llanes?
Irene: Well, it's a fairly quiet place in the winter, so it has quite a relaxed atmosphere, but it's got wonderful beaches nearby and it's surrounded by lovely countryside. Also, I've got lots of friends in the area, so I have a very active social life. And of course, most of my family and relations live nearby, too.
Examiner: And you, Peter, where are you from?
Peter: Bremen, in northern Germany.
Examiner: And what do you like about Bremen?
Peter: My friends, the shops, the sports centre …
Examiner: Do you come from a large family?

---

4 *It is:* a, d, e
It has: b, c, e, f, g, h, i, j, k, l

Pronunciation: word stress (1)

5.1 in<u>dus</u>trial, re<u>lax</u>ed, <u>at</u>mosphere, <u>won</u>derful, fa<u>cil</u>ities, his<u>tor</u>ic

5.2 ▶ **CD 1 Track 04**
See page 15.

Writing Part 1   An essay

1 *Suggested underlining*
Teenagers and young people, share housework equally with their parents, agree, has more time, better, own idea

4 Para. 1: e Para. 2: b Para. 3: c Para. 4: a
Para. 5: d

5 I believe, In my view, in my opinion, I think

6 1 Although 2 However 3 On the other hand
4 However 5 whereas

7 1 whereas 2 Although 3 However / On the other hand
4 Although 5 On the other hand / However
6 However / On the other hand

8 See sample in Exercise 3 in the Student's Book.

2 Leisure and pleasure

Listening Part 2

1 1 encourage 2 distract 3 concentrate 4 develop
5 solve 6 require 7 make 8 contribute 9 waste

3 *Suggested answers*
1 something you read or type of story 2 a job
3 something to do with games that he made with other students 4 a reason for working / something you can get from working 5 something which will help solve problems 6 qualities people have which are different from qualities he has 7 something one of his games has become 8 something that describes the information about the game 9 something large games need
10 a country or a city he travelled to

4 1 science fiction 2 computer programmer
3 (the) (Games) Creation Club 4 experience
5 experiments 6 skills and interests 7 film 8 detailed
9 (several years) 10 Japan

201

Answer key: Unit 2

▶ **CD 1 Track 05**

Mike: Hi! It's great to be visiting this school and talking to you. As you know, my name's Mike Selby and I'm a games developer. I'm here to tell you a bit about my work and how I got started. First of all, I think I can honestly say I have the coolest job in the world. I think I'm incredibly lucky to do what I love and get paid for it. Well, it'll be no surprise to you that when I was your age, I used to play computer games. I was also a huge fan of science fiction and used to read anything I could get my hands on. I spent hours reading and playing and I know my mum and dad hoped I'd grow out of it and become a bit more interested in school work at some stage.

Anyway, I never really expected to become a games developer, in fact my dream actually was to become a computer programmer. I mean, I thought I'd be good at developing software and things like that. And my parents would have approved, as in their view, it was a much safer choice. But games were my passion and while I was at school, I got together with a few of my friends and we set up something we called the 'Games Creation Club' – you know, we'd go through the process of having an idea, planning, sitting down and developing software and so on. At the time, it was the most exciting thing in my life, and I spent all my free time doing it. And then I had this opportunity which was even better. Word had got around that I was good at writing software, and a local company belonging to someone's dad offered me a summer job. Of course, I'd planned to spend the summer hanging out with my friends, but the chance to gain experience doing what I enjoyed was too good to miss. I worked much harder than I ever did at school and I loved every minute of it.

Games development is the most creative thing you can imagine. I love working on problems and I love carrying out experiments to work out how to deal with those problems. Also, it's a very rich environment and one thing which makes it so good is that I find myself working with colleagues whose skills and interests are completely different from mine. I think that it actually helps to have a good diverse range of people in the team and we all learn from each other. You probably have an image in your minds of a games developer sitting alone in front of a screen all day. In fact, it's an extremely social activity – we're always swapping ideas, playing games together, even going out to the cinema as a group and picking up ideas there. In fact, cinema is another of my passions and one of the biggest thrills for me was when one of my games, Dark Snake, was made into a film. Have any of you seen it? You have? Great, I hope you liked it! In the original game of Dark Snake, the players had to defend a medieval city that was being attacked by vicious reptiles. There were a lot of different characters, and there was a lot of detailed information about their adventures and life in the middle ages. Nowadays, I prefer to work on smaller games than that one, the reason being that those huge complex games take several years to make, and I don't want to spend so much time on things. I prefer a bit more variety.

I get to travel a lot as well, going to games conventions all over the world and meeting the people who play our games. Talking to them gives me an idea of what sort of things they're into, and what sort of things they'd like us to be doing. Last week, I was in Japan, and I learned a lot there.

Well, I hope I've managed to inspire a few of you. I should say that in the next few months, I'm planning to set up my own business developing games. One day, that's exactly what some of you may end up doing!

Grammar
Making comparisons

1 1 a bit more   2 much safer   3 most   4 better
5 much harder   6 most   7 biggest   8 so much

2 1 the healthiest   2 cheaper   3 more sociable   4 harder
5 the most thrilling   6 the least interesting   7 better

3 *Suggested answers*
1 difficult as it looks.   2 important thing is to participate, not to win.   3 skiing than skating.   4 nicer than I am.
5 as bad for you as some people say.

Reading and Use of English Part 1

2 *Suggested answers*
His dad gave him a motorbike and they rode it together. He instantly liked riding the motorbike and thought it was exciting.

3 1 B   2 D   3 A   4 C   5 D   6 B   7 A   8 A

Answer key: Unit 2

Vocabulary
Phrasal verbs and expressions

1 2 a 3 g 4 f 5 h 6 b 7 c 8 e

2 1 taking risks 2 sum up 3 have a go 4 make up
5 didn't have / hadn't got a clue 6 keep a promise / keep promises 7 taking up 8 get hold of 9 summing up 10 get hold of

Grammar
Adjectives with -ed and -ing

1 1 thrilled 2 exciting

2 1 amusing 2 irritating 3 bored 4 irritating
5 embarrassing 6 excited

3 1 astonishing 2 puzzled 3 motivating 4 worried
5 amusing 6 exhausted

4 g

> ▶ **CD 1 Track 06**
>
> **Young woman:** The whole experience was amazing actually. I mean, I'd been working really hard, studying, and so I was feeling pretty tired and nervous already, so when my best friend suggested I went along with her, I was like, shocked, like 'No way!' – I mean the thought of breaking a bone or something even worse just before an exam was terrifying. But you know, she just kept on at me, so for the sake of a bit of peace, in the end I said yes. When we were up there in the sky, I was just so scared I can't tell you. I just wanted to get out of the plane. I felt trapped, but the only way to do that was to jump, and in fact, the jump itself was really thrilling. I'd love to do it again. And I didn't break a thing!

5 2 tired and nervous 3 shocked 4 terrifying 5 scared and trapped 6 thrilling

Reading and Use of English Part 4

1 one of the easiest 2 not as/so interesting as 3 play tennis so/as well as 4 is the noisiest person in 5 not as/so cheap as 6 more quickly than

Speaking Part 2

2 *Suggested answers*
Football: getting exercise, good for you, good for health, helps you relax, having fun, laughing, builds up social relationships and friendships, breaks down social boundaries between boys and girls
Chatting in a café: communicating, sharing ideas and experiences, talk about problems, relax, enjoy friendship

> ▶ **CD 1 Track 07**
>
> **Examiner:** In this part of the test, I'm going to give each of you two photographs. I'd like you to talk about your photographs on your own for about a minute, and also to answer a short question about your partner's photographs. Martyna, it's your turn first. Here are your photographs. They show people doing different activities in their free time. I'd like you to compare the photographs, and say how you think the people can benefit from spending their free time doing these different activities. All right?
>
> **Martyna:** Well, in the first photo, there's a group of children, both boys and girls, playing football together in the park. They don't seem to be taking the game too seriously and they seem to be enjoying themselves. I think they benefit from this in several ways. Firstly, they're getting some exercise, which is always good for you because it's great for your health and helps you to relax. At the same time, they're having fun together, which is important because it builds up their social relationships and their friendships. Also, it's good to see boys and girls doing a bit of sport together instead of separately, because I think it helps break down social boundaries between boys and girls.
>
> In the second photo, there are four girls chatting together in a café and laughing. They aren't so active as the children in the first photo because they're not doing a sport, but they are probably communicating more and sharing their ideas and experiences. I think they also benefit because they can talk about their problems, relax and also enjoy their friendship. Mm, all in all, I think they get a lot from both activities.
>
> **Examiner:** Thank you.

3 ✓ 3, 4, 5, 7

4 See recording script for Track 07.

5 a 1 b 2 c 3, 4, 5

203

Answer key: Unit 2

6 b First of all, To start with
c Besides, In addition, What is more

Pronunciation: sentence stress (1)

7.1 See underlining in recording script for Track 08.

> ▶ **CD 1 Track 08**
>
> 1 <u>Firstly</u>, they're getting some <u>exercise</u>, which is always <u>good</u> for you.
> 2 It's <u>great</u> for your <u>health</u> and helps you to <u>relax</u>.
> 3 At the <u>same</u> time, they're having <u>fun</u> together …
> 4 … which is important because it <u>builds</u> up their social <u>relationships</u> and their <u>friendships</u>.
> 5 Also, it's good to see <u>boys</u> and <u>girls</u> doing a bit of sport <u>together</u> instead of <u>separately</u>.
> 6 I think it helps <u>break</u> down social <u>boundaries</u> between boys and <u>girls</u>.

Writing Part 2 An article

1 *Suggested underlining*
magazine for teenagers, leisure-time activity, How did you get started?, Why do you enjoy it so much?

3 *Suggested answers*
1 Para. 1: I've always loved … simple tunes; Para. 2: I found I really enjoyed … any more; Para. 3: When I got back home … play something really well; Para. 4: I'd recommend … that anyone can have.
2 Para. 1: how I started; Para. 2: how I continued; Para. 3: why I enjoy it; Para. 4: why I'd recommend it

4 *Suggested answers*
1 I've always loved music; I first got interested in playing the electric guitar last summer.
2 I found I really enjoyed playing the guitar; I was soon trying things that were a little more complicated.
3 It wasn't always easy; my cousin was great and helped me so much.
4 When they come round to my house, we play music together; we find it satisfying and relaxing.
5 I'd recommend it as a hobby; for me it's one of the most sociable, creative and entertaining hobbies that anyone can have.

5 *Suggested answers*
2 I got interested in flying when I was about 14 because my father took me to an airshow.
3 My parents don't want me to fly because they think it is dangerous.
4 One of my friends is learning to fly and he's asked me to come with him because he thinks I'd like it.

6 *Suggested answers*
2 I was soon trying things. They / The things were more complicated.
3 She even gave me one of her old guitars. She didn't need it any more.
4 I got back home. My parents let me do guitar lessons.
5 They come round to my house. We play music together.

7 *Suggested answers*
1 I was 13 when I started running seriously / I started running seriously when I was 13.
2 My aunt, who is a keen athlete, encouraged me.
3 I go running most days when/after I've finished school and done my homework.
4 Running is a sport which/that gets you really fit.

8 *Suggested answers*
1 I started windsurfing when I was 13 and I was staying with friends by the sea.
2 One of my friends, who is a keen windsurfer, encouraged me to start because she thought I would enjoy it.
3 I kept falling into the sea to start with because it was a fairly windy day and there were a lot of waves.
4 I didn't enjoy it at first because I had to concentrate quite hard, but I carried on trying.
5 I started to windsurf quite fast, which was exciting, so I started to find it quite enjoyable.

9 1 satisfying, relaxing
2 sociable, creative, and entertaining
3 competent

10

Feelings about an activity:	The type of activity:
astonishing, delightful, depressing, dreadful, entertaining, exhausting, incredible, irritating, superb, tremendous, unbelievable	competitive, demanding, economical, popular, time-consuming

11 *Sample answer*
See the model in Exercise 3 in the Student's Book.

Vocabulary and grammar review Unit 1

1 2 bad-tempered   3 hardworking/hard-working
4 unreliable   5 anxious   6 sensitive   7 mature
8 concerned/anxious

2 1 clear; up   2 pick; up   3 get on with   4 worn; out
5 do up   6 went on

3 1 do   2 make   3 do   4 doing   5 do   6 made   7 made
8 making

4 1 won   2 have arrived; have been expecting   3 have spent; has turned up   4 have been having / have had; has been telling / has told; has not told; has seen   5 has lost / has been losing; has been getting   6 has finished; have been waiting   7 has eaten; has not   8 has looked; has been studying

Vocabulary and grammar review Unit 2

1 1 keep a promise / promises   2 to take / taking risks
3 taking up   4 make up   5 sum up   6 haven't / haven't got / don't have a clue; have a go

2 *Suggested answers*
1 Katya took up karate when she was seven years old because she was interested in it.
2 Her father, who is a professional karate instructor, taught her, so she progressed quickly and soon became junior regional champion.
3 She did karate with other children who were the same age as her, but none of them were as good as her, so she felt dissatisfied.
4 Last year, she participated in the national championship, but she did not win because she was injured during one of the matches.
5 She hopes to become a professional karate instructor and work in the same sports centre as her father because he has too many students.
6 Some of her father's students have been studying karate for several years, and her father thinks they would benefit from a different teacher because they are too familiar with his style of karate.

3 1 motorbike made more noise than   2 are not as/so dangerous   3 is the best player   4 as/so stressed as
5 much more clearly than   6 more comfortable than any of

4 1 amazing   2 exhausting   3 puzzling   4 disappointed
5 motivated   6 astonished

3 Happy holidays?
Starting off

1

types of holiday	holiday locations and places to stay	holiday activities
a camping holiday	at a campsite	walking and climbing
a beach holiday	at a luxury hotel	meeting new people
a sightseeing tour	on a cruise ship	sunbathing
a cruise	at a youth hostel	relaxing
backpacking	by the sea	visiting monuments
	in the mountains	seeing new places
	in the city centre	
	at the seaside	

Listening Part 3

1 *Suggested underlining*
A enjoy, at first   B didn't mind, discomfort   C know, people   D similar before   E low-cost holiday
F improved, language skills   G (not) in as much danger as, imagined   H a break from my parents

2 1 G   2 F   3 D   4 A   5 C

> **CD 1 Track 09**
>
> **Presenter:** One. Francesca.
>
> **Francesca:** I went on one of those journeys overland to Kenya. It was awesome to be able to go off with a group of people my own age. I mean, really, on family holidays we always used to go to the same campsite and lie on the same beach and things. This was a whole new thing – seeing completely different places and doing lots of things I'd never done before. We did have a driver and a guide to keep an eye on things, so I don't think there was anything particularly risky about it, even though my mum and gran worried from the moment I left to the moment I got back!
>
> **Presenter:** Two. Mike.
>
> **Mike:** I went on holiday with my family – we stayed in a campsite in a big forest near a lake. My brothers and I made friends with a French boy, Pierre, who was camping there with his parents. I'm doing French at school, so I practised with Pierre, and I think I've got

Answer key: Unit 3

quite a bit better! We got up at about nine every morning and went swimming in the lake, even on days when it was cloudy. One day, we went on a trip to the nearest town – it was only half an hour's drive away. We also went for walks in the forest at night, which was cool.

Presenter: Three. Sally.

Sally: I went off with a couple of my friends in March. We were out in the open air in these amazing mountain landscapes and doing some awesome climbing. We all complained about what we cooked, though, and the weather caused a few problems. We were on our way back down the mountain when we got caught in this really big storm, so that was a bit scary. But I'd done that sort of thing quite a lot with my dad when I was a kid – um, my dad used to be a climber when he was younger – so I knew what I was doing.

Presenter: Four. Paul.

Paul: Well, it wasn't really my idea of a good time at all. The meals were good, if you don't mind sitting around with a lot of middle-aged adults in smart hotels. It was just really dull. And Mum and Dad dragged me round looking at paintings and sculptures, which was just so boring! Still, there was an upside, because while we were going round yet another museum, I got to meet this Polish girl called Jolanta. She was about as fed up as I was, so we just dumped our parents and went off for the day together. We had a really great time and, actually, we're still in touch.

Presenter: Five. Katie.

Katie: It was my first holiday without my parents, but I enjoyed myself so much I didn't really miss them at all! I went to Italy with my best friend and her parents. My parents aren't really into foreign travel, so it was the first time I'd ever been abroad. We stayed with her aunt in a small town near Rome, and there were plenty of other people our age there so I made lots of new friends. Luckily, they all spoke English, because my Italian's rubbish! We were allowed to go out to cafés together in the evenings, as long as the grown-ups knew what we were doing.

Grammar
Present perfect simple and continuous

1 1 used to go 2 used to be 3 was 4 were going
5 got 6 dumped 7 went 8 had 9 stayed
10 were doing

2 1 was walking 2 used to do 3 got; jumped; rode
4 used to spend 5 were walking; began
6 used to visit; was

3 developed, enjoyed, happened, mentioned, occurred, opened, planned, preferred, stopped, studied, travelled (BrE) / traveled (AmE), tried

Vocabulary
travel, journey, trip and way

1 1 trip 2 Way 3 travel 4 journey

2 1 trip 2 way 3 trip 4 trip 5 travel 6 journey
7 trip 8 journey 9 way

3 1 pleasant/safe/successful 2 overnight
3 outward 4 shopping 5 forthcoming
6 safe/pleasant

Reading and Use of English Part 3

1 2 adventurous 3 friendly 4 memorable
5 mysterious 6 risky 7 crowded 8 thrilled/ thrilling
9 doubtful 10 successful 11 remarkable 12 accessible

2 artist – artistic; caution – cautious; colour – colourful, colourless; educate – educational, educated; emotion – emotional; energy – energetic; mass – massive; predict – predictable; reason – reasonable; respond – responsible; storm – stormy; thought – thoughtful, thoughtless; wealth – wealthy

3 1 uncomfortable 2 thoughtful 3 colourful
4 unforgettable 5 optimistic 6 considerable
7 anxious 8 sympathetic

Grammar
at, in or on in time phrases

1 1 at, on 2 at 3 in 4 in

Answer key: Unit 3

Reading and Use of English Part 7

2 *Suggested underlining*
1 hide from danger   2 employee intimidating
3 didn't have time to appreciate, places   4 missed, home comforts   5 worried, strong   6 unsympathetic
7 painful experience   8 unhappy, weather   9 unaware, danger   10 on arrival, trip, mistake

3 1 B   2 C   3 D   4 C   5 B   6 D   7 A   8 C   9 A
10 C

Grammar
Past perfect simple and continuous

1 1 A
2 had organised (past perfect)
3 In the first sentence, her father organised the trip before they arrived; in the second sentence, he organised it when they were already in the country.

2 A Pauline Vernon: *until that point, no one* **had bothered** *to mention the sea-snakes* – before she got stung
B Sandy Henderson: *we'***d passed** *a small cabin a little way back on the trail* – they'd already seen the cabin once
C Nora Tracey: *It* **had seemed** *like such a good idea three months beforehand* – she was actually on the trip; *I'd* **persuaded** *my parents to let me go on the geography trip* – she was actually on the trip; *we'd* **tidied** *our rooms* – before she checked; *they'd* **imagined** *us all walking in the hills in glorious sunshine* – before they went on the trip
D Harry Green: *I'd* **wondered** *what the weather would be like* – before he went on holiday; *even though I'd* **had** *a great night's sleep* – before he struggled to keep up

3 1 had eaten   2 had never been   3 organised / had organised   4 arrived; had lost   5 recognised; had never spoken   6 had damaged

4 1 A
2 A past perfect continuous, B past perfect simple

5 1 had been living   2 had been walking; began
3 had already finished; offered   4 had only been speaking   5 got; had been walking

Speaking Part 3

2 **A city sightseeing tour:** you learn about architecture and history, other cultures and visit somewhere different.
A weekend camping trip in the mountains: you have exciting experiences and adventures, and learn to be independent, learn to work together to solve problems, learn teamwork, educational.
A beach activity day: you learn something from doing different sports and activities.

> ▶ **CD 1 Track 10**
> **Miguel:** Shall we start with this one?
> **Antonia:** OK.
> **Miguel:** How do you think doing a sightseeing tour might be good for students?
> **Antonia:** I think you can learn a lot about architecture and history and things like that.
> **Miguel:** Yes, and also you can visit somewhere very different and learn about other cultures.
> **Antonia:** Right. What about this sort of activity holiday in the mountains? I think it can give young people exciting experiences and adventures, things they don't get in their everyday lives.
> **Miguel:** Yes, and they learn to be more independent because they're away from home and their families, don't you think?
> **Antonia:** I think that's right. Also, they learn to work together to solve problems, so it's good for learning teamwork.
> **Miguel:** That's an important point, because if the school's organising the trip, it should be educational, shouldn't it? I mean, students have got to be learning something. And the beach activity day: what about that?
> **Antonia:** It sounds great, doesn't it? And I think just by doing sports and activities they don't normally do at school, students learn something.
> **Miguel:** I agree.

3 1 Shall; this one   2 think   3 What about
4 don't you   5 about that

Pronunciation: intonation (1)

4.1 1 good for students ↘   2 architecture ↗, history ↗, things like that ↘   3 different ↘, cultures ↗   4 activity ↗, mountains ↘   5 experiences ↗, adventures ↗, lives ↘

Answer key: Unit 3

▶ **CD 1 Track 11.** See page 38.

6 *Suggested answers*
1 N – There is not time – you need to reach a decision in one minute.
2 Y – It gets the discussion started and your partner involved.
3 N – It prevents further discussion.
4 Y – This is a possible way of creating more discussion.
5 Y – It creates further discussion.
6 N – You only have a minute and you will get higher marks if you can have a natural conversation.

7 Miguel does 2; Antonia does 4; Irene and Nikolai both do 5.

▶ **CD 1 Track 12**
Miguel and Antonia
Miguel: Well, Antonia, in my opinion, the best choice for the trip is the camping and walking activity in the mountains, because it will be an adventure for everyone, and if it goes well, everyone will enjoy it. What do you think?
Antonia: Hmm, I think your suggestion would be fine if the weather is good, but no one will enjoy it if it rains all the time, and it's a lot of responsibility for the teachers who are supervising the trip. I think the beach-activities trip is a better option because at least the kids will be staying in a hostel if the weather turns bad.

Irene and Nikolai
Irene: OK, I think we should choose the theme park because all teenagers enjoy the thrill of a theme park, and it gives everyone plenty to talk about and discuss before and after they go.
Nikolai: Yes, I think you're right, but I think we should also consider the visit to the museum because that might be more popular with the teachers, and we have to take their preferences into consideration as well.
Irene: Hmm, you might be right, but I think we should put the students' tastes first because it is their trip.
Nikolai: Maybe, but they can go to a theme park in their own time.
Irene: Yes, of course they can, but sometimes it's important to do these activities as a school group.

8 1 a 2 a 3 b 4 e 5 e 6 d 7 c

Writing Part 2 — A story

1 *Suggested underlining*
It was a trip I'll never forget; a group of people; a surprise; English-language magazine at your school

2 1 B 2 C 3 E 4 D 5 A

▶ **CD 1 Track 13**
Jean
Jean: Just coming to France for two weeks on a language course is a really big adventure for me. It's the first time I've ever been away from home, so to be away from my family just for a couple of weeks is an interesting experience. And of course I miss them, but it's OK. And it's the first time I've ever been anywhere by air, so for me it's all pretty amazing. Especially as I come from a pretty small village in Scotland.

Mark
Mark: I can remember a trip I made when I was younger – I was probably only about eight years old. Anyway, it was one of the first times I'd travelled anywhere without my mum and dad. I was with the other kids from my class and a trip had been organised to a nearby wildlife park. Well, the bus broke down in the middle of it and while we were all sitting inside waiting for the bus to be repaired, two lions came incredibly close to the bus. We kids thought it was terribly funny and all screamed with laughter, but I think some of the teachers were pretty scared actually. We could see them so close up!

Maya
Maya: For me it has to be something that happened quite recently. My mother's family comes from India and if you count all my uncles and aunts and cousins there are lots of us. In fact I have family living all over the world in lots of different countries. For example, I have an uncle in Canada and a cousin in Kuwait and so on. You name the place, there's probably some uncle or cousin living there. But this is a time when we all got together – nearly 40 of us – for my grandma's 80th birthday at her house. We had organised a surprise party for her. People had made a real effort to get there and we had an unforgettable weekend together.

Patrick

Patrick: Oh, I can tell you about a trip we made across the River Plate from Buenos Aires to Montevideo on a rather old ferry when a storm came up. I lived there as a child and I was with some friends from school. We'd been invited to someone's house there for a few days during our summer holidays – that's in December, you know. Anyway, it was very rough and we all got quite ill.

Luckily, it all blew over in a few hours, but when we got on dry land again, my legs were shaking.

Sarah

Sarah: I can tell you about a magical trip we did when I was quite small. I still remember it because it was like one of those things which makes a big impression on you when you're small. Anyway, we all took a train, my mum and dad, various relatives and myself and when we got to the station we walked what seemed a really long way to me. Of course it can't have been very far, but I didn't know where we were going or how far we'd have to walk.

Suddenly we got to this really nice lake where we had a picnic. Then afterwards we played football together. I'll never forget that day!

3 1 all of them 2 Mark, Patrick, Sarah

5 2 had decided 3 had only read 4 had entered
5 had 6 were waiting 7 approached
8 had never seen 9 started 10 managed

6 1 three paragraphs: Para. 1: where we were going on the trip and how we were feeling; Para. 2: the animals we saw; Para. 3 the puncture and what happened while we waited
2 excited, ancient, noisy, nervous, crowded, fascinating, brilliant, thrilled, relieved
3 going to a wildlife park, seeing animals in real life for the first time, the puncture, the monkeys on the bus, his/her classmates' excitement

7 *Sample answer*
See the model in Exercise 4 in the Student's Book, page 39.

Answer key: Unit 4

4 Food, glorious food

Starting off

1 1 c 2 b 3 a 4 c

Reading and Use of English Part 6

2 Para. 1: what the research is about
Para. 2: measuring brain power
Para. 3: quantity of chocolate needed to be cleverer
Para. 4: why and how you should eat more chocolate
Para. 5: other possible reasons for cleverness apart from chocolate
Para. 6: Do clever people eat more chocolate?

3 *Suggested underlining*
C It only shows, the two are connected
D Otherwise, so obvious E the two are linked
F In short G Instead, I found my information

4 1 G 2 E 3 F 4 B 5 C 6 A

Vocabulary
food, dish and *meal*

1 1 food 2 meal 3 dishes

2 2 dishes 3 dish 4 food 5 food 6 dish 7 meals

3 1 food 2 food 3 meal; dish 4 meal

4 2 food shortages 3 heavy/filling meal 4 food source
5 convenience food 6 balanced meals 7 food supply
8 organic food

Grammar
so and *such*

1 1 such a 2 so 3 such 4 so

2 1 such 2 so 3 such a 4 so 5 so 6 such a

3 1 I'll always remember that meal because it was so delicious. 2 I can't study in such a noisy place. 3 It was such fun for all of us to be together. 4 My best friend makes such funny jokes. 5 I'm glad to see you after such a long time. 6 What a pity there were so few spectators at the football match.

209

Answer key: Unit 4

4 1 never eaten such a good   2 so quickly that we
3 answered the question so well/excellently
4 with so little food   5 had so much fun at
6 make so much noise

Listening Part 4

2 *Suggested underlining*
1 British people's attitudes, eating insects   2 Why, choose insects as a topic   3 early human beings, other animals   4 surprised   5 like best, energy bar   6 insect farms, will increase in   7 advice, finding insects

3 1 A   2 C   3 B   4 C   5 B   6 C   7 A

CD 1 Track 14

Interviewer: Hi, everybody. It's great to have Lisa Fletcher in our school internet radio studio today. Lisa, you're planning to study Food Science at university, and you already know a lot about one aspect of food science, don't you?

Lisa: Hi! Well … quite a lot … I've been finding out about insects as a source of food for humans.

Interviewer: That's an unusual idea, isn't it?

Lisa: Not really, actually. It's unusual here in Britain, but in some parts of the world it's absolutely normal. Some people estimate that about two billion people worldwide eat insects and their larvae. And things like red food colouring and some flavourings, for example, are made from insects, so they're already ingredients in many people's diets, even if they don't realise it. It's generally recognised now that insects and insect products will play a very important role in ensuring that we have enough food to feed the world's population in the future.

Interviewer: And why did you choose this particular topic for your project?

Lisa: You may be surprised to hear that I used to be quite scared of insects. In fact I can't believe how much I've changed! But we had to choose a topic for a project about food at school, and I saw an article about people eating insects on a website. Even though it made me feel a bit uncomfortable and nobody else in the class was doing anything like that, I decided to do my project on it.

Interviewer: So, have human beings always eaten insects?

Lisa: It seems so. They may in fact have been a large part of early humans' diets all over the world, because in prehistoric times it was easier to find insects to eat than to go out hunting for larger animals. I mean if they could just find enough caterpillars or something and throw them on the fire, then they had an instant meal – lots of protein without too much effort.

Interviewer: And how about nowadays? Is there anything you discovered that you found particularly surprising?

Lisa: There was, though it's something that's pretty obvious really – I just hadn't thought about it before. It's the fact that people who eat some types of insect feel disgusted by the idea of eating certain other types of insect. So just because you eat termites, for example, doesn't mean you'll think it's OK to eat beetles. It's really a question of what you're used to.

Interviewer: And have you ever eaten an insect yourself?

Lisa: Not a whole one, because I'm still just a little scared of insects – I'm not brave enough, basically. But I have tried an energy bar made from insect flour. You know they're usually made with cereal and honey and nuts and raisins and things? Well this one contained flour made from ground insects. It didn't taste too bad, and was full of healthy ingredients, but the most exciting thing for me is that it might get people in the West to begin to accept the idea of insects as a source of protein.

Interviewer: And are insects farmed on a large scale, like we farm cows and sheep in Britain?

Lisa: Yes. There are farms in the US and in China, and there are plenty in other countries, like Thailand, too. People also breed them for food on a smaller scale, you know like in their apartments because it's cheap. But in the future, there'll probably be more and more farms like the ones I saw pictures of – they're about as big as football pitches.

Interviewer: Do you have any advice for British people who want to eat insects?

Lisa: Well you should really ask an expert about that, but I wouldn't recommend just going out and finding them yourself. It's like picking mushrooms, isn't it? You wouldn't just go and pick one and eat it without knowing what it was – that would be far too dangerous because it might be poisonous. There's also the risk that you might have a severe allergic reaction. I'd stick to the ones that are commercially available, though there aren't too many insects on the shelves at the moment in Britain.

Interviewer: Thanks very much, Lisa, and good luck with your studies!

Lisa: Thank you!

Answer key: Unit 4

Grammar
too and enough

1 1 enough 2 enough, too much 3 enough 4 too
5 too many

2 1 too many, enough 2 enough 3 too 4 too
5 enough

3 1 there wasn't enough food 2 not much 3 enough money 4 comfortable enough 5 much too long
6 very 7 much too

4 1 is too expensive for 2 enough petrol to get
3 was too astonished by 4 was not / wasn't warm enough for

Speaking Part 4

1 b balanced diet c cut down d junk food
e dairy products f live on g lifestyle

2 1 in other words 2 because 3 On the other hand
4 then 5 but 6 which 7 what

 CD 1 Track 15

Examiner: Do you think fast food is bad for you?

Martyna: I think it depends. I think the most important thing / is to have a balanced diet, / in other words, you eat a variety of / vegetables, / meat, / cereals and so on. I'm not sure it matters so much / how long it takes to prepare, / because I think fast food is / just / food which is prepared quickly. On the other hand, / if you just live on / what's it called / junk food, / for instance hamburgers and pizzas and things like that, / then you probably need to cut down / and have a more balanced diet.

Examiner: And Miguel, what do you think?

Miguel: I agree with Martyna. / I think it's fine to eat fast food occasionally, / but you have to balance it with other things like / fresh fruit and / vegetables which are in season and / cut down on dairy products and fat. / Also I think that what you eat is only one part of a / healthy lifestyle.

Martyna: I agree.

3 1 in other words 2 because 3 for instance, like
4 but, on the other hand

Pronunciation: grouping words and pausing (1)

4.1

 CD 1 Track 16

Examiner: How can families benefit from eating together?

Miguel: Well, / the important thing is not eating, / it's spending time together / so that they can talk about / what they have been doing during the day. / They get the chance to / exchange opinions / and make plans as well, / because everyone can contribute and / that's what makes a / rich, / meaningful family life. / Children learn ideas and attitudes from their parents, / while parents keep up to date with their children / and what they are thinking and doing.

Reading and Use of English Part 1

1 The surroundings, the service, the food, the price

2 1 B 2 B 3 C 4 B 5 A 6 D 7 C 8 A

Writing Part 2 A review

1 *Suggested underlining*
local English-language newspaper, know, local restaurant, café or snack bar, review, what, place, food, like, whether, family, enjoy eating there

2 2 a, b, c, d, f, h, i

3 & 4 *Suggested answers*
the waiters / the service: rushed, welcoming, helpful, cheerful, (a bit) slow, exceptional, satisfactory, rude
the interior: airy, cosy, modern, attractive, cheerful, colourful, elegant, exclusive, original, old-fashioned, welcoming
the food and menu: delicious, fresh, satisfying, tasty, wonderful, attractive, colourful, poor, elegant, exceptional, limited, original, satisfactory
the price: reasonable, competitive, expensive
the restaurant in general: modern, attractive, colourful, exceptional, elegant, exclusive, original, old-fashioned, expensive, welcoming

5 *Suggested underlining*
school magazine, restaurant, café or snack bar, review, 'Free Time' section, what it is like, whether, recommend it

Answer key: Unit 5

Vocabulary and grammar review Unit 3

1 1 journey 2 trip 3 travel 4 way 5 journey 6 way 7 trip 8 journey

2 1 while I was visiting 2 I had lost 3 used to go to school 4 she was still going to 5 had never met 6 used to be more

3 1 considerable 2 exclusive 3 dramatic 4 unacceptable 5 disorganised 6 unhelpful 7 remaining 8 preferable

Vocabulary and grammar review Unit 4

1 1 meal 2 food 3 dish 4 food 5 dish 6 food/meals 7 meal 8 food

2 1 too hot (for us) to 2 slowly enough (for us) to 3 was so full (that) 4 such delicious food that 5 cook well enough 6 such a long time / so much time

3 1 filling 2 convenience 3 increasingly 4 organisations 5 discourage 6 balanced 7 disappearance 8 choice

5 Study time

Listening Part 1

1 1 h 2 d 3 b 4 a 5 i 6 e 7 f 8 c 9 g

2 *Suggested underlining*
1 How does he feel, now 2 What, problem
3 What, like most 4 most difficult 5 Why, talking
6 What surprised her, school 7 think about, lesson
8 What, advice about

3 1 C 2 B 3 B 4 A 5 A 6 C 7 C 8 B

CD 1 Track 17

Presenter: One. You overhear a student talking about a course he has been doing.

Will: Actually, at the beginning of term, I was a bit lost. You know, my family has only just moved to this country, so I was new in this school, and I felt that everyone else knew more about the subject than I did. Listening to them, I got the impression that some of them felt this particular course was a bit of a waste of time. In my case, I was having problems not just with the language but also with the ideas. But I managed to get over all that and, in fact, the course has lived up to my original expectations, so I feel all the hard work's been worth it. I mean, we've got an exam next week, which I expected to feel a bit anxious about, but in fact I'm feeling fine about it.

Presenter: Two. You hear a student complaining about a problem she has had.

Mike: Oh, Helena! What's up?

Helena: Do you know what just happened? I was given an essay to write at the beginning of the month and I spent lots of time researching it. Anyway, Valerie – you know her – she came round to my place and while she was there she must have copied all my notes! All my research! I only found out in my tutorial just now when the tutor handed my essay back to me. He said he couldn't mark it because my essay repeated all the same key points that Valerie had made in hers. I'm absolutely furious, and she's going to get away with it, too!

Presenter: Three. You hear a student at a language school in Japan.

Boy: So, what are you doing here in Japan?

Girl: I'm learning Japanese at a language school. I go to classes for just two hours a day, which is good because I learn Japanese from Japanese teachers, and then I'm free to practise it during the rest of the day.

Boy: That sounds a good idea.

Girl: It is. You see, it's not all academic work. They also organise lots of other things for us learners to take part in after school. There are clubs we can join if we're interested, and they really are the best part. For example, I'm also doing a karate course taught in Japanese, which is great fun. I'm learning something completely different in the language I'm studying and I'm getting to know lots of local people.

Boy: Fantastic!

Girl: Yes, if you speak a bit of the language, it's much easier to make friends.

Presenter: Four. You hear a boy talking about revising for his exams.

Boy: I hate revising for exams, so I always put it off until the last minute, which I know I shouldn't. I'm hoping to study geography at university, and of course I won't be able to do that unless I do well in my exams at school. I have so many different lessons to attend – if I could drop some subjects, I'd have more time for geography, but I know it's important to learn about lots of different things. My mum says if I gave up football, I'd have more time to study, but exercise is important too. And so is sleep – I'm sure that helps me remember things better!

Presenter: Five. You hear a teacher talking to her class about their school sports day.

Teacher: Before you go off and take part in all your different sports events today, I'd like to point out a couple of things. First of all, if you're not sure when your event starts, check the programme. Every teacher has one, so all you have to do is ask. There's no excuse for missing a race. And secondly, if there are any changes to the programme, the teachers will tell you straight away. Do you remember last year, when it rained for half an hour in the middle of the day? Anyway, this year, luckily, there isn't a cloud in the sky. So good luck, and have fun!

Presenter: Six. You hear a girl leaving a message about her first day at a new school.

Carrie: Hi, Mum! I'm just calling to say I'm back and I'm still alive! You know how worried I was because I wouldn't know anyone, and you said there'd be lots of other kids in the same situation – and you were right, so we all sort of mixed in. Classes were fine – you know, the usual sort of stuff you do on the first day like course requirements and so on. One or two of the teachers might turn out to be monsters, but most seem fine. Oh, and the classrooms are nice, very bright and lots of technology like electronic screens and we're all connected up with wifi and stuff, so a lot better than I expected.

Presenter: Seven. You hear two students, a boy and a girl, talking about a lesson.

Jan: Hi, Max. So you got into trouble in maths again for staring out of the window!

Max: Yeah! I reckon Mr Drew's got it in for me! I mean, you don't have to look at the teacher to be listening to him.

Jan: So, unlike most of us, you were actually finding the lesson useful, you mean?

Max: Sure. Mr Drew knows what he's talking about, and there are some interesting concepts, but unfortunately it's all rather chaotic, and it takes him such a long time to get to the stuff we really need. His classes could do with a bit more planning, in my opinion.

Jan: Hmm, perhaps that's why the rest of us all get lost, while you're staring at the kids outside – and taking it all in!

Presenter: Eight. You hear a teacher talking to a student.

Teacher: Well, it's fine to study history or archaeology if that's the area you're planning to work in when you finish, but you must remember, you'll only find the sort of job you want in research if you get a really good degree – and the job itself won't be very well-paid either.

Girl: I know.

Teacher: I mean, you've got a good brain and if you applied yourself, you could study anything. I'd hate to think of you looking back in 20 years' time and thinking, I wish I'd studied IT or accountancy or something with better job prospects.

Vocabulary
Phrasal verbs

1 1 g   2 a   3 c   4 e   5 f   6 b   7 d

2 1 put off   2 gets away with   3 handed; back; gets over   4 live up to; looks back   5 turned out; point / pointed / have pointed out

find out, get to know, know, learn, teach and study; attend, join, take part and assist

3 1 study   2 found out   3 learn   4 attend   5 getting to know   6 take part   7 join   8 taught

Grammar
Zero, first and second conditionals

1 a 3, 5, 6   b 2, 4   c 1

2 1 f   2 a   3 h   4 e   5 g   6 d   7 b   8 c

3 1 said   2 lived, would go   3 did, would   4 have   5 have, ask   6 travelled, would be

4 1 you assist (us) with the   2 if you join   3 would take part in   4 will have to put off   5 better unless your teacher pointed   6 I get over my cold

Answer key: Unit 6

Reading and Use of English Part 7

1 *Suggested answers*
1 unfamiliar food and a difficult/strange host family; food the student doesn't like   2 not having friends; feeling lonely   3 not knowing their way around; feeling lost   4 difficulty understanding people / the teacher / the lessons

2 *Suggested underlining*
1 surprised, different approach to education
2 cooperating, host family   3 more adult as a result
4 helped, make a decision   5 responsibility, take as much advantage as possible   6 different attitude, getting up early   7 change from, normal school life   8 had not expected, go abroad   9 mixed feelings, type of school
10 change, opinion of people

3 1 D   2 C   3 C   4 A   5 B   6 C   7 A   8 A   9 D   10 B

Reading and Use of English Part 3

1 2 intention   3 response (responsibility)
4 adjustment   5 comparison   6 existence
7 demand   8 development   9 behaviour
10 advice/advisor   11 appearance   12 knowledge

2 2 assess   3 feel   4 involve   5 investigate
6 confuse   7 prefer   8 approve

3 1 friendships   2 variety   3 expectations
4 comparison   5 unprepared   6 independence
7 behaviour   8 welcoming

Speaking Part 1

1 1 because   2 if   3 when (if)   4 who   5 if   6 and

▶ **CD 1 Track 18.** See page 59.

2 *Suggested answers*
1 three
2 three
3 Candidates receive marks based on their ability to manage grammar and longer units of discourse. Candidates also achieve a higher score for longer, more complex sentences.
4 It creates a good, positive impression.

▶ **CD 1 Track 19.** See page 59.

Pronunciation: word stress (2)

4.1 ne<u>c</u>essary, nec<u>ess</u>ity

4.2 sat<u>is</u>fying/satis<u>fac</u>tory, <u>ed</u>ucate/edu<u>ca</u>tion, ex<u>am</u>/exami<u>na</u>tion, ex<u>plain</u>/expla<u>na</u>tion, <u>poss</u>ible/possi<u>bil</u>ity, pre<u>fer</u>/<u>pref</u>erence

4.3 The stress is always on the syllable before the suffix (-tion, -ity).

▶ **CD 1 Track 20.** See page 59.

Writing Part 1   The set text

2 *Suggested answers*
The second essay is better than the first because the writer gives specific examples from the book justifying their opinion of the character. The first essay is vague and it doesn't give a detailed description of the character.

3 1 b   2 a

5 1 although   2 For example   3 As a result   4 like
5 such as / like   6 For all these reasons

6 *Sample answer*
See second essay in Exercise 2, page 60

6 My first job

Listening Part 3

1 *Suggested answers*
B I didn't expect to have to work so hard   C I get a lot of new ideas from the people I meet   D I might get the chance to do something I've always wanted to
E I'm learning to do new things   F I work alone, mostly
G I'd like to go back and do the same job in the future
H I get annoyed when there are problems I can't solve

2 1 A   2 E   3 B   4 H   5 D

Answer key: Unit 6

CD 1 Track 21

Speaker 1: This is my first holiday job and I'm helping my aunt and uncle in their grocery shop for two weeks this July. I help carry boxes, put things on the shelves, and help serve the customers. Some of it's hard physical work, but I think I expected that when I started. The shop's quite small and for me, the best thing's all the different people who come in during the day – especially the old people who've lived in the area all their lives. I think they like the opportunity to talk to someone different, who hasn't heard all their stories before, and some of them are pretty interesting!

Speaker 2: My friend's dad has a small hotel and I'm helping in the reception there two days a week this summer. I'm normally quite shy, but I'm really happy to be doing this job because it's great to be getting some work experience. Anyway, my colleagues have given me a bit of responsibility even though I'm so young and only part-time, and I've learned things which you need to know for lots of jobs – practical things like how to answer the phone correctly – you know, not just saying 'Hey' or whatever. On some occasions, I've even been left on my own in charge of the whole hotel for a short time!

Speaker 3: Well, nobody expects babysitting to be a complete doddle, at least not when there are three small kids to look after. But, well, their mum's very nice and she did warn me – and she's paying me over the usual rate because she knows what it's like – she has to have them when I'm not around – but I really think I've let myself in for a lot more than I bargained for. I've done babysitting before, but it's never been like this. They never stop running around and shouting, and bath time – well, that's just chaos. I reckon I get wetter than they do!

Speaker 4: It isn't a very well-paid job, but then lots of holiday jobs aren't, I suppose. My mum and dad said they didn't want me to spend the whole summer just hanging out with my mates, so I'm working with a neighbour who repairs computers, going round to people's houses with him and fixing problems. Sometimes when he's very busy I take calls for him on his mobile. I often end up having to help people sort something out over the phone. If it's quite simple, that's fine, but obviously I don't have any training in computer skills, so sometimes I can't help them and I hate that.

Speaker 5: My big sister makes jewellery to sell at a local market and this summer she's actually paying me to work with her three days a week. She isn't paying me much, though, and if I can, I'll do something else next year instead. But even though the days are long, it's fun to chat to all the different people who work in the market selling different things. Sometimes famous people come and visit the market, too, because our town is quite touristy. There's always the possibility that I'll actually meet a film star – you never know – and that, well, that'd be a dream come true!

Vocabulary

work or *job*; *possibility*, *occasion* or *opportunity*; *fun* or *funny*

1 1 job 2 work 3 job; jobs 4 opportunity
5 occasions 6 possibility 7 fun

2 1 funny 2 fun 3 possibility 4 occasions
5 opportunity 6 job 7 work 8 jobs

3 2 badly paid 4 challenging 5 demanding 6 tiring
7 tough 9 office 11 manual 13 holiday 14 part-time
15 permanent 16 temporary 17 weekend 19 pleasant
20 responsible 21 worthwhile

Reading and Use of English Part 5

2 1 She was a waitress.
2 The special role her dad created for her, creating packed lunches, cakes and puddings.

3 *Suggested underlining*
1 None of us had ever worked in a hotel before.
2 impressive chef's hat and a terrifying ability to lose his temper and get violent
3 I … always grabbed the dishes he set down with a forbidding expression on my face which was transformed into a charming smile in the brief space between kitchen and dining room.
4 and I took pleasure in my ability to get on with the people at each table. It was funny how differently people behaved in the evenings, dressed up and talking with louder, colder voices, not always returning my smile.
5 the most extraordinary collection of puddings, cakes and other desserts ever to grace a Scottish hotel. Most were things I had invented myself and I had cooked all of them. Some – Jacobite Grenades, Mocha Genghis Khan and Goat's Milk Bavarios to name a few – were undeniably strange.

Answer key: Unit 6

4 1 C 2 B 3 D 4 B 5 D 6 B

Speaking Part 2

2 See recording script for Track 22.

3 a B b B c B d 2 e 1 f 2 g 2 h 1 i 2

> **CD 1 Track 22**
>
> **Examiner:** Here are your photographs. They show young people doing jobs. I'd like you to compare the photographs and say what you think the people are learning from doing these two types of work.
>
> **Nikolai:** Well, OK, so firstly I can say that <u>both photos show</u> young people, perhaps teenagers, working. Er, <u>both the jobs in the photos involve</u> working in situations where they need good skills in dealing with people in the correct way. I'm sure <u>neither of them</u> is very well-paid. <u>Anyway, the first photo shows</u> a girl serving young people in a restaurant, <u>whereas in the second photo</u> a boy is working with children and coaching them to play football. The girl's job may be full-time, <u>whereas the boy's</u> is probably part-time. <u>I think both can</u> learn a lot from these jobs. The girl can learn how to keep customers happy, while the boy has to keep children in order. The girl has to learn to work efficiently under pressure. <u>On the other hand</u>, the boy has to learn to keep cool. He'll probably learn <u>not just</u> to deal with children, <u>but also</u> their parents.
>
> **Examiner:** Thank you. Antonia, which of these jobs would you prefer to do?
>
> **Antonia:** I'd prefer to coach children than work in a restaurant because really I enjoy being in the fresh air more than being indoors. And I like kids.
>
> **Examiner:** Thank you.

4 b

5 See recording script for Track 22 (Nikolai does not use the phrases *While the girl in the first photo … , Another thing in the second photo is …*).

Pronunciation: sentence stress (2)

6.1 first, girl, young people, restaurant, second, boy, children

6.2 See underlining in recording script for Track 23.

> **CD 1 Track 23**
>
> Anyway, the <u>first</u> photo shows a <u>girl</u> serving <u>young people</u> in a <u>restaurant</u>, whereas in the <u>second</u> photo, a <u>boy</u> is working with <u>children</u>.

6.3 See underlining in recording script for Track 24.

> **CD 1 Track 24**
>
> The <u>girl's</u> job may be <u>full</u>-time, whereas the <u>boy's</u> is probably <u>part</u>-time.
>
> The <u>girl</u> can learn how to keep <u>customers</u> <u>happy</u>, while the <u>boy</u> has to keep <u>children</u> in <u>order</u>.
>
> He'll probably learn not just to deal with <u>children</u>, but also their <u>parents</u>.
>
> I'd prefer to <u>coach</u> <u>children</u> than work in a <u>restaurant</u> because really I enjoy being in the fresh <u>air</u> more than being <u>indoors</u>.

Grammar
Countable and uncountable nouns

1 1 information 2 some advice 3 a job
4 accommodation was 5 furniture 6 any damage
7 much luggage 8 music

2 *Students should circle:* 2 advice; information; knowledge; news 3 damage; transport 4 furniture 5 food
6 homework; work 7 equipment 8 music

3 1 piece/bit 2 number 3 piece/bit 4 piece/bit
5 deal 6 number; amount

4 2 c 3 f 4 d 5 e 6 a

5 1 the 2 an 3 the 4 – 5 a 6 a 7 a 8 the
9 the 10 the 11 – 12 the 13 a

Reading and Use of English Part 2

1 rock climbing, rafting, trekking, designing and implementing a volunteering project

2 1 get 2 If 3 the 4 every 5 So 6 away 7 such
8 just/only

Answer key: Unit 7

Writing Part 2 — A letter or email

1 *Suggested underlining*
weekend jobs teenagers do, describing, in your country, problems, how people find part-time jobs

4 1 *It's good …* indicates that he is answering the email + being friendly; *I hope …* rounds off the email in a friendly way. In the exam, both these sentences will make the email sound more authentic.
2 The first sentence of the paragraphs tells us the subject of the paragraph.

5 ~~restaurans~~ restaurants; ~~neibours~~ neighbours; ~~studing~~ studying; ~~wich~~ which; ~~payed~~ paid; ~~usefull~~ useful; ~~becaus~~ because; ~~especialy~~ especially

6 The spelling of these words should be corrected as follows:
embarrassing, opportunity, comfortable, grateful, environment, necessary, beginning, communicate, excellent, forward, prefer, received, recommend, which, easily, course, advertisement

7 *Suggested underlining*
part-time jobs, describing a part-time job you've done, someone you know well, what, learned, any problems

8 *Sample answer*
Hi Bob,
It's nice to hear from you again.
I have a part-time job in my uncle's café. I work there every Saturday afternoon for four hours, when it gets particularly busy because everyone's in town doing their shopping. I help in the kitchen, preparing salads and snacks and doing the washing-up. During the holidays, my uncle sometimes calls me and asks if I can come in for a few extra hours if a staff member is off sick or there are just a lot of customers that day.
It's good work experience for me because I'm learning how to work quickly under pressure in a small kitchen, which isn't always easy, and how to get on with different kinds of people.
I don't really have any difficulties except when I'm having to rush so much that I break a glass or a plate, but luckily my uncle doesn't get angry about things like that. I suppose it's difficult when I've got a lot of homework to do as well, but I usually manage.
I hope this information is useful and good luck with your project!
Louise

Vocabulary and grammar review Unit 5

1 1 get away with **2** put off; got over **3** live up to **4** look back; turned out **5** handed back; pointed out

2 1 learn **2** study **3** teaching **4** join; get to know **5** attend **6** take part

3 1 harder, he would / he'd **2** study abroad, you will become / you'll become **3** she would not / wouldn't attend **4** look after my book **5** knew the answer, I would **6** he wasn't / was not so tired

4 1 preference **2** knowledge **3** behaviour **4** comparison **5** activities **6** assistance **7** measurement **8** ability

Vocabulary and grammar review Unit 6

1 1 occasion **2** work **3** job **4** occasion **5** fun **6** opportunity **7** funny **8** possibility

2 1 had such / so much / a lot of fun on **2** have/get/take the/an opportunity to speak **3** have the possibility of studying **4** was much better than **5** with a good / great deal of **6** on one occasion

3 1 deal **2** bit/piece **3** bit/piece **4** bit/piece **5** number

4 1 – **2** a **3** the **4** a **5** – **6** a **7** – **8** a **9** the **10** a **11** a **12** – **13** a **14** an **15** the **16** an **17** –

7 High adventure

Starting off

1 1 mountain biking **2** rock climbing **3** snowboarding **4** windsurfing **5** canoeing/kayaking **6** parasailing

Listening Part 2

1 *Suggested answers*
1 a person or group of people **2** a time or place **3** a type of person **4** a type of person **5** a type of (probably natural) place **6** people, place or thing **7** a title **8** a time (duration) **9** a type of ability or activity **10** a descriptive adjective / an opinion

Answer key: Unit 7

2 1 family   2 (early) 1990s   3 men and women / women and men   4 specialists   5 mountains or deserts / deserts or mountains   6 inhabitants   7 South Island   8 ten/10 days   9 staying awake   10 (very) motivating

▶ CD 1 Track 25

Gary: … so I'm going to talk to you about adventure racing as my part of the project. Adventure racing's a sport you do in teams, and I got interested in this because I actually took part in one for the first time last year in the north of England with the rest of my family, and we were racing against lots of other teams made up of people of different ages. Anyway, I've done some research and what I've found out turns out to be much more interesting than I expected. The sport's been around for some time. There were races as far back as a hundred years ago and some newish ones which were started in the 1970s and 80s, but really people have been doing adventure racing in large numbers since the early 1990s, and it's one of the toughest sports you can imagine. Unlike marathons or pentathlons or those sorts of things, where the winner's the individual runner who finishes first, in adventure races the winners are the first team of four to six people, depending on the race, to all get over the finishing line together, and in many races one of the rules is that the team must be made up of an equal number of men and women – two or three of each depending on the size of the team. Anyway, it's not like just going jogging or running or something like that. These races combine a mixture of different activities or sports – running, swimming, kayaking, climbing and cycling to name just some of them. I've been looking a bit at the teams who win, and one of the things I've noticed is that the winning teams tend to contain specialists in different skills, such as climbing and kayaking, and that seems to give them an advantage. The races are organised in all sorts of different places. Occasionally, they're organised in cities – there's a very famous one which takes place in Chicago – you know, in North America – but the majority are held in mountains or deserts. This apparently heightens the sense of adventure and actually makes the race more hazardous because the course runs over an area which has little in the way of roads, certainly no telephones or hotels, and probably very few inhabitants, so competitors are really isolated and on their own. Of course, they do carry a radio so they can call for help if they run into real trouble. Well, perhaps it won't surprise you, but I want to do more of these races, and one of the goals I've set myself is to go to New Zealand and do one of the most spectacular races in the world, the South Island Race, where you run, cycle and kayak for 160 miles through mountains and down rivers. If that race sounds hard to you, and I guess it is, remember it only takes about 24 hours to do the whole course. I say 'only' because some of them go on for as long as ten days. Now that's really extreme. At the moment, I'd say that two or three days would be my absolute maximum in terms of endurance. Competitors have to carry everything they need with them – clothes, food and drink, the lot – and if they run out, they just go hungry or thirsty. On long races, my impression is that the greatest problem is just staying awake, because there are no fixed times for breaks, so teams tend to go on racing for as many hours as they can. In fact, I've heard of people falling asleep while they're riding a bike and that, as you can imagine, can be really dangerous. Just to finish off, another interesting fact: many people who are at the top of their sport in other fields are now taking part because they find that, rather than competing as individuals as they've done all their lives in sports stadiums and the like, they need to work as a team and help each other, and they find this very motivating. I think there's often quite a learning curve for other sports professionals.

Vocabulary
Verb collocations with sporting activities

1 1 do   2 going   3 organised   4 held   5 taking part; competing

2 1 organise/hold; compete / take part / enter
2 go; doing/taking   3 play; play; go

Reading and Use of English Part 6

1 *Suggested answer*
The title and the subheading suggest that we are going to read about what adventure racing involves.

2 *Suggested answers*
Para. 2: type of team which is successful
Para. 3: Rebecca's first race
Para. 4: Training for Australia
Para. 5: How they started the race in Australia
Para. 6: their result in the race
Para. 7: conclusion

Answer key: Unit 7

3 *Suggested underlining*
A Another, his feet   B followed them   C We won it even so, Eco-Challenge in Australia   D His, it
E That (was how much I had prepared)   F When I did it
G To achieve this
1 G   2 F   3 C   4 E   5 B   6 A

Grammar
Infinitive and verb + *-ing*

1 2 f   3 g   4 b, i   5 i   6 d   7 a   8 c   9 h   10 a

2 2 to go   3 to hold   4 Training
5 to get   6 injuring   7 running   8 pushing

3 1 to do   2 to learn   3 doing   4 taking part in

5 1 ~~running~~ to run   2 ~~spending~~ to spend
3 ~~to live~~ living   4 ~~to run~~ running   5 correct
6 ~~take~~ taking   7 ~~to win~~ in winning
8 ~~to sit and read~~ (with) sitting and reading
9 correct   10 ~~ride~~ riding / ~~for~~ to

Reading and Use of English Part 4

1 1 A too many words
B correct
C *suggest* is not followed by the infinitive, and the option doesn't use the word given without changing it
D doesn't use the word given

2 A correct
B too many words
C changes the word given
D doesn't use the word given

2 1 (in order / so as) to get ready   2 could not / couldn't help laughing   3 are not allowed to use

3 & 4
1 taking part in   2 more expensive to hire
3 to give her a ring/call   4 succeeded in winning
5 to lose his temper with   6 had no difficulty (in) learning

Listening Part 4

2 *Suggested underlining*
1 try paragliding   2 choose, in France
3 advantage of learning, sand dune   4 spend the first morning   5 started, instructor   6 when you land, it feels like   7 best reason

3 1 A   2 C   3 B   4 A   5 B   6 A   7 C

 CD 1 Track 26

Interviewer: So, Hannah, what made you want to go on a paragliding course? It sounds like an extremely risky thing to want to do, even for a journalist like yourself.

Hannah: Well, I thought it was a bit risky too. I mean, as a sports journalist, I spend my life watching people do different sports and I've done a fair number of them myself. It's one of the qualifications for the job, I suppose. Anyway, a couple of years ago, I was actually in Switzerland playing golf with friends. I was researching for an article on golf courses and, you know, golf isn't the most exciting of sports. Anyway, I was looking down the course, planning my next shot or something, when I saw these paragliders floating down from the heights. I thought to myself, that looks like fun. Perhaps I should have a go at it myself.

Interviewer: So you went on a course in France, I believe.

Hannah: That's right. I'd actually tried to go on a paragliding course in England a few years ago. I'd even paid the course fee – about £500 – but every time I went down to do the course, it was either too windy or it was raining, so in the end I got fed up and asked for my money back. Anyway, looking on the Internet, I found this rather wonderful place, called Dune du Pyla on the coast in south-west France. It's actually the highest sand dune in Europe – and they run courses there. The price was a bit higher with the travel, but it was a really nice place, and since sunshine was almost guaranteed, I went for it.

Interviewer: Great! And can you tell me, are there any advantages to jumping off a sand dune? I imagine it's rather less dangerous than jumping off a mountain, isn't it?

Hannah: Well, it isn't so high – only about 150 metres, in fact – but wherever you fall, it's going to hurt, so from that point of view, it doesn't necessarily make a lot of difference. But the good thing is that the beach guarantees you a relatively soft landing. Too soft if you go off the beach and into the water, because then you'll need rescuing, although there's usually a steady breeze to keep you from going into the sea.

Interviewer: And what's the main difficulty for a beginner? I imagine it's taking off and landing.

Hannah: The major problem for a complete beginner like myself is actually learning how to hold your paraglider up in the air – er, you know, so that both sides open properly. They only allow you to run

219

Answer key: Unit 7

off the edge and fly when you've mastered that technique, so I didn't get to fly till after lunch on my first day. Getting your paraglider open is quite tricky to start with. It makes you feel a bit silly when you see other people happily flying around below you or above you all morning!

Interviewer: And when you actually start flying, how does your teacher tell you what to do? Does he fly along beside you?

Hannah: No, it sounds a nice idea, and I'd have felt a lot safer if I'd had someone beside me. In fact, I listened to my instructor, Chantalle, through an earphone – she stayed down below and spoke into a small microphone device to tell me what to do. It was generally very quiet, calm and civilised, except when she raised her voice to shout at other flyers to keep away from me. And then you really heard her!

Interviewer: And is landing a problem?

Hannah: Surprisingly not. I was expecting something rather violent – you know, I've come off a horse in my time and that's a lot rougher, I can tell you. This was a relatively soft landing – the sand cushions you a bit – so hardly more of a bump than hopping off a park bench. And you're wearing a helmet, of course, rather like a biker's, so the danger's minimal.

Interviewer: But is it really as safe as you make out?

Hannah: They say it is. I mean, there are a couple of serious accidents every year, but the people I know who do it are very safety-conscious. Most sports, including slow earthbound ones like golf, have some element of risk – I've known a few people get hit by golf balls – some of my own even! Most of all, though, I was taken by the silence. I mean, you're not disturbing anybody in your rather strange eccentric quest for thrills and new sensations. That for me's the best thing and something I've rarely come across before.

Interviewer: Hannah, thank you.

Hannah: A pleasure.

Vocabulary
look, see, watch, listen and hear

1 1 watching   2 looking; saw   3 listened   4 heard

2 1 looked at   2 watching   3 hear   4 looking at
5 see   6 watching   7 hear   8 listening to

Speaking Part 3

3 Miguel and Irene did 2, 3 and 4.

▶ CD 1 Track 27

Examiner: I'd like you to imagine that the director of your school is interested in getting students to do more sport. Here are some ideas. Talk to each other about how each of them might encourage students to do more sport. You have some time to look at the task.

Irene: So, shall I start? How do you think a visit to the national athletics championship would encourage students to do more sport?

Miguel: Um well, perhaps seeing elite athletes doing their sports will inspire students to take up the sport and imitate them.

Irene: Yes, and I imagine students would see how fantastic these people look and how much they enjoy the activity.

Miguel: Maybe, but it might only interest some of the students, but not others. And what about a talk by a professional footballer? I suppose that might be interesting because he'll probably describe what life's really like for a footballer and how – what's the word – how glamorous he is.

Irene: I suppose so, but I don't think it would encourage me to start playing football myself. There are lots of people like me who aren't really interested in football at all.

Miguel: Yes, I see what you mean. And what about the next one – a weekend doing adventure sports? That's just the sort of thing I'd enjoy, and I think lots of students would get interested in adventure sports if they tried them.

Irene: That's a good point, and it could be a good, fun weekend, but do you really think many people are going to get involved in adventure sports as a result? They're quite expensive, you know, and you can't do them every day, not living in a big city.

Miguel: That's true – but you can always go to one of those sports centres with a … a climbing wall, I think it's called.

Irene: Maybe, but I don't think it's the same as going to the mountains to do these things, and not everyone can afford to do that. Now what about a school sports day? To me, that just sounds – mm, what's the word – childish. We used to do sports days at primary school.

Miguel: Well, perhaps this could be organised in a more adult way – you know, with some serious sports for people who were interested and less serious activities for other people. That way everyone could get involved.

Irene: Yes, good idea, and people could be organised into teams and it could all be made quite competitive and enjoyable at the same time. When I think about it, it could be really successful.

Miguel: You're right. And the idea of free membership of a sports club is also a great idea. Hm. Lots of students would be interested in that.

Irene: Yes, but I think that would mainly interest people who already do sports, so I'm not sure it would encourage other people to start.

Miguel: No … unless it was also a social club at the same time. I think that would be extremely effective.

Examiner: Thank you.

4 suggesting ideas: Well, perhaps … ; I imagine students would see … ; What about … ?; I suppose that might be …
asking your partner's opinion: How do you think …?; Do you really think … ?
agreeing: Yes, and … ; Yes, I see what you mean; That's a good point, and … ; That's true; Yes, good idea; You're right
disagreeing: Maybe, but … ; I suppose so, but … ; Yes, but …

Pronunciation: intonation (2)

5.1 ▶ CD 1 Track 28. See page 81.

Writing Part 2   An article

1 *Suggested underlining*
School magazine, sporting activity, exercise you enjoy, how you started, why, recommend it to other people, article

2 being in a team, being outdoors, keeping fit

3 not as rough as football, competitive, being outdoors, keeping fit, great for spectators

4 1 para. 2   2 para. 1   3 para. 3

5 1 Although   2 Despite / In spite of   3 Although / In spite of the fact that   4 despite / in spite of   5 Despite / In spite of   6 However

6 1 competitive   2 rough   3 athletic   4 opponents   5 coach   6 spectators   7 trophy

7 See sample answer in Exercise 3.

8 Dream of the stars

Reading and Use of English Part 7

2 *Suggested underlining*
1 accept negative comments   2 learned a lot from people who work in the theatre and TV   3 other people's suggestions improves their acting   4 variety, performing in the theatre   5 prepared, initially disappointed   6 satisfied, need to impress   7 Underline the whole question.   8 won't mind different sorts of work   9 Underline the whole question.   10 worried, performing in front of some important people

3 1 B   2 C   3 B   4 A   5 C   6 B   7 D   8 D   9 A   10 D

Vocabulary

Verb collocations with *ambition, career, experience* and *job*

1 1 pursue   2 achieve   3 offered   4 turn it down   5 gained

2 1 experience   2 a job   3 a career   4 an ambition

3 1 make/pursue   2 achieve/fulfil/realise   3 gain/get   4 find / apply for / look for   5 build   6 offers   7 launches

play, performance and *acting; audience, (the) public* and *spectators; scene* and *stage*

5 1 stage   2 plays   3 audience   4 performance   5 acting

6 2 play   3 acting   4 performance   5 audience   6 scene   7 stage   8 spectators

Grammar

at, in and *on* in phrases expressing location

1 1 at   2 in   3 on   4 in   5 at

2 1 in   2 on   3 at   4 in   5 at; at; at   6 on   7 in; on   8 at   9 on   10 in; in

Answer key: Unit 8

Listening Part 2

1 *Suggested answers*
1 a place, noun   2 a feeling, adjective   3 means of transport, noun   4 something he didn't bring, noun   5 something you learn, noun   6 a place, noun   7 noun describing an occupation   8 adjective, subject matter, noun   9 period of time, noun or adverb   10 a prize, noun

2 1 shop   2 nervous   3 hired car   4 tie
5 trivial facts   6 Green Room   7 university lecturer
8 general knowledge   9 two months
10 (big) television/TV

▶ **CD 1 Track 29**

Julie: So, I'm going to tell you about my dad's ten minutes of fame. It was when he starred on a TV show a few years ago and it happened like this. The family had a small shop just round the corner from where we live, and one day my aunt was working there on her own when a TV producer just happened to walk in and ask her if she'd like to take part in this quiz show called *The Big Question*. That was a big show, you remember, when we were small kids. I suppose he thought she'd look good on TV, sort of photogenic. Anyway, when she was asked, she just refused to even consider it. She said she was afraid she'd get so nervous that she'd be unable to say a word when a question came to her! My elder sister, who was only 11 at the time, told her she should go because it was the chance of a lifetime, but no one could say anything that'd make her change her mind. Just by chance, at that moment, my dad walked in. Well, he saw his opportunity and offered to go on the show himself! Anyway, the producer agreed, and a couple of weeks later, my father took a hired car – because ours was very old – and he drove to the TV studios. I don't think he trusted the trains to arrive on time, but I reckon there must have been quite a chance he'd get stuck in traffic. You know what it's like round London. Well, anyway, when he got there, he suddenly realised that he'd left his tie behind, so he had to ask the producer if they'd got a spare one at the studio he could borrow. Anyway, he was told he didn't need one – or a jacket for that matter either. Oh, and I forgot to say, he didn't really study for the show – you know, by reading encyclopedias and so on. In fact, I don't think we've ever had an encyclopedia in the house, though I did suggest buying one for the occasion. I suppose he could've gone online, but as far as I know, he didn't. He told me later that, the only thing he'd done was what he always did in the evening, which was read the popular press that we hadn't sold during the day and pick up lots of trivial facts. Anyway, later, what he told me was that before the show, he stood around with the other participants in somewhere called 'The Green Room', where they chatted to each other and were given something to eat and drink, and they got to know each other a bit. My dad felt a bit intimidated, I think, because the other competitors seemed very confident and looked really keen. My dad was expecting them to be doctors or lawyers or something, but in fact, although one of the women really was a university lecturer, the others were a bus driver and somebody who worked in a bank, so quite a mixture. When the show started, I think my dad felt quite lucky and very surprised to be able to answer his questions, which were all about general knowledge and nothing too specialist, because he actually managed to win. Anyway, he did the show, which was recorded, and all of us were longing to see him in it, especially as we knew he'd won. We thought it'd be broadcast like the following week, so it'd be really up to date, but in fact it came on nearly two months later and we almost missed it because we'd almost forgotten about it by then. But it was good, because for weeks after, people were stopping my dad in the street and saying, 'Didn't I see you on *The Big Question*?' Finally though, my dad didn't become a millionaire or come home in a sports car unfortunately, but he did win a big television with a wide screen – we've still got it at home, and it's great for the football – and a big fluffy elephant, which he gave to me. They were pretty impressive prizes for us then – well, for me, because I was still quite small. So, that was my dad's ten minutes of fame. I wonder what mine'll be.

Grammar
Reported speech

1 1 a   2 b

2 1 previous night he had seen   2 she would (get/come) back   3 would arrive (on/in)   4 wasn't allowed to borrow
5 (had) made several mistakes   6 (had) found the play

3 1 to even consider   2 to go   3 if they'd got
4 buying

Answer key: Unit 8

4 1 stealing / that she had stolen 2 lying 3 to buy
4 breaking 5 to visit 6 to buy 7 to visit
8 installing 9 send 10 not to use

Reading and Use of English Part 1

2 Through advertisements.

3 1 B 2 C 3 A 4 C 5 A 6 D 7 D 8 B

Speaking Part 4

1 generally speaking, generally, on the whole

▶ **CD 1 Track 30**

Examiner: Do you think schools should teach subjects such as dance, drama or music?

Antonia: Well, / I think generally speaking / schools should teach these subjects to small children / so that they can find out / if they like them. / I think these subjects / help children to learn / how to express themselves. / But I don't think generally it's so important for older children / or teenagers to do these subjects because / they tend to have lots of other things to study. / So, / on the whole, / I guess these subjects should be / voluntary, / not compulsory, / as children get older.

Examiner: Peter, do you agree with Antonia?

Peter: Generally, yes, but / I feel it's a pity when students / don't have time / for the subjects they enjoy.

2 *Answers and suggested answers*
1 She talks about teaching young children these subjects and then balances it with *but* and her views on older children and teenagers.
2 Young children: to discover if they like the subjects and to learn self-expression; Older children and teenagers: so many other subjects to study.
3 b

Pronunciation: grouping words and pausing (2)

4.2 See recording script for Track 30 above.

5 *Suggested answers*
1 a compulsory/voluntary activity, develop musical abilities, develop artistic expression, develop their musical knowledge
2 develop their artistic expression, work in a team

3 interrupt a film with advertisements, when the film is released
4 a celebrity, avoid/cause a scandal, disturb/protect someone's privacy, the media, a tabloid (newspaper)
5 help society develop, make people aware of problems

Writing Part 1   An essay

1 *Suggested underlining*
famous, film star, both advantages and disadvantages, media attention, lifestyle, your own idea

6 2 *Suggested answers*

	advantages (Para. 1)	disadvantages (Para. 2)
1	if actors are well-known … they will be offered more jobs	film stars have little privacy or time to themselves
2	they live exciting and glamorous lives with plenty of foreign travel and luxury	people with glamorous lifestyles meet other glamorous people; this can sometimes cause problems with, for example, their family relationships
3	fame and success go together	they have to work very hard to be successful and this may lead to considerable stress

3 The underlined sentences and phrase say what the paragraph will contain. This helps the reader know where the essay is going.
4 *Students should highlight:*
However, which, Firstly, if, and if, Also, with, Finally, On the other hand, First, because, Next, and this, Finally, and this, To conclude, because, However
5 in the final paragraph
6 It is required by the writing task, which asks *Do you agree?*

8 *Sample answer*
Many young people's ambition is to go into the music industry or the theatre. However, careers in these fields have both advantages and disadvantages.
There are two main advantages to these professions. Firstly, you can earn a living from a hobby. For example, if you enjoy playing a musical instrument, becoming a member of a band or an orchestra appears to be the perfect job. The second advantage is that if you are successful, you may become famous, and people will admire you for your professional abilities.

223

However, there are also two disadvantages. Being well-known means that you may have less privacy. Many actors, for example, are continually followed by photographers, so they have to be very careful what they do or say in public. Also, the majority of actors and musicians do not earn very much money from their work and may have to teach music or drama in order to survive. In my opinion, unless you are very talented, the best thing is to pursue your music or acting interests as free-time activities and concentrate on studying for a safer, more conventional profession instead.

Vocabulary and grammar review Unit 7

1 1 unpredictable   2 patience   3 preparations
4 inexperienced   5 simply   6 unwilling   7 realistic
8 valuable

2 1 taking   2 to get   3 to invite   4 changing   5 to wear
6 finishing   7 to finish   8 to become   9 helping
10 asking   11 working   12 spending

3 1 aren't allowed / are not allowed to go   2 to avoid getting   3 can't bear windsurfing   4 you mind turning
5 you (may) risk having   6 no/little point (in) going

Vocabulary and grammar review Unit 8

1 1 C   2 B   3 A   4 C   5 A   6 D   7 C   8 B

2 1 Although / Even though   2 despite / in spite of
3 While/Whereas   4 Despite / In spite of   5 However
6 while/whereas   7 although / even though   8 while/whereas

3 1 of the danger   2 the tickets were expensive   3 despite not feeling (very)   4 even though her salary is   5 she had slept the / she had been asleep the   6 would call at/after the

9 Secrets of the mind

Starting off

1 1 c   2 a   3 b   4 d   5 e   6 g   7 f   8 h

Reading and Use of English Part 5

1 She learned to meditate and explore important issues in life; to discover and accept who she really was; to be happy doing what was important for her

2 1 D   2 A

3 3 C   4 D   5 B   6 A

Vocabulary

achieve, carry out and *devote*

1 1 achieve   2 carried out   3 devoted

2 1 achieve: an aim, an ambition, an objective, success
2 carry out: an improvement, an instruction, an order, research, a test, a threat
3 devote: energy, one's life, time

3 1 achieved; ambition   2 carrying out research/tests
3 devote; time   4 devoted; energy
5 carry out; threat   6 carry out orders/instructions

stay, spend and *pass*; *make, cause* and *have*

4 1 have   2 caused   3 spent   4 spent   5 stay   6 made

5 1 spend   2 pass   3 stay   4 had/made   5 spend
6 spent   7 causing   8 makes/made   9 have
10 spent

6 **make:** a change, an impact, an impression, trouble
cause: an accident, a problem, trouble
have: an effect, an impact, an impression, a problem

7 1 caused an accident   2 made; impression
3 caused; (any) trouble / problems / a problem
4 have the impression   5 makes / made / has made; change   6 have; impact/effect

Listening Part 1

2 *Suggested answers*
1A intonation   1B body language, appearance, gestures, mirror   1C actual words
2A character   2B people we like   2C things in common, hobbies

3 1 B   2 C
Words and phrases used: appearance, intonation, mirror, things in common, character

Answer key: Unit 9

▶ CD 2 Track 02

Presenter: One. You hear an expert giving advice about meeting people for the first time.

Dr Bazey: When you meet people for the first time, there's a general belief that it's the words you use that count most, so people tend to spend lots of time preparing how they're going to start a conversation – you know, their opening gambit, so to speak. However, research shows that before we've even opened our mouths, people've already made up their minds about us just from our appearance alone. Then after that, it's things like our intonation and the tone of our voice. Our choice of words actually counts for very little. So, time spent in front of the mirror is probably time well spent!

Presenter: Two. You hear two girls talking about their friendship.

Mandy: We've been best friends for ages, haven't we, Sue?

Sue: Yeah, since we started primary school! Why do you think that is?

Mandy: Well, I guess we've always had lots of consideration for each other. I mean even if I don't get on with all your friends, I put up with them and I try not to show it. And we don't take each other for granted either. Also, we've got lots in common – I'd say that's vital – things we enjoy doing together, even though we're not too alike in terms of character. I mean, I'm rather outgoing and dominating and I tend to go to extremes.

Sue: While I'm more sensitive and cautious, which probably helps because we complement each other quite well.

4 3 B   4 C   5 C   6 A   7 B   8 B

▶ CD 2 Track 03

Presenter: Three. You hear a psychologist in the UK talking about intelligence.

Psychologist: Psychology's quite a young science, which means psychologists haven't had time to measure how or whether our minds are evolving, or whether in fact we're getting cleverer. It's hard to prove that our intelligence is actually increasing, even if young people nowadays tend to get higher marks in intelligence tests than they did 50 or 60 years ago. There are a variety of factors which could have an impact on this: better diets, our minds are stimulated more, or just getting more practice in tests of this type. At the same time, many people think that while exam results have been improving across the country, that's because the exams themselves aren't as demanding as they used to be.

Presenter: Four. You overhear a boy calling a friend on his mobile phone.

Jess: Hi, Ade.

Ade: Oh, hi there, Jess.

Jess: Um, Ade. I was (*yawns*) … Sorry, I'm just so tired.

Ade: Oh, me too – who wouldn't be after all those mid-year tests we've been doing!

Jess: Yeah, I've been up studying most nights, so sorry if I haven't been all that friendly.

Ade: No problem. Anyway, you weren't irritable with me, so I don't mind. Look, can we meet up some day next week instead of tomorrow, 'cos my mum's just told me I've got a dentist's appointment?

Jess: Poor you. Have you got a toothache or something?

Ade: No, just my annual check-up.

Jess: Oh, that's all right, then. Let's catch up at school, shall we?

Ade: OK, see you then. Bye.

Presenter: Five. You overhear a man talking about things which frighten people.

Man: Oh, yeah, you know, I'll do anything to avoid them.

Woman: Including going up several flights of stairs?

Man: Oh, yes. I mean, I just won't go in them, so I sometimes arrive at places a bit breathless.

Woman: I bet!

Man: I think I must have got the problem when I got trapped in one as a kid. I can't have been there for more than ten minutes, but I was trembling when I came out. It's totally irrational, because we all know that they're completely safe. I suppose it's like planes – I mean they terrify lots of people, though statistically they're very safe.

Woman: Well, see you upstairs, then!

Presenter: Six. You hear a girl talking to a boy about a dream.

Boy: Have you ever had a recurring dream – you know, one of those dreams which repeats itself from time to time?

225

Answer key: Unit 9

Girl: Yeah, I have, actually. I'm in one of those high places, a mountain top or the top of a building, and suddenly, for no reason, I'm falling. It's terrifying because I fall for some time, but then suddenly I wake up.

Boy: Wow, that's weird. Do you think it means anything?

Girl: Well, the interpretation I've read is that it's some sort of fear of failure. You know, there are all sorts of interpretations for other dreams. For example, that you could find something subconsciously threatening and your dream might be sort of pointing that out to you.

Presenter: Seven. You overhear two students talking about a classmate.

Rob: Cathy's been behaving a bit strangely lately, hasn't she? I mean, she's been very quiet and not talking much.

Ellie: Yes, she looks pretty stressed out and I guess it's been giving her bad nights.

Rob: What's the problem, do you know? Is it to do with her exams or something?

Ellie: Well, she had a maths exam last week, so she must have studied hard for it. But she's always been pretty hard-working, so she can't have got stressed by that. Anyway, she finds maths easy.

Rob: Lucky her! Hey, do you think she might've had a row with her boyfriend? He can be a bit difficult sometimes, don't you think?

Ellie: Yeah, it must be something like that. Now you come to mention it, I haven't seen him around recently. Perhaps we'd better ask her about him.

Rob: And try and cheer her up.

Presenter: Eight. You hear a boy and a girl talking about the boy's free-time activities.

Boy: I read this thing on the Internet that says your free-time activities say lots about you. If you like sport, you probably like being with other people. On the other hand, I'm someone who prefers doing things on his own, like playing computer games, and that probably shows the opposite, you know, that I'd rather be by myself.

Girl: And you don't feel so comfortable with other people, you mean?

Boy: Hmm, could be. Then again, people who enjoy travelling are often people who like taking risks, doing new things, if you see what I mean.

Girl: Well, you're obviously a stay-at-home type.

Boy: I sure am.

Grammar
Modal verbs to express certainty and possibility

1 1 must   2 can't   3, 4 and 5 may, might, could
2 Present: *may* and *could*; past: *must have* and *can't have*.

2 1 ~~may have~~ must have   2 ~~mustn't be tired~~ can't be tired   3 ~~can have~~ may/might/could have   4 correct   5 ~~can't~~ must

3 1 must have worked   2 must be   3 must have had / must have been having   4 may/might/could have had to; may/might/could have stopped   5 can't be   6 may/might/could rain

4 *Suggested answer*
In the first picture, the girl must have just performed at a concert because she's bowing to the audience and holding a violin. She must have played well, because the audience looks really enthusiastic. It might be a school concert and the audience may be parents and teachers. She must be feeling very pleased and she could also be feeling quite relieved that her performance went well.

In the second picture, the two boys must have broken the window while they were playing football. The man looks as if he might be going to tell them off or punish them. The boys may be feeling embarrassed about what they've done, or they could even be a bit frightened of the man's reaction. The man may be a little bit angry, but he might also remember his childhood and think that this was just an accident.

Reading and Use of English Part 4

1 1 a This is more than five words.
  b correct
  c It's correct English, and it means the same, but it doesn't use *had*.
2 a *despite* is not followed by *of*.
  b correct
  c *despite* is followed by a noun or a verb + *-ing*, not a verb in a tense.
3 a doesn't use the word given
  b *remind* means 'make someone aware of something they (may) have forgotten'.
  c correct
4 a The answer contains six words – the maximum is five.
  b The word given should not be changed in any way.
  c correct

Answer key: Unit 10

5 a *collected up* is not correct in this context.
  b *taken up* is not the correct phrasal verb and does not use the word given.
  c correct – *picked up* means 'collected'.
6 a *do* is not used with *effort*.
  b correct
  c *advise* is followed by an infinitive.

2 1 stand people making a noise   2 reminded him to lock
3 didn't / did not manage to see
4 can't/cannot have been   5 did you spend writing
6 may have found

Speaking Part 2

2 1 seem   2 must   3 perhaps   4 very different
5 exactly what   6 could be   7 who appears
8 may have decided   9 looks as if   10 unlike

▶ **CD 2 Track 04.** See page 102

3 *Suggested answers*
1 they are celebrating the old man's birthday party.
2 very happy.   3 sing 'Happy Birthday' to him.   4 at a football match.   5 cheering their team.   6 they're outside and making a lot of noise.   7 really happy.

Pronunciation: sentence stress (3)

4.1 a seems, exactly, could   b equipment, factory, doing, machine
In a) he emphasises the fact that he's speculating, while in b) he emphasises the different possible activities.

5 a bit, quite

▶ **CD 2 Track 05.** See page 103.

4.3 A: first, experience, being, though, second, job, warm, first   B: first, may, new, perhaps, mountains, looks, second, looks, job, looks, unlike The boy (A) sounds more certain about what he is saying. The girl (B) sounds less certain and emphasises that she is speculating.

▶ **CD 2 Track 06**

Boy: The girl in the <u>first</u> photo may have decided to climb the mountain because she wants a new <u>experience</u>, or perhaps she just enjoys <u>being</u> in the mountains even <u>though</u> she looks a bit tired. The girl in the <u>second</u> photo looks as if she's starting a new <u>job</u> and learning to do something. She looks as if she's quite <u>warm</u> from her work, unlike the girl in the <u>first</u> photo.

Girl: The girl in the <u>first</u> photo <u>may</u> have decided to climb the mountain because she wants a <u>new</u> experience, or <u>perhaps</u> she just enjoys being in the <u>mountains</u>, even though she <u>looks</u> a bit tired. The girl in the <u>second</u> photo <u>looks</u> as if she's starting a new <u>job</u> and learning to do something. She <u>looks</u> as if she's quite warm from her work, <u>unlike</u> the girl in the first photo.

Writing Part 2   A story

3 Para 2. starts *Now, however, …*
Para 3. starts *The tickets were VIP tickets, …*

4 1 he'd entered   2 hadn't heard   3 had sold out
4 'd been listening   5 'd received   6 was listening
7 included   8 walked   9 spent   10 made

7 *Sample answer*
Barbara just couldn't stop smiling. She'd just received a text message from her cousin in Australia, inviting her to stay there during the summer holidays! Her cousin had also sent her a photograph of Barbara's aunt and uncle's new house, right by the beach. They'd been living in Australia for three years now, and Barbara hadn't seen Anna, her cousin, since they'd left. She really missed her, because before they moved abroad, Barbara and Anna had done almost everything together.

Barbara's parents were watching TV when she showed them the text. They laughed and told her they were going too, and they'd already bought the tickets, but had wanted it to be a surprise. There were only three weeks of term left, and Barbara spent them dreaming of Australia and seeing Anna again at last.

Her mother took her shopping for presents to take with them for the family, and soon it was time for them to leave. The journey was exciting, but nothing like as exciting as the moment when she saw Anna and her family waiting for her in the arrivals hall at Sydney airport!

10 On the money

Reading and Use of English Part 2

2 The writer prefers going to shops with friends because it's more sociable, fun and exciting. It's also a good idea to try things before buying them.

227

Answer key: Unit 10

3 1 least 2 as / being 3 out 4 how 5 rather / sooner 6 like 7 what 8 on

Grammar
as and like

1 1 as 2 like

2 1 as 2 as 3 as 4 like 5 as 6 as; as 7 as 8 like 9 as; as 10 as

Reading and Use of English Part 5

3 1 B 2 D 3 B 4 C 5 C 6 A

4 1 b 2 b 3 a 4 a 5 b 6 a 7 a 8 a 9 b

Vocabulary
arrive, get and reach

1 1 get 2 arrived 3 reached

2 1 reached 2 get 3 gets/arrives 4 get 5 arrived 6 reach

3 1 safe and sound 2 in time 3 on time 4 shortly 5 unannounced 6 finally

Listening Part 4

1 *Suggested answers*
There are many shops in one place, easy parking, places to relax, customers are protected from the weather, etc., there is usually good security, so customers feel safe. There are usually more things you can do there, e.g. go to a restaurant, the cinema, bowling alley, the gym, have a haircut, see an arts event, etc.

2 Reasons the interviewees mention: access (station and motorway), good shops, good quality, caters for every taste including people who don't want to shop, family fun, safe and crime free, luxurious surroundings, reduce family conflicts.

CD 2 Track 07

Interviewer: Hi! I'm in a new shopping centre with some guys who've been finding out a bit more about the place. Kerry?

Kerry: Yeah – first, let me tell you where it is. You know you'd expect to drive for miles out into the countryside to a place among green fields. When they build them in the country, everyone has to get there by car, but at least then the parking's easy. This new one's taken over some abandoned industrial land on the outskirts of the city and it's pulling in young people, families, everyone, so there's a really great atmosphere.

Interviewer: So why do you think they went for this particular site? Salim?

Salim: Well, apparently, they were offered a place in the country and the plans were approved, but they chose this place for its convenient access from the station and the motorway. The locals did start kicking up a fuss about traffic noise and fumes and that sort of thing, so it took quite a long time to get things started, but they managed to get permission in the end.

Interviewer: But why do you think there are such masses of people here now? What's behind its popularity?

Salim: Well, you see, people don't just come to shop. They come to spend the day. There are tons of good stores with branches here, so even though you end up spending quite a bit, in general the stuff's good quality and there's something here for everyone. It caters for every taste, including people like myself who'd rather not shop at all but would prefer to take in a film or hit the gym instead. So you see lots of families having fun here too, without having to hang around with each other the whole time. Dad goes off to look at sports equipment or electronics, while mum hunts for clothes. You know, that sort of thing.

Interviewer: From where I'm standing now I can see trees and fountains. There are cafés, music for chilling out and even a free fashion show. It's a bit of a change from your normal high street, isn't it?

Kerry: Yeah, it's incredible, isn't it? You know, these places are pretty safe. There's never any trouble. But what I really like is that the place feels a bit like a palace. You know, I can spend all day here with my friends surrounded by all this expensive stuff without it costing me a penny. People treat you pretty well and you don't have to spend anything unless you want to.

Answer key: Unit 10

Interviewer: We're always hearing about families having arguments when they go shopping. Why's that?

Salim: Apparently, it's because they're spending the day together and their tastes in how to spend their free time are different, so they get irritable with each other, and this breaks down into arguments about which shops to go to and so on.

Interviewer: And this place is organised to cater for different tastes, isn't it?

Kerry: Well, yeah, what they've done is organise the shops, cafés and other places so there's a wide range of quite different shops in each section. This means that families can still be fairly close to each other, even though they're up to different things. You know, mum can wander into the clothes shop if that's what she wants to do, while dad can pop into the computer shop next door and the kids can go to a games shop or a music shop. They're all nearby and they can find each other easily.

Interviewer: And what else have they done, Salim?

Salim: Well, they've come up with ways of making shopping less tiring. You know, a day's shopping wears people out. They thought of hiring out small electrically driven cars to shoppers to cut down the amount they walk. They came up against problems of space – there just wasn't enough room for them all – so they also thought about those moving walkways you see at airports and that would've involved redesigning everything. What they actually came up with is a new technology which sends everything you've bought to your exit point, and you just pick it up there.

Interviewer: Awesome. Thanks, Kerry and Salim.

Kerry: Cheers.

3 & 4
1 B   2 C   3 B   4 A   5 A   6 B   7 C

Vocabulary
Phrasal verbs

1 1 j   2 a   3 g   4 h   5 l   6 k   7 d   8 c   9 f
10 e   11 i   12 b

2 1 came up with   2 cut down on   3 pop into
4 caters for   5 hanging around with   6 wore us out
7 pulling in   8 taken over   9 come up against
10 pick up   11 been up to   12 chill out

Grammar
Modals expressing ability

1 1 d; f   2 c; g   3 a; e   4 b; h

2 1 were able to   2 couldn't sleep   3 could
4 Can you   5 could have played   6 were able to

4 1 able to cut down   2 you could have had   3 you able to pick up   4 can't cater for

Speaking Part 1

2 1 T   2 B   3 T   4 A

CD 2 Track 08

Examiner: Thomas, are you ever given money by people in your family?

Thomas: Well, I have a lot of brothers and sisters, and my grandparents and my aunt and uncle live a long way away. My parents can't give us all money every week, but when we go and see my grandparents in the holidays, they give us some money to spend. I also get money from all my family on my birthday.

Examiner: And Anna, what do teenagers in your country typically spend their money on?

Anna: I think it really depends because teenagers are all different and so they spend their money in all sorts of ways. I guess some people spend more money on clothes and magazines, while others spend more on music and things like sports equipment. In general though, I think most teenagers spend money on things like going out to cafés or cinema tickets.

Examiner: Thomas, do you have a favourite shop?

Thomas: Hmm, I'm not sure, because I don't go shopping much really. Umm, but there is one shop I really like. It's one of a chain of sports shops and what's cool about it is I can just wander round and see all the clothes and equipment and stuff they sell … I look at clothes and equipment I'd like to buy – when I can afford it, I mean.

Examiner: Anna. Is there anything you'd like to buy that you can't afford?

Anna: Of course! Lots of things! I mean, I don't have a lot of money. My parents give me an allowance, and other people in my family give me money for my birthday. At the moment, I'm saving up for a pair of jeans I'd really like – maybe I'll be able to get them in the sales!

229

Answer key: Unit 10

Pronunciation: linking (1)

4.1 ▶ CD 2 Track 09. See page 113

4.2 ▶ CD 2 Track 10. See page 113

4.3 1 We don't pronounce final 't's and 'd's when the word which follows begins with a consonant.
2 We link the word to the following word when the word ends with a consonant and the following word begins with a vowel.

4.5 See recording script for Track 11.

> ▶ **CD 2 Track 11**
>
> **Thomas:** Hmm, I'm not sure, because I don't go shopping much really. Umm, but there is one shop I really like. It's one of a chain of sports shops and what's cool about it is I can just wander round and see all the clothes and equipment and stuff they sell. I look at clothes and equipment I'd like to buy … – when I can afford it I mean.

5 Thomas uses strategy 1; Anna uses strategy 3.

> ▶ **CD 2 Track 12**
>
> **Examiner:** Thomas, what sort of shops do you go to regularly?
>
> **Thomas:** Well, umm … I don't do a lot of shopping, at least not regularly, and my mum and dad do all the shopping for the family. … There's a place where they sell snacks and takeaways that I like and I've been there a few times with my friends. And when I'm at my grandparents in the holidays, I go to the shops with them in their town. I go to food shops with my grandparents and to sports shops and music shops on my own.
>
> **Examiner:** And Anna, what sort of shops do you go to regularly?
>
> **Anna:** My dad and I love cooking together at the weekend, making these really exotic dishes. There are plenty of shops in the area which sell good vegetables, food from different parts of the world, and spices, so we often go to those shops together to get what we need. My dad's a great cook. I'm learning a lot from him and we have a great time!

Writing Part 2 A review

1 *Suggested underlining*
website for teenagers, have been given, bought, gadget, a piece of clothing, describing, like it and why, recommend it to other people

4 *Suggested answers*
Para. 1: what the thing is: a bike – description of appearance – compare it with old bike
Paras. 2 and 3: description of features – suitable for?
Para. 4: where it can be found + price/colours
Para. 5: why I recommend it

5 *Suggested answers*
2 Apart from being very easy to use, this camera takes excellent pictures.
3 Although it's blue, which isn't my favourite colour, the camera still looks very smart.
4 It has a strong case, which is very important, because I am such a clumsy person that I would soon damage it while carrying it around.
5 My brother showed me how to use all the different functions, but don't worry if you have to work it out yourself, as it comes with a very good instruction manual and DVD.

6 *Sample answer*
See sample answer in Student's Book Exercise 4, page 115.

Vocabulary and grammar review Unit 9

1 1 spent 2 have 3 causes 4 pass 5 had 6 made
7 spent

2 1 may be 2 could just 3 might be doing it
4 very different 5 look 6 appear to 7 look as if
8 perhaps 9 both

3 1 must have switched 2 can't have turned
3 may not have heard 4 could have left 5 might answer
6 might have forgotten 7 can't have forgotten

Vocabulary and grammar review Unit 10

1 1 C 2 B 3 D 4 A 5 C 6 B 7 B 8 A

2 1 was not / wasn't able to finish   2 down (on) the amount of   3 was/felt so worn out by   4 could not / couldn't come up with   5 able to pick Paz up   6 get to the cinema until

3 1 as   2 as   3 as   4 as   5 like   6 as   7 as   8 Like   9 like   10 like

11 Medical matters

Starting off

1 1 active   2 workout   3 catch; infection; get over   4 check-up; treatment   5 illness   6 balanced diet; putting on

2 B 4   C 6   D 1   E 5   F 3

3

> **CD 2 Tracks 13 and 14**
>
> **Speaker A:** I love exercise and so does my Dad! We get up pretty early, about 6.30 and / I do an hour's workout in the morning before school and in the evening I usually have time for a couple of hours' football, so I really think I'm very fit.
>
> **Speaker B:** I take my health pretty seriously. I think you have to. / I visit the doctor regularly once a year for a check-up. Once or twice I've needed treatment for something she's found, but it's never been anything very serious.
>
> **Speaker C:** I think I'm healthy, but then I take good care of myself because I believe that old saying: 'Everything in moderation'. So / I'm very careful to eat a balanced diet – only a little meat and plenty of fresh fruit and vegetables – and I'm careful about not putting on weight, so I do a reasonable amount of exercise as well.
>
> **Speaker D:** I think I'm pretty healthy. I mean, I have a lovely life. I've been retired now for nearly 20 years on a nice pension, so no financial problems, and / here I am, in my 80s, still quite active – I mean, I go shopping, visit my friends and go to the cinema when I want to. What more can you ask for?
>
> **Speaker E:** I'm just a naturally happy, relaxed person and I think that's a large part of the secret of good health. / I never go to the doctor and in fact, I don't even know my doctor's name. I'm lucky: I've never had a day's illness in my life.

> **Speaker F:** Me, healthy? I should think so. I've never been stopped from doing anything I want to do because of an illness. Of course, / I do catch the occasional cold or other infection. I'm a doctor, so I can't really avoid them, but I get over them pretty quickly and they don't usually stop me going to work.

Listening Part 3

1 1 five; eight   2 read and think about the meaning of each option

2 1 f   2 c   3 e   4 g   5 b   6 a   7 h   8 d

3 Speaker 1: surgery, prescribe, treat
Speaker 2: cure(d), diagnose
Speaker 3: examination, sick note
Speaker 4: –
Speaker 5: heal

> **CD 2 Track 15**
>
> **Speaker 1:** Well, Dad got me to the surgery at a quarter past eight for an appointment at eight-thirty, but in fact I had to hang around there till nearly half past nine to see the doctor, so I was feeling pretty bored because there were only a couple of other people ahead of me. Anyway, when I finally saw the doctor he said I'd just got a slight infection, which is what I was expecting, and he prescribed some antibiotics to treat it. But I did find it a bit annoying to have to wait so long, especially as I was missing my favourite class of the week!
>
> **Speaker 2:** I've been feeling a bit off-colour for some time now and my dad's taken me to the doctor several times to try to get to the bottom of it. The last time I went, the doctor who normally sees me was on holiday so I saw a different one. She was just so sympathetic! She asked me all sorts of questions about my medical history and my family background and she took lots of notes. She spent a really long time talking to me and sounded so interested that when I left, I felt almost cured! Not that she was able to diagnose my problem straight away, but she did send me off for tests.
>
> **Speaker 3:** My mum took me to see the doctor the other day because we thought I'd got flu and needed a few days off school. Anyway, the doctor gave me quite a thorough examination and then he told me I was hardly ill at all and he refused to give me a

Answer key: Unit 11

sick note. I was quite surprised and pretty annoyed, because I'd been coughing and sneezing all week and feeling very under the weather. Anyway, there was nothing I could do to change his mind, so it was back to school the same morning, worse luck!

Speaker 4: When my mum and I went in, the doctor just asked me a few questions but didn't examine me. Then he said that if the symptoms persisted, I should come back the following week. My mum is never intimidated by doctors because her father was one. So she told him she wanted him to examine me properly straight away. I must say he looked a bit taken aback, but then he got up from his desk and came and gave me a really thorough check-up. In the end, he apologised and said he'd been up all night on duty in the local hospital, where he'd been rushed off his feet.

Speaker 5: My mum took me to the doctor because I'd been complaining of neck pains. We were there for what seemed like hours. She gave me a very complete check-up and took ages over it. She looked at my neck, asked about my medical history and my daily routine. Then she told me that the problem was probably caused by too much sitting in front of the computer studying, and with a good rest, my neck would heal itself. She suggested that I should make sure I spent time away from my desk to unwind and then the pain would just go away on its own.

4 *Suggested underlining*
A wasn't given enough attention B needed to relax
C irritated   D wish, hadn't gone
E felt better after, visit   F asked for a specialist
G agreed, diagnosis   H arrived late
1 G   2 E   3 C   4 A   5 B

Vocabulary
Idiomatic expressions
1 b   2 c   3 d   4 e   5 a

Reading and Use of English Part 6

1 He's not sure, but he's interested in medicine, biochemistry and race driving.

2 1 e   2 b   3 a   4 d   5 j   6 m   7 k   8 h

3 1 caught a cold apart from   2 was far longer than
3 succeeded in persuading   4 is unlikely to be   5 led to some patients being   6 long as I keep taking

Grammar
Relative pronouns and relative clauses

1 1 which   2 who   3 who   4 where

2 1 D   2 ND   3 D   4 D   5 ND   6 D

3 3, 4 and 6

4 3 and 4, because they are the object of the clause.

5 2 He studied hard for his maths exam, which he found quite easy. / He found the maths exam, which he studied hard for, quite easy.
3 The man (who/that) they sold the car to is a taxi driver. / They sold the car to a man who is a taxi driver.
4 Could you give me the newspaper (which/that) you were reading earlier?
5 That white house over there is the house where he was born.
6 Where's the envelope (which/that) I put the money in?
7 Every morning I go running in the park with Patricia, whose brother you know.
8 Karen and Teresa, whose dog we're looking after, are on holiday in the Caribbean at the moment.

Reading and Use of English Part 3

1 1 a

2 1 b   2 a

3 *mis-*: it means *to do something wrongly*

4 1 undo   2 disappoint   3 misuse   4 untie
5 misspell   6 disappeared   7 undressed
8 misinformed

5 inability/disability, disagreement, disappear, unaware, uncertain, inexperienced, informal, unhappiness, unhelpful, dishonest, dislike/unlike, impatient, unpredictable, unreliable, dissatisfied/unsatisfied, misunderstand

6 1 unexpected   2 security   3 occasionally
4 medical   5 height   6 calculation   7 assistance
8 uneasy

Answer key: Unit 11

Speaking Part 2

1 *Suggested answers*
When you need time to think: Let me think …
When you can't think of the word: I can't think of the word, but it's a type of … ; I'm not sure how to say it, but it's used for … ; What's the word?
When you've made a mistake: I'm sorry, what I meant was … ; No, I mean … ; What I want to say is that … ; Sorry, I mean …

2 Antonia did all the things on the checklist.

> ▶ **CD 2 Track 16**
>
> **Examiner:** In this part of the test, I'm going to give each of you two photographs. I'd like you to talk about your photographs on your own for about a minute, and also to answer a question about your partner's photographs. Antonia, it's your turn first. Here are your photographs. They show people doing healthy activities. I'd like you to compare the photographs and say how important you think each activity is for staying healthy. All right?
>
> **Antonia:** OK, so <u>both</u> photographs show people doing things which might be good for their <u>sanity</u>, sorry, I mean their <u>health</u>. In the <u>first</u> photo, I can see someone who looks as if he's, <u>what's</u> the <u>word</u>, he's <u>commuting</u> by <u>bicycle</u> in busy <u>traffic</u>. So, he's getting some exercise, which must be good for his general fitness. In the second photo, there are some young people who are doing some cooking – well, not exactly cooking because what they're doing is preparing a salad. What I want to say is, they're going to eat something quite healthy. I mean, it's not like eating pizza or hamburgers. So both photos show people doing something healthy – getting exercise and eating a good deeat, sorry, I mean diet. I'd say there are some <u>problems</u> with the idea of <u>health</u> in the <u>first</u> photo because of the <u>danger</u> from the <u>traffic</u>, especially because he's cycling in the <u>night</u>, I mean in the <u>dark</u>, and the, I can't think of the <u>word</u>, but it's a type of <u>smoke</u> which comes from the <u>cars</u>. On the other hand, if you live in the <u>city</u>, it's a good way of getting <u>exercise</u>. In the <u>second</u> photo, the kids should <u>remember</u> that they need to eat a <u>mixed</u>, um, sorry, a <u>balanced</u> diet, not just <u>salad</u> and <u>fruit</u>.
>
> **Examiner:** Thank you.

3 2 **a** Nikolai **b** Miguel **c** Peter

Pronunciation: intonation (3)

4.1 Underline on: both, sanity, health, first, what's, word, commuting, bicycle, traffic

▶ **CD 2 Track 17.** See page 125

4.2 The speaker is more confident in a). Her voice falls on the final stressed words. In b), her voice rises on the final stressed words, making her sound uncertain.

▶ **CD 2 Track 18.** See page 125

4.4 Stressed words: a) problems, health, first, danger, traffic, night, dark, word, smoke, cars b) city, exercise, second, remember, mixed, balanced, salad, fruit

▶ **CD 2 Track 19.** See page 125

4.5 b Her voice falls at the end of phrases.

5

> ▶ **CD 2 Track 20**
>
> **Examiner:** In this part of the test, I'm going to give each of you two photographs. I'd like you to talk about your photographs on your own for about a minute, and also to answer a question about your partner's photographs. Student A, here are your photographs. They show people doing healthy activities. I'd like you to compare the photographs and say how important you think each activity is for staying healthy. All right?

6

> ▶ **CD 2 Track 21**
>
> **Examiner:** Student B, which activity would you prefer to do to keep healthy, and why?

7

> ▶ **CD 2 Track 22**
>
> **Examiner:** Now, Student B, here are your photographs. They show two people with minor health problems. I'd like you to compare the photographs and say why it is important for these people to deal with their problems. All right?

8

> ▶ **CD 2 Track 23**
>
> **Examiner:** Student A, which problem do you think is more serious, and why?

233

Answer key: Unit 12

Writing Part 1 An essay

2 *Suggested underlining*
modern lifestyles, endanger, health, food, physical activity

3 *Suggested answers*
Strong points: It is clearly written in paragraphs, covers the notes in the task and is well linked together.

Weak points: The writer's opinion is not clear; there is no concluding paragraph.

5 1 c 2 a 3 b

6 1 a an explanation of healthy aspects of our lifestyles
  b things which stop people living healthily
  2 *However* (contrasts information and ideas with the paragraph before)

7 *Suggested answers*
1 There are three main advantages to living in the country.
2 On the other hand, there are several disadvantages to a country life.
3 Exercise is important for the following reasons.
4 However, there are some dangers attached to taking too much exercise.

9 *Sample answer*
Everyone knows that a healthy lifestyle when you are young is essential for staying well as you grow older. However, many young people could do more to look after their health.

Like everyone else, teenagers should take regular exercise. In my town, perhaps half of the young people I know go running or play football or do some other form of sport, but I have many friends who only do sporting activities occasionally, so they are not really fit. This may be because of the amount of time they have to spend studying.

On the other hand, it is becoming increasingly common for young people to have a healthy balanced diet, so few people become overweight, which is very important. Finally, it is important to remember to relax and have fun. Young people can become very stressed by exams, but they need to be organised and find time to do things they enjoy. Stress can be a major factor in ill-health.

In conclusion, I believe young people take a reasonable amount of care of themselves although many would benefit from following a regular exercise routine.

12 Animal kingdom

Starting off

Suggested answers
The horse is used in a competitive sport. There's a very close relationship between the horse and the rider.
The dog is a working animal and it's role is to guide and help blind people. The owner relies on the dog on a daily basis.
The guinea pig is a pet and the boy is probably its owner. The boy spends his leisure time playing with the hamster.
The lions are wild animals. The tourists admire and respect them in their leisure time / while on holiday, but there isn't a close relationship between man and animal.
The cow is a farming animal and it provides people with milk.
The camels are working animals and the men in the photo depend on them to carry goods across the desert.

Listening Part 1

1 1 eight; different subjects 2 twice 3 read but don't hear 4 in the question only 5 after you have heard the whole of each piece

2 1 C 2 B 3 C 4 B 5 C 6 B 7 A 8 A

> ▶ **CD 2 Track 24**
>
> **Presenter:** One. You overhear a conversation between two women about animals.
>
> **Woman 1:** My husband is always saying he wishes he had a dog to go for walks with.
>
> **Woman 2:** So do you think you'll get one?
>
> **Woman 1:** I don't know. It's such a commitment. I mean, we'd have to take him with us on holiday, that sort of thing, so I'd rule that out. Then my daughter, Patsy, would really like to have a horse.
>
> **Woman 2:** But that's even more of a commitment!
>
> **Woman 1:** I know, which is why I hesitate. I mean, we'd have to supervise her quite closely to start with to make sure she was safe. At least until we know she can control it.
>
> **Woman 2:** What about a cat?
>
> **Woman 1:** Well, they're definitely the easiest to look after – not that they interest any of us. In the end, we'll probably let Patsy have her choice – it's a mistake to deny your kids the things they really want.

Answer key: Unit 12

Presenter: Two. You hear part of a television programme about zebras.

Man: To us, every zebra looks alike. During their migration, all the stripes form a confusing pattern which helps to protect them from lions and other predators. But while to the untrained eye they appear identical, each individual's pattern is unique, helping others to identify them. While male zebras have wider, darker, shinier stripes than females, at a distance and in a mass they may all look the same. Even so, young zebras who go off to play can always pick out their mums from thousands of others.

Presenter: Three. You overhear a conversation between a boy and a girl about birds in the girl's garden.

Boy: Hi, Trish. What've you been up to this weekend?

Girl: Oh, I've been helping my mum in the garden a lot of the time.

Boy: So working hard.

Girl: You're telling me! But my mum loves the garden, especially the birds which go there to feed – you know, on insects and berries and things.

Boy: Uh-huh.

Girl: Yeah, and when she's not in the garden, she's watching the birds from the window and keeping an eye out to make sure the cats don't get them. There are tons of cats in our neighbourhood, and she hates the idea of them catching birds. And she's right: dead birds are gross!

Presenter: Four. You overhear part of a conversation in which a girl and a boy are talking about dogs.

Girl: Have you still got that lovely dog of yours?

Boy: We sure have!

Girl: Lucky you! I wish I had a dog.

Boy: Well, he is nice to look at, but we really got him to protect us from burglars. Probably, if we lived in a safer area, we wouldn't have bought one. In fact, he barks at everything, which doesn't make us very popular in the neighbourhood.

Girl: Well, all that barking might prevent a burglary. And I bet he's good fun to play with, isn't he?

Boy: Sure, he's great for that, but I'd be happier if my parents had bought a house in the country. Then we wouldn't worry about neighbours or burglars.

Presenter: Five. You hear a woman giving part of a lecture about animal rights.

Woman: It would, I think, be ignorant to suggest that zoos no longer serve a useful purpose. Many of them do quite valuable work conserving rare species. What I do think, and I'm sure you'd agree with me here, is that those old-fashioned zoos which were designed and built in the 19th century just don't give animals enough space. There's no feeling that animals are in a natural habitat. Those zoos should all be closed and banned, while the more modern zoos need to be strictly inspected to make sure that the animals are kept in the best conditions possible. That way, diseases and other problems can be avoided.

Presenter: Six. You hear a girl talking about some animals she worked with.

Girl: Last summer, you see, I went as a volunteer on a wildlife conservation project in Africa and I was asked to look after these young lions which had been orphaned – you know, they'd lost their mother. It's curious, because I'd expected to feel quite anxious – I mean, they're dangerous animals, aren't they? In fact, after I'd spent a few days feeding the lion cubs and playing with them, we had a very easy, comfortable relationship. I had to keep an eye on them as well, because they could be quite rough when playing with each other, and we didn't want them to harm each other, but I never felt they were going to attack me.

Presenter: Seven. You hear a boy talking about hippos.

Boy: I always thought hippos spent their day hiding in the water, but then I saw this awesome video on YouTube of a guy on holiday in South Africa. It shows him walking along a river bank – he's being filmed by a friend – when suddenly there's this crashing noise in the grass and a hippo rushes out. Wow! Anyway, the guy just manages to leap to one side and run while his mate screams and drops the camera. If he hadn't reacted quickly, the hippo would've killed him, for sure, trampled him underfoot! Anyway, I got sort of interested in this and Googled 'hippos'. Apparently, they get nervous if someone walks between them and the river, which is their natural habitat, and more people are killed by hippos in Africa every year than by any other animal just because they get between the hippo and the water.

Presenter: Eight. You hear a woman talking to her husband about a circus.

Woman: Brian!

Man: Yes?

Answer key: Unit 12

> **Woman:** I've been looking in the paper and it's given me an idea. Why don't we take the kids to the circus in the holidays? That's something we haven't done for a few years.
>
> **Man:** Hmm, I'm not sure. I mean, the last time we went, it wasn't exactly fun, was it?
>
> **Woman:** Yes, but that's because they had all those acts with tired-looking animals and things. If they'd had more acrobats, we'd have enjoyed it more. Anyway, this one's different. It might be much better.
>
> **Man:** OK, well, let's ask them if they'd be interested in going.

Vocabulary
avoid, prevent and protect; check, control, keep an eye on and supervise

1 1 protect   2 prevent   3 avoided   4 keep an eye on
5 supervise; control

2 1 protecting   2 prevents   3 checking   4 avoid
5 protect   6 supervise   7 check   8 control

3 1 successfully prevented   2 narrowly avoided
3 properly protected   4 strictly controlled
5 closely supervised   6 avoid; at all costs
7 check; carefully   8 heavily protected

Grammar
Third conditional and mixed conditionals

1 1 T   2 F   3 T

2 1 b   2 a   3 b   4 a   5 b   6 a   7 a

3 1 would have finished   2 had known; would have caught
3 would have gone   4 had not been
5 had sat   6 would have enjoyed   7 would not have made   8 would not have heard

5 1 a second – refers to present time
b third – refers to past time
2 a second – refers to present time
b third – refers to past time

6 1 had; would have driven   2 had studied; would not feel / would not be feeling   3 did not bark; would have taken
4 had not been; would still be

Reading and Use of English Part 1

2 1 eight   2 the text quickly   3 after   4 the options
5 you have finished   6 all the questions

3 horses

4 1 A   2 C   3 D   4 B   5 D   6 A   7 D   8 C

Grammar
wish, if only and hope

1 1 a, b, d and e   2 a, b and d   3 b   4 past tense and would + infinitive   5 c   6 past perfect   7 f
8 present simple

2 1 ~~wish~~ hope   2 ~~wish~~ hope   3 correct   4 ~~wish~~ hope
5 correct   6 ~~wish~~ hope   7 correct   8 ~~wish~~ hope

3 1 was a better   2 I'd / I had studied harder
3 would make less OR wouldn't / would not make so much   4 hadn't / had not called off   5 wish you'd / you had met

Reading and Use of English Part 7

1 1 F (There are ten.)   2 T   3 F (Read the questions carefully first.)   4 T   5 F (Answer all the questions.)

3 *Suggested underlining*
1 didn't immediately react, to injury   2 unwilling, injure, animal   3 believes, behaviour caused, attack   4 advice, ignored   5 was helped, quick reaction   6 no pain, injury
7 regrets, result, encounter   8 thinks, animals behaviour, unusual   9 happy at first, animal, attacked   10 surprised, eventually escape

4 1 B   2 C   3 D   4 A   5 B   6 B   7 D   8 B   9 D
10 A

Speaking Parts 3 and 4

1 1 Miguel is doing all the speaking and not giving Irene a chance to participate.
2 *Suggested answer:* Irene needs to find an opportunity to interrupt.

Answer key: Unit 12

CD 2 Track 25

Examiner: Now I'd like you to talk about something together for about two minutes. I'd like you to imagine that a famous animal expert has offered to give a talk to students at your school about some aspect of animals and the natural world. Here are some of the subjects he has said he can talk about and a question for you to discuss. First, you have some time to look at the task. Now talk to each other about what students would find interesting and useful about each of these subjects.

Miguel: I think choosing a pet could be interesting and useful for students who are thinking of adopting a cat or a dog or some other animal to share their home, so they can find the right one, or one that suits them and not one which is going to give them problems. And the talk about animals in danger is important for learning to look after the environment so that animals don't become extinct or disappear. But on the other hand, we see this sort of subject on television all the time and for students it might not be too interesting. Also, I suppose if there are students who are thinking of becoming farmers or vets, then working with animals might be quite interesting, though it wouldn't really interest me …

2 Yes, I agree, and; Yes, you're right, but

CD 2 Track 26

Miguel: I think choosing a pet could be interesting and useful for students who are thinking of adopting a cat or a dog or some other animal to share their home, so they can find the right one, or one which suits them—

Irene: Yes, I agree, and, and it will help them to learn a bit about what common pets are like, you know, er, their characteristics and perhaps a bit about how to look after them properly as well.

Miguel: And the subject of animals in danger is important for learning to look after the environment so that animals don't become extinct or disappear. It will make students more aware of the problem—

Irene: Yes, you're right, but, but we see this sort of thing on television all the time, so unless he has something new or unusual to say, this might be a subject students already know quite a lot about …

4

CD 2 Track 27

Examiner: Now you have about a minute to decide which two subjects it would be best for the expert to speak about.

5 1 c

2 **comment on the question:** That's a difficult question; That's quite interesting

introduce other people's opinions: People often suggest that … ; Some people say that …

say whether you agree or disagree with other people's opinions: I think that's true; I'm not sure that I agree

CD 2 Track 28

Examiner: Irene, do you think animals should be kept in zoos?

Irene: That's a difficult question. Some people say that it's cruel to keep animals in zoos where they don't have the freedom that they'd have in their natural habitat. They say that animals get stressed and can't relax, but I'm not sure that I agree. I think they can. If animals have some space, they can have a nice relaxed life in a zoo because no other animals will attack them, and they don't have to look for food either.

Examiner: And what can children learn from keeping animals at home as pets?

Irene: That's quite interesting. People often suggest that children learn to be responsible because they have to look after the animal. I think that's true and also, from my experience, I think it's an extra relationship which develops children's ability to love and care about the animals and the people around them.

Examiner: And Miguel, what can people learn from watching programmes about animals on television?

Answer key: Unit 13

Pronunciation: word stress (3)

6.1 See underlining in recording script for Track 29.

> **CD 2 Track 29**
>
> <u>That's</u> a difficult question. <u>Some</u> people say <u>that</u> it's cruel to keep animals in zoos where they don't have the freedom <u>that</u> they'd have in their natural habitat.
>
> They say that animals get stressed and can't relax, but I'm not sure that I agree. I think they <u>can</u>. If animals have <u>some</u> space, they <u>can</u> have a nice relaxed life in a zoo …
>
> <u>That's</u> quite interesting. People often suggest <u>that</u> children learn to be responsible because they have to look after the animal.
>
> I think <u>that's</u> true and also, from my experience, I think <u>that</u> it's an extra relationship which develops children's ability to love <u>and</u> care about the animals <u>and</u> the people around them.

Writing Part 2 A letter or email

1 *Suggested answers*
1 where to go, what to see and the best way of getting around to see countryside, scenery and wildlife
3 informal style – it's a letter to a friend – he has written to you in an informal style.

3 1 I'm very glad to hear that you're thinking of visiting my country this summer. 2 yes – advice about visiting Asturias, what to see while there, and hiring a car
3 yes – he adds information
4 quite informal

4 1 I'd advise you to go to Asturias 2 You should visit the 'Picos de Europa' 3 If I were you, I'd hire a car to get around. 4 The best idea would be to hire it online
5 Make sure that you take warm clothes and a raincoat

6 *Sample answer*
See the model letter in Exercise 3, page 137.

Vocabulary and grammar review Unit 11

1 1 diagnosed 2 heal 3 treatment 4 infection
5 put on 6 fit 7 prescription 8 cure 9 check-up
10 get over

2 1 misunderstood 2 disapprove 3 dissatisfied
4 inexperienced 5 dislikes 6 unwilling 7 unnatural
8 misleading 9 unfashionable 10 unacceptable
11 unreliable 12 dishonest

3 1 whose arm is broken has 2 one the injury (which/ that) / the one (which/that) the 3 whose inhabitants are (all)
4 in a/the way (that/which) 5 from his email what
6 (which/that) Chiaro tells do not / don't

Vocabulary and grammar review Unit 12

1 1 B 2 C 3 A 4 D 5 A 6 B

2 1 had not / hadn't been 2 was/were 3 wasn't, would have had 4 would not / wouldn't make 5 lived
6 has not / hasn't missed 7 would speak
8 would be 9 will change / are going to change
10 had studied 11 would have got 12 had eaten

3 1 had not / hadn't left 2 had paid her
3 have made a/any difference 4 had a better relationship with 5 would help him once in
6 had not / hadn't turned him down

13 House space

Starting off

1 1 c 2 b 3 a 4 d 5 f 6 e

Reading and Use of English Part 5

2 1 six 2 the text quickly before reading the questions
3 after

3 *Suggested answer*
It's conveniently situated close to the Grand Canal, the district is interesting, it's near the city centre and easy for clients to find, the printing trade has many roots in the area.

4 1 C 2 B 3 C 4 D 5 D 6 A

Vocabulary

space, place, room, area, location and *square*

1 1 place 2 square 3 location 4 area

Answer key: Unit 13

2 1 space 2 room 3 location 4 area
5 space 6 square 7 space 8 room

3 1 place 2 space 3 room 4 area

4 1 personal space 2 green space 3 legroom / leg room
4 market place 5 picnic area

Listening Part 2

2 1 F – You hear a talk given by one person.
2 F – It has ten questions. 3 F – You will need between one and three words. 4 T 5 T
6 F – You should read and try to predict the type of information and type of words you need. 7 T

3 *Suggested answers*
1 a number / duration 2 probably a noun 3 a person
4 name of a room 5 probably a verb / verb phrase
6 another type of room 7 another type of building / something that was there before 8 a machine or other facility 9 a noun 10 an adverb

4 1 eight/8 years 2 (strange) experiences 3 uncle
4 kitchen 5 (standing) behind 6 (old) garage 7 battle
8 tennis court 9 blood 10 at weekends

▶ CD 2 Track 30

Jeff: Hi, so as part of our project on historic local buildings, I thought I'd tell you about the house where I live. My mum and dad bought it when I was about seven, so we've been there for about eight years now. It isn't all that old – it was built about 15 years ago – but it's on the site of a much older place dating back to the 15th century which fell down. Anyway, why I'm telling you all this is 'cos we're pretty sure the house is haunted – I mean, it's got ghosts. Yeah, you can laugh, but I'm not joking. I know 'cos I know several people, myself included, who've had some strange experiences there. Yeah, yeah, you may think I'm just telling you a story, but a couple of years ago I remember, my mum and dad had invited all sorts of relatives to one of those big family celebrations and we were all sitting round after lunch – I was playing some game with my cousins, and my grandma was telling everyone about her visits to the doctor or something, when my uncle suddenly went pale and dropped his coffee cup. Grandma thought he'd been taken ill or something 'cos of her stories, but he said he'd just seen a group of men dressed up as medieval soldiers go past the window.

We cousins ran outside to take a look, but there was nobody there. Anyway, when he'd calmed down, he described their appearance in quite a lot of detail, so he wasn't just making it up. Then, a couple of months later, a friend of my mum's was staying with us. My mum was busy in her study and I was watching football on the telly in the sitting room when the friend came rushing out of the kitchen shouting and hollering that he'd seen the table sort of float across the room. I've never seen a grown-up tremble like he did, so when we went to look, the table had actually moved and it's one of those really heavy old oak ones. It took three of us to push it back, so he couldn't have done it on his own. Anyway, I'm not sure if it's because of the things which've happened, but when I'm studying in my room, I sometimes feel as if there's someone standing behind me, sort of breathing down my neck and checking what I'm doing like it's one of my teachers – I mean, I can feel the breath – but when I turn round, there's no one there. That shakes me up a bit! Anyway, my mum complained that she was experiencing the same thing, so she got the builders in and she had the old garage at the back of the house turned into a study so she could work there instead without being interrupted by these uninvited visitors! Then my dad got the whole house checked by a specialist in supernatural phenomena, a sort of ghost hunter. She checked local history records and apparently the house is actually located somewhere where, after one of those invasions, a battle took place a few hundred years ago with lots of fighting, so there could be quite a few bodies buried there. Weird, isn't it? A bit later, my dad decided to have a tennis court built in a corner of the garden, so he and I could play together. Anyway, one of the workers was on his own there one morning when he felt someone watching him. When he turned round, he saw something which literally made his hair stand on end: a man standing there with a white shirt covered in blood. The lad shouted and the man just disappeared. When we questioned him – you know, he was gibbering and shaking – he didn't know anything about the other supernatural experiences people had been having. My mum's getting a bit fed up with all these happenings, but my dad doesn't mind them so much. You see, he's only down here at weekends 'cos he works in London during the week.

Answer key: Unit 13

Grammar
Causative *have* and *get*

1 His mother had the garage converted into a study, and his father had a tennis court built.

2 1 b
2 a – He/She did it himself/herself; b – He/She asked someone else to do it for them
3 Other people – an architect and/or builders (1); a ghost hunter (2)

3 1 to have/get (your passport) renewed   2 had/got (a tooth) pulled out   3 having/getting (the house) painted   4 have/get (it) cut down   5 have/get (the house) extended   6 have/get (pizzas) delivered

4 1 had my bag stolen while   2 is having/getting his picture taken   3 have/get her hair dyed   4 his application turned down

Reading and Use of English Part 2

2 1 eight   2 grammar   3 general idea   4 before and after   5 one word ONLY   6 the completed text

4 1 as   2 spite   3 since   4 hardly   5 According   6 takes   7 out   8 come/pop

Speaking Part 2

1 1 T   2 F – two photos   3 F – compare the main ideas and discuss the question   4 T   5 T

3 *Suggested answers*
Photo 1: close to nature, fresh air, organic food, a rural setting
Photo 2: hi-tech, sophisticated entertainment, pollution
Both photos: environment, maintain a lifestyle, occupants, spend quality time, social life

5 1 F   2 T   3 T   4 T   5 T   6 T   7 T   8 F   9 F

> **CD 2 Track 31**
>
> **Examiner:** Peter, it's your turn first. Here are your photographs. They show two different places to live. I'd like you to compare the photographs and say what you think it is like for the people to live in each of these places. All right?
>
> **Peter:** OK. The first photo shows a traditional country cottage with the occupants, a family, standing in the garden where they grow their own vegetables, whereas the second photo shows a young family living in a smart luxury flat with a view of the city. I guess both photos show a lifestyle which the people have chosen and which they like, so for both families, it must be very pleasant to live where they do. Living in the country cottage must be very peaceful, with very little stress, no pollution and plenty of physical work, healthy organic food and fresh air. On the other hand, living in the city flat might be quite exciting because you're at the centre of things, with entertainment and friends close by. I think the first photo shows a way of life where money and success in your career are not so important as being close to nature and the countryside. The people living in this sort of environment probably have plenty of time to spend together. The family in the second photo must need to earn quite a lot of money to maintain their lifestyle, which is probably busier and more stressful.
>
> **Examiner:** Thank you. Martyna, which place would you choose to live in?
>
> **Martyna:** I'd choose the city flat because I can only fulfil my ambitions in a city, so I'd have to live there as well.
>
> **Examiner:** Thank you. Now, here are your photographs. They show …

Pronunciation: linking (2)

6.1 a y [j]   b r [r]   c w [w]

▶ **CD 2 Track 32.** See page 146

6.3 1 further-r-away; the-y-old   2 he-y-ever-r-answer   3 Our-r-aunt; stay-y-at; now-w-and   4 fewer-r-and; our-r-area; are-r-open

▶ **CD 2 Track 33.** See page 146

Grammar
Expressing obligation and permission

2 1 a I have to   b I can't; they won't let me   c I can; They let me   2 b

3 1 Michael: D   2 Irene: E   3 Mary: C   4 Luke: B   5 Laura: A

Answer key: Unit 13

CD 2 Track 34

Antonia: So, what's your host family like, Michael? Are they friendly?

Michael: Yeah, they're great fun, especially the mum. She's always cracking jokes and suggesting interesting things to do. And Hans, my exchange partner, never stops laughing! The house is always full of his friends too, so it's like a permanent party, and that's great. The only drawback is that they don't like me to stay up too late because we all have to be up so early every morning. I don't have to do anything around the house – though I do help from time to time, just to fit in and be part of the family, because they've really made me feel at home. What about you, Irene?

Irene: You sound really lucky with your family, Michael. Mind you, I haven't got any complaints. Karen, my exchange partner, is lovely, but her family is always very busy. I mean, they didn't let me go to a party in the evening the other day. Karen would have come too, of course, but they told me they just didn't have time to drive us there and then pick us up later. But they are very friendly. I mean, they said they were happy for my best friend to come round every day, because her exchange partner has hockey practice in the afternoon. Are you staying with a nice family, Mary?

Mary: Well, they're not too bad. I get on fine with my exchange partner Johanna. But the other day, her mum told me off after I'd got home a bit late and missed the family dinner. Apparently, I was supposed to phone to say I was going to be late back. Then when I went to see if there was anything left over in the fridge, I got into trouble again. She told me I couldn't just help myself to things without asking her first.

Michael: So, what did you do? Call your parents?

Mary: No, I apologised and she immediately said 'Never mind, I'm sorry, I'm just rather tired at the moment' and then she cooked me a really nice little meal. So we were all friends again.

Luke: Great. Still, your families sound really nice to me.

Mary: And what's yours like, Luke?

Luke: Well, they're all right, I suppose. Extremely tidy, though. I'm not the tidiest person myself, and nor are the rest of my family. So maybe that's why it's a bit of a shock – I'm simply not used to it. Anyway, all the kids in the family, and that includes me while I'm there – must do their share around the house – you know, like clearing up a bit, setting the table, doing some washing-up. I don't have to do any of the cleaning at all, fortunately, because I'd really hate that. How about you, Laura?

Laura: Well, I'm lucky. All the family are great. Sofie's parents are both teachers and they really want to help me improve my German, which I do appreciate. But it was hard when I was really tired the other evening and I had to make conversation in German – all I wanted to do was relax and say nothing! They don't allow me to spend much time online talking to my English friends for the same reason. But they've also told me that if I want to talk to my parents, I'm welcome to use their phone whenever I want, and for as long as I want. That's so nice, I think.Michael: It sounds as if we're all quite lucky, then. Not like a friend of mine who went to …

4 1 Michael 2 Laura 3 Laura 4 Mary 5 Irene

5 **obligation (present):** I must, I'm supposed to, I have to
obligation (past): I had to, I was supposed to
prohibition (present): I can't, I'm not allowed to, They won't let me, They don't allow me to
prohibition (past): They didn't let me
permission (present): I can, They let me
no obligation (present): I don't have to

Writing Part 2 — An article

1 a 6 b 4 c 1 d 3 e 2 f 5

4 *Suggested answers*
1 readers of the school magazine, i.e. other students, teachers, etc. 2 informal 3 conditional – it asks you to imagine your ideal home 4 the type of house, its location and features of the house 5 for example, by surprising the reader, by saying interesting things about yourself

5 2 Yes – type of house: small, stylish, modern flat; location: Barcelona, conveniently close to cafés, cool shops and modern cinemas; features: hi-tech gadgets, enormous sofa, big windows, etc.

Answer key: Unit 14

6 *Suggested answers*
Para. 1: Type of flat and location; my present accommodation; advantages of ideal flat
Para. 2: Characteristics of flat
Para. 3: Conclusion: room for my friends

7 1 from 2 where 3 own 4 what/whatever/anything
5 have 6 long 7 few 8 If

8 1 T 2 T 3 F 4 T – She would like to live alone and make her own decisions, she enjoys art and reading, she wants an active social life. 5 T
6 F – She lives in a small suburban house.

9 *Sample answer*
See the model answer in Exercise 5, page 149.

14 Fiesta!

Starting off

1 1 celebrate 2 dress up; perform
3 march; commemorate 4 hold 5 play/perform
6 gather round 7 let off 8 wearing

2 Photos: 1 traditional costumes, parade
2 fireworks 3 traditional costumes, traditional dances
4 street parties 5 parade, bands, traditional costumes
6 disguises, traditional costumes 7 street performers

Listening Part 4

2 1 an interview 2 seven 3 underline; different words
4 general ideas

3 1 C 2 A 3 B 4 A 5 B 6 A 7 C

> **CD 2 Track 35**
>
> **Interviewer:** Today, *South Live* visits the Winchester Hat Fair, an extravaganza of processions, fireworks and street theatre with performers from as far away as Australia and Brazil. And we're talking to a veteran performer at the Hat Fair, Mighty Max, who's come all the way from Canada once again. Max, why's the festival called the Hat Fair?
>
> **Max:** Well, I've been told the fair was only started in 1974, as a way of encouraging street performers like myself. It's not like there was one of those great old English traditions like hat-making here in the 18th century or anything. Lots of people come to the fair wearing funny hats because of the name, but that wasn't its origins. It was always supposed to be about street theatre, and during the act, a hat's passed around so that the performers can earn a living. And that, in fact's where the name comes from.
>
> **Interviewer:** Now, you've been coming here for a number of years. Why do you keep coming back?
>
> **Max:** Oh, I just love performing here. There are artists like myself from all over the world who come here year after year and we get to know each other and stuff. But what makes the fair unique is the people who come to watch. You know, you jump around and do your act and they really let their hair down and love it when they're being made a fool of by other people in the crowd, and that's really what makes it such fun.
>
> **Interviewer:** So, how did you get involved in street theatre in the first place?
>
> **Max:** Well, you know, my big ambition was to be a circus performer. I actually went to quite a famous circus school in Canada as a teenager where I was taught juggling and acrobatics. My dad was dead against it, but he paid for the classes on the condition that I went to university and got myself what he called 'a proper education' as well. It was ironic, really, because if I hadn't gone to university, I might never have got into street theatre. You see, every vacation I had time to travel and I found I could pay for my trips by performing in the street and making a collection.
>
> **Interviewer:** Fantastic! Your act's been attracting tremendous crowds here in Winchester. How do you explain your popularity?
>
> **Max:** Well, it's a combination of high-class acrobatics, which are performed without any safety equipment at all, and some quite risky stunts. So it gives the audience a thrill – you know, there are plenty of oohs and aahs, but what I think really gets them into it is that I make them laugh. There's a lot of clowning in my act, which builds a sort of two-way communication with the audience, and they love it.
>
> **Interviewer:** The acts I've seen around town today have been pretty high quality. Why do you think that is?
>
> **Max:** Well, there's plenty of money around this town, which certainly attracts the best people from around the world, but you know, none of that money's going to go in the hat unless your act is a good one, and so you've gotta make sure people have a really great time watching you work.
>
> **Interviewer:** And what difficulties do street performers come up against?

Max: Good question. In a place like Winchester, not many. We're each given a place and a time to perform. As you've seen, I attract pretty large crowds and I need plenty of space, so narrow streets are no good. Here, we're given the main shopping street, which is fine. In other places, if you haven't got permission, you'll get moved on by the police, so I always make sure that I've got the right permits. Actually, what's most likely to stop things happening the way you'd like is usually the rain or even just a bit of drizzle. I mean, where's the fun in standing around getting cold and wet?

Interviewer: None at all. But what about Winchester? Has the Hat Fair put the town on the map? I mean, does it attract a lot of visitors from outside?

Max: I'm not the best person to answer that question. I get the impression that the people who come here tend to be from the surrounding area rather than tourists. What Winchester gets is an amusing party – something they can do which is just plain fun. They gather in the streets and parks and unwind and forget about the other stuff in their lives.

Interviewer: Mighty Max, thank you, and I hope the rest of the fair goes well for you.

Max: Thank you.

4 *Suggested answers*
Some residents may find it annoying or noisy, it interrupts traffic, it may encourage pickpockets and crime, it may be dangerous, etc.

Grammar
The passive

1 a I've been told; was only started   b 's passed around
c they're being made a fool of   d was taught
e we're given; you'll get moved on

2 *Suggested answers*
2 a   3 b, d, first passive in e
4 a, b, c, d, first passive in e

3 1 Our school was founded in 1904.
2 My wallet has been stolen
3 You won't be able to email me while my laptop is being repaired
4 Have you heard? I've been given second prize!
5 If you hadn't done the work, you would have been told off (by the teacher).

4 People go out in the open air in the early morning; they eat traditional foods; young men swim in the Nile.

5 1 are   2 as   3 been   4 to   5 is   6 being   7 by
8 have   9 doing   10 were (Note: *fish* can be singular or plural, depending on the context.)

6 1 a
2 A large number of contemporary Egyptian traditions are said to have their origins in very ancient times. For example, offerings of fish are believed to have been made to the ancient gods …
3 It is said that a large number of contemporary Egyptian traditions have their origins in very ancient times. For example, it is believed that offerings of fish were made to the ancient gods.

7 1 It is thought that Sham el Nessím marked the start of the spring festival in ancient Egypt.
2 It is known that eating salted fish was a custom of the ancient Egyptians.
3 Five thousand people are reported to have joined in the festivities.
4 Our festival is said to have the best fireworks in the world.

8 1 is believed to have originated   2 expected to be chosen   3 said that the festival is   4 is thought to be
5 is considered to be   6 to go/date back more than

Reading and Use of English Part 6

1 1 F – There are six questions and no example.
2 T   3 T   4 T   5 F – Read the completed text again to check it reads logically.

3 *Suggested answers*
Para. 2: people who attend festival; Para. 3: where the festival happens; Para. 4: the writer's arrival; Para. 5: the market; Para. 6: festival activities

4 1 F   2 C   3 E   4 G   5 B   6 A

Reading and Use of English Part 3

1 1 tourists   2 dancers

2 1 designer   2 novelist   3 researcher   4 collector
5 survivor   6 consultant   7 motorist   8 comedian
9 salesman/saleswoman/salesperson
10 specialist   11 refugee

Answer key: Unit 14

3 1 eight 2 Read the whole text quickly before answering the questions 3 think what type of word you need 4 Make sure you have spelled the word correctly 5 read the completed text again

4 1 organisers 2 arrangements 3 activities 4 participants 5 surrounding 6 energetic 7 unusually 8 impressive

Speaking Parts 3 and 4

1 1 T 2 T 3 T 4 F – You should try to reach a decision, but if you don't succeed, don't worry.
5 F – It's the same subject. 6 T 7 T 8 T

2

> **CD 2 Track 36**
>
> **Examiner:** I'd like you to imagine that you are having a class discussion on the role festivals play in modern life. Here are some aspects of festivals that you could discuss. Talk together about whether festivals are important in the modern world. You now have some time to look at the task. All right? Could you start now please?

3

> **CD 2 Track 37**
>
> **Examiner:** Now you and your partner have a minute to decide which two aspects are most relevant to consider in the discussion.

4

> **CD 2 Track 38**
>
> **Noelia:** OK, let's see, do you think you can learn about history by going to festivals?
>
> **Denis:** Well, I think some of them are based on significant historical events, like winning things.
>
> **Noelia:** You mean, remembering victories in battles?
>
> **Denis:** Yes, thank you, victories, and also, probably more often, important days in the religious calendar. The way people celebrated these can show us how people lived in the past.
>
> **Noelia:** That's a very good point. I think we can learn how they enjoyed themselves in the past, erm …
>
> **Denis:** Good, let's move on to that: having fun. Do you think that's a reason for having festivals these days?
>
> **Noelia:** Hmm, well, I, er …
>
> **Denis:** I mean, do you think festivals are important because they are an opportunity for people to enjoy themselves not just with their families at home, but with other people in the area where they live?
>
> **Noelia:** Yes, it probably is a reason why they're important. Nowadays, people can find plenty to entertain themselves at home, so it's easy to forget about all the other people who live around us. Festivals bring people together who might otherwise rarely meet. I mean kids go to school together locally, but my parents spend all day at work, quite far from home.
>
> **Denis:** Yes, that's true, because of course all sorts of people go to festivals and walk around together …
>
> **Noelia:** You mean you can mix with different kinds of people.
>
> **Denis:** Exactly, mix and exchange ideas. And of course that also means people of different ages.
>
> **Noelia:** An interesting point. There's a festival in the summer here every year, and my whole family always go together–
>
> **Denis:** Oh great!
>
> **Noelia:** –and my grandmother really looks forward to it and so do my little brothers and sisters. I think it's great fun too.
>
> **Denis:** I think that's an important point: that festivals really, what's the word, appeal to all age groups.
>
> **Noelia:** Well that means they play a role in individual people's lives as well as that of a community at any given time …

5 1 *Suggested answer*: They help each other with vocabulary and expressing ideas, they react to what the other person says, they invite the other person to speak and express ideas. This is important because they should try to have a normal conversation.

2 a That's a very good point; Yes, that's a good idea; An interesting point; I think that's a very interesting general idea …

b You mean … ; In other words

c I mean … ; So that (i.e. Noelia continues where Denis dries up.)

244

Answer key: Unit 14

6

▶ **CD 2 Track 39**

Examiner: I'd like you to imagine that you are doing a class project on celebrations. Here are some things people often celebrate and a question for you to discuss. First, you have some time to look at the task. Now talk to each other about how you think we should celebrate each of these occasions.

7

▶ **CD 2 Track 40**

Examiner: Now you have about a minute to decide which two occasions it would be most enjoyable to celebrate.

8

▶ **CD 2 Track 41**

Examiner: Antonia, how do towns and cities benefit from having festivals and other celebrations?

Antonia: Hmm, that's a good question. Some people say that it's good for, what's it called, community spirit, but I think the main benefit is for local businesses because tourists and visitors are attracted to the town to spend their money in shops and restaurants.

Examiner: Nikolai, do you agree with Antonia?

Nikolai: Yes, I partly agree with her. I think in many places, people spend a lot of time during the year preparing for their festival and I think it really encourages a feeling of cooperation and a community feeling.

Examiner: And, Nikolai, do you think festivals should be organised more for tourists or more for local people?

Pronunciation: improving fluency

9.1–9.3 See underlining, pause marks and intonation arrows in recording script for Track 42.

▶ **CD 2 Track 42**

Hmm, that's a good question. / Some people say that it's good for, / what's it called, / community spirit, / but I think the main benefit is for local businesses / because tourists and visitors are attracted to the town / to spend their money in shops and restaurants.

9.4 See underlining, pause marks and intonation arrows in recording script for Track 43.

▶ **CD 2 Track 43**

Yes, I partly agree with her. / I think in many places / people spend a lot of time during the year preparing for their festival / and I think it really encourages a feeling of cooperation / and a community feeling.

Writing Part 1 An essay

1 1 140–190 words; 40   2 you must deal with three points, one of which is your own idea   3 write a plan first   4 you should check your answer carefully when you finish

2 *Suggested underlining*
better, live, recorded music, quality, convenience, own idea

5 *Suggested answers*
Although people can listen to recorded music on their music players when they are travelling, working or studying, music festivals and concerts are becoming more and more popular. This is because, I believe, they offer two main advantages.
The first advantage is that the quality of the sound is much better at live concerts, where the music and voices come directly from the performers. This makes it a much more emotional experience because you have direct contact with the musicians and you react to them and they react to you.
The second advantage is the atmosphere. Instead of listening to a recording alone on your personal music player, you are listening with a huge crowd of people and enjoying the music together. This means it is a social as well as an artistic experience.
The main disadvantage is that you cannot listen to live music whenever you want, like you can on a personal device. Apart from that, the noise from the audience sometimes spoils the quality of the sound.
In my opinion, however, the best way to enjoy music is the spontaneous atmosphere of a live concert. It is more exciting because you are surrounded by other enthusiastic fans, who are dancing with you.

6 2 music festivals and concerts are becoming more and more popular
3 music festivals and concerts
4 the music and voices come directly from the performers

245

Answer key: Writing and speaking references

5 listening to music at live concerts
6 the musicians
7 you are listening with a huge crowd of people and enjoying the music together
8 The main disadvantage is that you cannot listen to live music whenever you want
9 a live concert

7 1 It/This 2 it 3 they 4 they; that 5 that
6 This 7 that/this 8 that/this

8 *Sample answer*
Films are now as popular as they were when my grandparents were young. However, now with the Internet and DVDs we have much more choice about when and where we can watch them.
There's no doubt that for the quality of the experience the best place to watch a new film is in the cinema on a wide screen with excellent sound. What is more, you can see films which everybody is talking about because they have recently been released.
The drawback of the cinema is the price of the tickets. If they were cheaper, people would go more often. This means that if, like me, you are a cinema fanatic, you have little choice but to download films off the Internet if you want to see them frequently.
I also believe that it is worth seeing a good film several times. The best way of doing this is to see it first in the cinema, then later at home, when you can appreciate other aspects of the film.
For me, however, going to the cinema is a far better experience because it is a special location.

Vocabulary and grammar review Unit 13

1 1 space 2 room 3 place 4 location 5 area 6 place
7 space 8 square 9 room 10 place

2 1 since 2 made 3 out 4 than 5 enough 6 there
7 one 8 What

3 1 have a tennis court built 2 you have the car checked
3 to clear up 4 have to do 5 are supposed to pay
6 are not allowed to speak

Vocabulary and grammar review Unit 14

1 1 lawyer 2 possibilities 3 especially 4 suitably
5 responsibility 6 appropriately 7 demanding
8 representative

2 1 reputation 2 safety 3 amazement 4 dissatisfaction
5 existence 6 truth 7 width 8 addition 9 difference
10 obligations

3 1 is expected to arrive 2 was broken into by 3 are reported to have 4 has not / hasn't been tidied for
5 are said to be 6 cake was / had been eaten

Writing reference

Part 1

1 1 All young people, stay at school until, 18, qualifications for jobs, don't find it interesting, own idea

2 Para. 1: should continue (my opinion)
Para. 2: jobs more specialised; more training gives more opportunities
Para. 3: many students don't find it interesting; prefer to earn money
Para. 4: uninterested students cause problems; should only study things they like after 16
Para. 5: shouldn't leave school at 16; miss opportunities

3 visit, your own country, foreign country, holiday, cheaper, more interesting, own idea

4 *Suggested answer:* The sample answer in Exercise 4 deals with each of the notes in order in separate paragraphs. This essay deals with each of the three notes in paragraph 2 with reasons for staying in your own country, and then each of the notes again in paragraph 3 with reasons for travelling abroad.

Part 2

Emails and letters

1 1 An English friend, Pat
2 What a typical family in your country is like, what families do together when they have free time
3 Pat's project, different countries

2 1 families close, spend time together, help each other, get together at weekends, young people leaving to find work
2 go for walks, have lunch together, go to street celebrations

Answer key: Writing and speaking references

Stories
1 1 both
2 The style is formal, but the use of speech is informal; Yes, it answers the question.

Reviews
1 1 what it's about, why we would all enjoy it
2 everyone would enjoy, film or book
3 readers of your school's English-language magazine, i.e. other students; in the magazine

2 1 first and second paragraphs
2 third paragraph

Articles
1 1 g 2 d 3 e 4 h 5 c 6 b 7 a 8 i 9 f

2 Para. 1: c Para. 2: b Para. 3: a Para. 4: d

Speaking reference
2 e 3 c 4 h 5 f 6 g 7 d 8 i 9 a

Acknowledgements

Development of this publication has made use of the Cambridge English Corpus (CEC). The CEC is a computer database of contemporary spoken and written English, which currently stands at over one billion words. It includes British English, American English and other varieties of English. It also includes the Cambridge Learner Corpus, developed in collaboration with Cambridge English Language Assessment. Cambridge University Press has built up the CEC to provide evidence about language use that helps to produce better language teaching materials.

The Cambridge Advanced Learner's Dictionary is the world's most widely used dictionary for learners of English. Including all the words and phrases that learners are likely to come across, it also has easy-to-understand definitions and example sentences to show how the word is used in context. The Cambridge Advanced Learner's Dictionary is available online at dictionary.cambridge.org © Cambridge University Press. Reproduced with permission;

The authors and publishers acknowledge the following sources of copyright material and are grateful for the permissions granted. While every effort has been made, it has not always been possible to identify the sources of all the material used, or to trace all copyright holders. If any omissions are brought to our notice, we will be happy to include the appropriate acknowledgements on reprinting.

p. 35: Guardian News & Media Limited for the adapted article (a) 'My crap holiday, so that's why the beach was deserted' by Pauline Vernon *The Observer* 22 November 2009, p. 144: adapted article 'My kitchen' by Tamsin Blanchard *The Observer* 10 June 2001. Copyright © Guardian News & Media Limited 2009, 2001;

p. 35: Ninemsn Pty Ltd for the adapted text (b) 'Reader story: attacked by a bear' by Sandy Henderson, 18 June 2009. © 1997-2013 ninemsn Pty Ltd - All rights reserved;

p. 41: Kasey Edwards for the adapted text 'How chocolate makes you smarter'. Reproduced with permission. Kasey Edwards is the best-selling author of 4 books *30-Something and Over It, 30-Something and The Clock is Ticking, OMG! That's Not My Husband,* and *OMG! That's Not My Child;*

p. 47: Manchester Evening News for the adapted article 'Moso Moso' by Kyla *Manchester Evening News* 17 August 2005. Used by permission of Manchester Evening News;

p. 64: Lucy Irvine for the heavily adapted text 'Lucy's first job' from *Runaway*. Copyright © Lucy Irvine 1987. Used by kind permission of Lucy Irvine;

p. 69: The Independent for the adapted article 'The teenagers who may yet bring big society to life' by Oliver Wright, *The Independent* 28 August 2012. Copyright © The Independent;

p. 76: Adventure Sports Journal for the adapted text 'Are you ready for an adventure race?' by Rebecca Rusch *Adventure Sports Journal 2006*. Used by permission of Adventure Sports Journal;

p. 90: The Daily Mail for the adapted article 'You Tube 'geek' one day, millionaire celeb the next' from *This is Money online* 10 December 2010. Copyright © Associated Newspapers Limited;

pp. 96–97: Marilyn Price-Mitchell for the adapted text 'Happiness or Harvard' which appeared in *Psychology Today*, 3 October 2012. Copyright ©2012 Marilyn Price-Mitchell. All rights reserved;

p. 108: Teen Ink for the text 'My greatest influence' by Rachel S., Colleyville, Texas. Reprinted with permission of Teen Ink Magazine and Teenink.com;

p. 132: adapted article 'Circus life, Neil and Toti Gifford run the show' *The Daily Telegraph* 6 July 2005. Copyright © Telegraph Media Group Limited 2013;

pp. 134–135: News Syndication for the adapted article 'Surviving an animal attack' *The Sunday Times* 23 April 2006. Copyright © News Syndication;

p. 141: Darley and Anderson Literary Agency for the adapted text 'my new home in Venice' from *The Cemetery of Secrets* by David Hewson, published by Pan Macmillan 2009. Reproduced with permission.

Photo acknowledgements:

p. 8 (tl): Altrendo/Juice Images/Corbis; p. 8 (tr): Radius Images/Alamy; p. 8 (l): iofoto/Shutterstock; p. 8 (bl): XiXinXing/Shutterstock; p. 11 (tl): Jon Feingersh/Blend Images/Getty Images; p. 11 (tr): Ocean/Corbis; p. 12: Piti Tan/Shutterstock; p. 13: Kiselev Andrey Valerevich/Shutterstock; p. 14: Ocean/Corbis; p. 15 (cr): vario images GmbH & Co.KG/Alamy; p. 15 (bl): Brian Kinney/Shutterstock; p. 16 (bl): Andrey Armyagov/Shutterstock; p. 16 (br): PicturesofLondon/Alamy; p. 17: Don Bayley/Getty Images; p. 18 (tl): Corbis; p. 18 (tr): Jacek Chabraszewski; p. 18 (cl): SnowWhiteimages/Shutterstock; p. 18 (bl): Oliver Furrer/Alamy; p. 18 (br): Kevin Dodge/Corbis; p. 19: Horizons WWP/Alamy; pp. 20–21: Rally-Pics.com/Alamy; p. 22: iStockphoto/Thinkstock; p. 23: Mettus/Shutterstock; p. 24 (t): Lifesize/Thinkstock; p. 24 (b): Kathrin Ziegler/Taxi/Getty Images; p. 25 (t): KidStock/Blend Images/Getty Images; p. 25 (b): Outdoor-Archiv/Alamy; p. 26: BA LaRue/Alamy; p. 27: Design Pics/Superstock; p. 30 (tl): Photo Network/Alamy; p. 30 (tr): Justin Kase zsixz/Alamy; p. 30 (cl): Fuse/Getty Images; p. 30 (cr): Jutta Klee/Corbis; p. 30 (5): NAN728/Shutterstock; p. 32: Marka/Superstock; p. 33: Ben Pipe/Robert Harding World Imagery/Corbis; p. 34: Hemis/Alamy; p. 35 (tr): chris mcloughlin/Alamy; p. 35 (tl): Atlantide Phototravel/Corbis; p. 35 (b): David Lobos/Shutterstock; p. 35 (br): visuall2/Shutterstock; p. 36: Doug Perrine/Alamy; p. 37 (t): Blend Images/Alamy; p. 37 (b): PT Images/Shutterstock; p. 38: Robert Fried/Alamy; p. 39 (b/g): Adrian Sherratt/Alamy; p. 39 (tr): CHAINFOTO24/Shutterstock; p. 40 (tl): Maximilian Weinzierl/Alamy; p. 40 (tc): nexus 7/Shutterstock; p. 40 (tr): anyaivanova/Shutterstock; p. 42: Jack Hollingsworth/Getty Images; p. 44: Adrian Lascom/Alamy; p. 45: photopalace/Alamy; p. 46 (l): GlowImages/Alamy; p. 46 (r): paulaphoto/Shutterstock; p. 48 (l): Ilpo Musto/Rex Features; p. 48 (r): blickwinkel/Alamy; p. 49: Blend Images/Alamy; p. 52 (tc): Martin Shields/Alamy; p. 52 (tl): wavebreakmedia/Shutterstock; p. 52 (tr): Blend Images/Alamy; p. 52 (cl): Fuse/Getty Images; p. 52 (bl): Corbis/Superstock; p. 52 (tl): VikramRaghuvanshi/Getty Images; p. 52 (bl): michaeljung/Shutterstock; p. 52 (tr): Blend Images/Alamy; p. 52 (br): Big Cheese Photo/Superstock; p. 52 (t): VanHart/Shutterstock; p. 53: Golden Pixels LLC/Alamy; p. 61: Paul Burns/Corbis; p. 62 (tr): SHOUT/Alamy; p. 62 (tl): Radius Images/Corbis; p. 62 (bl): Jaimie Duplass/Shutterstock; p. 62 (br): Innershadows Photography/Shutterstock; p. 63: Constantine Pankin/Shutterstock; p. 64: iStockphoto/Thinkstock; p. 65: Courtesy of Summer Isles Hotel, Achiltibuie; p. 66 (l): I Love Images/Corbis; p. 66 (b): Alistair Berg/Getty Images; p. 67 (t): LatinStock Collection/Alamy; p. 67 (b): Big Cheese Photo/Superstock; p. 68: Frank Perry/AFP/Getty Images; p. 69: Siegfried Kuttig - RF -2/Alamy; p. 70 (r): Monkey Business Images/Shutterstock; p. 70 (l): Photofusion Picture Library/Alamy; p. 74 (1): Cultura Limited/Superstock; p. 74 (2): LumiImages/Mauritius/Superstock; p. 74 (3): Konstantin Shishkin/Shutterstock; p. 74 (4): Karl Weatherly/Getty Images; p. 74 (5): Vladimir Piskunov/Getty Images; p. 74 (6): SFL Travel/Alamy; p. 75: Arnd Hemmersbach/NordicFocus/Getty Images; p. 76/77 (t): imago/Actionplus; p. 77 (insert): Hyoung Chang/The Denver Post via Getty Images; p. 80 (t): Nicolas Thibaut/Photononstop/Getty Images; p. 80 (b/g): Protasov AN/Shutterstock; p. 81: Nick Hanna/Alamy; p. 82: PCN Photography/Alamy; p. 84 (tl): Javier Soriano/Getty Images; p. 84 (ul): Karim Jaafar/Getty Images; p. 84 (ll): ZUMA Press, Inc./Alamy; p. 84 (bl): PictureGroup/Rex Features; p. 85 (tl): Samuel Borges Photography/Shutterstock; p. 85 (tr): Iancu Cristian/Shutterstock; p. 85 (bl): Tetra Images/Alamy; p. 85 (br): Blend Images/Alamy; p. 86: Caspar Benson/fstop/Corbis; p. 87 (t): John Eder/Getty Images; p. 87 (c): Jung Yeon-Je/AFP/Getty Images; p. 87 (b): Nathan King/Alamy; p. 88: ITV/Rex Features; p. 89: elkor/Getty Images; p. 90: William Perugini/Shutterstock; p. 91 (tl): Ariel Skelley/Blend Images/Corbis; p. 91 (br): Helene Rogers/Art Directors & TRIP; p. 91 (tr): MBI/Alamy; p. 91 (bl): Multi-bits/Getty Images; p. 92: Johannes Eisele/AFP/Getty Images; p. 96 (1): Corbis; p. 96 (2): Jiri Hubatka/Alamy; p. 96 (3): Baran Azdemir/Getty Images; p. 96 (4): Daniel Koebe/Corbis; p. 97: Tetra Images/Alamy; p. 98: Sabphoto/Shutterstock; p. 102 (tl): picturegarden/The Image Bank/Getty Images; p. 102 (bl): Juice Images/Alamy; p. 102 (tr): Cusp/Superstock; p. 102 (br): Pegaz/Alamy; p. 103: Rechitan Sorin/Shutterstock; p. 104 (tl): Blend Images/Superstock; p. 104 (tr): Vicki Beaver/Alamy; p. 104 (bl): Chris Cooper-Smith/Alamy; p. 104 (br): Sharie Kennedy/LWA/Corbis; p. 105: Corepics VOF/Shutterstock; p. 106 (tl): Robert Stainforth/Alamy; p. 106 (tc): MO_SES/Shutterstock; p. 106 (tr): Andrey

Armyagov/Shutterstock; p. 106 (cl): vnlit/Shutterstock; p. 106 (c): Maxx-Studio/Shutterstock; p. 106 (cr): David Pearson/Alamy; p. 106 (br): Gjermund/Shutterstock; p. 106 (br): Michel Tcherevkoff/Getty Images; p. 109: Anna Hoychuk/Shutterstock; p. 111: Photononstop/Superstock; p. 112: Peter Cade/Getty Images; p. 114 (br): BrandX Pictures/Jupiterimages/Thinkstock; p. 114 (bl): Flirt/Superstock; p. 114 (cr): John Giustina/Getty Images; p. 116 (t): iStockphoto/Thinkstock; p. 116 (b): Erik Isakson/Corbis; p. 118 (tl): Blend Images/Superstock; p. 118 (tc): RK Studio/Shea Pollard/Getty Images; p. 118 (tr): michaeljung/Shutterstock; p. 118 (bl): Shestakoff/Shutterstock; p. 118 (bc): IgorGolovniov/Shutterstock; p. 118 (br): Samuel Borges Photography/Shutterstock; p. 119: VStock/Alamy; p. 120: Jochen Tack/Alamy; p. 121 (l): Artisticco/Shutterstock; p. 122: BSIP SA/Alamy; p. 124 (t): Peter Cade/Iconica/Getty Images; p. 124 (b): Tim Hall/cultura/Corbis; p. 125 (t): Image Source/Getty Images; p. 125 (b): ColsTravel/Alamy; p. 126 (tl): Tim Graham/Getty Images; p. 126 (tr): Pegaz/Alamy; p. 126 (bl): YanLev/Shutterstock; p. 126 (br): Jacek Chabraszewski/Shutterstock; p. 128 (tl): Peter Llewellyn/Alamy; p. 128 (tc): Markus Altmann/Corbis; p. 128 (cr): Ulrich Doering/Alamy; p. 128 (cl): Images of Africa Photobank/Alamy; p. 128 (bl): imagebroker/Alamy; p. 130 (l): Jason Prince/Shutterstock; p. 130 (r): Thomas Dressler/Gallo Images/Getty Images; p. 132: Mary Evans/Retrograph Collection; p. 133: Corey Hochachka/Design Pics/Rex Features; p. 134 (t): Karine Aigner/National Geographic/Getty Images; p. 134 (b): Roberto Nistri/Alamy; p. 135 (tl): Steven Kazlowski/Science Faction/Superstock; p. 135 (bl): Jenny Zhang/Shutterstock; p. 135 (tc): PT Images/Shutterstock; p. 135 (tr): Blend Images/Alamy; p. 136: imagebroker/Alamy; p. 137: F. J. Fdez. Bordonada/age fotostock/Superstock; p. 140 (1): Tupungato/Shutterstock; p. 140 (2): blickwinkel/Alamy; p. 140 (3): Derek Meijer/Alamy; p. 140 (4): iStockphoto/Thinkstock; p. 140 (5): picturesbyrob/Alamy; p. 140 (6): Greg Balfour Evans/Alamy; p. 141 (r): Honza Hruby/Shutterstock; p. 141 (tl): Bridge of Sighs, Venice (La Riva degli Schiavoni) c.1740 (oil on canvas), Canaletto, (Giovanni Antonio Canal) (1697-1768)/Toledo Museum of Art, Ohio, USA/Giraudon/The Bridgeman Art Library ; p. 144: Peter Horree/Alamy; p. 145 (t): moodboard/Alamy; p. 145 (b): OJO Images Ltd/Alamy; p. 146 (t): Blend Images/Superstock; p. 146 (b): frans lemmens/Alamy; p. 147 (t): Christine Webb/Alamy; p. 147 (b): Rachel Lewis/Getty Images; p. 148: Howard Oates/Getty Images; p. 149: ailenn/Shutterstock; p. 150 (1): Kirsty McLaren/Alamy; p. 150 (2): KIKE CALVO/VWPICS/Alamy; p. 150 (3): Richard Wayman/Alamy; p. 150 (4): Peter Titmuss/Alamy; p. 150 (5): Geoff Burke/Getty Images; p. 150 (6): Curt Wiler/Alamy; p. 151: Photogenix/Alamy; pp. 152–153: mhatzapa/Shutterstock; p. 153: Megapress/Alamy; p. 154: Bjorn Svensson/Alamy; p. 155: Bjorn Svensson/Alamy; p. 156: JLImages/Alamy; p. 157: Michelle Pedone/Corbis; p. 158 (l): Jilly Wendell/Getty Images; p. 158 (r): Erik Isakson/Corbis; p. 159 (t): Norbert Schaefer/Corbis; p. 159 (b): Stockbroker/Superstock; p. 196 (t): Pablo Paul/Alamy; p. 196 (b) Blend Images/Shutterstock

Cover image by biletskiy/Shutterstock

Illustration acknowledgements:
Jeff Anderson (Graham-Cameron Illustration) p. 23; John Batten (Beehive Illustration) p. 20; Moreno Chiacchiera (Beehive Illustration) p. 56; Fay Dalton (Pickled Ink) p. 108; Elisabeth Eudes-Pascal (Graham-Cameron Illustration) pp. 43, 101; Kevin Hopgood (Beehive Illustration) pp. 13, 41, 45, 55, 107, 131, 147; Joanna Kerr (New Division Illustration) pp. 9, 54, 78, 122, 133, 142; Dusan Pavlic (Beehive Illustration) pp. 22, 99; David Shephard (The Bright Agency) pp. 79, 100; Mark Turner (Beehive Illustration) pp. 31, 44, 60

Installing the CD-ROM on your hard disk

- Insert the *Complete First for Schools* CD-ROM into your CD/DVD drive. The CD-ROM will automatically start to install. Follow the installation instructions on your screen.

- On a Windows PC, if the CD-ROM does not automatically start to install, open My Computer, locate your CD/DVD drive and open it to view the content of the CD-ROM. Double-click on the Complete First for Schools Application file. Follow the installation instructions on your screen.

- On a Mac, if the CD-ROM does not automatically start to install, double-click on the CompleteFirstforSchools CD icon on your desktop. Double-click on the Complete First for Schools Application file. Follow the instructions on your screen.

System requirements

Windows

- Intel Pentium 4 2GHz or faster
- Microsoft® Windows® XP (SP3), Vista® (SP2), Windows 7®, Windows 8®
- Minimum 1GB RAM
- Minimum 750MB of hard drive space
- Adobe® Flash® Player 10.3.183.7 or later

Mac OS

- Intel CoreTM Duo 1.83GHz or faster
- Mac OSX 10.5 or later
- Minimum 1GB RAM
- Minimum 750 of hard drive space
- Adobe® Flash® Player 10.3.183.7 or later